The Making of a Tory Evangelical

The Making of a Tory Evangelical

Lord Shaftesbury and the Evolving Character
of Victorian Evangelicalism

DAVID FURSE-ROBERTS

Foreword by
CAROLINE COX

◥PICKWICK *Publications* · Eugene, Oregon

THE MAKING OF A TORY EVANGELICAL
Lord Shaftesbury and the Evolving Character of Victorian Evangelicalism

Copyright © 2019 David Furse-Roberts. All rights reserved. Except for brief quotations in critical publications or reviews, no part of this book may be reproduced in any manner without prior written permission from the publisher. Write: Permissions, Wipf and Stock Publishers, 199 W. 8th Ave., Suite 3, Eugene, OR 97401.

Pickwick Publications
An Imprint of Wipf and Stock Publishers
199 W. 8th Ave., Suite 3
Eugene, OR 97401

www.wipfandstock.com

PAPERBACK ISBN: 978-1-5326-5429-9
HARDCOVER ISBN: 978-1-5326-5430-5
EBOOK ISBN: 978-1-5326-5431-2

Cataloguing-in-Publication data:

Names: Furse-Roberts, David, author. | Cox, Caroline, 1937–, foreword writer

Title: The making of a Tory evangelical : Lord Shaftesbury and the evolving character of Victorian evangelicalism / David Furse-Roberts, with a foreword by Caroline Cox.

Description: Eugene, OR: Pickwick Publications, 2019 | Includes bibliographical references and index.

Identifiers: ISBN 978-1-5326-5429-9 (paperback) | ISBN 978-1-5326-5430-5 (hardcover) | ISBN 978-1-5326-5431-2 (ebook)

Subjects: LCSH: Shaftesbury, Anthony Ashley Cooper,—Earl of,—1801–1885 | Evangelicalism—Great Britain—History—19th century | Social reformers—Great Britain | Great Britain—Social conditions—19th century | Church of England—History—19th century | Evangelicalism—Church of England

Classification: BR1642 F87 2019 (paperback) | BR1642 (ebook)

Manufactured in the U.S.A.   04/24/19

Contents

Foreword by Caroline Cox | vii
Acknowledgments | xi
Abbreviations | xiii

Introduction: Identifying the "Inner Impulse" | 1

Part I: Ashley and the Anglican Evangelical Tradition
1 Ashley's Expression of Anglican Evangelicalism | 23
2 Continuity and Change from Clapham | 47

Part II: Ashley and the Tradition of Paternalism
3 Surveying the Contours of Ashley's Paternalism | 77
4 Imbibing Paternalism: St Giles, Southey, and Sadler | 93
5 The Place of Ashley's Paternalism within the Tory and Whig Traditions | 127

Part III: Ashley and the Emerging Synthesis of Evangelicalism and Tory Paternalism
6 A Convergence of Tory Paternalism and Early Victorian Evangelicalism | 141
7 Ashley and the Factory Reform Movement | 183
8 "Something Admirably Patrician in His Estimation of Christianity" | 204

Part IV: Ashley and the Milieu of Victorian Evangelicalism
9 Locating Ashley's Place within the Victorian Evangelical Terrain | 215
10 Premillennialism: Thy Kingdom Come, Thy Will be Done | 226
11 Desire for the Nations | 233

12 Repudiating "Romanism," "Ritualism," and "Rationalism" | 248
13 Home and Hearth | 268
14 Sanctifying Sundays | 282
15 Evangelical Benevolence and Tory "Self-reliance" | 288

Conclusion: A Conservative and a Reformer | 296

Bibliography | 307
Index | 323

Foreword

> Is not this the fast that I have chosen? To loose the bands of wickedness, to undo the heavy burdens, and to let the oppressed go free, and that ye break every yoke? Is it not to deal thy bread to the hungry, and that thou bring the poor that are cast out to thy house? When thou seest the naked, that thou cover him; and that thou hide not thyself from thine own flesh? (Isaiah 58: 6–7, *Holy Bible*, KJV)

In what became one of the great mercy ministries of all time, a fledgling Salvation Army adopted this prophetic charge as its "Isaiah Charter" in the 1860s. Even before William Booth's bands of Hallelujah Lads and Lasses descended on the slums of London's East End to minister to the spiritual and physical needs of poverty-stricken Londoners, a sensitive and reserved aristocrat from rural Dorset had felt a similar calling as he was likewise confronted with the acute suffering and poverty left in the wake of the Industrial Revolution. In an 1856 speech to the Young Men's Christian Association, the Earl of Shaftesbury enunciated his life mission to help the poor of Victorian Britain, commending this charge to his young audience:

> If you consider yourselves in relation to man, and consider the duties you owe to your fellowmen, the purpose for which you were sent on earth, the duties you have to perform—to defend the fatherless, to plead for the widow, to enlighten the ignorant, to solace the suffering, to spread the knowledge of God among those who know it not, and to give a helping hand to all in need.

Lord Ashley (later Lord Shaftesbury) was arguably the pre-eminent social reformer of the Victorian Age. Whilst he never held a cabinet post in his fifty years of parliamentary service, his impact on British society surpassed that of any of his parliamentary contemporaries. In addition to his contribution to the factory reform movement, he energetically committed himself to an almost exhaustive catalog of causes aimed at advancing the material and spiritual wellbeing of humanity. He took a leading role in initiatives for the more humane treatment of the mentally ill; sanitary reform; the banning of animal vivisection; the outlawing of "chimney sweepers" and other degrading forms of child labor; the rescuing of women and girls from sexual servitude; the education of poor children through "Ragged Schools"; the provision of job opportunities in the navy for young boys; the construction of adequate housing and sanitation for England's working poor; the inclusion of a Christian influence in British imperial policy in India; the strengthening of the evangelical contribution to the Church of England; the promotion of Christian mission abroad through the Church Missionary Society and support at home for societies committed to evangelism and Bible distribution.

In this volume, David Furse-Roberts provides a contextual study of Lord Shaftesbury and the evolving character of the Victorian evangelical faith he came to personify in so many ways. Owing to his seminal contribution to social reform in Victorian England, most notably to the Factory Acts, Shaftesbury has been justifiably portrayed as a man of action. The aim of his study, however, is to discuss the spiritual and political impulses behind the work for which he became famous. The evangelical tradition of Christianity that the young Shaftesbury imbibed from his nursemaid is explored and the impact his maturing faith had on arousing his social conscience and call to action is made better known to readers.

In attributing Shaftesbury's manifold endeavors to his evangelical faith, this book also explores how his evangelicalism was tinged with a conservative, patrician hue. By virtue of his aristocratic birth, Shaftesbury had been imbued with an abiding sense of *noblesse oblige*. That is, those who were blessed with the endowments of wealth and property had an inherent obligation to use these in the service of the poor and disadvantaged. As both a Tory and an evangelical in parliament, Shaftesbury eschewed the alternatives of *laissez-faire* liberalism on the one hand and socialism on the other to favor a conservative yet humane society of social order and personal obligation, strong families, volunteerism, and free enterprise tempered by moderate state intervention.

I am very pleased to recommend David Furse-Roberts' contextual study of Lord Shaftesbury, because I hope that readers will be reminded afresh that despite the human imperfections and mistakes of its adherents, the Christian faith has been a great spiritual and moral force for good in our society. Through the legacy of such figures as Wilberforce, Buxton, and Shaftesbury, it has contributed immeasurably to freedom, justice, progress, civilization, and the dignity of every individual.

Foreword

May this well-researched study not only educate and inform, but also inspire and challenge all people of faith and goodwill to champion these ideals in our own time where human suffering, oppression and injustice still abound and where there is an urgent need for help to alleviate suffering and for effective advocacy to promote justice, peace and freedom for all.

Caroline (Baroness) Cox
House of Lords
London
June 2018

Acknowledgments

In the composition of this tome, I wish to acknowledge the following people for their invaluable assistance and personal support. First, I wish to recognize the Reverend the Honorable Fred Nile MLC to whom my personal interest in Anthony Ashley Cooper is indebted. My appreciation also goes to the late Professor Michael Roberts of Macquarie University who gave me preliminary guidance on how I should approach a contextual study on Lord Ashley. I would particularly like to thank the Right Honorable Baroness Caroline Cox for graciously agreeing to contribute a foreword, which provides a fitting adornment to this volume.

Throughout the composition this project, I am particularly grateful for the generous input of some distinguished UK scholars in the field of Victorian British history. First, to Professor David Brown of the University of Southampton who met with me in person on a number of occasions to discuss the focus and themes of my study. Secondly, to Professor David Bebbington of the University of Stirling who also met with me in person to point me to some crucial historical sources relating to Lord Ashley. Finally, to Professor Stewart J. Brown of New College, University of Edinburgh, for his abiding interest, warm encouragement, and constructive input whilst studying abroad. With the collation of primary source material, I also give thanks to the respective library staff of the University of Southampton, the University of Cambridge, the British Library, and the Bodleian Library of Oxford for their professional assistance. Across the Atlantic, I acknowledge the input from Professor Donald M. Lewis of Regent College (Vancouver, Canada) who read carefully over my chapter structure to offer some welcome advice.

Returning to Australia, I wish to express my heartfelt gratitude to Professor John Gascoigne and Dr Geoffrey Treloar for their generous time, personal encouragement and academic professionalism in the supervision of my doctoral thesis on which this book is based. Not least, my gratitude extends to the dedicated team at Pickwick Publications for bringing this volume to print. I conclude by offering my profound appreciation to my family and friends who have helped sustain me through this endeavor with their love, support, good humor, interest and encouragement.

David Furse-Roberts
Sydney, Australia
June 2018

Abbreviations

BFBS	British Foreign and Bible Society
CIS	Christian Influence Society
CMS	Church Missionary Society
CPAS	Church Pastoral Aid Society
EA	Evangelical Alliance
HC	House of Commons
HL	House of Lords
LCM	London City Mission
LDOS	Lord's Day Observance Society
LMS	London Missionary Society
LSPCJ	London Society for the Promotion of Christianity amongst the Jews
RSU	Ragged School Union
SICLC	Society for Improving the Conditions of the Labouring Classes
SPCK	Society for Promoting Christian Knowledge

Introduction
Identifying the "Inner Impulse"

In 1905, the Archdeacon of Westminster and grandson of William Wilberforce, Basil Wilberforce, pondered, "What was the inner impulse that stimulated the founder and pioneer of this noble work, the Great Lord Shaftesbury, whose statue stands at the west end of the Abbey?"[1] Claiming to have known the Victorian statesman, who stood in the same tradition of Evangelical social reform as his grandfather, the Archdeacon suggested one of the secrets to his "moral nature" was his "personal devotion to the living Christ."[2] In chronicling the life and legacy of Ashley, manifold obituaries, eulogies, lectures, articles, biographies, and historical narratives have variously alluded to the prominent Anglican layman's evangelical Christianity as the great impetus behind his philanthropy and social reforms. Whilst the contours of Ashley's long life and keynote achievements have been extensively documented, with due attention given to his motivating Christian faith, a contextual and thematic study of the theological doctrines, political traditions, and philosophical currents that historically and contemporaneously molded the mind and worldview of Ashley is yet to emerge. Previous biographical studies have justifiably focused on such exploits as his seminal contribution to the factory reform movement, his mission to advance the welfare of children through education, and his pioneering advocacy for a Jewish homeland in Palestine. The objective of this study is, by contrast, to comprehend better the "mind behind the man" by examining the religious and ideological milieu from which this key Victorian imbibed his guiding principles.

With this study endeavoring to examine Ashley's place in the evolving character of Victorian Evangelicalism, it will begin, in Part One, by

1. Wilberforce, "The Awakening," 326.
2. Ibid.

discussing the influence of *Anglican* Evangelicalism on the religious outlook of the young Ashley through the examination of significant British evangelical individuals and movements.[3] In the second part, it will assess the contribution of Tory paternalism to the maturing political philosophy and worldview of Ashley. In today's discourse, the very notion of "paternalism" invariably grates against modern ears with its illiberal connotations, yet amid the harsher realities of nineteenth-century life it was welcomed by many as an ameliorating check on exploitation. In Part Three, it will be argued that, despite some differing premises and points of conflict, evangelical Anglicanism and Tory paternalism found a great deal of common ground in their shared vision for a hierarchical and communitarian Christian social order eschewing the excesses of *laissez-faire* liberalism, individualism, and utilitarianism. With Ashley's own worldview indebted to each of these two traditions, he ordinarily drew upon this coalescence to agitate for his various social reform causes, notably lunacy-patient treatment, factory legislation and public health. Part Four will contend that, as well as molding Ashley's personal philosophy, this confluence of Tory paternalism and Evangelicalism came to define the ensuing character of Victorian Evangelicalism which was evident in a number of key aspects: namely, its attitude towards imperialism, its staunch Sabbatarianism and its idealization of the family. As such, Ashley was well poised to exemplify this evolving temperament of Victorian evangelical religion.

In addition to appreciating the intellectual origins of Ashley's religious and political thought, this study seeks to explore some of the defining trends and epochs of the Victorian era, particularly those relating to the much debated "Condition of England" question. As the studies of Theodore Hoppen, Boyd Hilton, and Stewart Brown have illustrated,[4] Ashley's lifetime coincided with rampant industrialization and urbanization, rapid population increase, constitutional reform (with the removal of political disabilities for Nonconformists, Roman Catholics, and Jews), the emergence of a working-class consciousness with the rise of the socialist and Chartist movements, the expansion of education, the advances of science and rationalism, and the sharpening of divisions within the Church of England. This study does not promise to shed light on the era in its entirety, as to borrow Lytton Strachey's memorable phrase, "it would be futile to hope to tell even a précis

---

3. Hereafter, capital 'E' Evangelicalism will refer to Evangelicalism specifically within the Church of England, while small 'e' evangelicalism will refer to evangelicalism more broadly as a movement across all Protestant denominations. The same principle applies to the capping of Evangelical and evangelical.

4. Hoppen, *The Mid-Victorian Generation*; Hilton, *A Mad, Bad and Dangerous People* and Brown, *Providence and Empire*.

of the Victorian age, for the shortest précis must fill innumerable volumes."[5] Moreover, this study does not claim to provide a definitive portrait of the era with Asa Briggs having observed that "there was no single Victorian England" owing to the innate complexity and protean character of the age.[6]

Indeed, one of the themes of this work is the multi-faceted character of the two major traditions which, it is argued, shaped the reforming outlook of Ashley: Evangelicalism and paternalism—a diversity that was compounded by the changing circumstances over Ashley's long lifetime (1801–85), which encompassed much of the century. Notwithstanding the need to engage with this extent of change and diversity, this contextual study of Ashley continues the task of Strachey and Briggs to better understand Victorian worthies by due historical contextualization. By examining Ashley in the context of the prevailing religious and political currents of his time, it is the intention that appreciation of the Victorian era will be advanced by analyzing a particular fragment of it, in the life and thought of this Victorian aristocrat, Anglican layman, Evangelical activist, social reformer, statesman, and philanthropist.

As one of the keynote social reformers of the Victorian age responsible for factory reform, the expansion of educational opportunities for underprivileged children and the provision of adequate housing and sanitation for England's growing urban communities, Ashley's social reform endeavors require such contextualization—both for the light they caste on this major figure and on the larger movements of the age. Notwithstanding his status as a Tory of the landed aristocracy, his longstanding contribution to social reform legislation exemplified much of the reforming spirit behind the Victorian age. Indeed, this juxtaposition of Ashley as a 'Tory reformer' typified the broader paradox of Victorian Britain, an era arguably as noteworthy for its energetic innovation and far-reaching reform as for its apparent staidness and proclivity to uphold traditional values. Ashley's visions for a humanely-regulated industrial labor force, an educated populace and salubrious living conditions for urban inhabitants represented the reforming outlook which went beyond his own tradition of Tory Evangelicalism. Such reform was also the outcome of other major currents of thought: Benthamite utilitarianism, working-class radicalism, and, to a lesser extent, a surviving tradition of Foxite Whiggism. Collectively these movements inspired the defining social reforms of the Victorian period.[7] Despite Ashley's

5. Strachey, *Eminent Victorians*, 9.

6. Briggs, *Victorian People*, 15. Although Strachey's and Briggs' works were published some decades ago, their respective summations of the Victorian age remain pertinent to contemporary studies of the period.

7. Mandler, *Aristocratic Government*, 220–23. Despite the widely perceived indifference of early Victorian Whiggism to social reform, Mandler argued that there was a

Evangelical convictions being at odds with Benthamite free-thought and his instinctive Toryism clashing with working-class radicalism, his agenda for social reform, at various times, had the capacity to accommodate interests from a broad spectrum of Victorian social reform traditions. This was particularly evident in Ashley's collaboration with Edwin Chadwick on the General Board of Health in 1848, where the Evangelical social concern of the former intersected with the utilitarian interests of the latter in a common project to elevate the living standards of the urban poor.[8]

Given that so much of Ashley's social reform agenda represented the various responses to the "Condition of England Question" famously posed by Thomas Carlyle in 1839, his personal interaction with this key theme of Victorian Britain also warrants historical contextualisation. Pre-occupying both Whig and Tory administrations during Ashley's time in public office, the 'Condition of England Question' became a popular expression for the parlous economic and social conditions besetting the working classes of Britain during the 1830s and 1840s. Eliciting the first waves of Victorian social reform, the Question gave rise to what Geoffery Finlayson identified as three "recognizable responses": namely, Tory paternalistic social amelioration, Whig political reform, and conservative economic improvement and modernization.

To varying degrees, Ashley engaged with each of these responses to the Condition of England Question. Being a Tory-aligned aristocrat with an evangelical social conscience, it was in his parliamentary efforts to secure socially ameliorative measures such as the humane treatment of the mentally ill and the reform of the factory system that his response to the Question was most pronounced. With respect to Whig political reform, Ashley's legislative approach was noteworthy with his support for the Catholic Emancipation Bill in 1829. Despite representing the landed interests of his Dorset constituency which ordinarily favored protectionism, Ashley also supported economic reform efforts to address the Question by siding with the free-trading Peel over the repeal of the Corn Laws in 1846—a move which, it was hoped, would bring with it cheaper food for the masses. Thus, far from standing on the periphery of the political discourse accompanying the Question, Ashley was intimately engaged with the various political attempts to deal with the "Condition of England." His engagement, however, was often less impelled by pragmatic considerations than by his Tory paternalism, his fervent evangelical Protestantism or indeed a combination of

'Foxite' tradition in the Whig party that was sympathetic to entertaining social reform in accordance with the philosophy of Whig-founder, Charles James Fox, to give precedence to the 'common weal' of the people.

8. MacDonagh, *Early Victorian Government*, 34–35.

both. Hence, exploring these currents of Tory paternalism and Evangelicalism are critical to understanding the Victorian intellectual context of Ashley's response to the Question.

Finally, Ashley's *lay* status within the Established Church is also worthy of particular attention and historical contextualization. How was it that a life-long layperson in a highly clericalized denomination such as the Church of England was able to exert such a far-reaching influence on the character of Victorian evangelicalism at large? Part of the answer surely lies in the historic emphasis of evangelical Protestantism on lay-agency, a tradition dating back to Martin Luther's Reformation doctrine of the "priesthood of all believers." As Mark Noll observed, this trait of evangelicalism was particularly evident during the Victorian age when an energized evangelical laity led the charge in "active evangelism, active benevolence and active missionary service."[9] Despite evangelicalism's historic penchant for lay activity, however, Deryck Lovegrove has argued that prevailing historiography in the field of evangelicalism, and religion generally, has tended to overlook "the contribution and role of the religiously committed laity over a wide historical canvas."[10] To remedy this omission, Lovegrove produced a comprehensive study of the part played by non-ordained men and women in the life of the church. Whilst this renewed focus on "lay evangelicalism" is certainly a welcome development, little has emerged in the way of specific case-studies on prominent evangelical laymen and women, particularly from the Victorian age. It is thus timely for a contextual study such as this to focus on the extent to which Ashley's much-noted support of mission societies, voluntary associations and evangelistic enterprises typified the robust lay activity behind Victorian evangelicalism.

Before proceeding to the thematic outline for this study, it will be useful briefly to introduce the two key subjects of the volume: Lord Ashley (1801–85) and the religious movement of Evangelicalism, otherwise known as "vital religion." A descendent of Anthony Ashley Cooper, the First Earl of Shaftesbury (1621–83), Ashley was born into the Shaftesbury earldom in 1801 to his father Cropley Ashley-Cooper (later the Sixth Earl of Shaftesbury) and his mother Lady Anne, the daughter of George Spencer (the Fourth Duke of Marlborough). After the death of his father in June 1851, Ashley assumed the title as Seventh Earl of Shaftesbury.[11] Despite his privileged aristocratic pedigree, Ashley's childhood encountered considerable

9. Noll, "National churches," in Lovegrove, *Rise of the Laity*, 140.

10. Lovegrove, *Rise of the Laity*, 7.

11. The title 'Ashley' will be used in all references to the Victorian social reformer up until 1851. Thereafter, he shall be referred to as 'Shaftesbury' to reflect his post-1851 title.

suffering and his relationship with his parents, particularly his father, remained problematic. These details of his early personal life are by no means irrelevant as they had profound implications for the religious and political ideals he would imbibe in early adulthood. The tepid and formalistic nominal Anglicanism of his upbringing propelled him towards the embrace of a decidedly different Anglican tradition, an Evangelicalism he esteemed as warm, lively, and heartfelt. Meanwhile, Ashley's idealistic and benign form of Southey-inspired Tory paternalism, to a large degree, represented a deliberate counterpoise to the aloof and self-interested aristocratic superintendence of his father. The relationship of his religious and political worldviews to his family background will be explored in further depth throughout the study.

The evangelical Protestant faith to which Ashley gradually assented in his early manhood dated back to the 1740s evangelical revival within the Church of England led by John Wesley and George Whitefield. As a religious movement within Protestantism at large, however, evangelicalism transcended conventional denominational boundaries and both its multifaceted doctrinal essence and fluidity have given rise to a number of definitions in recent evangelical historiography. The leading historian of British evangelicalism, David Bebbington, identified four defining characteristics of this religious movement: conversionism, activism, biblicism, and crucicentrism.[12] According to Bebbington, evangelicalism and evangelicals have manifested all four of these traits, but each one to varying degrees, depending on the historical time and place.[13] Complementing the "Bebbington quadrilateral" definition of evangelicalism (as it became known), Timothy Larsen formulated his own "pentagonal" characterization of evangelicalism which, in short, defined an evangelical according to the following five points: an orthodox Protestant, an heir to the eighteenth-century Wesley-Whitefield revival, an adherent to the primacy of Scripture, a believer in the atonement, and, finally, somebody who stressed the work of the Holy Spirit in the life of the believer and the church.[14] It is evident from the definitions that the "Bebbington quadrilateral" and "Larsen pentagon" overlapped considerably, with Robert Warner also proposing "Christocentrism," the "transformed life" of the believer and "revival aspirations" as three important additions to the canon of evangelical characteristics.[15]

---

12. Bebbington, *Evangelicalism in Modern Britain*, 3.

13. Ibid.

14. Larsen, "Defining and Locating Evangelicalism," in Larson and Treier, *Companion to Evangelical Theology*, 1.

15. Warner, *Reinventing English Evangelicalism*, 19.

In addition to these doctrinal formulations, Mark Noll contended that evangelicalism could be defined not merely by a set of doctrinal convictions but also by its heterogeneous constitution of individuals, associations, books, practices, perceptions, and networks of influence shared by the promoters of the eighteenth-century revivals and their descendants.[16] Thus, as John Wolffe observed, evangelicalism did not represent an organized form of religion in institutional terms, but rather a broad movement generating a multiplicity of institutions.[17] Given this denominational plurality of evangelicalism, John Stackhouse was correct to identify "trans-denominationalism" as an organizing principle for the movement, whereby evangelicals tended to relativize their own denominational identity in favor of pan-evangelical co-operation.[18] This was particularly pertinent in the case of Ashley who, despite his avowed Anglican identity, remained committed to the cause of pan-evangelical unity.

These definitional frameworks of evangelicalism will be eminently useful tools in identifying and explaining Ashley's own form of evangelicalism in this study. In Part One, it will be argued that Ashley embodied all of the requisite doctrinal characteristics comprising both the Bebbington and Larsen prisms of evangelical identity as well as engaging with the various literature, individuals, and networks that Noll stressed as being so integral to the movement. It will, however, be contended that some evangelical traits were certainly more pronounced in both Ashley's personal piety and public witness than others. The lingering uncertainty surrounding the time and nature of Ashley's conversion to Christianity, coupled with his robust defense of biblical authority and sustained advocacy for mission and philanthropy, point to the conclusion that Ashley's evangelicalism was characterized more by its activism and biblicism than by its conversionism. The distinctive contours of Ashley's Evangelicalism will be explained by a combination of factors including his personal background, his avowed Anglican identity, his Tory paternalist creed, and indeed the broader Victorian evangelical context.

With the overarching aim of establishing Ashley as a specimen of Victorian Evangelicalism, the first part of this volume focuses chiefly on the religious tradition of Evangelical Anglican Christianity in Britain and charts the extent to which it accounted for the evolution of the social reformer's religious outlook. Although Ashley's Evangelicalism, to a large degree, came to reflect the vital religiosity of his own Victorian age, it will be argued that

---

16. Noll, *Rise of Evangelicalism*, 3–4.
17. Wolffe, *God and Greater Britain*, 23.
18. Stackhouse quoted in Warner, *Reinventing English Evangelicalism*, 19.

the original form of British Evangelicalism he imbibed from the 1820s was essentially that of the robust but measured and reasoned variety championed by the Clapham Sect and the *Christian Observer*. In exploring Ashley's assent to vital religion, this part will pinpoint relevant Clapham-aligned Evangelicals and explain the direct influence of their religious tradition *specifically* on the emerging spirituality of the young Ashley. As a starting point, Edwin Hodder's 1886 biography provided some valuable clues as to how some of the Clapham Evangelicals were perceived through the eyes of Ashley.[19] The author, pioneering educationalist and philanthropist, Hannah More (1745–1833), was one such Clapham figure for whom Ashley accorded high praise in his diary.[20] Accordingly, this volume will closely study More's writings to appreciate the bearing she had on Ashley's Evangelical outlook. The second Clapham figure to whom Ashley owed much inspiration in both his outlook and work was Thomas Fowell Buxton (1786–1845), Wilberforce's parliamentary successor in the anti-slavery movement. Upon reading Buxton's own accounts of the slave trade, Ashley instinctively felt the same horror and disgust against the practice of slavery which had so impelled the Clapham anti-slavery campaigners.[21] In agitating for an end to these more domestic forms of 'white' slavery, the extent to which his thoughts were attributable to those of his anti-slavery predecessor will be assessed by a study of Buxton's accounts, speeches and correspondence. Despite citing some historical figures behind the inspiration of Ashley's Evangelicalism, Hodder did not discuss the extent to which his Evangelicalism was indebted to these individuals.

While much of the existing literature points to the influence of Claphamite Evangelicalism generally, few works discuss in any length, specific *figures* outside of Clapham who directly shaped the young aristocrat's spirituality. Aside from Ashley's nursemaid, Maria Millis, the primary contributor to Ashley's emerging Anglican Evangelicalism was undoubtedly the Church of England clergyman, Edward Bickersteth (1789–1850). Gareth Atkins published a recent article exploring the Evangelical doctrine and practice of Bickersteth within the wider context of developments in the British Evangelical world during the 1830s and 1840s. While Atkins' article helpfully contextualized Bickersteth's theology, it did not attempt to gauge his *longer-term* influence on Ashley's rising generation of Evangelicals.[22]

19. Hodder, *The Life and Work of the seventh Earl* (Vols: I–III).
20. Hodder, *Life and Work of the Seventh Earl*, Vol. I, 200.
21. Ibid., 258.
22. Atkins, "Anglican Evangelical Theology," 1–19. The only mention Atkins made of Ashley was his close friendship with Bickersteth dating back to 1835 (at 15).

Biographies of Ashley, meanwhile, have made passing reference to Bickersteth as a spiritual mentor to the young Ashley.[23] However, no biographical study to date has explored in any great depth the nature of Bickersteth's own religious principles and the extent to which these molded the spiritual consciousness of Ashley.[24] Based on his own writings and sermons, the Evangelical Bickersteth's defining beliefs included a pre-millennial eschatology accompanied by the "urgency" of Christian mission, a staunch anti-Catholicism, the priority of pan-evangelical solidarity, and an abiding sense that God worked directly through contemporary national events. Bickersteth's articulation of these doctrines in various publications of his such as *Practical Remarks* (1832) and the *Divine Warning* (1842) will be discussed in order to appreciate the roots of much of Ashley's breed of Anglican Evangelicalism.[25]

In addition to Bickersteth's influence, the Evangelicalism of Ashley was molded to a significant degree by his friend and Victorian contemporary, Alexander Haldane (1800–1882). As the proprietor of the influential Anglican newspaper, *The Record*, Haldane's editorial tone and pronouncements typified the outlook of an emerging Victorian Evangelical generation decidedly more strident and defensive in temperament than the older, temperate Evangelical voices of the Clapham Sect and *Christian Observer*. The theological hallmarks of this new "Recordite" Evangelical generation included a staunch Protestantism, an uncompromising biblical literalism and a premillennial eschatology, all of which the Evangelical Ashley embodied. Whilst their origin could be traced back to Bickersteth, who had a historical affinity with the Clapham Sect through his early activity with the Church Missionary Society (CMS), they were arguably reinforced by the Recordite apostle. For this reason, various references will be made to Haldane and the *Record*

---

23. Battiscombe in *Shaftesbury: A Biography*, discussed the influence of Bickersteth on Ashley's evolving Evangelicalism, particularly with regard to his eschatology, at 99–104. In *Shaftesbury: The Great Reformer*, Richard Turnbull likewise explained, briefly, the influence of Bickersteth on Ashley's Evangelical convictions concerning premillennialism and the priority of Christian mission amongst the Jews, in particular, at 50–52.

24. In his voluminous biography *The Seventh Earl of Shaftesbury*, Geoffrey Finlayson acknowledged the significance to Ashley's evolving Evangelicalism of his meeting with Bickersteth in 1835 at 104 and recognized the clergyman's "great influence on Ashley" (at 320). Like Ashley's other biographers such as Battiscombe and Turnbull, however, Finlayson did not extensively survey the contours of Bickersteth's own theology which contained so many of the seeds of Ashely's evangelicalism.

25. Bickersteth's key works included *Practical Remarks on the Prophecies* (1832), *A Treatise on Baptism* (1840), *Family Prayers* (1841), *The Restoration of the Jews to their own Land* (1841), *Divine Warning to the Church* (1842) and *The Signs of the Times in the East: A Warning to the West* (1845).

in this part's discussion of Ashley's significant status as a 'transitional' Evangelical figure between the Claphamite and Recordite generations.

Together with Evangelical Anglicanism, paternalism was arguably one of the key belief-systems that shaped Ashley's basic worldview and approach to religious affairs, politics, and society. Accordingly, this second part of the volume will explore the various spheres from which Ashley imbibed the tradition of paternalism and the contexts in which he manifested its ideals. In two volumes, David Roberts provided an invaluable background to this core philosophy embodied by Ashley.[26] As with evangelicalism, paternalism represented a complex, multifaceted and essentially protean concept, subject to a variety of historical definitions and explanations. Appreciating this innate complexity, Roberts identified a variety of paternalist traditions arising from disparate contexts ranging from the landed aristocracy, to the church and even the modern factory. Paternalism also transcended political ideology with the Whig, Tory, and radical movements all exhibiting a strand of paternalist philosophy. With Ashley's own breed of Tory paternalism shaped by a variety of influences such as his friendship with Robert Southey, his troublesome relationship with his father, his strained relations with his own Tory party, and, of course, the continual interplay of his politics with his evangelical religiosity, it could not be squarely compartmentalized into one of Roberts' categories.

Nonetheless, it can be deduced that Ashley's Tory paternalism was indebted to some contexts and traditions more than others. Of the several paternalist sub-categories Roberts identified, Ashley's breed of paternalism was chiefly drawn from the aristocratic, "country-squire" school and the ecclesiastical school, thereby giving it a predominantly, but not exclusively, "high Tory" character. Expressed politically, his Tory paternalism favored an interventionist and ameliorative style of governance that was frequently at odds with the liberal-Toryism of Prime Minister Robert Peel and his Home Secretary, James Graham, in the 1840s. In short, Ashley's Tory paternalism entailed belief in a divinely-ordered hierarchical society, a sense of public duty and *noblesse oblige*, the inheritance or ownership of land as a basis for performing paternal duties, the idealization of rural life, a romanticized view of the past and the preservation of traditional institutions including the Crown and Established Church. It is evident Ashley publicly manifested many of these attitudes to varying degrees with Roberts describing the Earl as "Parliament's most complete paternalist."[27]

---

26. Roberts, *Paternalism*; Roberts, *Social Conscience*.
27. Roberts, *Paternalism*, 218.

After critically analyzing the various strands of Ashley's paternalist philosophy, this part will closely explore the distinctive breed of Tory paternalism embodied by the Lake poet, Robert Southey, and how this influenced the political thought of Ashley. Given that Ashley enjoyed a close personal friendship with Southey, with no evidence of a similar relationship existing with either Coleridge or Wordsworth, discussion will be chiefly confined to the influence of the Bristol-born Southey on Ashley. This relationship between the two men has been acknowledged in recent historiography. Richard Turnbull's recent biography, for instance, is to be given credit for appreciating the paternalist streak in Ashley's tradition of Evangelicalism and attributing much of this to his friendship with Southey.[28] Finlayson, meanwhile, had observed Ashley's great admiration for Southey and identified the poet as "an exponent of the Tory paternalist school of thought."[29] While biographers on Ashley to date have made mention of the Dorset aristocrat's significant relationship with the Poet Laureate, they have not focused on Southey's romantic conservative philosophy in any great detail, thereby restricting their capacity to assess its thoroughgoing impact on the emerging Tory paternalism of Ashley. Conversely, there have been comprehensive studies on Southey's intellectual and political thought but none have alluded to the influence of this on Ashley.[30] Thus, to remedy this lacuna in the historiography, this second part will closely examine the key publications of Southey, including his *Book of the Church* (1824), *Colloquies* (1829), and *Essays Moral and Political* (1832), in addition to his personal correspondence with Ashley, to reveal the intellectual roots of this social reformer's Tory paternalism.[31]

In addition to examining Southey's thought as the primary prism through which Ashley imbibed his Tory paternalism, this part will discuss Ashley's difficult relationship with his father. It will be pointed out that Ashley's father's jurisdiction of the St Giles estate fell well short of the classic paternalistic virtues esteemed by Southey, and, later, Ashley himself. Instead of exercising a benevolent and attentive superintendence over his estate's workers, the Sixth Earl displayed palpable neglect towards the welfare of his charges with their lodgings and amenities falling into a state of disrepair. In an effort consciously to distance himself from the poor stewardship of his father, Ashley made radical changes to the management of St Giles once he

28. Turnbull, *Shaftesbury*, 44, 77.
29. Finlayson, *Seventh Earl*, 74.
30. Andrews, *Robert Southey*, 2011; Eastwood, "Robert Southey," 308–31.
31. The principal publications in which Robert Southey articulated his Tory paternalist ideals were *Sir Thomas More, or, Colloquies on the Progress and Prospects of Society* (1829) and *Essays Moral and Political* (1832).

assumed ownership of the estate in 1851. It will be argued that, in remedying his father's oversights, Ashley sought to exercise the Tory paternalist leadership of the kind he had brought to his more public endeavors of factory reform legislation and improved public health. This part will conclude by examining the broader political influences on Ashley's Tory paternalism and the extent to which his Tory paternalism was either typical or atypical of the prevailing Tory party philosophy, particularly during the second Peel administration of 1841–46. The enigmatic nature of Ashley's Tory party identity will be discussed within the broader context of political party realignments over social reform during the early Victorian period. On the one hand, Ashley's personal philosophy remained firmly wedded to the paternalist tradition of the high Tories, an affinity that was cemented through his friendship with the romantic conservative Southey. On the other hand, Ashley had moved into Whig political circles, at least at a personal level, through his marriage to Lady Emily Cowper in 1830 who was most likely the natural daughter of future Liberal Premier, Lord Palmerston. Moreover, on social reform issues such as factory legislation, Ashley had enjoyed decidedly more cooperation with the Whig Premier, Lord John Russell, than with his Tory predecessor, Robert Peel.[32]

After establishing Ashley's indebtedness to the tradition of Evangelical Anglicanism on the one hand, and Tory paternalism on the other, this third part of the volume explains the confluence between some elements of each and how this synthesis reached its apogee in the life and work of Ashley on the cusp of the Victorian age. In providing the basis for a study of how Ashley represented a bridge between Tory paternalism and Evangelicalism, Geoffrey Finlayson published a chapter discussing Ashley's guiding principles.[33] Therein, Finlayson made reference to the "stirring of two forces which were to undergird his [Ashley's] life," identifying each of these as "paternalism" and "evangelicalism."[34] Finlayson went on to observe that Ashley's "paternalism and evangelicalism combined . . . to ensure that it was always the responsibilities of rank which he emphasized." Although Finlayson appreciated the convergence between paternalism and evangelicalism in Ashley's own life and outlook, his chapter did not contextualize this development in the broader context of the ideological realignments taking place in early Victorian England that helped to account for such a symbiosis.

In terms of illuminating this broader context, Boyd Hilton's monumental *Age of Atonement* explored the complex interplay between

---

32. Mandler, *Aristocratic Government*, 240.
33. Finlayson, "Shaftesbury," in Hollis, *Pressure from Without*, 159–82.
34. Ibid., 160.

Evangelicalism and political thought, particularly on economic policy and the role of government in society.[35] Focusing on the period 1795–1865, Hilton's study covered the very time frame in which Ashley was formulating his own religious and political outlook. For the purposes of understanding Ashley's synthesis of Evangelicalism and Tory paternalism, the most critical insight to be gained from Hilton's study was that, between the 1820s and 1840s, a significant body of opinion within the Anglican Evangelical movement revised its philosophy of state intervention. Departing from the earlier tradition of Wilberforce and the Clapham Sect, which had defended the *laissez-faire* orthodoxy of political economy, an emerging generation of Evangelicals, including Edward Bickersteth, Henry Drummond, the leaders of the factory reform movement, and Ashley himself, came to support ameliorative state intervention and thus the notion of a paternalist government. Accounting for this shift in outlook, Hilton cited many pertinent factors such as constitutional reforms and economic turmoil, coupled with a changing theology of providence and eschatology amongst Evangelicals.[36] Despite occasionally mentioning Ashley as part of this new Evangelical generation,[37] Hilton's study did not venture into a specific discussion of how Ashley himself was able to reconcile his deeply-held Evangelical beliefs with paternalist ethics.

Hence utilizing Hilton's *Age of Atonement* as an invaluable contextual study, this part will discuss how the Evangelical Ashley assented to a predominantly 'high Tory' form of paternalism through the influence of his mentor, Bickersteth, and his subsequent acquaintance with similarly paternalist-minded Evangelicals such as Robert Benton Seeley and Charlotte Elizabeth Tonna. While Hilton's volume sheds light on the critical political and economic realignments taking place within pre and early Victorian Evangelicalism, Kim Lawes' study of *Paternalism and Politics* explored the practical implications these realignments had for Tory perspectives on economic policy and the role of government. In particular, Lawes provided some invaluable discussion of the emerging tensions between liberal utilitarianism and aristocratic paternalism in the 1820s and 30s.[38] Within the Tory paternalist critique of economic liberalism, Lawes identified a strand of social reform activism led by Evangelical parliamentarians such as Michael

---

35. Hilton, *Age of Atonement*.
36. Ibid., 10, 15–17.
37. Ibid., 15, 17–18, 95, 212–13.
38. Lawes, *Paternalism and Politics*, 64–96.

T. Sadler and Ashley who preached the responsibility of the state to protect the poor.[39]

While an appreciation of the synthesis between evangelicalism and paternalism undergirding Ashley's worldview is considerably indebted to the background scholarship of Finlayson, Hilton, and Lawes, this third part of the study will focus especially on the evolving relationship between the two streams of thought in early Victorian society and, in particular, the specific implications this had for the evolving political and religious outlook of Ashley. Accordingly, this volume will identify relevant historical and contemporaneous factors that enabled common ground to be forged between the traditions of Evangelicalism and Tory paternalism underpinning Ashley's worldview. These included a distinctively Anglican tradition of paternalism, the growing appeal of a benignly interventionist state for Evangelicals aggrieved by the seeming deficiencies of *laissez-faire* political economy to address social disadvantage, the common zeal of Evangelicals and high Tory paternalists to preserve the Protestant constitution of England in the face of recent 1828–29 reforms, the emergence of a distinctive strand of premillennial Evangelical eschatology reinforcing the merits of paternalist state intervention, the publication of Evangelical treatises by R. B. Seeley and C. E. Tonna advocating paternalist social reform measures and the infiltration of Evangelical religion through the ranks of the aristocracy where it occasionally melded with traditional patrician values.

Drawing attention to the factory reform movement where both Tory paternalist ideals and Evangelical social concern featured conspicuously in campaign discourse, this third part will investigate how the leading lights of the factory reform movement managed to integrate high Tory ideals into their Evangelical belief-systems. Owing to the peculiar political and religious vicissitudes of Yorkshire in the early decades of the nineteenth-century, reformers such as Richard Oastler, George Stringer Bull, and Michael Thomas Sadler emerged as a new breed of "Tory-Evangelicals." By studying each of these reformers and their common zeal for the cause of factory reform, this volume will illustrate how they represented the forerunners to the "Tory-Evangelical" Ashley. This was instanced by their ability similarly to harness an alliance of Tory paternalist and Evangelical social objectives as a powerful driving-force for social reform. Thus, with Ashley surfacing as the natural successor to these reformers, this part will conclude with a study of how the Victorian social reformer himself personified the alliance of Evangelical Protestantism and Tory paternalism which had occurred over the preceding two decades. Particular attention here will be given to how

---

39. Ibid., 2, 150.

Ashley's Evangelical and paternalist sensibilities informed his recommendation of bishops under the premiership of Lord Palmerston.

Having established Ashley as personifying this synthesis of Tory and Evangelical threads of thought, Part Four will seek to locate Ashley's place within the milieu of Victorian Evangelicalism. It will also discuss the extent to which the Victorian Ashley represented the defining tendencies and preoccupations of this religious movement. With Part One having examined both the historic background and internal characteristics of Ashley's Evangelicalism, this fourth part will return to the religiosity of Ashley but assess it in its contemporary Victorian context. Given that the Evangelicalism of Ashley was shaped to a considerable degree by his mentor, Edward Bickersteth, and subsequently, his Victorian contemporary, Alexander Haldane, Ashley was arguably well-placed to identify closely with the prevailing temperament of Victorian Anglican Evangelicalism.

The specialized studies of Kenneth Hylson-Smith and Nigel Scotland each succeeded in illuminating the defining contours of Victorian Anglican Evangelicalism.[40] Whilst Bebbington's *Dominance of Evangelicalism* and Bradley's *Call to Seriousness* each provided a comprehensive overview of Victorian evangelicalism *generally*, Hylson-Smith and Scotland specifically examined the nature of *Anglican* Evangelicalism in the Victorian period. This is crucial, given the fact that Ashley's avowed Church of England identity colored much of his Evangelicalism, thereby distinguishing it from the evangelicalism of Victorian Nonconformists. As Timothy Larsen demonstrated in his study on Victorian Nonconformity,[41] despite consensus on core Protestant doctrines, Dissenters frequently differed radically from Churchmen on social and political questions. These included political party allegiance, religious liberty, Catholic and Jewish emancipation, the merits of free trade versus protectionism and church disestablishment. Predictably, the outlook of Ashley on such issues accorded with that of his co-religionists in the Established Church. For this reason, the explicit focus of Hylson-Smith and Scotland on Victorian Evangelicalism within the Church of England provided the most apposite contextual background to appreciating the religious temperament of Ashley.

---

40. Hylson-Smith, *Evangelicals in the Church of England* and Scotland, *Evangelical Anglicans*. Carter in *Anglican Evangelicals* also touched on some aspects of Anglican Evangelicalism during the Victorian Age. While Carter's study contained a relevant chapter on eschatological developments in early Victorian Anglican Evangelicalism (152–93) and a case study on Anglican Evangelical responses to the Tractarian-instigated 'Gorham Affair' (312–55), it did not provide the same broad overview of Victorian Anglican Evangelical interests and preoccupations as Hylson-Smith and Scotland.

41. Larsen, *Friends of Religious Equality*.

Drawing on these two volumes, together with more specialist studies on such concerns to Victorian Evangelicals as premillennialism,[42] imperialism and race,[43] Christian Zionism,[44] anti-Catholicism and anti-Tractarianism,[45] anti-rationalism,[46] pan-evangelical cooperation,[47] family and gender,[48] the Sabbath,[49] philanthropy and social welfare,[50] this part will discuss the salient preoccupations of Victorian Anglican Evangelicalism and the extent to which Ashley (later Shaftesbury) reflected these in his pronouncements and activities. In examining Ashley's posture on each issue of popular Evangelical concern, it will become evident as to with which generation of Anglican Evangelicalism the Victorian social reformer most closely identified, given that his faith was indebted to both Claphamite and Recordite influences. On matters such as Sabbath observance and philanthropic enterprise, it appeared that Ashley stood very much in the tradition of the Claphamites. On the other hand, Ashley's premillennialism and anti-Catholicism strongly suggested he had imbibed the Evangelical temperament of his Recordite Evangelical contemporaries. Meanwhile, on the priorities of mission, evangelism, and family life, it could be deduced that Ashley represented both generations, given the perennial nature of these Evangelical preoccupations from the Clapham-aligned Simeon to the Recordite Haldane.

In examining the Evangelical interests of the Victorian Ashley, the significance of the romantic Tory-based paternalism he imbibed largely from Robert Southey does not fade into the background. On the contrary, the inflow of paternalist thinking into Ashley's Evangelicalism becomes very apparent as he frequently invoked the paternalist themes of tradition, authority, protection, and guidance in his perspectives on issues as diverse as imperialism, Jewish emancipation, the Sabbath, family life, philanthropy and social welfare. Accordingly, the purpose of this part is not only to examine Ashley's Evangelical attitudes in their Victorian social and cultural context but also to illustrate the degree to which his Evangelicalism, and that of Victorian society at large, reflected the infiltration of romantic

---

42. Spence, "The Renewal of Time and Space," 81–101; Brown, "Evangelical Social Thought,": 126–36 and Spence, *Heaven on Earth*.

43. Elbourne, "Religion in the British Empire," in Stockwell, *British Empire*, 131–56.

44. Lewis, *Origins of Christian Zionism*.

45. Wolffe, *Protestant Crusade*.

46. Larsen, "Bishop Colenso and his Critics," 433–58.

47. Wolffe, "Evangelical Alliance in the 1840s," in Sheils and Wood, *Voluntary Religion*, 340.

48. Davidoff and Hall, *Family Fortunes*.

49. Wigley, *Rise and Fall of the Victorian Sunday*.

50. Finlayson, *Citizen, State, and Social Welfare*.

paternalism which had accompanied the Evangelical thought of social reform advocates such as Bickerseth, Seeley, Tonna, Oastler, Bull, Sadler, and Ashley. Given the culturally conditioned nature of Evangelicalism, Bebbington rightly identified romanticism as a major influence on the evolving character of nineteenth-century Evangelicalism.[51] Although Bebbington had discussed premillennial eschatology and the use of art and emotion in worship and liturgy as manifestations of the romantic inflow into Victorian Evangelicalism,[52] this part appreciates that high Tory paternalism, popularized by the likes of Southey, was also a critical import from the romanticism that Ashley exhibited in the Evangelicalism of his time.

Turning to the biographies on Ashley published to date: their respective narratives of his life did feature some commentary on the social reformer's religious outlook and political sympathies. Geoffrey Best's 1964 biography contained a welcome chapter on the ever pertinent themes of "Church, State and Empire":[53] Battiscombe's biography managed to accommodate an insightful discussion of Ashley's premillennial eschatology[54] and, most recently, Turnbull's 2010 biography helpfully alluded to the themes of paternalism and premillennialism,[55] albeit in brief and fairly general terms. It was Finlayson's voluminous account of 1981, however, that arguably provided the most extensive coverage of these matters.[56] Finlayson discussed the evolution of Ashley's Evangelicalism in the 1820s and 30s as well as the manifestation of his Tory paternalist creed in his early political life.[57] Finlayson's biography proceeded far beyond merely recounting the minutiae of Ashley's personal and domestic life to discuss extensively his political career and its broader historical significance in Victorian public affairs. In so doing, Finlayson shed invaluable light on Ashley's relationship with key public figures from the Duke of Wellington in the late 1820s to William Gladstone in the early 1880s. This study is thus indebted to Finlayson for weaving such a meticulous portrait of Ashley within the broader tapestry of Victorian British life.

The contemporaneous context of Ashley's pivotal *ideas* and their historical origins, however, remained largely unexplored by Finlayson. Readers of his biography would be furnished with limited knowledge and appreciation

---

51. Bebbington, *Evangelicalism*, 81.
52. Ibid., 84; Bebbington, *Dominance of Evangelicalism*, 140–53.
53. Best, *Shaftesbury*, 52–80.
54. Battiscombe, *Shaftesbury: A Biography*, 99–103.
55. Turnbull, *Shaftesbury*, 210–12, 219–23.
56. Finlayson, *Seventh Earl of Shaftesbury*.
57. Ibid., 74–76.

of such themes as Edward Bickersteth's and Alexander Haldane's distinctive Evangelical theology, Southey's romantic conservative philosophy, the emerging Tory-Evangelicalism of thinkers and writers such as R. B. Seeley and C. E. Tonna, and the extent of Ashley's indebtedness to the radical Tory politics of the early factory reformers, Sadler, Oastler, and Bull. Of course, given the forgoing acknowledgment of Finlayson's biography, it would be a little unrealistic to have expected his already comprehensive study to have covered all of the above ground. Hence this study fulfills a specific purpose by adding this important historical and contemporaneous context to the evolving religious and political thought of Ashley.

Accordingly, this fourth part will extend its focus beyond the mere biographical narrative to discuss the extent to which Ashley's own mindset typified at least a part of the complex character of Victorian Evangelicalism. As for the published works covering Victorian-period Evangelicalism generally, their treatment of this religious movement is very thorough, replete with references to key Evangelical figures, including Ashley. The Evangelical Tory is typically well-introduced and his significance as a lead social reformer is appreciated, but discussion is fairly brief with the narratives understandably conscious of incorporating other noteworthy individuals, networks, events, traits, and trends within the Victorian evangelical matrix.[58] Thus to shine the narrative spotlight more closely on Ashley, this part draws on primary materials that include Parliamentary Papers recording Ashley's speeches and debates in the House of Commons and the House of Lords, Ashley's letters and general correspondence, as well as articles from journals, periodicals, and publications to which he was a contributor.

As for the personal diary entries of Ashley, these are generally treated with caution given the frequently emotive and subjective nature of his firsthand observations; nevertheless, they warrant substantial consideration given his lifelong reputation as an avid diarist. Though some insightful entries have been gleaned from the original diary manuscripts in the Broadlands collection at the University of Southampton (along with other items in this archive), Shaftesbury's virtually indecipherable handwriting and the tyranny of distance for an Australian-based researcher have increased the utility of the diary extracts reproduced and published in 1886 by the British biographer, Edwin Hodder (1837–1904). The diary extracts transcribed in Hodder's near contemporary biography have both advantages and disadvantages. On the negative side, the selections made by Hodder naturally reflect his own concerns and those of his contemporaries. On the other hand,

---

58. For references to Ashley, see for example, Brown *Providence and Empire*, 162–64; Wolffe, *Expansion of Evangelicalism*, 105–7; Bebbington, *Dominance of Evangelicalism*, 93–94; Hylson-Smith, *Evangelicals in the Church of England*, 139–41.

they have the merit of being recorded by somebody who was personally acquainted with Ashley. From Hodder's biography, it was evident that the author had engaged in personal conversations with Ashley about important themes and issues, such as Ashley's own childhood.[59]

In its methodology, Hodder's biographical account stood firmly in the tradition of biography famously pioneered by James Boswell (1740–95) who published his *Life of Samuel Johnson* in 1791. As Boswell had done with Johnson, Hodder directly incorporated his conversations with Ashley into his biographical work and arguably included more personal details than those which would have otherwise come to light from Ashley's own diaries. With Hodder following Boswell's example of note-taking conversations with his biographical subject, he largely succeeded in capturing a similarly vivid portrait of Ashley. While Hodder's transcriptions cannot be always treated as infallible authority, given his own inescapable proclivities towards personal bias, the author nonetheless had the advantage of been privy to Ashley's own thoughts and communications. In addition, Hodder's publication is widely available and this has made it possible for subsequent biographers, from the Hammonds (1939) to Turnbull (2010), to verify and duly contextualize Ashley's quotations within the broader narrative of his whole life. In drawing from these original sources, it is anticipated that this publication will formulate a fresh analysis of how Ashley emerged as a key figure within the context of Victorian Evangelicalism, thereby adding a new insight to that provided by the existing literature.

In desiring to make this volume a *contextual study* of Ashley and not merely another biography,[60] it will go beyond the narrative of Ashley's life to study the prevailing intellectual ideas absorbed by Ashley as a young man and manifested subsequently in his public career. Anglican Evangelicalism and Tory paternalism, of course, represented the two dominant wellsprings of Ashley's thought. His advocacy of these twin pillars of his reforming creed helped to color at least some elements of Victorian Evangelicalism more generally. In providing a study of Ashley that is both chronologically and

59. See, for example, Lord Shaftesbury in conversation with Edwin Hodder, cited in Hodder, *Life and Work of the Seventh Earl*, Vol. I, 51.

60. Following Edwin Hodder's official 1886 biography of *The Life and Work of the Seventh Earl* which drew heavily on the primary sources of Ashley, there has been a periodic output of subsequent biographical works. These have included Kirton, *True Nobility* (1886); Bingham, *Life of the Seventh Earl of Shaftesbury* (1899); Hammond, *Lord Shaftesbury* (1923); Blackburn, *Noble Lord* (1949); St Fancourt, *The People's Earl* (1962); Best, *A Biography of A. A. Cooper: 7th Earl* (1964); Battiscombe, *Shaftesbury: A Biography* (1974); Finlayson, *Seventh Earl of Shaftesbury* (1981); Pollock, *Shaftesbury: The Reformer* (2000); and most recently, Turnbull, *Shaftesbury: The Great Reformer* (2010).

thematically contextual, it is anticipated this publication will present fresh insights into this prominent Victorian figure as well as a renewed appreciation for the crucial juncture he occupied in the course of British religious and social history. Thus the objective of this volume, as a contextual study, is to produce an original work that adds to an understanding of both Ashley and Victorian Evangelicalism, thereby filling a void between the existing biographies and the general historical narratives on Evangelical Protestantism in the Victorian era.

Part I

Ashley and the Anglican Evangelical Tradition

1

Ashley's Expression of Anglican Evangelicalism

In the twilight of his long life in 1884, Ashley described himself as an "Evangelical of the Evangelicals."[1] The Evangelical identity of this Victorian social reformer and philanthropist is widely appreciated by both the biographical works and the historiography of Evangelical religion in the Victorian period. Given the fluid and heterogeneous nature of Evangelicalism in eighteenth- and nineteenth-century Britain, however, this first section will seek to explore the manner and extent to which Ashley embodied the various Evangelical characteristics as identified by the historians of this religious movement.[2] Identifying the Established Church of England as the institution through which the Evangelicalism of Ashley was conditioned, this section will discuss some of the key Anglican institutions, networks, and leaders primarily responsible for configuring both the *praxis* and theology of the Evangelicalism that Ashley came to imbibe as a young man in the 1820s and 1830s. This period of British history during which Ashley assented to Evangelicalism is particularly significant given the historiographical consensus that this was also the precise point at which Evangelicalism

---

1. Hodder, *Life and Work of the Seventh Earl,* 3. In 1884, Shaftesbury told his biographer, Edwin Hodder: "I am an Evangelical of the Evangelicals. I have worked with them constantly, and I am satisfied that most of the great philanthropic movements of the century have sprung from them. I stand fast by the teachings of the party, but I am not, and never have been, a leader of that party."

2. Historians of British Evangelicalism including David Bebbington, Timothy Larsen, John Wolffe, Mark Noll, Mark Smith, and Rob Warner have been chiefly responsible for formulating working definitions and thematic analyses of this religious movement.

underwent considerable ferment and transformation.³ According to the accepted narrative, Evangelicalism, whilst retaining its fundamentals of belief and practice, changed appreciably in *temperament* and *disposition* during the second quarter of the nineteenth century from being the rationalist, measured, and postmillennial variety of Charles Simeon and the Clapham Sect generation to the more strident, ultra-Protestant, and premillennial version of Alexander Haldane and the *Recordites*.⁴ Evangelicalism thus experienced a combination of change and continuity during this generational transition. This essentially accorded with Bebbington's theory that the relationship between successive Evangelical generations "was one of continuity as well as discontinuity."⁵

With the earlier half of Ashley's life spanning these two generations, he witnessed first-hand this Evangelical transformation and his personal faith accordingly reflected elements of each. This was captured by Edwin Hodder who catalogued a string of Evangelical figures from both the Clapham and Recordite traditions with whom Ashley was seen to be connected.

> Lord Shaftesbury belonged to the older order of Evangelicals, to the Venns, Romanie, Topladys, Berridges, Simeons, Grimshaws, Herveys, Scotts and Newtons of a former day-to the school represented by Hugh Stowell, Haldane Stuart, Edward Bickersteth, Hugh McNeile, Henry Venn, William Marsh, Alexander Haldane, in his own day.⁶

Of the first generation, Hodder appropriately associated the fellow of King's College Cambridge, Charles Simeon, and the Bible commentator, Thomas Scott, with Ashley and his Evangelicalism. Although Ashley was not known to have enjoyed a personal acquaintance with Simeon, the Cambridge leader's zeal for overseas mission and evangelism amongst the Jews was transmitted through another Anglican clergyman, Edward Bickersteth, who became a personal mentor to Ashley. Meanwhile, Ashley inherited Scott's reverence for the divine inspiration of scripture through the reading of his influential Bible commentaries. The other 'older order' Evangelical figures that Hodder

---

3. See for example, Bebbington, *Evangelicalism*, 75–104; Wolffe, *Expansion of Evangelicalism*, 204; Hilton, *Age of Atonement*, 10–22 ; Lewis, *Origins of Christian Zionism*, 93–95 and Turner, *John Henry Newman*, 29.

4. Hilton, *Age of Atonement*, 10. 'Recordite' was a term popularly assigned to the succeeding generation of Victorian Evangelicals who identified with Alexander Haldane's *Record* newspaper, established in 1828, and its promulgation of a militantly Protestant and premillennial form of Evangelicalism.

5. Bebbington, "Response," in Haykin and Stewart, *Emergence of Evangelicalism*, 427.

6. Hodder, *Life and Work of the Seventh Earl*, Vol. III, 5.

cited, on the other hand, were peripheral and not closely connected with Ashley's spiritual formation. Of the more recent school, again, it was a select number, namely Bickersteth and the *Record* proprietor, Alexander Haldane, with whom Ashley was closely acquainted.[7] Although Ashley was initially cool towards the *Record* for what he saw as its polemical tone, he came to appreciate Haldane as a kindred spirit in his similarly premillennial and uncompromisingly Protestant expression of Evangelicalism.[8] It was Hodder's reference to Bickersteth, however, that was particularly noteworthy, not only on account of his intimate friendship with, and far-reaching influence on Ashley, but also on his status as a 'transitional' Evangelical bridging the Claphamite and Recordite gulf. Accordingly, this section will conclude that chiefly by virtue of Bickersteth's influence, Ashley similarly represented an intermediary figure in the transformation of British Evangelicalism during the 1820s and 1830s.

The emergence of Anglican Evangelicalism and Ashley

The Evangelical Protestant expression of Christianity took root with a religious revival bursting forth on the English scene from the 1730s through the dynamic preaching activity of the Wesley brothers and Whitefield.[9] Notwithstanding the diversity of theological perspectives and emphases within evangelicalism, not least the Arminian-Calvinist controversy between the movement's two figureheads John Wesley and George Whitefield, Bebbington was able to formulate a 'quadrilateral' of doctrinal hallmarks underpinning this religious tradition. First, Evangelicalism could be defined by its *conversionism* with the belief that lives needed to be transformed by the power of Christ and his Holy Spirit; second, the movement was characterized by its *activism* with the practical application of the gospel in activity such as mission and philanthropy; third, this religious tradition was marked by *biblicism* with its high view of the Bible; and fourth, Evangelicalism was distinctive because of its *crucicentrism* which stressed the sacrifice of Christ on the cross to atone for the sins of humanity.[10] Appropriately, Bebbington's quadrilateral had Victorian roots with two earlier formulations of

---

7. Ashley enjoyed a close personal friendship with Edward Bickersteth from 1835 until his death in 1850. Thereafter, Alexander Haldane took Bickersteth's place as Ashley's closest confidant until his death in 1880.

8. Finlayson, *Seventh Earl of Shaftesbury*, 102–5, 160–61.

9. Bebbington, *Evangelicalism in Modern Britain*, 1.

10. Ibid., 3.

Evangelicalism proposed by the Anglican reviewer, W. J. Conybeare, in 1853 and the Anglican Evangelical leader, J. C. Ryle, in 1867.[11]

Far from representing a static formulation of evangelical thought or a one-size-fits-all descriptor of evangelicals, however, Bebbington appreciated that the shape of this quadrilateral was subject to change according to the broader historical context and recognized that different evangelical figures and movements would emphasize some characteristics to a greater degree than others.[12] John Wesley, for example, gave special emphasis to conversionism and activism with his sermons extolling the importance of being reborn in Christ and his itinerant preaching activity exemplifying the activist temperament of evangelicalism. Turning to a Victorian example, Bishop (J. C.) Ryle arguably championed the biblicism and crucicentrism strands with his sermons hammering home the "absolute supremacy" of Holy Scripture and the imperative of justification by faith through the atoning death of Christ. Thus Warner correctly observed that within the Bebbington quadrilateral, axes could frequently form between two of the four characteristics in the case of Evangelical sub-movements, institutions or individuals.[13] Of the possible number of axis combinations, however, Warner only identified and discussed, two, namely the "conversionist-activist" axis and the "biblicist-crucicentric" axis.[14]

Given the enduring currency of the Bebbington quadrilateral in evangelical historiography, with Mark Noll crediting it as "the most serviceable general definition of evangelicalism,"[15] it would be apposite to apply it here to this study of Ashley's Evangelicalism. Such an analysis is especially due, given that neither of the two biographies of Ashley published since Bebbington's *Evangelicalism in Modern Britain* (1989) engaged with this definition of Evangelicalism.[16] Whilst Pollock, and especially Turnbull, each appreciated the rich Evangelical religion of Ashley, neither biographer referred to,

11. Hutchinson and Wolffe, *Global Evangelicalism*, 6–7, 8; Conybeare, "Church Parties," 276. Whilst not identical to Bebbington's formulation in 1989, Conybeare had identified 'conversion,' 'justification by faith' and the 'sole of authority of scripture' as the 'watchwords' of the Evangelical camp. Similarly, J. C. Ryle observed that Evangelicalism emphasized the 'absolute supremacy' of 'Holy Scripture,' the saving 'work and office of our Lord Jesus Christ' and the 'inward work of the Holy Spirit in the heart of man.'

12. Bebbington, *Evangelicalism in Modern Britain*, 2–4.

13. Warner, *Reinventing English Evangelicalism*, 33–34.

14. Ibid.

15. Noll, *American Evangelical Christianity*, 185 cited in Larsen, "The Reception Given Evangelicalism," in Haykin and Stewart, *Emergence of Evangelicalism*, 28.

16. Pollock, *Shaftesbury: The Reformer* and Turnbull, *Shaftesbury: The Great Reformer*.

nor utilized, the landmark Bebbington quadrilateral as a tool of analysis. Applying the quadrilateral to Ashley, it was apparent all four characteristics variously manifested themselves in Ashley's theological outlook and activity as the following summation of his religious faith illustrated:

> He [Ashley] believed in the doctrine of the total depravity of the human heart by nature; in the necessity of a "new birth" through the "revelation to each individual soul, by the agency of the Holy Spirit and the Word, of the great saving truths of the Gospel of the grace of God, by which the understanding is spiritually enlightened and the character transformed." He believed in the Christian life as a humble, "continuous trust in the Atoning Blood," a simple faith in Scripture, a constant prayerfulness, and a recognition of the Hand of God in all the events of life.[17]

Whilst this observation represented a fairly general and simplified description of Ashley's evangelicalism, it nonetheless touched upon all the quadrilateral points of conversionism, activism, biblicism, and crucicentrism. Importantly, it also captured the core evangelical belief of the Holy Spirit's work in the life of the believer as emphasized by Larsen in his 'pentagonal' formulation of Evangelicalism.[18] Additionally, it also made reference to eternal salvation solely through personal trust in Christ, an Evangelical conviction Warner and Marsden regarded as a necessary supplement to the Bebbington quadrilateral.[19]

Taking conversionism as the starting point of the quadrilateral, it was evident the Victorian social reformer accorded great importance to the necessity for individual lives to be transformed by the power of Christ. The precise date and immediate circumstances of Ashley's own conversion remain unclear with no record of his experiencing anything approximating either the 'Road to Damascus' epiphany of St Paul or the 'strangely warmed heart' of Wesley. Nonetheless, Ashley believed in the reality of personal conversion with the impressionable years of childhood and youth representing the ripest opportunity for the gospel to inspire a change of heart. Thus in his 1848 speech to parliament on the progress of the Ragged School Unions (RSUs), Ashley pointed out that it was indeed the Christian conversion and ensuing moral transformation of working-class children which represented one of the crowning achievements of his RSUs enterprise: "They are received ragged, but they are turned out clothed—they are received as heathens, and

---

17. Hodder, *Life and Work of the Seventh Earl*, Vol. III, 4.

18. Larsen, "Defining and Locating Evangelicalism," in Larsen and Treier, *Companion to Evangelical Theology*, 1.

19. Warner, *Reinventing English Evangelicalism*, 18.

in many instances, I thank God, they go out as Christians."[20] Typical of Evangelicals across all denominations, Ashley saw prayer, evangelism, and Christian instruction as the primary channels through which individuals could be converted. For Ashley, the pan-evangelical Ragged Schools provided one such forum where souls could be led to Christ through the provision of Christian instruction.

As an avowed Churchman, however, Ashley's own very gradual conversion experience was peculiarly Anglican and somewhat less typical of evangelicals from some Nonconformist traditions, particularly Methodism. Conceding that conversion could be gradual as well as sudden, Bebbington observed that "Anglican Evangelicals, commonly more educated, sober and respectable than their brethren in other denominations, never had qualms about accepting the validity of gradual conversions."[21] This was a view shared by the Anglican Simeon who insisted that of conversions, "we require nothing sudden" in the spiritual journey of the believer.[22] Certainly this was also the case with Ashley who first encountered Evangelical Christianity as a young boy under the care of his nurse-maid, Maria Mills, but noted in his diaries that it was not until he reached the age of twenty-five that he credited the works of Philip Doddridge as the "first thing that opened his eyes" and the Bible commentaries of Thomas Scott as prompting him to start "thinking for himself."[23] By these remarks, Ashley was essentially implying that, whilst he never had any cause to challenge the Evangelical presuppositions he had imbibed as a young child, it was through his voluntary reading of such Evangelical authors that he positively received their theology on his *own terms* as an independent, thinking adult who was at liberty either to accept or reject their propositions about God according to his own conscience.

While biographers of Ashley have all agreed that he underwent a gradual conversion to Evangelicalism, differences of opinion emerged as to *when* this journey completed its course. Battiscombe concluded that it was in 1835 when he was acquainted with Bickersteth,[24] Finlayson deduced that it was in 1834 when his theological convictions became more explicit in his dairies,[25] whilst Turnbull, on the other hand, contended that it occurred as

---

20. Lord Ashley, "Juvenile Population," HC Debates, *Hansard*, 6 June 1848, Vol. 55, cc. 445–46.
21. Bebbington, *Evangelicalism in Modern Britain*, 7–8.
22. Ibid., 8.
23. Hodder, *Life and Work of the Seventh Earl*, Vol. I, 44.
24. Battiscombe, *Shaftesbury: A Biography*, 99.
25. Finlayson, *Seventh Earl of Shaftesbury*, 103.

early as 1826 when Ashley was just twenty-five.[26] Whilst it was certainly true that the doctrinal contours of Ashley's Evangelicalism became more pronounced from the mid-1830s, it seems apparent that his *conversion* to Evangelicalism was already evident in the previous decade. As Turnbull convincingly argued, the fact that Ashley in 1826 attributed his "independent thinking" to the Evangelical bible commentator, Thomas Scott, was a "likely indicator of a course leading to conversion to Evangelicalism."[27] This course progressed with Ashley remarking in his first diary volume of 1825–31 that "the numerous graces mentioned in the Bible are almost beyond belief"[28] and that the first chapter of Romans proved the insufficiency of "natural religion."[29] On the basis of these telling reflections, together with his frequent personal habits of prayer and scriptural devotion, there would be reasonable grounds for deducing, as Turnbull did, that Ashley had embraced the essentials of Evangelical religion whilst still in his twenties.[30] In so doing, Ashley arguably accomplished the "conversion journey" that began from his early boyhood encounters with Maria Millis.

Inextricably linked to conversionism, crucicentrism represented another touchstone of Ashley's evangelicalism. For Ashley and his co-religionists, there was simply no basis for Christian conversion aside from the cross of Christ. Without the cleansing of human sin and guilt through the penal substitutionary atonement of Christ on the cross, it was not only impossible for a person to be forgiven and reconciled to God, but also to be "born again" by the Holy Spirit and thereby converted. A century before Ashley emphasized the importance of the cross, Wesley had preached that there was nothing in Christianity that was "of greater consequence than the doctrine of Atonement."[31] Ashley continued this critical emphasis on the cross in both his private and public life. An Anglican minister, Rev Nehemiah Curnock, observed that "calmly and thoughtfully in the early morning of life," Ashley "determined to known [sic] nothing among men, save Jesus Christ, and Him crucified." He added "to that blessedly single purpose, by that simple creed, he [Ashley] steadfastly abode."[32] Ever conscious of the dearth of Christian influence from his own parents, Ashley as a father saw

26. Turnbull, *Shaftesbury*, 35.

27. Ibid., 36.

28. Lord Ashley, Diary Entry (1826), 15. [Broadlands Archives SHA/PD/1]

29. Lord Ashley, Diary Entry (February 11, 1827). [Broadlands Archives SHA/PD/1]

30. Turnbull, *Shaftesbury*, 36.

31. Bebbington, *Evangelicalism*, 14.

32. Curnock, *Three Famous Earls of Shaftesbury*, 871. Broadlands Archives [SHA/MIS/5/3].

to it that his own children understood the truths of Evangelical Christianity, not least the centrality of the cross. Speaking of Ashley's interaction with his children, R. Pengelly noted that the "great subjects of immortality and salvation through a crucified Lord were matters of daily and open conversation between them."[33]

If Ashley frequently discussed the importance of the cross for personal salvation, then for whom did he believe Christ died? This was a question that had long dogged the Evangelical movement since the latter eighteenth-century with the Arminian-leaning Wesleyans tending towards a doctrine of general (or universal) atonement, whereby Christ's death was for all of sinful humanity. By contrast, the more Calvinist followers of Whitefield held to a doctrine of particular atonement, which held that Christ had died for the elect. Between these two views, however, something of a reconciling synthesis emerged by the turn of the nineteenth-century with Anglican Evangelicals such as Charles Simeon and William Wilberforce expressing the view that redemption was both general and particular.[34] On the one hand, the potential reach of divine grace through Christ's atonement on the cross was universal; however, the capacity for human beings to either accept or reject this offer of redemption meant that its ultimate effect was particular. The Anglican Ashley himself assented to this view, suggesting that Christ's death had been for all. In a parliamentary debate on factory reform, he described the children of the factory system "as beings created, as ourselves, by the same maker, *redeemed by the same saviour* and destined to the same immortality."[35] For Ashley, it appeared axiomatic that if God had created *all* human beings, he could also redeem *all* people through the atoning sacrifice of Christ. Ashley was aware that not all the factory children he referred to were by any means regenerate Christians because of human agency to either reject or accept Christ as their personal savior. It was, nonetheless, his view that there was the *potential* for all to be redeemed given his belief in the universal bounds of divine grace.

The major characteristics within Ashley's Evangelicalism, however, were biblicism and activism. To a greater extent than conversionism and crucentrism, which he imbibed chiefly from the earlier Wilberforce-Simeon generation of Evangelicals, his biblicism typified the dominant trait of Evangelicalism amongst his own Victorian generation. Whilst the commitment of the pre-Victorian generation of Evangelicals to the authority and value

---

33. Pengelly (ed.), *Lord Shaftesbury*, 79–80.

34. Bebbington, *Evangelicalism in Modern Britain*, 17.

35. Lord Ashley, "Employment of Children," HC Debates, *Hansard*, 4 August 1840, Vol. 55, c. 1274.

of scripture was beyond contention, the "biblicism" of the succeeding generation was arguably more pronounced and this reflected broader changes within Evangelicalism during the second quarter of the nineteenth century. From the 1820s, the newer generation of Evangelicals began to insist on inerrancy, verbal inspiration, and the need for a literal interpretation of the Bible.[36] This trend towards a narrower construction of scripture manifested itself in the bitter disputes within the British and Foreign Bible Society in 1825–26 about the inclusion of the Apocrypha in Bibles distributed to Europe.[37] Contrary to the wishes of Simeon and some older-generation Evangelicals, the newer breed of Evangelicals led the charge to expunge the Apocrypha from the scriptures owing to its "lack of divine inspiration."[38] By 1841, Louis Gaussen had argued in *Theopneustia* that, since every part of the Bible was the word of God, it must be all equally inspired. According to Holmes, such views became common, if not the majority, within Victorian Evangelicalism.[39] The leading figure of this new generation was the fiery Scottish-born Alexander Haldane, an Anglican who stoutly defended the verbal inspiration of the scriptures. Responsible for founding the influential Anglican *Record* newspaper in 1828, Haldane and his disciples sought radically to recast British evangelicalism into a formidable Protestant force that was emphatically biblicist and vigorously opposed to Roman Catholicism, Tractarianism and theological liberalism.

Indeed, it was through Ashley's evolving friendship with Haldane in the 1840s that his personal Evangelicalism began to exude a distinctively biblicist flavor. Despite having imbibed his love of scripture from an earlier generation of Evangelicals, particularly Thomas Scott and Edward Bickersteth, the influence of Haldane appeared to accentuate his emphasis on the Bible and its supreme authority. Rejecting the view propounded by proponents of higher biblical criticism in the 1860s that some genres of the scriptures were more inspired than others,[40] Ashley articulated his position on the inspiration of the Bible.

> Men contend that one part of the Bible is inspired, and that another is not, or that there are differences in the degrees of

36. Bebbington, *Evangelicalism in Modern Britain*, 14.
37. Turner, *John Henry Newman*, 39.
38. Atkins, "Wilberforce and his Milieux," 241–43.
39. Holmes, "British (and European) Evangelical Theologies," in Larsen and Treier, *Companion to Evangelical Theology*, 247.
40. Turner, *John Henry Newman*, 133–37. Proponents of biblical higher criticism, propagated their views in *Essays and Reviews* (1860), which espoused a low view of biblical inspiration, judged parts of the Pentateuch unhistorical, and asserted that the essential truths of the Bible did not depend upon the historic truth of all its narratives.

> inspiration. The whole authority of the Bible is thus cut up from beginning to end. Depend upon it, my friends, that there is no security whatever except in standing upon the faith of our fathers, and saying with them that the blessed old Book is God's word written, from the very first syllable down to the very last, and from the last back to the first.[41]

As the views propounded by higher biblical criticism continued to circulate through the 1870s, with theologians questioning the historicity of the Pentateuch in parts and rationalizing various supernatural elements of the biblical narrative, Ashley remained unmoved with an even more stubborn affirmation of the Bible's inspiration and authority in 1874:

> believe as it stands before me, it [the Bible] is the Word of God. Take all the nonsense you can, and bring all the arguments you can, all the persuasion in your power, you shall not turn me from the position I have taken up, that this is the Word of God. I believe every syllable of it, and rest my salvation upon it.[42]

As his vehement opposition to the proposed revision of the Bible in 1870 would demonstrate, Ashley was by no means speaking in hyperbolic terms when he reiterated his belief in *every syllable* of the Bible. For Ashley, the Authorized Version of 1611 represented not only a literary masterpiece of the English language but the immutable Word of God. In a letter to Canon William Selwyn in 1870 remonstrating against the revision, Shaftesbury warned that "If the Bible is altered, it will cease to be the Bible . . . of every Protestant speaking the English language over the entire surface of the globe."[43] According to Ashley, the original 1611 translation had been conceived in an era of doctrinal purity when a consensus had existed on the Protestant truths of the Reformation; hence its truthful rendering of God's word was assured. The Victorian era, however, was a different *zeitgeist* with "the immense variety of opinion on doctrinal matters."[44] Thus Ashley feared that if the Bible was to be revised in the 1870s, its hitherto Protestant flavor would be invariably diluted by ritualist and Socinian influences. Accordingly, the biblicist strand of Ashley's evangelicalism was not only sharpened by the march of theological liberalism but also by the contemporaneous challenges of Tractarianism and Roman Catholicism. For Ashley, the Bible

---

41. Shaftesbury, *Address to the Church Pastoral Aid Society* (May 8, 1862) cited in Hodder, *Life and Work of the Seventh Earl*, Vol. III, 7.

42. Shaftesbury, "The Earl of Shaftesbury on Sunday-Schools," 3.

43. *Lord Shaftesbury and the Revision of the Bible*, 1.

44. Ibid., 4.

was not merely the supreme "Word of God" but also the sole authority for Protestants. In contrast to both the Tractarians and Roman Catholics whose theology drew heavily on the received traditions of the church, particularly on the works of the patristic fathers and church divines such as St Thomas Aquinas, it was the Protestants' boast that they were the religion of "one book." Ashley affirmed this when he told an audience "that the Bible and the Bible alone, is the religion of Protestants."[45]

Alongside biblicism, activism represented the most prominent strand of Ashley's Evangelical faith. Of the entire quadrilateral characteristics manifest in this social reformer's evangelicalism, activism was unique in that it was both rooted in an earlier generation of pre-Victorian Evangelicals and nourished by a contemporaneous generation of Evangelicals. Notwithstanding the considerable differences between the Clapham and Recordite generations of British Evangelicals, activism represented a continuous thread which Ashley personified to great effect. Bebbington appreciated that the activist nature of British Evangelicalism was present from the very beginning, describing the movement's fountainhead, John Wesley, as a "typhoon of energy." In his discussion of Evangelical activism, Bebbington accorded special attention not only to Wesley and the Methodists, but also to Wilberforce, Thomas Chalmers, and Ashley himself.[46] The characteristic which each of these disparate figures shared was the conviction that a saving faith in Christ impelled one to work tirelessly for the cause of the gospel in prayer, preaching, pastoral care, evangelism, mission, education, philanthropy, and social reform. This multifaceted activism bore fruit with the birth of the world-wide missionary movement, a proliferation of voluntary associations, and the social reform campaigns to humanize prisons, abolish slavery and phase-out child labor. As John Wolffe observed, it was this activism of British Evangelicalism which distinguished it from its seventeenth-century antecedent, English Puritanism.[47] To be sure, different Evangelical individuals and organizations were more active in some domains than others. The Scottish evangelical Presbyterian minister Thomas Chalmers devoted much of his time to preaching and pastoral care, whilst Wilberforce channeled a great deal of energy into philanthropy and social reform.

The Evangelical activism of Ashley in the endeavors of mission, education, philanthropy, and social reform has been widely cited.[48] However,

45. Shaftesbury, *Speech to Bible Society* (1877), 178.
46. Bebbington, *Evangelicalism in Modern Britain*, 11–12.
47. Wolffe, *God and Greater Britain*, 23.
48. For example, in their respective discussions of Evangelical activism, both Bebbington and Wolffe mentioned the significant place of Ashley. Wolffe, *Expansion of Evangelicalism*, 105–7; and Bebbington in both *Evangelicalism in Modern Britain*, 120;

several questions need to be asked? What was the wellspring for his activism and was it even peculiarly Evangelical? What particular form did it take and how did it express itself? Finally, to what extent was it indebted to both the proceeding generation of Evangelicals and to the contemporaneous generation? In spite of frequently invoking the Christian motifs of sacrificial love and redemption as rationales for pursuing causes such as factory reform, it is important to note that the initial impetuses for Ashley's social activism were not specifically Evangelical or even religious.

The first such impetus was his emotionally deprived childhood to which biographers such as Geoffrey Best have attributed his campaign to reform the factory system. This is certainly a plausible hypothesis as the shocking revelations of children suffering physically and emotionally in the factories would have evoked disturbing memories for Ashley of his own sorrowful childhood at the hands of his detached and indifferent parents. According to his biographers, Ashley recalled painful childhood memories of feeling cold, hungry and emotionally isolated.[49] Thus learning that factory children endured similar hardships, albeit in vastly different contexts, would have kindled a purposeful resolve for him to do all he could within his capacity as a legislator to ameliorate, if not altogether spare, the misery inflicted upon such children.

The second impetus was a more specific incident, also from Ashley's early life, where he witnessed the degrading spectacle of a pauper's coffin desecrated by a mob of drunken youth. According to Ashley's diarized recollections, his reaction of horror and indignation spurred him with a passion to better the lives of the poor and downtrodden.[50] This motivation for his activism could be likened to that of another eminent Victorian, Charles Dickens (1812–1870). Like Ashley, Dickens had experienced a traumatic childhood which similarly impelled him to agitate for the plight of poor children. Although scornful of some Evangelical causes such as sabbatarianism, Dickens admired Ashley's factory reform campaigns.[51] The fact that Dickens was not a particularly pious Anglican, and one even disdainful of particular Evangelical habits,[52] further demonstrated that the inspiration for Victorian social activism was by no means a uniquely Evangelical or religious one.

---

and *Dominance of Evangelicalism*, 93–94; Moreover, Hylson-Smith, in his chapter on "Evangelicals in Action," devoted six out of sixteen pages to the work of Ashley in Hylson-Smith, *Evangelicals in the Church of England*, 196–201.

49. Best, *A Biography of A. A. Cooper*, 15; Battiscombe, *Shaftesbury: A Biography*, 4.

50. Blackburn, *Noble Lord*, 21.

51. Letter of Charles Dickens to Edward Fitzgerald (December 29, 1838) cited in Hodder, *Life and Work of the Seventh Earl*, Vol. I, 227.

52. Pope, *Dickens and Charity*, 13.

Notwithstanding this non-religious inspiration for his social activism, Ashley encountered no difficulty reconciling this with the Evangelical faith he assented to from his twenties. He regarded his Evangelical convictions as eminently conducive to elevating the human dignity of poor and oppressed persons. Given, however, that his desire to advance human wellbeing predated his conversion to Evangelical Christianity, his activism maintained an eminently temporal focus. As well as entertaining an Evangelical concern for the spiritual destiny of the afflicted, he was very much committed to improving their material wellbeing for the more immediate term. For Ashley, it not only mattered that people were spiritually redeemed through Christ for eternity but also that they could be enabled to lead clean, respectable, and dignified lives free from the afflictions of poverty, squalor, and degradation. Agitating for an improved standard of public health and hygiene for city dwellers in the 1850s, Shaftesbury employed scripture to justify the body-and-soul dualism of his activism. Already appreciating that the soul needed to be redeemed from the corruption of sin, he added that the temporal body was in need of similar deliverance: "If St Paul, calling our bodies the temples of the Holy Ghost, ought not to be corrupted by preventable disease, ought not to be degraded by filth when it can be avoided, and ought not to be disabled by unnecessary suffering."[53] Ashley's emphasis on both the eternal soul and the temporal body in his activism enabled him to find much common ground with social reformers of the utilitarian, Benthamite tradition. Like Ashley, Utilitarians such as Edwin Chadwick (1800–1890) were committed to ameliorating the parlous living conditions of Victorian city-dwellers in their quest to maximise the happiness of the greatest number of people. Accordingly, the Evangelical Ashley was able to work collaboratively with the utilitarian Chadwick on the General Board of Health to deliver better sanitation to the urban poor of London.

The activism of Ashley was characteristic of both his Evangelical forbears and contemporaries. Like his mentor and friend, Bickersteth, Ashley continued the activist tradition of the pre-Victorian Clapham Sect, a coterie of upper middle-class Anglican Evangelicals who championed the causes of mission, philanthropy, and social reform. Although Bickersteth was not a member of the Clapham circle himself, he was recognized as the natural successor to the Clapham-aligned clergyman of Cambridge, Charles Simeon.[54] Bickersteth had followed Simeon's footsteps in his active patronage of

---

53. Shaftesbury, *Addresses of the Earl of Shaftesbury and the Hon W. F. Cowper*, 9–10.

54. Hylson-Smith, *Evangelicals*, 144. Although Bickersteth never experienced Simeon's classes first-hand, Michael Hennell in *Sons of the Prophets* argued that Bickersteth stood out as Simeon's successor and as leader of the Anglican Evangelical clergy from Simeon's death in 1836 to his own in 1850.

the Church Missionary Society and the London Society for the Proclamation of Christianity amongst the Jews (LSPCJ). With the examples set by Simeon and Bickersteth, Ashley, in turn, would play his own active role to support these causes in his various capacities as chair or president.[55] More generally, Ashley's activism captured the Clapham Sect's thrust of "Practical Christianity," the shorthand title commonly given to Wilberforce's treatise of 1797 which called for Christians of the higher and middle classes to model their faith in action.[56] In the tradition of the Clapham leader and parliamentary anti-slavery activist, Ashley exhorted an assembly of young men in 1841 to exercise a "practical Christianity":

> Christianity is not a state of opinion and speculation. Christianity is essentially practical, and I will maintain this, that practical Christianity is the greatest curer of corrupt speculative Christianity. No man, depend upon it, can persist from the beginning of his life to the end . . . unless he is drawing from the fountain of our Lord Himself. Therefore, I say to you, again and again, let your Christianity be practical.[57]

In so urging, Shaftesbury typified the activism of not only the Clapham generation of Evangelicals, but also those of his own generation. To a large degree, the activism of the Wilberforce-Simeon generation had been inspired by an optimistic belief in human progress derived from the Enlightenment.[58] Thus, notwithstanding the Evangelical belief in human sin, Clapham-sponsored campaigns such as prison reform and anti-slavery were largely aimed at realizing this vision for a higher state of civilization. The activism of the Recordite Evangelical generation, on the other hand, was chiefly propelled by a distinctive strand of premillennial eschatology which stressed proactive engagement in evangelism, mission and social reform before the imminent return of Christ.[59] As a premillennialist himself, Ashley typified this activism by immersing his energies in the missionary activity of the CMS, the evangelism of the BFBS and the factory reform movement as eschatologically purposeful causes. Hodder rightly noted that

---

55. Turnbull, *Shaftesbury*, 57. Shaftesbury accepted an invitation to serve as Vice-President of the CMS from 1837, an office he held until his death 1885.

56. Wilberforce, *A Practical View*.

57. Shaftesbury, "Address to Assembly of Young Men" (1841) in Hodder, *The Life and Work of the Seventh Earl*, Vol. I, 327.

58. Bebbington, *Evangelicalism in Modern Britain*, 60.

59. Spence, "The Renewal of Time and Space," 97. Spence argued that the comprehensive nature of the hope of universal restitution meant that premillennialists were willing to pay attention to the lives of communities, not just individuals.

belief in Christ's second coming stimulated Ashley in all his work.[60] Thus Evangelical activism was not solely the practical outworking of Christian charity but could also be the product of personal life experience, secular philosophical influences, and eschatological thinking.

The Bebbington quadrilateral and its serviceability from one historical context to another has proved eminently useful in analyzing the distinctive facets of Ashley's Evangelicalism. Even when taking into due consideration the additional Evangelical traits of "Christocentrism" and the "transformed life" proposed by Warner, the crucicentric vertex of the quadrilateral was capable of capturing Ashley's emphasis on the centrality of Christ whilst the conversionist point adequately touched upon Ashley's appreciation of the life-changing repercussions stemming from one's personal conversion to Christ. As an apparatus for scrutinizing the doctrinal basis, formation, and practical expression of the Victorian social reformer's Evangelical faith, it has been invaluable to identifying the priorities and emphases of Ashley's outlook within the religious movement. While exhibiting each dimension of the quadrilateral, Ashley succeeded in forging a new axis between biblicism and activism with both dimensions featuring most conspicuously in his pattern of Evangelical piety and practice. Amid the developments and changes in Evangelicalism over Ashley's long life, his two abiding concerns were always for an *activist* faith, expressing itself in practical deeds of mission, philanthropy, and social reform, and a biblicist faith, doggedly adhering to the received canon of scripture as "God's word written."

In addition to Bebbington's quadrilateral, there are additional frames of analysis that shed further light on key aspects of the Evangelicalism embodied by Ashley. The first is that of "trans-denominationalism," with Evangelicalism's fluid nature transcending conventional boundaries of denomination.[61] To highlight the trans-denominational mindset of Evangelicalism, Warner cited the earlier example of Whitefield who preached to Nonconformists against the wishes of his fellow-Anglicans.[62] Like the quadrilateral, this organizing principle can be readily adapted to the latter historical context of the Victorian Ashley, where the Evangelical social reformer and his co-religionists frequently exhibited a trans-denominational mode of thought.

Like both his mentor, Bickersteth, and his contemporary friend, Haldane, Ashley felt an acute sense of spiritual communion with evangelicals from other denominations. In spite of his avowed Anglicanism and

60. Hodder, *Life and Work of the Seventh Earl*, Vol. II, 523.
61. Warner, *Reinventing English Evangelicalism*, 19.
62. Ibid.

affection for the Established Church, Ashley desired to stand in solidarity with Nonconformists on shared doctrinal convictions and to collaborate with them in common causes and enterprises. Indeed, his first affinity with Nonconformity could be traced back to the first-stage of his conversion in the 1820s when he consulted the works of Philip Doddridge. Of the Congregationalist author's writings, he remarked that they were "the first thing that opened my eyes."[63] As Ashley's Evangelical faith matured in later adulthood, he sought to work constructively with Nonconformists in transdenominational enterprises such as the BFBS and Ragged School Unions (RSUs). Just four years after Evangelical Churchmen and Nonconformists had collaborated to form the Evangelical Alliance in August 1846, Ashley wrote in his diary of how his Evangelical convictions in 1850 transcended denominational boundaries:

> Grace be with all them that love the Lord Jesus Christ in sincerity. . . . God speed to all such, and to give them the right hand of fellowship in all works of love and charity. This overrides all ecclesiastical differences, all distinctions of form and human arrangement, all the modes and varieties of non-essentials; but it demands the full belief of Evangelical truth, the joyous reception of Christ's blessed atonement, his perfect work, His everlasting dominion, His faith, His fear, His love. It binds us to the true believers of the Lutheran and Presbyterian Churches; it binds us to the pious Nonconformists of England, to the Henrys and Doddridges wherever they may be . . . .[64]

For all his heartfelt congeniality with non-Anglican Evangelicals, it needs to be recognized that the transdenominational outlook of Ashley and early Victorian Evangelicals generally was aided by broader developments in the constitutional and religious landscape of Britain. Despite the resistance of Anglican high Tories, the repeal of the Test and Corporation Acts in 1828 did much to abate many of the old hostilities dividing Anglicans and Nonconformists, as Evangelicals outside the Established Church were now able to participate in English public institutions on more of an equal footing. This provided not only a favorable climate for pan-evangelical initiatives such as the Evangelical Alliance but also made it somewhat easier for Nonconformists to sympathise with Ashley's genuine piety and common evangelicalism whilst maintaining their own independent views of social and political

---

63. Conversation with Edwin Hodder, cited in Hodder, *Life and Work of the Seventh Earl*, Vol. I, 44.

64. Lord Ashley, Diary Entry (January 5, 1850), cited in Hodder, *Life and Work of the Seventh Earl*, Vol. II, 184.

matters.⁶⁵ For all the progress towards greater harmony between the Church of England and Dissent, however, tensions still lingered after 1828 over the contentious issues of church rates, burials, tithes, and of course the principle of establishment.

Another definitional framework of Evangelicalism which is eminently applicable to Ashley is that of Mark Noll, who proposed that the movement could be defined not simply by a matrix of doctrinal "essentials" but also by its composition of individuals, associations, literature, practices, and networks of influence shared by the progenitors of the Evangelical Revival and their heirs.⁶⁶ Holmes concurred, arguing that "in Britain at least, evangelicalism was a movement defined by relationships and activities at least as much by theology."⁶⁷ Atkins went even further, observing that the world of Evangelicals "was made up of far-reaching, fluid and sometimes ambiguous relationships—patronage, informal linkages, personal connections and overlapping networks—rather than being founded on subscription to a particular set of shibboleths."⁶⁸

Thus a study of fundamental institutions such as the Established Church of England; of critical associations such as the Clapham Sect; and of influential individuals including Thomas Scott and Edward Bickersteth, are all necessary to illuminate further the temperament of Ashley's Evangelicalism and its historical origins in particular. In assenting to Evangelicalism as a young man, Ashley did not simply imbibe a static creed of orthodoxy and practice, but rather a malleable and protean religious movement that was continually remolded by its influential groups and individuals at the same time as having been recalibrated according to its historical context. To be sure, British Evangelicalism remained broadly orthodox in Trinitarian and Christological matters;⁶⁹ however, the expression and application of these changed palpably over time, as did a whole range of "secondary matters" such as prevailing Evangelical attitudes towards economic policy and political party allegiances. Thus, by studying the institutions, associations, and individuals through which British Evangelicalism was continuously reconditioned, it is possible to appreciate something of the origin and character of the religious faith Ashley came to inherit as a young man in the 1820s.

65. Larsen, *Friends of Religious Equality*, 264.
66. Noll, *Rise of Evangelicalism*, 3–4.
67. Holmes, "British (and European) Evangelical Theologies," 241.
68. Atkins, "Wilberforce and his Milieux," 15.
69. Holmes, "British (and European) Evangelical Theologies," 242.

The relevance of the Anglican Evangelical tradition to Ashley's early life

The first such institution through which Ashley's form of Evangelicalism was filtered was of course the Church of England. According to Carter, the Established Church was primarily responsible for recalibrating a large part of British Evangelicalism into a conservative and hierarchical form of Protestant Christianity during the latter eighteenth century. This conservative flavor of Anglican Evangelicalism did not go unnoticed by Boyd Hilton who noted that "all Evangelicals were conservative at bottom, not only from their sense of man's sinfulness" but also from "a fundamental fear of the loneliness of liberty" and a "craving for authority and obedience."[70] Hence the instinctive conservatism of Ashley could be explained not simply by reference to his aristocratic birth, imbuement of Tory paternalist ideals and Tory Party allegiance, but also by his spiritual attachment to Anglican Evangelicalism. Theologically, Evangelicalism could certainly be regarded as a conservative form of Protestant Christianity in that it remained committed to the preservation of classic Reformation doctrines and principles. Church of England Evangelicals cherished what they regarded as the inherent doctrinal purity of the 1662 *Book of Common Prayer* and Thirty-Nine Articles.[71] The Articles were valued for reflecting the moderately "Calvinistic" theology held by most evangelicals and articulated the fundamental principles of the Protestant reformers in ways that avoided extremes.[72] The Anglican catechism was accepted for its affirming phraseology and the Anglican formularies of the Prayer Book were endorsed as not only scriptural, but as an effective prophylactic against the introduction of heresy into the Established Church.

The conservatism of Anglican Evangelicalism was also evident in its pattern of church government. Despite obviously repudiating many of the doctrines and practices of Roman Catholicism, not least its allegiance to the Pope, it nonetheless saw merit in continuing with Catholicism's form of episcopal church government. Hierarchical and deferential, episcopacy stood in contrast to the more 'grassroots' modes of church government favored by non-Anglican evangelicals. Episcopacy was esteemed as ancient, of apostolic origin, and with its principle of hierarchy, far more suited to the ordering of fallen human nature than the 'republican' synodical system of the Presbyterians and other Protestant churches.[73] The Anglican Evangelical

---

70. Hilton, *Age of Atonement*, 205.
71. Carter, *Anglican Evangelicals*, 14.
72. Ibid.
73. Carter, *Anglican Evangelicals*, 13.

Christian Observer claimed that the church had been governed by bishops, priests, and deacons from apostolic times: where these orders were to be found duly appointed, the word preached, and the sacraments administered, there the 'church of Christ' was to be found, with its form and authority.

It may well be easy to take the Anglican form of Ashley's Evangelicalism for granted given that the Established Church would have been the default religious affiliation for every aristocrat born in the land.[74] However, the Church of England's institutional association with the English aristocracy is the very reason that its influence merits examination in the particular case of Ashley. In a conversation with Edwin Hodder, Ashley recalled that he was "brought up in the old 'high and dry' school" of the Church of England.[75] What, then, was this "high and dry" milieu of Anglicanism into which Ashley was born at the beginning of the nineteenth century? The "high" referred to the high emphasis this school placed on the constitutional primacy of the Church of England, whilst the "dry" denoted a style of worship that was formal, dispassionate and typically perfunctory. According to William J. Conybeare, the high and dry culture of the Established Church was affluent and privileged, underpinned by an elite network of clerical patronage and nepotism.[76] The principal preoccupation of high and dry Anglicans was neither the dream of church catholicity nor the zeal for purity of theological doctrine, but rather "the comforts of an establishment" with its attendant social and political prestige.[77] It was thus a formalistic and spiritually nondemanding variety of Anglicanism that appeared palatable to the materialistic sensibilities and worldly aspirations of aristocratic landowners such as Ashley's parents. According to Hodder, Ashley "received no help from his parents in his religious life, leaving 'the boy' 'to grow up in the old 'high and dry school' in the cold, lifeless, formal orthodoxy of the times."[78]

Notwithstanding the evident dearth of religious enthusiasm in Ashley's immediate family, the young Ashley was nonetheless reared in several spheres where Anglican instruction took place, thereby exposing him to possible Evangelical influences. The first, and arguably the most formative of such spheres, was the care he received from his nanny, Maria Millis,[79] who is said to have imparted Christianity to the seven-year-old Ashley from

---

74. Lewis, *Origins of Christian Zionism*, 111.
75. Hodder, *Life and Work of the Seventh Earl*, Vol. I, 44.
76. Conybeare, "Church Parties," 328–29.
77. Conybeare, "Church Parites," 329.
78. Hodder, *Life and Work of the Seventh Earl*, Vol. I, 36.
79. Maria Millis was also the house-keeper and maid to Ashley's mother, Anne Spencer-Churchill, who had been acquainted with her before she married Cropley Anthony Cooper.

both the Bible and Anglican *Book of Common Prayer*.[80] Millis had imbibed her Evangelical faith from Woodstock Church and was then able to share this faith with the young Ashley. During her year-long residency at St Giles Wimbourne, Millis read Bible stories to Ashley and taught him a prayer that he would repeat until old age.[81] Ashley reflected on the indebtedness of his faith to the early family housekeeper: "She was an affectionate, pious woman. She taught me many things, directing my thoughts to highest [sic] subjects; and I can even now call to my mind many sentences of prayer she made me repeat at her knees. To her, I trace, under God, my first impressions."[82] It is evident the *Book of Common Prayer* also maintained a special affection in Ashley's heart throughout his long life. In a speech at the Annual Meeting of the Church Pastoral Aid Society in 1873, Shaftesbury reflected that "The Prayer Book is, indeed, pervaded with such a deep spirit of piety and truth that it is emphatically a sermon in itself."[83]

Ashley's subsequent education at Church-patronized institutions such as Chiswick Preparatory School, Harrow and Christ Church, Oxford, would have further instructed Ashley in the Anglican tradition.[84] Indeed, during his attendance at Harrow in the 1810s, Ashley came within the orbit of two identifiably Evangelical figures. The first was his contemporary, Harry Verney (1801–94), the son of an Evangelical baronet who became a lifelong friend. Subsequently serving as an Evangelical MP, Verney supported many of Ashley's reform efforts in parliament.[85] The second was the Anglican Evangelical clergyman John William Cunningham (1780–1861), who served as the school's vicar.[86] Representing the Evangelical Anglicanism of the Clapham Sect, Cunningham had worked as a curate to John Venn of Clapham before assuming his post at Harrow from 1811. In conjunction with his preaching and pastoring duties at Harrow, Cunningham served as life governor of both the CMS and BFBS.[87] Even before the Tractarian controversy erupted from the 1830s, Cunningham viewed himself as a standard-bearer of the Evangelical tradition within the Established Church. Despite having supported the Catholic Relief Act of 1829, he was profoundly suspi-

80. Duncan, "An English Nobleman," 2.
81. Hennell, *Sons of the Prophets*, 52.
82. Hodder, *Life and Work of the Seventh Earl*, Vol. I, 50–51.
83. Shaftesbury, *Speech of the Earl of Shaftesbury at the Annual Meeting of the Church Pastoral Aid Society*, Thursday, May 8, 1873 (London, 1873), 23.
84. Mohan, "The Seventh Earl of Shaftesbury," 132–33.
85. Lewis, *Origins of Christian Zionism*, 112.
86. Lewis, *Origins of Christian Zionism*, 112. John William Cunningham held the post as vicar of Harrow from 1811 until his death in 1861.
87. Rosman, "Cunningham, John William," 280.

cious of Catholicism in both its Anglican and Roman forms. In his capacity as a novelist, Cunningham penned a *Velvet Cushion* in 1815 in which he extolled the Protestant traditions of the English Church. Declaring "Popery and the Bible" to be 'not very strictly harmonizing'[88] he denounced Popery as "superstitious, formal, cold and cruel"[89] whilst lauding the theology of the Puritans as "in general pure" and their practice "correct."[90] In sentiments foreshadowing those of Ashley, Cunningham confidently pronounced that "Good old England" has a "Protestant Church, and a free State, with which a wise Papist, or a sober tyrant, find it almost impossible to quarrel."[91] Whilst the spiritual musings of Ashley in his diary suggest that it was not until his mid-twenties that he consciously appraised matters of faith on his own terms as an adult, it is plausible that, consolidating the earlier influence of Maria Millis, the Evangelical vicar of Harrow fertilized a latent Evangelical spirituality which would come to the fore in Ashley's mid-twenties and blossom from his mid-thirties. As a student at Harrow, Ashley would have been exposed to the Evangelical preaching from Cunningham's pulpit and the ensuing tenor of his own Anglican "vital religion" certainly suggested that the vicar's appeals to an emphatically Protestant cast of Anglicanism did not altogether go unheeded.

Making the invisible church visible: Evangelicalism, Ashley, and the Established Church

Unlike many of his Dissenting evangelical contemporaries, such as C. H. Spurgeon, with whom he was otherwise in firm agreement on general evangelical doctrine, Ashley maintained throughout his life the historic Anglican view that the Established Church was the supreme guardian over the nation's religion and morality. As such, it was esteemed as the instrument which had safeguarded and buttressed the wellbeing of England through times of turmoil and ferment. In a speech at his re-election for the County of Dorset in 1841, Ashley exhorted his audience to remember and honor the special role of the Established Church:

> Stand by your Church. . . . It was your Church that gave you the blessings of the Reformation. It was your Church that carried you through the perils of the French Revolution; and she will

---

88. Cunningham, *A Velvet Cushion*, 18.
89. Ibid., 22.
90. Ibid., 48.
91. Ibid., 112.

> still carry you through even greater dangers and trials than you have yet passed through if you stand by her. Where will you find any other body of men so truly the friends of the poor as the Clergy of the Established Church; and rely upon it; that if you will but hearken to her dictates, peace and unanimity will again be restored to these realms. . . .[92]

Like all other loyal Anglicans—be they Low, High, or Broad Church-aligned—Ashley envisioned the Established Church as the fulcrum upon which all of England's religion, morality, freedom, prosperity, and peace rested. Of the Established Church, he warned: "Her overthrow would be perilous to every institution, every class, every form of property, and of religious freedom and in the matter of religious liberty, to none more than to the Nonconformists themselves."[93] Ashley, therefore, was not only committed to preserving the *inward* piety, spirit, and doctrine of Anglican Evangelicalism, but also its *outward* institutional structures, not least the constitution and status of the Established Church. In an age of expanding constitutional plurality, with the repeal of the Test and Corporation Acts in 1828 followed by Catholic Emancipation in 1829,[94] the survival of the Established Church as a remaining pillar of the English Protestant constitution was deemed all the more essential for early Victorian Churchmen.

As such, Anglican Evangelicalism recognized the potential advantages of operating within a state-church but also its limitations. First, an Established Church was seen as the best, if not the only, means of providing religious education for the poor of England. This, the more so, given the fact that large sections of the country could not afford to support their own churches or did not chose to do so—as indicated by the lack of voluntarily supported churches in large swathes of the countryside.[95] The legal, parliamentary foundation of the Church's teaching also meant that its sacred formularies would be constitutionally safeguarded against the encroachments of what were seen as religious heresies, whether Socinian or popish.[96] Continuity of teaching would be maintained by its ordinances and, importantly, it seemed to them, at least in a formal sense, to be anchored in Reformation truth.[97] For these reasons, Anglican Evangelicals continued to affirm the

---

92. Ashley, *Speech at the Late Election* (1841).

93. Shaftesbury, *Speech at the Annual Meeting of the Church Pastoral Aid Society* (1873), 28.

94. Wolffe, *God and Greater Britain*, 45.

95. Carter, *Anglican Evangelicals*, 20.

96. Ibid.

97. Ibid.

establishment status of their Church, with fraternities such as the Clapham Sect seeking to avail themselves of its perceived advantages to propagate the gospel. For Evangelicals, including Ashley, Establishment was treasured not so much for being a "badge of privilege," but, rather, a God-given and state-sanctioned mandate for the Church of England to represent the *whole* of English society. For Shaftesbury in 1867, this meant the Church adopting the poorest of the poor as its own:

> It has ever been my heartfelt and earnest desire to see the Church of England the Church of the nation, and especially of the very poorest classes of society, that she might dive into the recesses of human misery and bring out the wretched and ignorant sufferers to bask in the light, and life, and liberty of the Gospel.[98]

The universality that establishment implied was therefore seen by such Evangelicals as neatly complementing their mission to claim the whole nation for Christ. However, this heightened sense of the Established Church's responsibility towards the poorer classes also stemmed from an "instinct of self-preservation" in the face of political attack.[99] In light of historic constitutional reforms such as Catholic and Jewish Emancipation, Evangelicals such as Ashley in the 1860s felt impelled to reaffirm the historic role of the Church of England.

Notwithstanding the above importance early Evangelicals vested in the Established Church as a convenient vehicle for furthering their mission, they were by no means oblivious to the limitations of the institutional Church. Quoting Lady Huntingdon, Best observed that, in common with all other evangelicals, their first allegiance was to the invisible "Church of Christ" rather than the more tangible Church of England.[100] For this reason, the cause of Christianity generally (especially that which was evangelical) was often put before the interests of the Established Church. Again, this attitude was reflected in the approach of Lord Shaftesbury to Church affairs. In his vision to make worship services more accessible to those unacquainted with the traditional parish church, Ashley went against the grain of Established Church opinion to legislate for the conduct of worship services in non-traditional venues such as theatres and halls. Thus, whilst the early generation of Evangelicals and their Victorian successor, Ashley, attached a firm importance to the Established Church, it was nonetheless a limited

---

98. Lord Shaftesbury, "Clerical Vestments Bill (No 2)," Second Reading, HL Debates, *Hansard, 14 May 1867, Vol. 187, c500.*

99. Wolffe, *God and Greater Britain*, 54.

100. Best, "The Evangelicals and the Established Church," 63–78.

one in their various religious, political, and social campaigns to advance Evangelical causes.

2

Continuity and Change from Clapham

With Ashley widely recognized as both a leading Anglican layperson and prominent Victorian, it is critical to ascertain the nature of the Anglican Evangelicalism he inherited as a young adult. What were the tradition's associations and leading figures through whom Ashley imbibed his personal Evangelical principles, practices, and key priorities? Even if never personally acquainted with the Victorian peer, what bearing did the ideas, literature, and activities of these influential men and women have on his religious outlook and work? First, it will be contended that the Clapham Sect fraternity, which was arguably the most visible expression of Anglican Evangelicalism in the pre-Victorian period, exhibited a fundamental and profound influence on the social reformer's lifelong work of political advocacy, philanthropy, and Christian mission. In addition to the legacy of Clapham, the character of Ashley's received Evangelicalism was profoundly conditioned by two pre-Victorian Anglican Evangelical figures. The first was Thomas Scott, whose works he knew through reading his *Commentary on the Bible* in the mid-1820s; and the second was Edward Bickersteth, a mentor with whom he cultivated an enduring friendship from the early 1830s. Whether it was Ashley's staunch biblicism, defensive Protestantism, Christian Zionism, or Sabbatarianism, each of these attributes, to varying degrees, could be attributed to the influences of Scott and Bickersteth.

Part I: Ashley and the Anglican Evangelical Tradition

The Clapham Sect and Anglican Evangelical activism

The Clapham phenomenon

As the first reservoir of Evangelical Anglicanism from which Ashley imbibed his religiosity, the Clapham Sect was particularly significant considering its reputation as both a hotbed of *lay* initiatives and its *activist* function as a wellspring for social reform and philanthropic causes. Given Ashley's status as a lay Evangelical activist and social reformer, it is crucial to appreciate the historical significance of the Clapham Sect as a forum where both lay-initiated and lay-dominated activity flourished. Rather than being dominated by Anglican deacons, priests, and bishops, the fraternity was chiefly comprised of politicians, lawyers, bankers, authors, and other middle-class professionals.[1] As Atkins has shown, the emergence of the Sect in the 1790s was symptomatic of a broader shift in British Evangelicalism away from clerical leadership towards lay initiative and autonomy. According to Atkins, the 1780s and 90s witnessed the ascendency of a new generation of lay activists drawn from among the professional and commercial classes and "bringing with them tactical awareness and an appreciation of the advantage of influence."[2]

Eschewing political quietism, the Claphamites stressed the importance of lay Evangelicals being able to exert their influence in public life. The publishing organ of the Sect, the *Christian Observer*, maintained that the practitioners of vital religion were to "use their talents of every kind, their time, their influence, their property, their suffrage, under a solemn sense of responsibility to God."[3] In retrospect, this phenomenon of lay agency should not be surprising given Noll's observation that the personal religion of Evangelicalism generally gave impetus to heightened lay activity.[4] The Clapham Sect thus represented the natural manifestation of Evangelical lay initiatives in philanthropy, evangelism, missionary service, and social reform which would be continued, to varying degrees, by Lord Ashley and

---

1. The Clapham Sect included the prominent anti-slavery MPs, William Wilberforce (1759–1833) and Thomas Buxton (1786–1845); the economist and banker, Henry Thornton (1760–1815); the author and philanthropist, Hannah More (1745–1833); the estate manager and editor of the *Christian Observer*, Zachary Macaulay (1768–1838); the chairman of the East India Company, Charles Grant (1746–1823); the Master of Chancery, James Stephen (1758–1832); as well as three Anglican clergymen, Charles Simeon (1759–1836), John Venn (1759–1813) and Thomas Gisbourne (1758–1846).
2. Atkins, "Wilberforce and his Milieux," 7–8.
3. *Christian Observer*, XXXII (1832), 555.
4. Noll, "National Churches," in Lovegrove, *Rise of the Laity*, 140.

the Victorian generation of lay Evangelicals in their patronage of numerous voluntary societies, mission agencies, and pressure groups.[5]

Appreciating the Sect's *activism* is similarly critical to understanding the origins of Ashley's activist "vital religion." Like its championing of lay agency, Clapham's activist temperament was also attributable to broader trends within British Evangelicalism; in this case, the shift from pietism to activism in the 1780s. While Wesley, Whitefield, and the pioneering figures of the Evangelical Revival had themselves personified an activist breed of "vital religion," the prominence of theological discourse within the movement had tended to blunt the public activism of Evangelicalism *at large* with much energy devoted to debating the Arminian-Calvinist controversy.[6] By the 1780s, however, a decidedly more doctrinally pragmatic generation of Evangelicals came to the fore which included the Clapham identities of Simeon, Wilberforce, and More. Rather than dwelling on the theological intricacies of predestined election, this generation of Evangelicals preferred to preach a straight-forward, practical theology of "justification by faith" which manifested itself in active works of service.[7] Promulgated through the literature of More, Wilberforce, and Gisborne, Atkins noted that this new "Practical Christianity" was "activist and deliberately untheoretical, and found a receptive audience among busy laypeople for whom arguments based on social interests, professional ambitions, reason and practicality carried much more weight than systematic abstractions."[8] Its approach was all about engagement with society, politics, and culture, as opposed to pietistic withdrawal and introspection. With the death of Wilberforce in 1833, Akins concluded in his epilogue that this breed of Evangelicalism "came to an end," noting that "Evangelicals in the 1830s and 1840s increasingly withdrew from public engagement."[9]

Whilst this observation is certainly applicable to the Clapham circle of Evangelicals, with the fraternity effectively rendered non-existent by 1833, it entirely overlooks the new wave of Evangelical activism accompanying the factory reform movement of the 1830s–40s.[10] The activist Evangelicalism incubated by the Claphamites did not altogether fade as a succeeding generation of Victorian Evangelicals assumed the mantle of social reform. Al-

---

5. Bradley, *Call to Seriousness*, 135.
6. Atkins, "Wilberforce and his Milieux," 8.
7. Ibid., 10.
8. Ibid., 10–11.
9. Ibid., 246, 252.
10. In the Epilogue to Atkins' thesis, any reference to the Evangelical leaders of the factory reform movement including Oastler, Bull, Sadler, and even Ashley himself, were conspicuously absent.

though the Yorkshire-based, radical Tory Evangelicals agitating for factory reform were well removed from the Clapham circle of London, Oastler and Sadler, at least, had been well-acquainted with Wilberforce. Indeed Sadler regarded himself as something of Wilberforce's parliamentary successor in continuing his tradition of sponsoring social reform legislation.[11] The Evangelical activism behind much of the factory reform campaign was not only embraced by Lord Ashley and the Tory radicals, but also the *Record*. Superseding the *Christian Observer* as the leading mouthpiece of Evangelicals from the early 1830s, the *Record* in 1844 lauded the Ten Hours bill as "a great boon to the most delicate and helpless portion of the community."[12] Hylson-Smith noted that, even though the "Recordite" generation of Evangelicals was reactionary in many respects, they were nonetheless activist in temperament.[13]

The continuity between the Evangelical activism of the Clapham Sect and that of the Victorian Ashley, in particular, was evident in both outlook and strategy. Ashley shared Clapham's affirmation of "Practical Christianity" with his personal remarks that, contrary to "being a state of speculation and opinion," "Christianity was essentially practical." In terms of specific Evangelical causes and ideals, the thread of activism between Clapham and Ashley was again discernible. Ashley's desire to bring a Christian influence to bear on British imperialism in India was a concern first entertained by Clapham's Charles Grant as early as 1793.[14] The efforts of Claphamites, such as Hannah and Patty More, to establish schooling for the poor in 1789 were continued by Ashley through his involvement in the Ragged School Union.[15] From 1837, Ashley assumed a lead role within the Church Missionary Society (CMS) just as Wilberforce, Grant and Thornton of the Clapham Sect had done in the preceding generation.[16] Likewise Charles Simeon's pioneering work with the London Society for Promoting Christianity amongst the Jews (LSPCJ) was continued in earnest by Shaftesbury, as were the activities of the British and Foreign Bible Society founded with the assistance of Clapham leaders. Even with the antislavery crusade, Ashley brought much of the same abolitionist zeal to the plight of "climbing boys" and other forms of domestic child-labor that Wilberforce and Buxton had successfully mo-

---

11. Sadler had assisted Wilberforce in his re-election bid for his seat of Yorkshire.

12. Editorial, *The Record*, March 25, 1844, 4.

13. Hylson-Smith, *Evangelicals in the Church of England*, 80.

14. Tomkins, *The Clapham Sect*, 120.

15. Ibid., 75–77.

16. Turnbull, *Shaftesbury*, 57. Shaftesbury accepted an invitation to serve as Vice-President of the CMS from 1837, an office he held until his death in 1885.

bilized against indentured servitude in Africa and the Americas.[17] Thus it is apparent that the Clapham Sect represented a nursery of Evangelical social and political causes that Shaftesbury and his generation of co-religionists would nurture through the ensuing Victorian age. Even through the decades succeeding the demise of the fraternity in the 1830s, the form and thrust of Shaftesbury's Evangelicalism would continue to exhibit the hallmarks of the original Claphamites.

Along with the Clapham Sect fraternity, there were a number of key Evangelical leaders, each steeped to varying degrees in the traditions of the Established Church, who had a considerable influence on forging the religious temperament of Ashley. Some of these figures were cited approvingly by Ashley in his speeches and writings, whilst others could be regarded as exerting a less conscious influence on their Victorian descendants, simply by formulating or popularizing key Evangelical principles to which Ashley would later assent and defend as "articles of faith." With the Clapham Sect, to a large extent, epitomizing the spirit of Anglican Evangelicalism in the pre-Victorian period, it is no coincidence that many of these figures were also active Claphamites. Others, however, either preceded or succeeded the fraternity but would no doubt have identified with its core values and vision. In either case, a study of these identities provides fundamental clues as to the religious impulses which energetically propelled Shaftesbury through a lengthy career of public devotion to the Evangelical cause.

William Wilberforce: A parliamentary forerunner to Ashley?

A comparative study between the lead Clapham identity, William Wilberforce, and Ashley reveals almost as much about the discontinuities between the two figures as it does about their commonly perceived relationship as 'heir and successor' in the tradition of Evangelical public engagement. In much of the historiography touching on nineteenth-century British church history, the names of Shaftesbury and Wilberforce are frequently mentioned in the same breath as the two great exemplars of evangelical-driven political activism and social reform. This was recognized as early as 1840 when the *London Times* observed that "Ashley was doing for the slave children working in Britain's mines and factories what Wilberforce had done for the sons and daughters of Africa."[18] After Shaftesbury's passing in 1885, the *Times* again eulogized his memory with the claim that "Lord Ashley, as he was then called, had evidently been strongly impressed by the example of Wil-

17. Hodder, *Life and Work of the Seventh Earl*, Vol. III, 153–58.
18. *The Times*, October 1840.

berforce, to whom in the double character of practical philanthropist and religious man he bore no little resemblance."[19]

On the face of it, the degree of analogy between the Yorkshire-based, Evangelical Abolitionist MP and the Victorian Evangelical parliamentary crusader for factory children is not difficult to appreciate. In addition to their shared religiosity and Tory-leaning politics, each figure was arguably the leading Evangelical Anglican layperson of their time and an active supporter of mission and philanthropy. Sharing much the same vision to advance Evangelical interests, ideals, and aims within the British parliament, it transpired that Wilberforce and Ashley advocated comparable causes and supported similar projects during their respective parliamentary careers. Taking the factory reform movement as a key illustration, Ashley has been widely recognized as the parliamentary standard-bearer of that cause; however, it was initially Wilberforce, amongst the Evangelicals, who was responsible for setting the movement in train.[20] The anti-slavery campaigner had united with Sir Robert Peel[21] to launch the first Factory Act in 1802, even protesting that the reform needed to be more far-reaching. In 1805, he took up the cause of the Yorkshire weavers; and in 1818 he supported Peel in a further extension of the Factory Act. In an assessment that could aptly apply to Ashley, Sir James MacKintosh judged Wilberforce to be a Tory by predilection, but by his actions "liberal and reforming."[22]

There are no surviving records of personal links between Wilberforce and Ashley, so it is unknown whether the two men actually met or were personally acquainted with one another. At least in parliamentary spheres, opportunities for the two politicians to have interacted would have appeared very limited given that Wilberforce resigned from his seat in the House of Commons as the Member for Bramber in 1825, one year before Ashley initially entered the House as the Member for Woodstock in 1826. Ashley's diaries revealed little about his personal attitudes to the Clapham Sect leader and none about his acquaintance, if any, with Wilberforce. The scant content that Ashley's diaries recorded of Wilberforce, however, revealed his estimation of the anti-slavery leader to be predictably favorable. Certainly, it was evident he saw himself as possessing something of a kindred spirit to Wilberforce: "Have been reading Seeley's abridgment of Wilberforce's Life. How many things have we felt alike, what similar disappointments,

---

19. "Death of Lord Shaftesbury," *The Times*, October 2, 1885, 11.
20. Hylson-Smith, *Evangelicals in the Church of England*, 91.
21. Sir Robert Peel, First Baronet (1750–1830).
22. Hylson-Smith, *Evangelicals in the Church of England*, 91.

misgivings, and disgusts!"[23] The like sentiments of the two men would have been felt across a range of matters including their common affirmation of a public-spirited and eminently practical form of Anglican Evangelical religion, a spirit of philanthropy as well as a shared disgust of immorality, injustice, slavery, and exploitation. Thus, even if Ashley rarely alluded to Wilberforce expressly, it was evident his instincts and outlook were, subconsciously at the very least, informed by Wilberforce. A further sign of Ashley's admiration for Wilberforce was his attendance at his funeral in 1833. Favorably contrasting Wilberforce's funeral with a ceremony he had just attended in Rome, Ashley remarked, "I could not but compare it with the funeral I had attended just previously to my departure from England, Mr Wilberforce's, in Westminster Abbey."[24]

The chronological disjuncture, albeit very brief, between the respective parliamentary careers of Wilberforce and Ashley symbolized some of the religious and political cleavages that existed between the two men. To be sure, Wilberforce had belonged to an earlier generation of Evangelicalism to that of Ashley which, despite embodying a similarly "practical theology" of social activism and engagement, was decidedly different in both its theological emphases and political outlook. Wilberforce was essentially a creature of the Clapham generation whose Evangelicalism was cultured, reasoned, measured and steeped in the rationalist epistemology of the Enlightenment. As such, the Claphamites held to a "Newtonian" or "natural law" conception of providence whereby the deity was seen to operate generally and predictably through natural and immutable laws of cause and effect.[25] For this reason, Wilberforce, Chalmers, and their contemporaries tended strongly to favor free-trade and limited government,[26] since state intervention was seen as an unwarranted human interference with the sovereign laws of God.[27] Accordingly, the *Christian Observer* in 1823 lauded free trade as "that truly Christian system of intercourse."[28]

---

23. Shaftesbury, Diary Entry (27 July 1843), in Hodder, *Life and Work of the Seventh Earl*, Vol. I, 498.

24. Shaftesbury, Diary Entry (13 January 1834), Hodder, *Life and Work of the Seventh Earl*, Vol. I, 186.

25. Hilton, "The Role of Providence," in Beales and Best, *History, Society and the Churches*, 228.

26. Hilton, *Age of Atonement*, 205.

27. Ibid., 121. For example, Thomas Chalmers saw interventionist policies as undesirable because they would obscure the providence of God apparent in the economic cycle.

28. *Christian Observer*, 22 (1823), 131.

The succeeding generation of Victorian Evangelicals, by contrast, was decidedly antagonistic towards free trade and minimalist state intervention, attributing much of the "Condition of England" to *laissez-faire* social theory.[29] Recasting Evangelicalism into a generally more militant, ultra-Protestant and premillennial movement, the succeeding generation distanced themselves from the "Newtonian" theory of providence held by the Claphamites to embrace an interventionist view which saw God as constantly directing earthly affairs by special warnings and judgments.[30] As such, it behooved earthly governments similarly to pursue an interventionist approach to social and economic problems. Adopting this paternalist conception of government, Ashley departed from the political and economic mindset of Wilberforce and his fellow Claphamites. According to H. S. Jones, Ashley "personified an alternative evangelical theodicy in which providence worked not naturally but miraculously."[31] Hence, for Wilberforce, factory reform legislation had represented a special dispensation from an otherwise non-interventionist government to address an egregious injustice, whereas, for Ashley, it was the logical application of normative paternalist policy seeking to emulate the paternal superintendence of the almighty. Therefore, notwithstanding the indebtedness of Ashley to the Evangelical activism of Wilberforce and the obvious continuities between the two, the differing Evangelical contexts and theological approaches of the two social reformers have generally been underappreciated. Understanding these is critical to appreciating the historical reality that British Evangelicalism was a fluid movement, simultaneously capable of maintaining continuity and embracing change from the generation of Wilberforce to that of Ashley.

Hannah More (1745–1833): Educator and progenitor of Victorian Evangelical values

A close confidante of Wilberforce, Hannah More was another Clapham identity similarly credited by historians and her biographers with helping shape the character of Victorian Evangelicalism that Ashley came to personify in so many respects.[32] Perhaps more than any other member of the Clapham Circle, More's identity as a woman underscored the dominant

---

29. Hilton, *Age of Atonement*, 92.
30. Ibid., 15.
31. Jones, *Victorian Political Thought*, 19.
32. See, for example, Stott, *Hannah More*. Stott's thesis is that Hannah More represented the "first Victorian."

lay-activism of the fraternity. With the clergy of all Evangelical denominations representing an exclusively male domain, Clapham's cultivation of a distinctively lay culture allowed women such as More to have an Evangelical voice in the public sphere. Best known as a pioneering educationalist, an author of several genres (including novels, treatises, religious tracts, and pamphlets) and also a philanthropist, More's influence on educating societal attitudes on moral and religious matters was profound with the broad dissemination and popular appeal of her literature. Described by one of her biographers as the "first Victorian," much of her literature could effectively be regarded as a manifesto of Victorian Evangelical religious beliefs, moral convictions, and social attitudes. For More, profligacy, luxury, moral laxity, spiritual complacency, lukewarm piety, and dissimulation were symptoms of a social and spiritual malaise, a practical irreligion more dangerous than outright skepticism, which filtered down through society, infecting "servants and inferiors," and contributing to rising crime.[33] In keeping with the conservative disposition of English Evangelicalism against the backdrop of the French Revolution, More, like Wilberforce, represented something of a counter-revolutionary who envisioned a hierarchical and paternalist society, whereby the ruling elite would set an example for the nation by modeling a robust, self-denying Christianity characterized by the hallmarks of punctuality, temperance, industry, thrift, Sunday observance, and philanthropic activity. Thus, in distancing herself from the prevailing habits and attitudes of the forgoing Regency age, More emerged as one of the trendsetters for Victorian Evangelical culture along with Wilberforce and other Evangelical contemporaries.

In both her activity and philosophy, More had a considerable impact on Ashley, not least in his sharing of her vision to extend Christian education amongst the poor. In his personal reflections of 1834, Ashley made no secret of his admiration:

> Read the memoirs of Miss Hannah More, amiable, virtuous, and wonderful woman! What a true, diligent, and (humanly speaking) useful servant of Christ was she. Ah, let those who rely on works for justification, cease to hope until they shall at least have equalled her, and then they will begin to despair; for, finding no consolation in self-meritousness, and neither foreseeing time, nor feeling strength to renew their efforts.[34]

---

33. Stott, *Hannah More*, 131.

34. Shaftesbury, Diary Entry, (7 September 1834) in Hodder, *Life and Work of the Seventh Earl*, Vol. I, 200.

Ashley was no doubt in awe of More's pioneering work with education. Like himself half a century later, More had regarded the provision of educational institutions as pivotal to the Evangelical mission to raise the moral and religious standards of the succeeding generation. Recognizing schools as the furnace through which the religious beliefs and moral attitudes of impressionable young minds were largely molded, More helped found several schools in the district of Mendip, Somerset, between 1789 and 1795. In these new establishments, pupils were taught basic literacy, enabling them to read the Bible and the catechism, as well as the socially desirable virtues of punctuality, cleanliness, and honesty.[35] In a letter to Wilberforce in 1791, More commented enthusiastically that in some of the schools; "much ground had been gained among the poor. . . . Many reprobates were, by the blessing of God, awakened, and many swearers and Sabbath-breakers reclaimed."[36] In one sense, these institutions represented the embryonic forerunners to the Victorian RSUs supported by Ashley. The mission and rationale behind More's Mendip Schools and the Ragged Schools were essentially analogous, namely, to bring a Christian-based education within the reach of poor families so as to instruct greater numbers of working-class boys and girls in basic learning skills together with Christian precepts. As Tomkins concluded, the activity of figures such as More in educational enterprises and moral reform campaigns shaped the essence of Evangelical Christianity in the succeeding Victorian age.[37]

Ashley exemplified this spirit in his campaigns for factory reform and sanitary provision as well as in his active support and patronage of numerous charities and mission organizations. To an Evangelical of patrician blood such as Ashley, More's construction of Christ's Talent Parable[38] and the creed of *noblesse oblige*, amongst some of the aristocracy, essentially represented natural bedfellows. In his mind, Christ's injunction to utilize his talents liberally and energetically to the glory of God was at one with his own Tory paternalist obligation to use the endowments of rank and property to protect the poor and weak. Whilst Ashley did not necessarily share More's argument that "poverty was ordained by providence,"[39] he shared her

---

35. Stott, *Hannah More*, 105.

36. Letter from Miss H. More to Mr Wilberforce (1791) in More, *Life of Hannah More*, 157–158.

37. Tomkins, *Clapham Sect*, 248–50.

38. More, *Christian Morals*, 74. Drawing heavily from the 'Parable of the Talents' recorded in chapter 25 of Matthew's Gospel, More concluded that the underlying principle of this parable was that everything derived from the hand of God. 'Every talent is a deposit placed in our hands, not for our exclusive benefit, but for the good of others'.

39. Hilton, *Age of Atonement*, 207. Embracing the same theory of Providence as

belief that those endowed with wealth had an obligation to use it in the service of the poor.

Thomas F. Buxton (1786–1845): Parliamentary anti-slavery campaigner and social reformer

The other Clapham identity with whom Ashley shared a historical affinity was the parliamentarian Thomas Fowell Buxton, Wilberforce's anointed successor in the anti-slavery campaign.[40] On the issue of slavery, Ashley readily identified a kindred spirit in Buxton, sharing the Whig MP's revulsion for the practice. Reading Buxton's personal accounts of the trade in 1839, Ashley recoiled with horror and indignation:

> Have been reading on the journey, Buxton's account of the actual state of the Slave trade. It is enough to make a man miserable for life; . . . But sympathy is useless, nay contemptible, without corresponding action; what we do to wipe out this damned spot, and mitigate this horrid tyranny? . . . Let those who believe in God, and have faith in him . . . wrestle as it were, for a blessing on those peoples and nations, black though they be.[41]

Although the long, protracted battle to end the slave-trade in the British colonies was eventually won in 1833 with the passage of the Slavery Abolition Act through the British Parliament, other forms of slavery did not escape the attention of Ashley.[42] On the domestic front, the social reformer continued his campaigns against not only child labor in factories and mines, but also against the use of 'climbing boys' as human chimney cleaners, the conscription of children into agricultural labor gangs; and, towards the end of his life, the exploitation of small children in circuses and pantomimes as gymnasts, acrobats, and dancers.[43] In agitating for an end to these more do-

---

her Clapham contemporaries, More believed that the 'divine laws' of economics determined the poorer state of some people. This differed from the view of Ashley who believed that poverty was the consequence of unjust economic practices which did not accord with the purposes of Providence.

40. Desiring to anoint a younger successor, Wilberforce finally entrusted the campaign against the slave-trade to his parliamentary protégé in 1821.

41. Shaftesbury, Diary Entry (August 13, 1839) in Hodder, *Life and Work of the Seventh Earl*, Vol. I, 258.

42. Lord Shaftesbury, Diary Entry (November 20, 1853) in Hodder, *Life and Work of the Seventh Earl*, Vol. II, 397. Casting his eye across the Atlantic in 1853, the new Earl of Shaftesbury denounced the continuing practice of slavery in the southern states of the USA.

43. Shaftesbury, "Introduction," in Barlee, *Pantomine Waifs*, x–xi.

mestic forms of 'white' slavery, Ashley devoted himself to the task in a like-minded fashion to that of his Clapham hero, Buxton, combining moral zeal with political pragmatism to yield gradual policy change. Although Ashley's dominant domestic focus may have marked something of a departure from the Wilberforce-Buxton approach, his essential campaign strategy and parliamentary tactics were heavily indebted to his Clapham predecessors.

Beyond Clapham: The theological influence of Thomas Scott and Edward Bickersteth on Ashley

Thomas Scott (1747–1821)

Whilst Clapham was chiefly responsible for shaping the *activist* dimension to Ashley's Evangelicalism, its *doctrinal* characteristics owed much to the theology of two Anglican Evangelical clergyman, namely Thomas Scott and Edward Bickersteth. Although Scott and Bickersteth had existed outside the Clapham Circle, each figure was profoundly influenced by the Claphamite preacher of Cambridge, Charles Simeon (1759–1836). Ordained a minister in 1773, Scott had worked closely with Simeon and other Anglican Evangelicals to found the CMS, of which he was the first secretary.[44] It was in his writings and biblical commentaries especially, however, that Scott really left an indelible impression on Ashley and Anglican Evangelicalism generally. Subsequently undergoing several revised editions, Scott published what was widely regarded as his *magnum opus*, his *Commentary on the Holy Bible*, wherein he enunciated a high view of divine inspiration and authority behind the scriptures. Scott contended that human beings needed a revelation which only God could give. Accordingly, the Bible was both inspired and authentic. Of the Scriptures' authorship, he wrote:

> The Holy Spirit communicates to the minds of the sacred writers . . . those things which could not otherwise have been known; and [exercises] such an effectual superintendency . . . as sufficed absolutely to preserve them from every degree of error. . . . Every sentence in this view must be considered as "the sure testimony of God."[45]

In addition to the divine inspiration of scripture, Scott's *Commentary* entailed a comprehensive Evangelical exposition of key doctrines such as the atonement, repentance, faith, the dispensation of grace replacing that of the

---

44. Hindmarsh, "Scott, Thomas," 591.
45. Scott, *Commentary on the Holy Bible*, 5.

law, and the necessity of obedience.⁴⁶ According to Hindmarsh, the ubiquity of the work was such that Scott's *Commentary* eventually became standard reading for Victorian Evangelicals.⁴⁷

Along with the literature of Doddridge, Ashley read Scott's *Commentary* just as his Evangelical convictions were starting to take shape. For Ashley, it marked a watershed moment in his spiritual life as the Evangelical theology of Scott contrasted sharply with the perfunctory Anglicanism of his upbringing. Whilst Ashley's father had taught him as a boy to recite catechisms from the Anglican Prayer Book, his recitations were assessed on the basis of their textual accuracy rather than on their authenticity as expressions of a living faith.⁴⁸ Reflecting on the commentary's impact, Ashley later recalled; "It was not till I was twenty-five years old, or thereabouts, that I got hold of 'Scott's Commentary on the Bible,' and, struck with the enormous difference between his views and those to which I had been accustomed, I began to think for myself."⁴⁹ The teachings of Scott that Ashley encountered in his *Commentary* included the premise that it was "highly reasonable to believe the Bible to be a divine revelation"⁵⁰ primarily because of the historical veracity of the scriptures when compared with "the most approved ancient writers,"⁵¹ the "contemporary fulfillment of the prophecies,"⁵² and the sufficiency of the scriptures with "no need of apocryphal additions."⁵³ Although Scott was a postmillennialist belonging to the Simeon-Wilberforce generation of Evangelicals, it was evident his theological views on the Bible's authority and inspiration laid a solid foundation for the enduring *biblicism* of Ashley's Evangelicalism. This was evident in the way in which Shaftesbury in 1874 professed his belief in "every syllable" of the Bible.⁵⁴ In an era where new scientific thought and higher biblical criticism were challenging traditional Evangelical modes of biblical interpretation, Hodder claimed Shaftesbury's "faith was never staggered by the difficulties involved

---

46. Turner, *John Henry Newman*, 35.

47. Hindmarsh, "Scott, Thomas," 593.

48. Hodder, *Life and Work of the Seventh Earl*, Vol. I, 36.

49. Ashley, "Reflections' (1826) in Hodder, *Life and Work of the Seventh Earl*, Vol. I, 44.

50. Scott, *Commentary on the Holy Bible*, b4.

51. Ibid., b7.

52. Ibid., b8.

53. Ibid., e2.

54 Shaftesbury, "The Earl of Shaftesbury on Sunday-Schools," 3.

in the acceptance of the whole of the Bible, from the first chapter of Genesis to the last chapter of Revelation."[55]

As well as promulgating a doctrine of scriptural infallibility, Scott's interpretation of prophecy arguably shaped Ashley's own theological outlook. Despite his postmillennialism differing from Ashley's premillennialism, Scott believed, like Ashley, that the fulfillment of the Bible's prophecies could be deduced from *present day* developments and events, as opposed to ones promised for the indefinite future. Writing his *Commentary* in the midst of the French Revolution, Scott witnessed the conversion of nations to Christianity with the extension of overseas mission to European colonies, the "long continued dispersion of the Jews," "the division of the empire into ten kingdoms" and what he perceived to be "the superstition, uncommanded austerities, idolatry, spiritual tyranny, and persecution, of the Roman [Catholic] hierarchy."[56] According to Scott, these occurrences coincided with the predictions of the New Testament, and, for him, it was this contemporary fulfillment of prophecy which vindicated the scriptures as "the unerring word of God."[57]

During the Victorian era, Ashley similarly interpreted contemporary events to be the fulfillment of biblical prophecy. With the movement to create a Jewish homeland in Palestine, beginning with the establishment of a British Consul in Jerusalem in 1834 and the Anglican-Lutheran bishopric there in 1841, Ashley saw the return of the Jews to their ancient homeland as a fulfillment of prophecy. Chairing a meeting of the London Society for the Promotion of Christianity amongst the Jews in 1845, Ashley remarked that this phenomenon represented "the fulfillment of a long series of prophecies, and the institution of unspeakable blessings, both in time and in eternity, for all the nations of the world."[58] In a similar vein, Ashley welcomed the advance of overseas missionary activity during the 1850s as a prophetic prelude to the Second Advent: "I see it . . . the Gospel will be offered where, in truth, it has never yet been fairly offered, in China and Japan; it will then have been preached for a witness to all nations, then will the end come! Come, Lord Jesus, come quickly."[59] According to Lewis, Ashley's beliefs in the contemporary fulfillment of biblical prophecy, particularly with respect to the restoration of the Jews to Palestine, drew considerably on "older

---

55. Hodder, *Life and Work of the Seventh Earl*, Vol. III, 6–7.
56. Scott, *Commentary on the Bible*, b8.
57. Ibid., b8.
58. Ashley, "Speech from the Chair of the Jews Society," May 1845, in Hodder, *Life and Work of the Seventh Earl*, Vol. II, 105.
59. Lord Shaftesbury, Diary Entry (September 3, 1852), in Hodder, *Life and Word of the Seventh Earl*, Vol. II, 440.

strands in Protestant biblical interpretation" such as the *Commentary* of Scott.[60]

While philosemitism represented a distinctive hallmark of the ultra-Protestant, premillennialist, Recordite Evangelicals,[61] it was in fact cultivated by members of the preceding Evangelical generation, particularly Simeon and Scott. Despite the suspicion of many Claphamites towards Christian Zionism,[62] Simeon had aroused Evangelical interest in Jewish evangelism through his work with LSPCJ. Furthermore, Scott's *Commentary* did much to popularize the notion of a Jewish return to Palestine among its numerous readers (including Ashley) throughout the English-speaking world in the nineteenth century.[63] Like his fellow postmillennialist Simeon, Scott believed that they had been honored by God, and made blessings to mankind above all other nations: and the descendants of Judah have been, and are, incomparably, the most illustrious of that favored race.[64] In view of what he saw as this divine favor on the Jews, Scott maintained that Christians had a responsibility to seek their greatest good, above all in fostering the Jews' return to their homeland and commending to them the Christian gospel. Scott articulated his position which could be regarded as a brief manifesto of Victorian Christian Zionism:

> I . . . honour the nation to whom God committed his ancient oracles, and by whom they have been communicated to us Gentiles. I honour the race whence prophets, whence apostles, whence Christ himself, arose. I feel myself a debtor, to a vast amount, unto the Jews, from whose Scriptures (for the most, at least, of the New Testament was written by Jews,) . . . and it would be a high gratification to me, could I, by any means, repay even a small part of the debt which I owe to that race, of whom it was of old predicted, "that in them should all the nations be blessed."[65]

For societies such as the LSPCJ, and leading Evangelical figures including Simeon, Bickersteth, and Ashley himself, such a mission statement would

---

60. Lewis, *Origins of Christian Zionism*, 17.

61. Ibid., 93.

62. Ibid., 45. Moderate Clapham Evangelicals such as William Wilberforce and Zachary Macauley shunned Christian Zionism as they were anxious to avoid the charge of 'religious enthusiasm' and did not want to mar their reputation for 'serious Christianity'.

63. Ibid., 41, 61.

64. Ibid., 61.

65. Scott, *The Jews a Blessing to the Nations*, 4.

come to represent the unofficial charter under which late eighteenth- and early nineteenth-century Evangelicals would mobilize to support such causes as the dissemination of the scriptures amongst English Jews, the dispatch of Christian missionaries to the Middle East, the creation of a Jewish homeland, the establishment of a Protestant bishopric in Jerusalem in 1841 and pleas for the persecution of Jews in Tsarist Russia and Poland during the early 1880s to cease. Whilst Scott's Evangelical theology remained generally characteristic of the Wilberforce-Simeon generation, his affirmation of the Bible's divine authority, his interpretation of prophecy and his call for Christians to work towards the restoration and ultimate conversion of the Jews exerted far-reaching influences on Ashley and the Victorian generation of Evangelicals.

A "transitional" Evangelical: Edward Bickersteth (1786–1850)

Together with Scott, the Reverend Edward Bickersteth proved profoundly influential in determining the calibration of Ashley's Evangelicalism. Above all, his status as a "transitional" Evangelical accounted for the amalgam of Claphamite and Recordite traits in the Evangelicalism personified by Ashley. Unlike Scott whom Ashley had only known through print, Ashley became personally connected with Bickersteth. After reading Bickersteth's literature, Ashley sought "a personal acquaintance" with the clergyman and stayed at his Watton rectory in Hertfordshire for the first time in August 1835.[66] A close friendship between the two men ensued and this all the more impressed Bickersteth's beliefs and practices upon the younger Ashley. In both a chronological and theological sense, Bickersteth represented a critical transitional figure between the Simeon-Wilberforce generation of Clapham Evangelicals and Lord Ashley.

Born in 1786, twenty-seven years after Simeon and fifteen years before Ashley, Bickersteth was born early enough fully to immerse himself in the prevailing Evangelical sub-culture of the Claphamites, yet lived long enough (until 1850) to exert a direct personal influence on the emerging Victorian generation of Evangelicals. As such, Bickersteth failed to fit neatly into either one of Hilton's two categories of "moderate" (Clapham) Evangelicals and 'extreme' (Recordite or crypto-Recordite) Evangelicals.[67] For this reason, the figure of Bickersteth has often escaped close historiographical analysis from narratives which focus either on the Clapham generation of Evangelicals or those of the ensuing Victorian period. Notwithstanding, there have

66. Hennell, *Sons of the Prophets*, 44.
67. Hilton, *Age of Atonement*, 10.

been some recent exceptions with Lewis aptly recognizing Bickersteth as "an interesting bridge between the older Claphamite evangelicalism with which he was identified and the newer Adventist movement."[68] A study of Bickersteth by Atkins also examined the role of this clergyman within the context of broader continuities in Evangelical thought between the 1820s and 1840s.[69] Discussion of the critical relationship between Bickersteth and Ashley, however, was minimal with just a brief reference to it in the context of the campaign for a Jewish homeland.[70]

Biographies of Ashley have discussed this formative relationship in more depth,[71] although the doctrines of Bickersteth are yet to be interrogated to a sufficient degree. Given Bickersteth's role as not only a close personal friend but also an adviser to Ashley, a study of these core beliefs and principles espoused by this clergyman is critical to appreciating the enduring ideals Ashley imbibed and proceeded to reflect throughout his public life. Upon perusing the various treatises, diary entries, letters, and pieces of correspondence penned by Bickersteth, it is apparent where much of the inspiration lay behind the public postures Ashley adopted on a range of issues including the importance of household piety, the honoring of the Sabbath, a distinctively premillennial eschatology, support for Christian mission, concern for the poor, an antipathy towards both Tractarianism and Roman Catholicism, and the embrace of a "denominationally inclusive" evangelicalism seeking to build bridges with fellow evangelicals outside the Established Church.

Bickersteth's pattern of personal piety in his earlier life certainly typified the Evangelicalism of the Clapham generation with its strong emphasis on "conversionism" and "activism." Converted to Evangelical Christianity in his twenties, again through the influence of Philip Doddridge, Bickersteth underwent a conversion experience similar to that of Wesley. Like Wesley, Bickersteth had essentially trusted in his own efforts and righteousness to earn favor with God before coming to embrace the Evangelical notion of trusting wholly in Christ for salvation and acceptance before God. In December 1806, Bickersteth reflected in his personal journal:

> As it is advised by the excellent Doddridge, as I may hope it will have some effect on my soul in making me ashamed of sin, and as it may be an additional tie to a life of holiness; as it will also

68. Lewis, *Origins of Christian Zionism*, 116.

69. Atkins, "Anglican Evangelical Theology," 5.

70. Ibid., 15.

71. Battiscombe, *Shaftesbury: A Biography*, 100; Finlayson, *Seventh Earl of Shaftesbury*, 104, 115–16; Turnbull, *Shaftesbury*, 35, 50–52.

> become evidence when I have departed this world, to my surviving friends, that I trusted alone in the name of Jesus and his Gospel for life and happiness, salvation and immortality beyond the grave.[72]

Once converted, Bickersteth practised an intense personal piety characterized by continuous prayer and regular journals of confession and self-admonishment to live more for Christ. Like Ashley, he was an avid diarist who frequently recorded his spiritual musings and petitions. Meanwhile, the activist dimension to Bickersteth's faith rose to the fore as he shared the Claphamites' zeal for promoting evangelism and mission. After entering the ordained ministry of the Established Church, Bickersteth took a lively interest in the CMS, eventually becoming principal of its missionary training college and serving as its secretary from 1824–30.[73] Like Simeon and his generation of Claphamites, the clergyman became a leader in garnering nationwide, grass-roots support for the multitude of religious societies mushrooming in Britain during the first quarter of the nineteenth century.[74]

Whilst Bickersteth was an Evangelical of the Establishment who regarded the Church of England as superior in doctrine, he entertained an open attitude to evangelical Dissenters who shared the same fundamentals of Reformation Christianity. In this respect, he also exhibited the transdenominational mindset of British Evangelicalism. Speaking of an "ideal" man's company and his religious affiliation, Bickersteth opined:

> I had rather he was a Churchman, because I am convinced the Church of England approaches nearer to Christian perfection in its Articles and Liturgy, than any Church with which I am acquainted. Yet I think it would be extremely narrow-minded to shun a man's company, merely because he was a Dissenter. The main essentials, such as faith, love, humility and piety, are what one ought chiefly to regard, and we should be fondest of the company of those who have most of these, however we may differ in lesser points.[75]

To give tangible form to this affinity with Nonconformists, he subsequently worked towards formalizing an alliance between Anglican Evangelicals and Evangelicals outside the Established Church through setting up the multidenominational Evangelical Alliance in 1846. Of the new alliance, he declared:

---

72. Bickersteth, Journal Entry (December 28, 1806), in Birks (ed.), *Memoir of the Rev. Edward Bickersteth*, 20.
73. Turnbull, *Shaftesbury*, 35.
74. Ervine, "Bickersteth, Edward," 92.
75 Edward Bickersteth, Journal Entry (9 April 1809) in Birks, *Bickersteth*, 55.

"The desire was thus increased for a purer union, not based on religious indifference, or the sacrifice of conscience even in lesser things, but on the real and substantial agreements of Evangelical Protestants in all the vital doctrines of the Gospel; and this gave birth to the Evangelical Alliance."[76]

Bickersteth's spiritual protégé, Ashley, reflected a comparable transdenominational mindset: upholding the primacy of the Established Church on the one hand, while also acknowledging the existence of a communion in "the gospel" between evangelicals of all denominations. There were few spheres in which this was more evident to Ashley than in the work of the British and Foreign Bible Society. As the Society's newly appointed President in 1851, he praised its denominationally inclusive approach:

> That it is catholic in its character, catholic in all its operations; that it enables vis [sic] to form in these realms, in times of singular distress and difficulty, a solemn league and covenant for all those who "love the Lord Jesus Christ in sincerity"; that it shows how, suppressing all minor differences, or treating them as secondary, members of the Church of England and Noncomformists may blend together in one great effort.[77]

In conjunction with leading the BFBS, Ashley supported the founding of the interdenominational Evangelical Alliance which Bickersteth had helped form in August 1846.[78]

Bickersteth's desire to collaborate with non-Anglican evangelicals was propelled not only by a sense of communion with those of like faith, but was seen as also the best strategy to counter the influence of Roman Catholicism and other perceived enemies of Evangelical religion. This latter motive reflected the increasing defensiveness of Bickerseth's Evangelicalism from the 1830s. Whilst the Evangelicalism of his earlier life up until the 1820s had been unmistakably Claphamite, it began to adopt both an outlook and tone which was more characteristic of the emerging Evangelicalism associated with the *Record*. With the successful passage of the Catholic Relief Act in 1829 supported by leading Claphamites such as Wilberforce, Bickersteth started to entertain some disquiet about what he saw as the Claphamites' too accommodating approach towards Roman Catholicism. In a letter to William Wilberforce's son in 1838, Bickersteth spoke very highly of his father's Evangelical character, but made his disappointment known about

---

76. Edward Bickersteth, Journal Entry (29 November 1846), in Birks, *Bickersteth*, 193–94.

77. Lord Ashley, "Address to Bible Society as Presiding Chair" (May 2, 1851), in Hodder, *Life and Work of the Seventh Earl*, Vol. II, 346.

78. Turnbull, *Shaftesbury*, 119.

his sympathetic stance on the "Roman Catholic subject."[79] In addition to Catholic Emancipation, the growing presence of Roman Catholics in Britain engendered fears amongst Bickersteth that the Protestant Constitution of Britain was under challenge,[80] thereby necessitating calls for a fresh Protestant 'offensive' to counter Catholic influence.[81] Convinced of a divide-and-conquer strategy amongst Evangelicalism's detractors, Bickersteth believed that a show of visible unity amongst evangelical Protestants would be crucial to mitigating the onslaughts of the enemy.[82] Aggrieved at so much of the infighting he witnessed amongst Protestants, Bickersteth appealed for unity:

> There is tremendous evil in this war of brethren, Protestant brethren, biting and devouring one another. It is the scoff of the Infidel and the Papist. . . . It is not necessary that all who have a heart-union should visibly unite, but it is needful that enough should do it, to produce the effect of a brotherly recognition.[83]

The Anglican clergyman's antipathy towards Catholicism ran deep, denouncing the church for its worship of images,[84] its "idolatrous" sacrifice of the mass,[85] its neglect of the Sabbath,[86] its addition of the Apocrypha to the "Word of God,"[87] and its system of priestly confession.[88] Accordingly, he deplored government measures seen as favoring Irish Catholics such as the 1845 Maynooth legislation to extend state aid to a Catholic seminary which he perceived to be Westminster's wrongheaded attempt to appease Catholic grievances in Ireland.[89] Despite supporting the Catholic Relief Act

---

79. Letter from Edward Bickersteth to Samuel Wilberforce, 13 June 1838, Wilberforce Manuscripts, C. 7, folio 137, in Lewis, *Origins of Christian Zionism*, 116.

80. Bickersteth, *Divine Warning*, 211. Bickersteth conceded that "much remains in our noble Constitution" but appealed for it "to be held fast."

81. Ibid., 211. Bickersteth lamented the "multiplication of Roman Chapels, now exceeding 500 in Great Britain."

82. Ibid. Bickersteth appealed for his readers to "rally then around each Protestant standard . . . and to help maintain unadulterated our national profession of the pure doctrines of the Word of God, handed down to us by our Protestant forefathers, and sealed with their blood."

83. Bickersteth, "Letter to a Clergyman" (January 29, 1846), in Birks, *Memoir of the Rev Edward Bickersteth*, 172.

84. Bickersteth, *Divine Warning*, 160.

85. Ibid., 162.

86. Ibid., 164.

87. Ibid., 165.

88. Bickersteth, *Divine Warning*, 170.

89. Bickersteth, *Signs of the Times*, 90–91.

in 1829, Ashley was similarly opposed to the Roman Catholicism of his day throughout his public career, often perceiving it as a threat to the traditional Protestant character of England. Like his mentor, he believed that a unified Protestant block was critical to neutralizing both the influence of Roman Catholicism in British religious life at large and Tractarianism within the Established Church.

Ashley's premillennial eschatology, together with the closely related special concern for the conversion of Jews to Christianity, was also heavily indebted to the outlook of his spiritual mentor. Bickersteth himself came to embrace premillennialism in the early 1830s believing that its view of prophecy best accorded with the scriptures.[90] In short, the doctrine of premillennialism affirmed that the second coming of Christ would *precede* the millennium (that is, the one thousand year reign of Christ on earth); that the first resurrection was literal, and that Christ would establish a glorious kingdom of righteousness on earth at his return before the resurrection of the dead and the final judgment.[91] Premillennialism gained currency in English evangelicalism broadly, with the perceived terrors and evils of the French Revolution helping to fan prophetic speculation about the "end times."[92] Owing to anxieties about such ferment, the premillennial doctrine of an imminent Second Coming appealed to such evangelicals who increasingly interpreted day-to-day political events in prophetic biblical terms. This outlook departed from the more postmillennial eschatology of the Clapham generation who maintained the second coming of Christ would *succeed* a fixed interval of a thousand years.

Meanwhile, Bickersteth had undertaken a study of biblical prophecy with a view to rethinking what he could personally affirm amidst all the apocalyptic speculation swirling around him in the evangelical subculture. Coming to his conclusion in 1833 after careful examination, he set aside his postmillennial convictions and declared himself in favor of a premillennial interpretation of scripture and propounded these views in an expanded version of his *Guide to the Prophecies* in 1835. Just prior to composing this guide, Bickersteth declared:

> I have found the doctrine of the personal coming of Christ before the millennium quickening and profitable to my soul; and believing it to be Divine truth, I pray that I may see it with greater clearness and power, hold it more firmly, confess it more

---

90. Bickersteth, Journal Entry (January 1833), in Birks, *Bickersteth*, Vol. II, 24.
91. Birks, *Bickersteth*, Vol. II, 25.
92. Lewis, *Origins of Christian Zionism*, 37.

> boldly, and live in its joyful hope, as well as in its awakening and stirring influence.[93]

On eschatological matters, Bickersteth was a key clerical thinker in this period and his premillennialism perhaps represented his most significant break from the older Claphamite Evangelical tradition. Drawing from the ideas of Bickersteth, Ashley typified this new Adventist spirit with his frequent and earnest petitions for the return of Christ.

> There is very little seeming, and no real, hope for mankind but in the Second Advent; . . . first, we have to contend against the various lets and hindrances which arise in the execution of every honest purpose, the abatements, the diversions, the overthrows of our schemes; next, we must consider how small a portion of our fellow-creatures can receive benefit from any policy of ours/ the widest plan and the fullest success of benevolence never yet affected the twentieth part of mankind/nothing can be universal but the reign of our blessed Lord on the throne of David, when there shall be "Glory to God in the highest, peace on earth, and goodwill towards men," even so come, Lord Jesus![94]

Although Ashley, by his life and example, stressed the imperative necessity of doing everything possible to better the human condition in the present world, he expressed the premillennial conviction that it was only in the second coming of Christ that the ultimate hopes of humanity would be realized.

Typically axiomatic in a premillennial outlook was a concerted drive to bring the original inhabitants of Israel, the Jews, to a saving faith in the gospel. This mission was embraced with equal fervor by Bickersteth and then Ashley. Like premillennialism, this resurgent interest in the Jews and Judaism was integral to the response of Evangelicals to the political turmoil of the French Revolution. Accordingly, prophetic commentators insisted that the Jews were "God's timepiece"—the key to understanding the prophetic speculations.[95] Even after the French Revolution had abated, Evangelical momentum for the Jewish cause remained strong with British evangelicals in the early nineteenth-century feeling with special power, the injunction that the Christian gospel should be preached (in the words of Paul in Romans 1:16 KJV), "to the Jew first." Such momentum could be attributed to three factors: first, the influence and notable impact of German-speaking Pietism in the English speaking evangelical world at the turn

---

93. Bickersteth, Journal Entry (27 March, 1834), in Birks, *Bickersteth*, Vol. II, 22.

94. Shaftesbury, Diary Entry (December 25, 1842), in Hodder, *Life and Work of the Seventh Earl*, Vol. I, 441–42.

95. Lewis, *Origins of Christian Zionism*, 41.

of the nineteenth century; second, the attitude of the older generation of English Evangelical leadership to the LSJ and to the issues of Jewish conversion and restoration; and third, the initiative and involvement of converted Jews whose leadership was crucial to the conversionist cause and to evangelical perceptions of the Jews as a group with a national, Hebrew identity.[96] This was all crucial for the 1809 founding of the London Society for the Promotion of Christianity amongst the Jews. It was commonly referred to in the nineteenth century as the Jews' Society and quickly became known as the leading British organization concerned with the evangelization of Jews.

According to Bickersteth, the prominence the scriptures gave to both the conversion *and* the restoration of the Jews to their own homeland was inescapable. As early as 1832, he concluded that "there are many expressions in the Old Testament which may lead us to expect not only the conversion of the Jews, but their national restoration from their present dispersion to their own land."[97] Composing a volume of prayers in 1842 that reflected his growing zeal for the Jewish cause, the clergyman petitioned the Almighty "to make known the good tidings of thy grace to thy people Israel,"[98] and to "let our attention be more directed to many prophecies respecting Israel, and a love of Jerusalem to be excited in all our hearts."[99] In practical efforts to support the mission to the Jews, Bickersteth immersed himself in the work of the London Jews' Society and, together with Ashley, would energetically support the establishment of a Protestant bishopric in Jerusalem in 1841. Conceding that he arrived somewhat later as a convert to the Jewish cause, Bickersteth reflected:

> Engaged for many years in the work of promoting missions to the Gentiles, my mind was but little directed toward the Jews; but having since been enabled to give more consideration to the Divine testimony concerning them, I have increasingly seen how plainly, in these momentous times, our God requires His people to care for Israel, and how great is the blessedness of helping forward their salvation.[100]

---

96. Ibid., 50.
97. Bickersteth, *Practical Remarks*, 12.
98. Bickersteth, *Family Prayers*, 383.
99. Ibid., 384.
100. Bickersteth, "Anniversary Sermon to the London Jews' Society" (1834), in Birks, *Bickersteth*, Vol. II, 33.

Indeed, Thomas R. Birks concluded that Bickersteth's devotion to the Jewish cause was such that it rivalled that of the Cambridge preacher and mission pioneer, Simeon, who had helped found the LSPCJ.[101]

From Simeon, Scott and then Bickersteth, the mantle of lead Evangelical advocate for the Jews passed to Ashley as Britain entered the Victorian age. Typifying the aspirations of various British evangelical and millenarian groups to reunite the Jewish people with their ancient soil, Ashley expressed his heartfelt desire to provide a homeland for the Jews in personal reflections and parliamentary speeches.[102] Ashley's interest in Jews and the possibility of their restoration to Palestine could be traced back to a remarkably early period in his diary, well before he was publicly identified as an Evangelical. As early as 1826, he began his diary entry with the following question, "Who will be the Cyrus of Modern Times, the second Chosen to restore God's People?"[103] Like Bickersteth, Ashley played an active role in the Society and was generally vocal in his support for evangelism amongst the Jews. He extended Simeon's original agenda by also supporting the creation of a Jewish homeland and the establishment of a Protestant bishopric in Jerusalem. Penning an article for the *Quarterly Review* in 1839, Ashley was ebullient about the progress made towards realizing this vision:

> A more important undertaking has already been begun by the zeal and piety of those who entertain an interest for the Jewish nation. They have designed the establishment of a church at Jerusalem, if possible on Mount Zion itself, where the order of our service and the prayers of our Liturgy shall daily be set before the faithful in the Hebrew language.[104]

In addition to his work with the LSPCJ, Ashley's abiding fidelity to the Jewish cause was evident in his approach to British foreign policy, particularly with respect to Middle-Eastern affairs. According to Joseph Adler, it was these intense religious feelings that motivated the Victorian social reformer in 1838 to urge Lord Palmerston to appoint a British vice-consul for Jerusalem and to extend the consulate's protection to the Jews of Palestine.[105]

---

101. Birks, *Bickersteth*, 33.

102. Adler, *Restoring the Jews to their Homeland*, 141.

103. Ashley, Diary Entry (July 30, 1826), Vol. I [Broadlands Archives SHA/PD/1]. The reference is to Cyrus, King of Persia, who sought to rebuild the Temple in Jerusalem for the Jews. See 2 Chr 36:22–23.

104. Ashley, "The State and Prospects of the Jews," *The Quarterly Review* 63.125 (1839), 186.

105. Adler, *Restoring the Jews*, 140.

The other characteristic of Bickersteth's Evangelical thought reflected in Ashley was that the "Condition of England" question demanded proactive efforts on the part of society and government to address the plight of the poor. Decrying the "idolatry of wealth" in 1843 as "one great and peculiar snare of Britain in this day,"[106] Bickersteth warned that unless "a large class of the wealthy" attended to the temporal and spiritual distresses of their fellow citizens, they would suffer condemnation in "the day of Christ."[107] In a statement reflecting Bickersteth's departure from the dominant Christian-political-economy thinking of Chalmers and the Claphamites, Bickersteth insisted that it was not merely the duty of private individuals and churches, but also "the duty of the nation and of its government to see that the poor are not neglected."[108] Advancing a case for state intervention to ameliorate the plight of child laborers, the clergyman argued that there was much sin against the poor in Britain, which it was "in the power of a Christian legislature to remedy."[109] Appreciating the afflictions of the poorer classes as one of "deep national importance," he maintained that they required "the aid of wise, righteous and merciful laws."[110] As Ashley's chief mentor, he encouraged the parliamentarian to agitate for appropriate state intervention in the factory system to relieve the suffering of juvenile industrial workers. Welcoming the introduction of the 1844 Factory Bill into the House of Commons, Bickersteth wrote: "it appears to me a very weighty duty on all faithful Christian ministers and Christians through [sic] our country to support the benevolent, the patriotic, and the truly Christian measures of the Lord Ashley, for the amelioration of the Working Classes of society."[111] Thus, whilst Ashley's program of moderate state intervention was bolstered by the leaders of the factory reform movement together with sections of the *Record*, it was fundamentally informed by the thinking and writing of the Watton rector.

From Ashley's initial acquaintance with Bickersteth in 1835 to the clergyman's death in 1850, the warm affinity between the two men was kept alive by a copious flow of correspondence. As well as endorsing Ashley's factory reform bills in his published literature and in letters to the *Record*, Bickersteth expressed his effusive praise for the work of his protégé in 1840 with this dedication to Lord Ashley in one of his published treatises:

106. Bickersteth, *Divine Warning*, 264.
107. Ibid., 266–67.
108. Bickersteth, *Signs of the Times*, 333.
109. Ibid., 334.
110. Ibid., 334.
111. Ibid., 423.

> To the Right Honourable Lord Ashley. MP for the County of Dorset. In grateful memory of his labours for the benefit of the factory children, for the maintenance of Christian education by the state, for the unimpaired continuance of our Protestant institutions, as well as of his efforts to communicate our highest blessings to others, and especially to the children of Israel....[112]

Bickersteth's high estimation of the Victorian social reformer was reciprocated in 1850 when Ashley paid tribute to his personal mentor, shortly after his death: "How I miss, and shall continue to miss, the warmth, the joy in good [sic], the sympathy, of dear Bickersteth. How many times his words have encouraged or consoled me."[113] With a deep personal friendship providing the foundation, Birks noted the "deep harmony of feeling and judgment" in the views between the Anglican minister of Watton and aristocrat of Wimbourne St Giles.[114] Similarly, Hodder reflected that Bickersteth was a "friend who, more than any other, had been a constant sympathizer and earnest coadjutor in Lord Ashley's labors."[115] Appreciating the visible continuity of thought and action between the two men, Hodder further concluded that "on almost every subject their views were identical."[116] Given the symmetry of their views on so many issues from premillennial eschatology to anti-Catholicism, therefore, it would be reasonable to conclude that much of the spiritual impetus for Ashley's social reforms sprang directly from the religious views and emphases of his mentor Bickersteth.

A son of the Clapham Sect or a brother of the Recordites?

By the time the Earl of Shaftesbury entered late middle-age in the 1860s, it was apparent that the flavor of his Evangelicalism palpably reflected that of the Recordite generation, owing to the enduring friendship he had cultivated with the *Record* proprietor, Alexander Haldane.[117] Scathing of

---

112. Bickersteth, *A Treatise on Baptism*, "Dedication."

113. Ashley, Diary Entry (28 February 1850), in Hodder, *Life and Work of the Seventh Earl*, Vol. II, 311.

114. Birks, *Bickersteth*, Vol. II, 56.

115. Hodder, *Life and Work of the Seventh Earl*, Vol. II, 310.

116. Hodder, *Life and Work of the Seventh Earl*, Vol. II, 310.

117. Altholz, "Alexander Haldane," 28. After the death of Ashley's mentor Bickersteth in 1850, Haldane took his place as his principal 'counsellor and friend'. Although Haldane initially had little interest in the factory reform legislation of Ashley, their shared opposition to Tractarianism, Romanism, and rationalism brought the two men closer together as co-campaigners.

higher biblical criticism,[118] skeptical of the promises rendered by scientific opinion,[119] and fiercely loyal to the Authorized Version of the Bible,[120] Shaftesbury stood for an Evangelicalism which was politically conservative and pro-Anglican establishment, philosemitic, premillennial, resolutely orthodox in its adherence to the scriptures, unaccommodating of theological modernism, and impenitently opposed to Catholic influence both inside and outside the Established Church.[121] As with Bickersteth, his premillennial eschatology represented his most significant departure from the thinking of the Claphamites. Beneath this steely Recordite exterior, however, the living core of Ashley's Evangelicalism essentially resembled that of the Clapham generation. The causes of Christian mission, education, philanthropy, and social reform which had animated the Clapham Sect from the 1790s remained with Shaftesbury right up to his death in 1885.[122] The frequent visits to Ragged Schools and the chairing of mission societies continued to dominate the elder Shaftesbury's evangelical witness as much as his parliamentary campaigns against Roman Catholicism and Tractarianism.

Given the elasticity for Ashley's Evangelicalism, like that of Bickersteth, to accommodate simultaneously both Clapham and Recordite traits, it is critical not to view these two schools as mutually exclusive. As Ralph Brown argued, there were overriding similarities between the two schools despite their differences: a moderate Calvinist theology cultivated by Simeon and Scott, an abiding loyalty to the established church, a devotion to Christian mission and a commitment to social reform were just some of the enduring commonalities personified by transitional figures such as Bickersteth and Ashley.[123] Notwithstanding Hilton's somewhat rigid dichotomy between

118. Hodder, *Life and Work of the Seventh Earl*, Vol. III, 163. Of Bishop Colenso's book on the Pentateuch, Shaftesbury was quoted by Hodder as describing this work of higher biblical criticism as a "puerile and ignorant attack on the sacred and unassailable Word of God."

119. Shaftesbury, "Diary Entry" (25 August 1868), in Hodder, *Life and Work of the Seventh Earl*, Vol. III, 18. Appraising the merits of Victorian scientific explanations for humanity's origin and purpose, Shaftesbury questioned 'how shall we be better, wiser, happier?'

120. Lord Shaftesbury, "Correspondence with Professor Selwyn" (1870) in Hodder, *Life and Work of the Seventh Earl*, Vol. III, 260. Decrying the revision of the Bible, Shaftesbury praised the Authorised Version as "that precious, inestimable and holy gift to England."

121. Lewis, *Origins of Christian Zionism*, 95.

122. Kirton, *True Nobility*, 385–86.

123. Brown, "Evangelical Social Thought," 127, 131. Brown suggested that owing to their moderate premillennialism, the Recordites in fact had more in common with the earlier Claphamite generation than with contemporaneous Evangelicals who held to the extreme premillennialism of Edward Irving and the 'Albury circle.'

"moderate" and "extreme" Evangelicals, Hilton's discernment of a theological and ideological divide between the two generations was nonetheless useful in underscoring just how Anglican Evangelicalism, and its practitioners such as Ashley, could adjust their core doctrines to the tumultuous economic and social vicissitudes of the nineteenth century. More generally, it highlighted the malleable nature of British Evangelicalism and its ability to recalibrate itself according to changing historical contexts and cultures. The adoption of premillennial eschatology from the 1820s and 1830s, for example, owed much to exogenous factors such as the permeation of romanticism, geopolitical upheaval in Europe, and wide-ranging constitutional reform between 1828–32.[124] As Bebbington observed, Evangelicalism (and its practitioners) "proved remarkably adaptable to a wide range of diverse societies, taking up aspects of their ways of life and merging them with the distinctive features of the faith."[125] The development of Ashley's Anglican Evangelicalism was indeed a case in point. It was a new synthesis bringing together Claphamite and Recordite elements in a perspective at once responsive to the changing conditions of the early Victorian era and calculated to address its distinctive needs. As an expression of evangelicalism, it embraced all the elements of the Bebbington Quadrilateral, but the emphasis on biblicism and activism forged a new axis reflecting how the priorities and emphases of the movement could be adjusting in the thinking of a sensitive and energetic proponent such as Ashley.

---

124. Lewis, *Origins of Christian Zionism*, 87–91.

125. Bebbington, "Chapter 1: Evangelicalism and Cultural Diffusion," in Smith (ed.), *British Evangelical Identities*, 18.

Part II

Ashley and the Tradition of Paternalism

3

Surveying the Contours of Ashley's Paternalism

Together with Anglican Evangelicalism, paternalism was arguably one of the key belief systems that shaped the basic worldview and approach of Ashley to religious affairs, politics, and society. With contemporary Western liberalism esteeming the primacy of individual autonomy, "paternalism" frequently evokes unsavory connotations of state control and coercion. Yet in the context of the Victorian era, paternalism was widely defended by evangelical Protestants, Roman Catholics, Tories, and even Whigs as not only a respectable creed with long traditions but as a humane shield offering protection to new classes of workers from the harsh impacts of unbridled industrial capitalism. Indeed, to the extent that it afforded industrial laborers freedom from commercial exploitation, this paternalism could be said to have represented an expression of the "negative liberty" identified by Isaiah Berlin, the twentieth-century liberal theorist.

In the 1800s, paternalists and "agrarian-minded Evangelicals" such as Ashley hoped "to see the restoration of a properly functioning, hierarchical society structured around patrician obligation and plebian deference, with private philanthropy as its vital social cement."[1] The paternalist outlook of Ashley has been widely acknowledged by his various biographers, most notably Finlayson and Turnbull, who credit it as one of the guiding philosophies behind his social reforms and philanthropy.[2] Even with this due

---

1. Lawrence, "Paternalism, Class and the British Path," in Gunn and Vernon (eds), *Peculiarities of Liberal Modernity*, 148.
2. Finlayson, *Seventh Earl of Shaftesbury*, 74–76; Turnbull, *Shaftesbury*, 13–15.

acknowledgement, however, questions remain as to the origins and inspiration behind this paternalist mindset, the precise essence and practical forms that his paternalism assumed and the extent to which it evolved over time.

In the most general sense, paternalism could be defined as the interposition of an individual or a state in the affairs of another party with the self-justification that the other party's welfare would be better off or protected from harm.[3] In Ashley's context of nineteenth-century Britain, however, paternalism in both theory and practice represented a fluid and heterogeneous amalgam of tendencies and traits that escaped simplified characterizations. Accordingly, this second part will begin by engaging closely with two seminal studies by David Roberts, the only comprehensive studies produced to date that examine paternalist philosophy and practice specifically within the Victorian context,[4] to identify the defining contours of Ashley's paternalist philosophy and the extent to which they surfaced in his pronouncements and policies. From this forgoing analysis, it will be concluded that Ashley's paternalism conformed *largely* to high Tory precepts that stressed the primacy of traditional institutions, the existence of landed property as the essential basis for performing public duties and the assumption that society was innately hierarchical and organic. Notwithstanding, it will also be acknowledged that Ashley's paternalism was by no means static but ever evolving, and as such, it also came to absorb distinctively Whig traditions of paternalist thought and practice. Contrary to popular perception, paternalist attitudes were by no means the sole preserve of Tories, with David Roberts, Richard Brent, and Peter Mandler each shedding invaluable light on the existence of a distinctive paternalist tradition in Whig circles.[5]

Ashley's place on the spectrum of nineteenth-century paternalism

The political philosophy of paternalism, like the religious tradition of Evangelicalism, represented a complex spectrum comprised of multiple strands and nuances. Despite paternalism's contested nature, its historiographical treatment to date, at least in the nineteenth-century British political context,

3. Dworkin, "Defining Paternalism," in Coons and Weber, *Paternalism*, 28–31.

4. Roberts, *Paternalism*. This was followed by Roberts, *Social Conscience of the Early Victorians*. In addition to examining paternalism, Roberts discussed other philosophies that he saw as major contributors to the formation of the early Victorian conscience. These included political economy, utilitarianism, philanthropy and humanitarianism.

5. Roberts, *Social Conscience of the Early Victorians*; Brent, *Liberal Anglican Politics*; Mandler, *Aristocratic Government*.

has been somewhat limited and its contribution to the political thought of Lord Ashley has been even less documented. Appreciating this dearth of commentary on paternalism in the late 1970s, David Roberts produced his pioneering study on paternalism as a political concept and its manifestation in early Victorian England. Roberts attributed the absence of forgoing studies to the fact that, like the medieval English Constitution, paternalism experienced a "nameless existence" during the earlier nineteenth century.[6] In addition, it is not possible to identify paternalism with a set of concrete, logical and clearly definable axioms which historians could readily identify and discuss.[7] On the contrary, it formed a set of varying beliefs and practices that could form different combinations in the minds of different people in differing times and places.

Notwithstanding paternalism's inherent heterogeneity, Roberts developed a working model of the concept in the Victorian context. According to Roberts, Victorian paternalism was firstly undergirded by four basic assumptions, namely, that society should be authoritarian, hierarchical, organic, and pluralistic.[8] Second, paternalism entailed the exercise of three principal sets of duties on the part of the paternalist, these included the responsibilities to rule, guide and help.[9] Satisfied that the ensuing course of historiography warranted no revision to his original paternalist formula posited in 1979, Roberts reiterated it in his section on paternalism as part of his broader 2002 study on philosophical currents shaping the Victorian age.[10] Whilst Roberts is to be credited for devising a working model of paternalism applicable to the Victorian period, neither of his two works discussed the extent to which Ashley's political outlook embodied the defining features of the Victorian paternalist paradigm even though he alluded to Ashley at various points in his studies.[11] This model of paternalism

6. Roberts, *Paternalism*, 1.
7. Ibid.
8. Ibid., 2.
9. Ibid., 4–5.
10. Roberts, *Social Conscience of the Early Victorians*, 9–10.
11. In *Paternalism*, Roberts referred to Ashley's "strong Evangelicalism" at 8, his reconciliation of philanthropy with paternalism at 35, his concern for the plight of factory children at 75, his appeal for the aristocracy to support philanthropic causes at 82, his reflection on the conditions of his recently inherited St Giles estate at 134, his paternalist rationale for the factory acts at 190, his responsibility for the Two lunacy Acts at 206, and finally, the difficulty of categorizing Ashley's form of paternalism at 218–19. Meanwhile in the *Social Conscience of the Early Victorians*, Roberts acknowledged the influence of the paternalist Robert Southey on Ashley but did not elaborate further at 29.

proposed by Roberts can thus be employed to identify and examine the Victorian paternalism of Ashley.

Turning to paternalism's four-fold assumptions about society, it was evident that Ashley himself envisioned British society as being authoritarian, hierarchical, organic and pluralistic. Given authoritarianism's connotations of despotism and antipathy to English notions of liberty, it is perhaps too strong a word to characterize the outlook of Ashley. Nonetheless, it is certainly true that Ashley entertained an acute sense of paternal authority which extended from the domestic sphere of the household to the civic life of the nation. Speaking of the family home in 1872, Shaftesbury desired "to maintain the great principle that the working man should be the master of his house, and the happy head of a moral and industrious family."[12] Thus, in its domestic context, "paternal authority" assumed an avowedly patriarchal character where fatherhood denoted sovereignty. In the public realm, meanwhile, paternal authority implied a disciplinary role for the government and its institutions to promote peace and good order. Admiring Britain's political institutions for their "effects of discipline acting upon the vigor of British character" in 1840, Ashley maintained that these "instruments" were indispensable for the "alliance and protection" of the people.[13]

Closely related to this notion of "paternal authority," Ashley shared the paternalist's conviction that God had created a hierarchical society which was necessary for its own well-being. According to Ashley, the key to a flourishing society was not the elimination or "leveling" of different ranks, but rather their harmonious co-operation. Introducing his 1842 bill to extend child labor restrictions to mines and collieries across the UK, Ashley expressed the "hope to see the revival of such a good understanding between master and man, between wealth and poverty, between ruler and ruled, as will, under God's good providence, conduce [sic] to the restoration of social comfort, and to the permanent security of empire."[14] Aspiring to revive the traditional social bonds between classes, Ashley reflected the paternalist's third assumption that society was "organic" in the sense that the existence of amicable class relations accorded with what he regarded as the "natural order of things" ordained by God. Finally, Ashley's reference to different contexts of paternal authority, such as the household, the school and the state, accorded with the "pluralist" assumption of British paternalists that

---

12. Shaftesbury, *Speech on laying the Memorial Stone*, 5.

13. Lord Ashley, Diary Entry (November 9, 1840) cited in Edwin Hodder, *The Life and Work of the Seventh Earl*, Vol. I, 316.

14. Lord Ashley, "Employment of Women and Children in Mines and Collieries," HC Debates, *Hansard*, 7 June 1842, c. 1321.

each sphere within society was vested with a distinctive paternal jurisdiction, be it that of the father, the landlord, the teacher or the parson.

As to the three sets of duties Roberts identified as the prerogative of the conscientious paternalist, Ashley's theory and practice of paternalism exhibited the distinctive roles of ruling, guiding, and helping. As a landowning peer, the duty to *rule* was primary and instinctive for Ashley, flowing directly from his privileged station. In the nineteenth-century House of Lords, political representation was a function of property and the composition of the House reflected its distribution. In addition to the bishops, the Lords consisted predominantly of wealthy landowning peers who had included successive Earls of Shaftesbury superintending the St Giles estate of Wimborne. In his speeches, Ashley spoke of the governing obligations that "alone can sanctify the possession of property, and render its tenure a joy to all classes, alike honourable, beneficial, and secure."[15]

For paternalists, such as Ashley, the duty to rule did not simply imply the exercise of control or superintendence but also an obligation to provide *guidance* to one's dependents. Such guidance typically took the form of instruction, training and education, particularly within the context of the Ragged School Movement with which Ashley was involved. Speaking on the education of children in 1840, Ashley told the House of Commons that "to ensure a vigourous [sic] and moral manhood, we must train them aright from their earliest years and so reserve the full development of their physical and moral energies."[16] For Ashley, such paternal guidance was not only appropriate in the classroom but also in the realm of colonial affairs. Of each British colony, he pledged that "I would protect and train it until its riper years, and then give it, like a full-grown son, free action and absolute independence."[17] This suggested, however, that Ashley regarded the paternalist duty to guide as one being for a "season" and by no means terminal.

Through his philanthropic activity, Ashley exhibited the third duty of the paternalist which was that of *helping* the poor in their afflictions and sufferings. Calling on the parliament to discharge what he saw as its duty of paternal care to the underprivileged in 1843, Ashley told his colleagues:

> We owe to the poor of our land a weighty debt. We call them improvident and immoral, and many of them are so: but that

---

15. Lord Ashley, Speech, December 1, 1843 cited in Hodder, *Life and Work of the Seventh Earl*, Vol. I, 309–10.

16. Lord Ashley, Education of Children, HC Debates, *Hansard*, 4 August 1840, Vol. 55, c. 1261.

17. Lord Ashley, Diary Entry (June 26, 1845), cited in Hodder, *Life and Work of the Seventh Earl*, Vol. II, 77.

improvidence and that immorality are the results, in a great measure, of our neglect, and, in not a little [sic], of our example. . . . Only let us declare, this night, that we will enter on a novel and a better course—that we will seek their temporal, through their eternal welfare—and the half of our work will then have been achieved.[18]

As a representative of the aristocracy, Ashley felt no small measure of contrition for the previous dereliction of duty to the poor exhibited by much of his own class. The English nobility's indulgent preoccupation with its own wealth at the expense of the poor, throughout the Regency era, did not quite square with the lofty aristocratic ideal of *noblesse oblige*. Elected to represent the various constituencies of Woodstock, Dorset, and Bath in the House of Commons,[19] Ashley was convinced of his responsibility to do all within his power to help arrest this pattern of neglect towards the poor. Accordingly, he viewed his agitation for factory labor reform, his involvement with the RSU and all his philanthropic initiatives as practical means to helping the underprivileged.

The Tory dimension to Ashley's paternalism

Given British paternalism's emphasis on the traditional values of authority, hierarchy, and duty, together with its tendency to idealize the past as a "golden age" of pre-industrial and pre-urban rural simplicity, it is not surprising that this philosophy has been widely understood to be synonymous with high Tory ideology. While Ashley's paternalism undeniably exhibited Tory characteristics, his classification as a *pure* Tory paternalist is perhaps an oversimplification. As Roberts pointed out, the nineteenth-century Tories by no means enjoyed a monopoly over paternalism with the philosophy transcending political party allegiances. The various strands of paternalism were malleable enough to be woven into other social philosophies and political traditions.[20] Given its multifarious nature, paternalism found not only a home in the Tory party but also the Whig tradition[21] and the emerg-

18. Lord Ashley, "Condition and Education of the Poor," HC Debates, *Hansard*, 28 February 1843, Vol. 67, c. 74.

19. Ashley initially entered the House of Common in 1826 as the MP for the pocket borough of Woodstock (Oxfordshire) prior to successfully contesting the electorate of Dorset in 1831. After resigning from his Dorset seat in 1846 over his support for the repeal of the Corn Laws, Ashley re-entered the Commons In 1847 as the elected member for Bath before finally transferring to the House of Lords in 1851.

20. Roberts, *Paternalism*, 211.

21. Ibid., 229–36.

ing Owenite socialist movement.[22] In addition to identifying "romantic," "Peelite," "Ecclesiastic," and "Country-Squire" sub-branches of paternalism clustered around the Tory stump of paternalism, Roberts also observed a distinctive Whig variety of paternalism which envisioned a proactive role for the government to advance the welfare of the public through government commissions and public programs such as housing and sanitation.[23] The origins of this Whig paternalism were drawn out by Richard Brent who discussed the infusion of a humanitarian philanthropy into the Whig party during the early decades of the nineteenth century through aristocratic figures such as Viscount Althorp and Lord Radnor who espoused a creed of *noblesse oblige*.[24] Paternalist philosophy, moreover, found a new lease of life in the nascent socialist thought of Robert Owen who proposed that an enlarged, centralized state adopt new paternalist powers, particularly in education, that had hitherto been the preserve of local authorities and non-government institutions.[25] As Robert Gray appreciated in his study of the nineteenth-century factory reform movement, "paternalism" was indeed a "widespread theme in early and mid-nineteenth-century public discourse" where the familiar "motifs of social responsibility, enlightened benevolence and reciprocal obligation cut across the established political spectrum."[26]

Given these forgoing varieties of paternalism, which clusters or combinations of these paternalisms did Ashley embody in thought and practice? Although Roberts technically classified Ashley as belonging to what he termed the "Ecclesiastic" or "Churchman" category of paternalists,[27] it becomes apparent that Ashley's paternalism was sufficiently multifaceted to have spanned several categories of paternalism and not simply those of the Tory variety. During the earlier phase of his career, it was certainly evident that Ashley exhibited most of the paternalist traits of the sub-branches existing beneath the Tory canopy. With the *romantic* paternalists of William Wordsworth and Samuel Taylor Coleridge, who idealized the rural simplicity of the pre-industrial world, the young Ashley shared their affection for the land and their distrust of city life. A native of rural Dorset, Ashley similarly relished a close affinity with country life matched with some degree of antipathy and suspicion towards the cities. During his otherwise difficult and melancholic upbringing, the young Ashley was known to thrive on

22. Lawes, *Paternalism and Politics*, 20–24.
23. Roberts, *Social Conscience of the Early Victorians*, 447.
24. Brent, *Liberal Anglican Politics*, 125–27.
25. Lawes, *Paternalism and Politics*, 22.
26. Gray, *Factory Question*, 50.
27. Roberts, *Paternalism*, 280.

the perceived pleasures and delights of country life. This characteristically Tory paternalist affection for the countryside remained with Ashley as he embarked on his political career in Westminster. In an 1841 diary entry, the Dorset MP praised the bucolic beauties of country life, comparing its virtues to the book of Ruth in the Bible:

> The book of Ruth is a beautiful picture of agricultural life, a happy peasantry and a good landlord. There are passages in it of unrivalled sweetness and beauty, exhibiting a state-of-things, and a simplicity of intercourse arising from and coloured by religion, such as this country tomorrow can never enjoy![28]

Conversely, Ashley was aghast at what he perceived to be the contaminating influence of the cities: "Counties are befouled by the filthy people of their capitals, it is from them that impiety emanates and on them that punishment descended; God be praised that London no longer wields an irresistible power over her kindred cities."[29] Although conscious as a professing Evangelical Christian that sin and corruption were to be found everywhere, he nonetheless perceived the cities to be particular hotbeds of vice and immorality. In common with the Lake poets, he singled out the burgeoning cities of the industrial age where the social evils of slave labor, prostitution, delinquency, drunkenness, vagrancy, and homelessness appeared most acute. He thereby entertained fears about the infiltration of these maladies throughout the broad expanses of rural England. Thus, in the early stage of his political career, the romantic flavor of Ashley's paternalism was still strongly pronounced.

Owing to Ashley's later status as a landowning aristocrat, the romantic disposition of his paternalism was augmented by a distinctive *country-squire* outlook. For authentic country squire paternalists, the stewardship of property had, at its heart, a fiduciary duty whereby landowners and squires had an obligation to exercise a protective authority over their workers.[30] In turn, it was expected that the workers would honor their landowners with an attitude of deference and loyalty. Such a hierarchical relationship would ensure a necessary degree of order and stability. Esteeming the sanctity of the privately owned estate, country-squire paternalists invoked property as a bulwark protecting not only one class but all classes from chaos. They

---

28. Lord Ashley, Diary Entry (July 4, 1841), in Hodder, *Life and Work of the Seventh Earl*, Vol. I, 340.

29. Lord Ashley, Diary Entry (1826), in *Personal Diary* (1825–31), 16. [Broadlands Archives SHA/PD/1]

30. Roberts, *Paternalism*, 6.

distinguished sharply between a traditional rooted property of service and a grasping, rootless property, not yet mellowed by time.[31]

To a considerable degree, the country squire's conception of property owed much to Edmund Burke's doctrine of "stewardship," whereby the steward *served* rather than *owned* his property. Accordingly, Burke emphasized the obligations as well as the rights of property ownership.[32] He feared the transfer of political power from landholders to the new industrial capitalists, chiefly because their utilitarian denial of moral obligation and duty, as guides to action, represented a threat to the continuation of a stable social order. In the new economic order, which had accompanied the Industrial Revolution, country-squire paternalists similarly expressed concern that the new "utilitarian" conception of landed property could lead to the fragmentation and atomization of property into impersonal shares that would never inspire allegiance or lead to stability.[33] Ashley himself came to lament the modern, commercial trend of detaching landed property from "all notions of ancestral feeling, of attachment to hereditary estates, and of long connections between property and peasantry."[34] By the mid-nineteenth century, Ashley regretted that landed property was looked upon by many "merely as a negotiable article of merchandise, to be sold and shifted with as little of affection and difficulty as a five-pound note."[35]

Characteristically of paternalists from the country-squire stable, Ashley opposed the measures of the 1832 Reform Bill, believing, like William Wordsworth, that it would unduly tip the balance of power too much in favor of large urban centres at the expense of rural communities. In an address to his Dorset constituents, Ashley gave this assurance to his concerned audience:

> I have opposed the Reform Bill in the House of Commons, because I believed it to be a sudden and presumptuous Innovation, destructive of the nice balance hitherto maintained between the Interests of the Land and Manufactures, and subversive of our Civil and Religious Ministers; but the Measure they have produced, I must ever regard as violent in its provisions, miscalculated in its effects, and eventually injurious to the whole

---

31. Viereck, *Conservatism*, 14.
32. Roberts, *Social Conscience of the Early Victorians*, 17.
33. Newby et al., *Property, Paternalism and Power*, 24.
34. Hodder, *Life and Work of the Seventh Earl*, Vol. II, 446.
35. Hodder, *Life and Work of the Seventh Earl*, Vol. II, 446.

Part II: Ashley and the Tradition of Paternalism

Community, by the aggrandizement of the Towns at the expense of the Agriculturalists.[36]

As a self-identified "agriculturalist" representing his rural constituency, Ashley was convinced that a redistribution of electoral power in favor of the towns and cities would diminish the electoral clout of rural landowners and their ability to maintain an authentically agrarian paternalist voice within the parliament. His stance was characteristic of Tories who had deployed a plethora of arguments against reform. As Hilton observed, opponents of reform feared that the Bill's abolition of parliamentary boroughs would render the Commons uncontrollable and jeopardize property in general.[37]

In addition to the romantic and country-squire schools of paternalism, Ashley's early outlook was heavily indebted to that of the *ecclesiastical* variety, as already appreciated by Roberts. Whilst the first two forms of paternalism were incidental to Ashley's rural credentials, his ecclesiastical streak of paternalism owed much to his enthusiastic embrace of Anglican Evangelicalism as a younger adult. Ashley envisioned an expanded and more active role for the Church of England, and sought to realize this through his support and patronage of Church organizations such as the CMS and the Church Pastoral Aid Society. His vision for an enlarged Established Church, however, was not merely driven by his Evangelical zeal for national mission but also by the same ecclesiastic paternalist ideals as Southey, Coleridge, and Sir Robert Inglis. Despite his form of Anglicanism differing radically from the High Anglican tradition of these paternalists, he shared their hope that the national Church would be a good and powerful paternal role-model to England and the world. "I have ever desired that the Church of England should in her wisdom, her piety, her strength, and her moderation be a model to all the nations of the earth. It has ever been my most ardent desire that in all the great dependencies of this vast empire the Church of England should be powerful and beneficent."[38]

Speaking in reference to the parliamentary debate over the Clerical Vestments Bill in 1867, Lord Shaftesbury was arguing that the advance of "ritualism," with the recent revival of Convocation and the introduction of vestments such as surplices, represented an aberration from what he understood to be the Church's Protestant foundations. Mindful that he was unapologetically campaigning for the Evangelical cause within the Church, Shaftesbury concluded that whatever his own theological position may have

---

36. Ashley, *Address to the Gentry* (1831)

37. Hilton, *A Mad, Bad and Dangerous People*, 429.

38. Shaftesbury, Clerical Vestments Bill (No 2), Second Reading, HL Debates, *Hansard*, 14 May 1867, Vol. 187, c. 501.

been on internal Church affairs, his paternalist vision for an expansive and nurturing Church of England whose "children should rise up and call her blessed" would prevail regardless of doctrinal loyalties.

As Ashley became progressively involved in the great parliamentary debates of the day, especially over factory reform; his idealistic paternalism began also to take on a more pragmatic form. In this respect, it reflected elements of the *Peelite* school identified by Roberts. Notwithstanding Ashley's personal frustrations with Peel regarding the dearth of liberal Tory support for his factory acts, he nonetheless shared the pragmatic focus of the Peelites to resolve present day problems by the enactment of appropriate legislation. Although Ashley's boyhood affinity with the old agrarian life represented the first basis of his paternalist instincts and remained a lifelong trait of his character, he demonstrated more of a pragmatic amenability to adapt his principles to the conditions of contemporary industrial life. This approach of Ashley's became particularly evident in his evolving position on Britain's protectionist Corn Laws, repealed by the Peel administration in 1846. At the General Election of 1841, Ashley characteristically defended the Corn Laws as a necessary measure to protect the interests of rural landholders who formed the backbone of his Dorset constituency.[39]

By 1845, however, his position changed as he came to regard the policy as an impediment to realizing his objective of passing a ten-hour factory bill.[40] In Ashley's mind, defending the retention of such protectionist measures in the agricultural sector would imply doing the same for the industrial sector. With a protectionist regime impairing the free intercourse of trade and the capacity to compete with foreign markets, it was deemed highly plausible that manufacturers would lack sufficient confidence in their markets to concede a ten-hour day.[41] Accordingly, Ashley accepted Peel's policy of repealing the Corn Laws as a necessary concession to maximize the possibility of enacting his factory reform legislation. In so doing, Ashley broke ranks with many of his fellow Tory paternalists, who would have regarded his capitulation to commercial interests as an act of class treason. Protectionism represented a *sine qua non* for country-squire Tories and their outrage at his stance on the Corn Laws was palpable. Faced with the dilemma of either representing the staunch protectionism of his constituency or supporting Peel's policy, Ashley elected to resign from his seat of

---

39. Ashley, Diary Entry (December 28, 1844) [Broadlands Archives SHA/PD/3], in Finlayson, *Seventh Earl of Shaftesbury*, 239.

40. Ashley, Diary Entry (December 28, 1844) [Broadlands Archives SHA/PD/3], in Finlayson, *Seventh Earl of Shaftesbury*, 239.

41. Finlayson, *Seventh Earl of Shaftesbury*, 240.

Dorset in January 1846 so he could vote for the repeal of the Corn Laws with a clear conscience.[42]

Thus, even in cases where Ashley was under intense political pressure to uphold the interests of his fellow agriculturalists, whom Tory paternalists traditionally esteemed as the pillar of society, he accommodated the needs of those in the cities—particularly the growing mass of urban inhabitants afflicted by poverty and homelessness. In so doing, Ashley did not forsake his agrarian-derived paternalist principles but simply applied them to new contexts and areas of need as they arose. Indeed, redirecting his political strategy to ensure that the new, urban class of industrial laborers could eventually receive due legislative protection from exploitation, in the form of a ten-hour bill, became his *overriding* paternalist duty. Accepting that England's march to mass-industrialization and urbanization was inexorable; Ashley came increasingly to see the poor communities of England's towns and cities as the paternalist's new "tenement." Accordingly, he contributed to the urban projects of sanitary infrastructure and housing estate construction, as new means of discharging his paternalist duties to those deemed in such need of care and protection.

Ashley's pragmatic breed of paternalism was again conspicuous in his parliamentary agitation for factory reform. The social reformer was every bit as committed as the romantic paternalists to preserving the traditional relationship between employer and employee. He accepted, however, that the industrialization of Victorian England was irreversible and hence the old ideals typifying agricultural life needed to be imported into the new manufacturing system. Unlike Wordsworth and the Young England movement of Lord John Manners, Ashley did not object to the manufacturing system outright as an evil *per se* to be eradicated. On the contrary, he appreciated the indispensability of the manufacturing system to England's modern economy but simply desired it to reflect what he valued as the more paternal and humane ideals underpinning the old agrarian order. In an 1844 speech to the Commons, Ashley flatly denied that his campaign for factory-labor reform was motivated by an agenda to destroy the commercial, manufacturing system:

> are you reasonable to impute to me a settled desire, a single purpose, to exalt the landed, and to humiliate the commercial aristocracy? Most solemnly do I deny the accusation; if you think me wicked enough, do you think me fool enough, for

---

42. Shortly after resigning from his Dorset seat, Ashley decided to contest the seat of Bath and was re-elected to the House of Commons in July 1847 where he served until June 1851. Thereafter, he assumed his hereditary peerage in the House of Lords.

such a hateful policy? Can any man in his senses now hesitate to believe that the permanent prosperity of the manufacturing body . . . is essential, not only to the welfare, but absolutely to the existence of the British empire? No, we fear not the increase of your political power, nor envy your stupendous riches. . . . We ask but a slight relaxation of toil, a time to live, and a time to die; a time for those comforts that sweeten life, and a time for those duties that adorn it.[43]

Reflecting on his factory reform campaign almost four decades later, Shaftesbury explained in 1882 that his underlying objective was always to restore a sense of paternal affection to contemporary labor relations:

> I have always labored to bring the employer and employed, the capitalist and labourer, face to face, mind to mind, heart to heart. Half the mischief in England arises from people not knowing each other; half the mischief arises from one class not knowing what is demanded by the other. I wish there could be more friendly intercourse; and much might be done to promote this if everyone did what he could.[44]

Like Thomas Carlyle, he accepted that the captains of industry were a new industrial class of 'aristocracy' who could emulate the traditional values of their agrarian counterparts.[45] Through the assistance of such reforms as the Ten Hour Factory Act, Ashley had faith in the possibility of being able to transmute the paternal virtues of the old agricultural paradigm to the new industrial order which increasingly defined Victorian life. Some of Ashley's fellow paternalists in the romantic movement did not necessarily share this leap of faith, convinced that such virtues would inexorably be swept away by the tide of commercialism and industrial capitalism.

Having firmly established Ashley as manifesting traits from each of the schools belonging to the Tory cluster of paternalisms, it would be remiss not also to examine the distinctively Whig dimension to Ashley's paternalist thought and practice. Although Ashley remained a Tory by both philosophical predilection and party identity, he grew disaffected with the liberal Toryism of Peel and his Home Secretary, James Graham, particularly over their reluctance to support his factory reform measures.[46] Disillusioned and

43. Ashley, "Hours of Labour in Factories," HC Debates, *Hansard*, 15 March 1844, Vol. 73, c. 1101.
44. Shaftesbury, "Chapter II: Work and Influence," in Bullock (ed.), *Talks with the People*, 19.
45. Roberts, *Social Conscience of the Early Victorians*, 17.
46. Roberts, "Tory Paternalism and Social Reform," 328–29.

frustrated at not being able fully to execute his paternalist ideals through the prevailing parliamentary program of Peel's Tory party in the earlier 1840s, Ashley found the succeeding Whig administration of Lord John Russell decidedly more amenable to his paternalist objectives. Accordingly, he was willing to collaborate with Whig MPs to realize his policy objectives and relied heavily on their support to pass successfully his factory reform legislation.[47]

The relative cooperation Ashley enjoyed with the Whigs was no doubt aided by the fact that the Tory-aligned Ashley, to a significant degree, entertained paternalist ideals not incompatible with those practiced by the Whig party in the 1840s and 50s. As Peter Mandler observed, there were a sizeable number of Whig parliamentarians who had an unfashionable desire for paternalist intervention stemming from a lingering "Foxite sense of aristocratic responsibility," or what Roberts termed a "Whig *noblesse oblige*."[48] Like the equivalent ethos in sections of the Tory party, this primarily derived from the pre-eminent sphere of landed property with its attendant obligations. Indeed, the Whig prime ministers, Russell and Palmerston, were two such landholders who appreciated the responsibilities of government to rule, protect, and guide its subjects.[49] This paternalist streak in the Whig party helped to explain the legislative reality that "hardly a single measure of social reform, factory legislation pre-eminently, was enacted between 1830 and 1852 without the support of the Whig leadership."[50]

Within Whig circles, Ashley's paternalism found not only an affinity with the traditional aristocratic paternalism embodied by Russell and Palmerston but also a newer variety of centralized, state paternalism inspired by the utilitarian philosophy of Jeremy Bentham (1748–1832). In his *Constitutional Code* (1830), Bentham maintained that a collectivist state led by a centralized government was eminently conducive to realizing the utilitarian objective of maximizing the greatest happiness for the greatest number.[51] Although Bentham was pre-eminently a utilitarian, his proposals for the establishment of numerous government schemes, agencies and inspectors to oversee improvements in public health and education accorded with the vision of a more paternalist government espoused by Russell and like-minded Whigs. One of the leading Victorian practitioners of utilitarianism, Edwin Chadwick, dedicated his public career to give effect to many of Bentham's

---

47. Ibid., 329.
48. Mandler, "Cain and Abel," 97.
49. Roberts, *Social Conscience of the Early Victorians*, 447.
50. Mandler, "Cain and Abel," 100.
51. Roberts, *Social Conscience of the Early Victorians*, 435.

ideas. Appointed by Russell's Whig administration to the General Board of Health in 1848, Chadwick sought to execute the government's paternalist and utilitarian objectives by developing schemes for inspectors and boards to oversee the provision of potable drinking water, adequate sanitation, and the municipal management of gas and water.[52]

With Chadwick believing that it was the government's mission to care for the welfare of the people, Ashley found his utilitarian paternalism congenial to his own philosophy of benign state intervention. Accordingly, Ashley worked constructively with Chadwick as a fellow commissioner on the General Board of Health to improve sanitation and urban hygiene.[53] Although he never abandoned the localized, rural paternalism of the Tory romantics, country squires, and ecclesiastics, he believed that the "micro-paternalism" of the family household, the school, the church, and the country estate needed to be *supplemented* by a larger-scale state paternalism of the kind championed by the Whig utilitarians. As Roberts pointed out, Ashley's 1845 lunacy bills made provisions for both the empowerment of local JP's *and* the exercise of central government inspection.[54] Like Whig paternalists inspired by Benthamite utilitarianism, Ashley believed that state mechanisms such as parliamentary legislation and government commissions could be employed to discharge the appropriate duties of authority, protection and practical assistance.

As well as his partnership with commissioners Chadwick and Thomas Southward Smith on the General Board of Health, Ashley worked collaboratively with Whig commissioners on the Lunacy Commission of 1845. As Roberts noted, most of these commissions were indeed Whig initiatives.[55] In contrast to Tories such as Peel and Graham who were less than enthusiastic about government commissions, Ashley created an expanded Lunacy Commission and a Mining Inspectorate. Whilst he maintained faith in the old, localized mechanisms for exercising paternal authority, Ashley appreciated that the new complexities of industrialized life gave rise to vulnerable classes of people warranting additional forms of protection. For wide-scale groups, such as child factory labourers, it was most desirable and indeed most practicable for a centralized agency, such as the government, to render the necessary protections. Certainly in this respect, Ashley's evolving paternalism was more in tune with that of the Whigs than the somewhat staid and strictly localized variety of the Tory country squires. Thus, Ash-

52. Ibid., 438.
53. Ibid., 453.
54. Ibid., 430.
55. Roberts, *Paternalism*, 25.

ley's breed of paternalism, in its capacity to exhibit the traits of multiple sub-groups of paternalist tradition in Victorian Britain, displayed an almost unparalleled catholicity and malleability to reconcile such a diverse, and occasionally conflicting, tapestry of threads into its philosophical outlook.

4

Imbibing Paternalism
St Giles, Southey, and Sadler

The fundamental wellspring of Ashley's distinctive paternalism was his childhood experience of the St Giles family estate, where he witnessed firsthand, the exercise of paternalist authority divorced from the much-extolled virtues of care and guidance. Ashley's father, the Sixth Earl of Shaftesbury, had represented a forbidding authority figure but his palpable lack of filial warmth and solicitude was something Ashley was determined to redress in his own pattern of paternal rule. The evolution of Ashley's paternalism, however, was not merely the consequence of his family upbringing and desire to recast a decidedly different paternalist philosophy and approach from his father, but also the product of circulating social and political ideas he imbibed primarily from personal relationships. The two most significant of these connections were his warm friendship with the romantic Lake poet, Robert Southey, and his political links with the parliamentary leader of the factory reform movement, Michael Thomas Sadler. Southey and Sadler each espoused a high Tory form of paternalism that profoundly shaped the political conscience of Ashley. Recoiling with alarm at the Condition of England Question which highlighted the maladies of rural and urban pauperism, industrial and agricultural child labor, social dislocation, and commercial exploitation, high Tories such as Southey and Sadler proposed a revivified paternalism with its medicine of benign state intervention providing a timely remedy to these social ills plaguing pre and early Victorian Britain. As Roberts, Harold Perkin, and Kim Lawes observed, the messages of Southey and Sadler represented a broader revival of 'aristocratic' paternalist thought in Britain during the 1830s as the liberal orthodoxies of political economy came under sustained critique from social reformers of both Tory and Radical persuasions.[1]

Paternalism and practice: The interplay of Ashley's paternalism with that of his aristocratic background

Considering Ashley's status as the heir to one of Britain's prestigious earldoms, it could readily be taken for granted that his predominantly Tory-inclined paternalism was something this Dorset aristocrat ordinarily imbibed from birth. With the Shaftesbury heraldic motto of "love-serve" adorning a stained-glass window in the chapel of St Giles estate, it would seem apparent that the family ideal of 'noble public service' ran deeply through his veins. Accordingly, to exercise the paternalist duties of benign authority, protection, guidance, and succor to those subordinate in rank would appear second-nature to somebody of his pedigree and station. The forgoing historiography on paternalism in the nineteenth-century British context, albeit limited, suggested, however, that the concept of paternalism was often more imagined rather than actual, and idealized rather than practiced. Notwithstanding the authentic and practical paternalism of Lord Ashley himself, this historiographical understanding of the concept emerges as eminently applicable to the arguably notional paternalism typifying his immediate family background. Therefore, what effect did this paternalism have on the decidedly different form exhibited by Ashley?

As an ideal, E. P. Thompson observed that paternalism suggested a mutually assenting relationship of 'human warmth' where the father (figure) is conscious of his duties and responsibilities towards his son, whilst the son is acquiescent or actively complaisant in his filial station.[2] To what extent, however, was this ideal actually real and was it ubiquitously practiced? According to Thompson, the very use of the term confused the actual and the ideal since it tended to offer a model of the social order as it appeared from 'above.'[3] As such, it failed to do justice to portraying a *holistic* portrait of the social order and thus the grittier realities of the paternal compact often escaped attention. Thompson proceeded to note that the common practices of landlord absenteeism;[4] the emergence of the three-tier system

---

1. Perkin, *Origins of Modern English Society*, 237, 239; Roberts, *Paternalism*, 57–59; Lawes, *Paternalism and Politics*, 2.
2. Thompson, *Customs in Common*, 22.
3. Ibid., 24.
4. Ibid., 43.

of landowner;[5] the isolation of Justices of the Peace from the main industrial areas;[6] the erection of forbidding fences around country estates;[7] and the impersonal, perfunctory manner in which landowning masters rewarded their servants tended to suggest an absence of the warm, filial relationship between master and servant that paternalism professed to champion. Whilst not wholly denying the practice of authentic paternal responsibilities, Thompson concluded that paternalist gestures were often employed as a theatrical veneer to mask a less savory reality.[8]

Likewise, Roberts conceded that the pattern of rural life in early nineteenth-century Britain was often starkly at odds with paternalist ideals. Far from representing the benevolent and solicitous shepherd of his property and its workers, country landlords frequently displayed hauteur, imperiousness, and aloofness in their management of estates.[9] The oversights and abuses of rural superintendence were brought to light in the 1843 report on women and children in agriculture submitted to the Poor Law Commissioners and in the 1847 report of the Select Committee on Settlement and Removal. Before the committees, multiple witness bore testimony to widespread incidences of dilapidated workers cottages and parlous living standards which landlords failed to rectify.[10] As Roberts noted, these rural maladies were even conspicuous to the most ardent apologist of paternalism with Sadler railing against landlord absenteeism in his treatises and Southey decrying the "landlords who rack rent their tenants and farmers who grind the laborers."[11]

Turning to the paternalist stewardship of Ashley's own family, the Sixth Earl of Shaftesbury's superintendence of the St Giles estate appeared to conform to some of the less sanguine realities of rural estate ownership highlighted by Thompson and Roberts. Ashley's father, Cropley Ashley Cooper (1768–1851), became the landlord of St Giles estate in 1811 upon assuming his seat in the House of Lords as the Sixth Earl of Shaftesbury. The impersonal and neglectful manner with which he managed St Giles could be traced back to his control of the family household, the very sphere from which paternalists derived their theory of paternal authority. As a

---

5. Ibid. The 'three-tier' system of landowner was comprised of the landlord himself, the 'middle-men' and then the labourers.

6. Ibid., 44.

7. Ibid., 45.

8. Ibid., 64.

9. Roberts, *Paternalism*, 136.

10. Ibid., 139.

11. Ibid., 37.

father to his children, the Sixth Earl accepted and displayed the paternalist premises of authority and hierarchy but not the benevolent duties of protection, guidance and nurture. The dearth of these paternal qualities in Ashley's father was recognized by Ashley and confirmed by his biographers. From his earliest diary entries as a young man to his reflections in old age, Ashley's less than flattering appraisals of his father remained consistent. As a younger man in 1828, Ashley wrote that his father's approach was censorious, fault-finding and abusive.[12] In a conversation with his biographer, Edwin Hodder, towards the end of his life, Shaftesbury recalled that he and his siblings were brought up with "very great severity, moral and physical, in respect both of mind and body, the opinion of our parents being that, to render a child obedient, it should be in a constant fear of its father and mother."[13] George Howard, a visitor to Ashley in the 1820s, noted the "uncommon awe and reserve" in which the whole Ashley family stood for the Howards.[14] Subsequent biographers confirmed these first-hand impressions, in even more severe terms, with Geoffrey Best characterizing Ashley's father as a "repulsive parent" whose "treatment of his children was callous and peremptory."[15] Thus, the Sixth Earl's example appeared to square with Roberts' identification of a paternalism that entailed patriarchal authority without the benevolence.[16]

The aloof but stern patriarchal severity with which Ashley's father ruled his children appeared to extend to his management of the St Giles estate. Although recognized for his competent chairmanship and good business acumen, his stewardship of the estate and its workers left much to be desired with the workers' cottages falling into disrepair and the basic needs of the labourers unattended to. The poor condition of workers on family estates in districts such as Dorset was suspected in parliament during the early 1840s when questions were raised about the system of 'truck,' whereby the wages of agricultural laborers were made up 'in kind.'[17] Considering the cavalier approach of the Sixth Earl to managing domestic affairs, there were reasonable grounds for supposing that the St Giles estate was no exception.[18] Given, however, that St Giles was still under the jurisdiction of

12. Ashley, Diary Entry (November 16, 1828). [Broadlands Archives SHA/PD/1]

13. Shaftesbury in conversation with Hodder, cited in Hodder, *Life and Work of the Seventh Earl*, Vol. I, 51.

14. Finlayson, *Seventh Earl of Shaftesbury*, 15.

15. Best, *A Biography of AA Cooper*, 14.

16. Roberts, *Paternalism*, 134–35.

17. Finlayson, *Seventh Earl of Shaftesbury*, 198.

18. Hodder, *Life and Work of the Seventh Earl*, Vol. II, 368. After careful examination of the estate he inherited in 1851, Ashley discovered that the Truck-System was in

his father, Ashley's concessions of 'vice' and 'misery' in agricultural districts before a Quarter Sessions hearing in 1843 were deliberately couched in general terms to avoid any explicit references to his family's estate. In light of a recently restored relationship with his father, Ashley was aware of the dangers in reigniting conflict if he were specifically to censure St Giles. When the social reformer's vocal campaigns for the plight of factory children have been counterpoised with his seeming inaction on the condition of agricultural laborers, not least those on his family's property, it has brought understandable allegations of moral double-standards. Hilton, for example, noted that Ashley's "lachrymose concern for the victims of industry went with an apparent indifference to the fate of his own Dorset laborers."[19] The reality is, however, that, despite his hesitancy about usurping his father's then jurisdiction of St Giles, Ashley was consciously cultivating a new, practical form of domestic paternalism that would become manifest after assuming control of the estate in 1851.

In a studious effort radically to distance his leadership style from that of his father, it is evident Ashley sought to preach and practice a decidedly different form of paternalism in both his family household and superintendence of St Giles. The basic pillars of authority and hierarchy would stand, but added to these would be the personalized embellishments of paternal care, guidance and protection. With Ashley vividly remembering the indifference of his father towards his own boyhood, Finlayson observed that Ashley "had taken a keen interest in his [son's] education and in particular, his spiritual instruction."[20] In habits more characteristic of his nursemaid than his own father, Ashley spent time with his son reading the Bible and engaging intimately with his life. To a considerable degree, Ashley's domestic paternalism was sustained by a desire to spare his son from the same inattention and emotional deprivation that he had painfully endured as a child. This domestic paternalism extended to his eventual oversight of the family estate following his father's death in 1851. Even before his management of St Giles, however, glimpses of Ashley's guiding paternalist principles were evident in an 1843 speech to an annual Dorset agricultural festival, where he admonished all landholders to exercise the following duties:

> . . . begin a more frequent and friendly intercourse with the labouring man. We have lost much in departing from the simplicity of our forefathers; respect his feelings; respect his rights; pay him in solid money; I say it again, emphatically, pay him

---

fact 'nourishing' on St Giles.
19. Hilton, *Mad Bad and Dangerous People*, 585.
20. Finlayson, *Seventh Earl of Shaftesbury*, 197.

> in solid money; pay him in due time; and, above all, avoid that monstrous abomination which disgraces some other counties, but from which, I believe, we are altogether free, of closing your fields in the time of harvest; give to the gleaner his ancient, his Scriptural right: throw open your gates, throw them wide open, to the poor, the fatherless, the widow.[21]

In a thinly-veiled criticism of the 'truck system' believed to be widely practiced in his own county and even under his father's own watch, he implored landowners to pay their workers "solid money" in "due time." Interpreting his son's speech in Sturminster as a reproach to his superintendence of St Giles, the Sixth Earl of Shaftesbury took exception to Ashley's call for a new approach to managing the estate.[22] While Ashley maintained that his exhortations were fair and humane, his father regarded them as "inducing the people to make extortionate demands."[23] Such disagreements only served to highlight the radically different philosophies of superintendence existing between father and son.

Discovering the full extent of the appalling conditions besetting the St Giles estate he inherited in 1851, including evidence of the notorious truck-system, the new Earl of Shaftesbury found compelling cause to put his paternalism swiftly into practice. Accordingly, he set about eradicating the truck-system, renovating the cottage accommodation, restoring the chapel and introducing new initiatives for the estate's laborers with plans for garden allotments, cricket clubs, and scripture readers.[24] With the death of the Seventh Earl in 1885, the *Times* credited Shaftesbury with transforming St Giles into a "model village" with renovated cottages and the provision of alms-houses for those unable to work.[25] In effecting such a transformation, Shaftesbury sought to showcase the fruits of a radically reformed agricultural paternalism which was beneficent, solicitous, personalized, and eminently practical. Again, Shaftesbury was resolved to personify a paternalism that stood in stark contrast to the insouciant, impersonal, perfunctory and harsh patriarchal authority found to be exercised by his father and numerous other contemporaneous landholders across the country. Thus, Ashley sought to lend material substance to a paternalist ideal that was often more

---

21. Lord Ashley, Speech to the Sturminster Agricultural Society at Sturminister, Dorset (December 1, 1843), in Hodder, *Life and Work of the Seventh Earl*, Vol. I, 521.
22. Finlayson, *Seventh Earl of Shaftesbury*, 201.
23. Ibid.
24. Hodder, *Life and Work of the Seventh Earl*, Vol. II, 370.
25. "Death of Lord Shaftesbury," *The Times*, October 2, 1885, 11.

a guide to an imaginary ideal than a reality in the agrarian world of early Victorian Britain.

The revival of aristocratic ideals in the 1820s: Proposing Tory paternalism as an alternate pathway to political economy

The context in which Ashley's paternalism was forged extended far beyond the domestic realm to the broader political and economic currents circulating in pre and early Victorian Britain. By the 1820s and 30s, the *laissez-faire* orthodoxy of political economy had permeated both the Whig and Tory sides of British politics. Economic liberalism had been the creed of Pitt and during the first three decades of the nineteenth century it made considerable inroads into British political discourse. On the one hand, the classical economics of the Smith-Ricardo school exerted a powerful influence on the Whigs through organs such as the *Edinburgh Review*; whilst, on the other hand, the philosophy of Christian political economy, popularized by Chalmers and Malthus, infiltrated the Tory side of politics through the agency of liberal Tories such as Huskisson and Peel.[26] Thus, with the steady shift towards more of a free-trade economic paradigm, both Whig and Tory dominated parliaments presided over the repeal of protective legislation in crafts and industry.[27]

Although the Industrial Revolution gave birth to a new urbanized mercantile class possessing more liberal, utilitarian ideals, the traditional values of the old landholding aristocracy never really died out with the advance of the Industrial Revolution. On the contrary, they held sway across many parts of the country and experienced a renaissance in the 1820s and 30s.[28] Indeed, the re-galvanizing of Tory paternalist forces was, in no small measure, a reaction to the new entrepreneurial ideals of *laissez-faire* political economy, free trade and industrial capitalism. Proponents of the old paternalism contended that in its preoccupation with generating maximum profit and industrial efficiency, the new economic order was inclined to jettison age-old notions of paternal duty and responsibility towards the welfare of the subordinate laboring classes. Hence a healthy injection of paternalist ideals into the new industrial culture would be welcomed as a humanizing corrective.

---

26. Jones, *Victorian Political Thought*, 18.
27. Stewart, *Foundation of the Conservative Party*, 167–68.
28. Perkin, *Origins of Modern English Society*, 239.

As well as social reform advocates been moved by the plight of factory workers, the revival of aristocratic ideals was sustained by a steady output of political opinion decrying the inhumanity of the new industrial capitalism. Periodicals such as the *Quarterly Review*, *Blackwood's* and *Fraser's* readily became a platform for such agitators publicly to reaffirm the paternal virtues of the old aristocratic paradigm.[29] As the most outspoken proponent of Tory paternalism, *Blackwood's* consistently maintained that the "poor had a right to be cared for" and that the poor laws ought to be retained, not only to prevent revolution but to keep wages high and maintain demand. In addition, the new Tory periodicals frequently advocated measures to expand education and elevate living standards as antidotes to overpopulation and other social problems. Determined to recalibrate late Hanoverian Toryism into an avowedly paternalist creed, *Blackwood's* articulated its guiding philosophy.

> As Tories, we maintain that it is the duty of the people to pay obedience to those set in authority over them: but it is also the duty of those who are placed in authority to protect the people who are placed below them. They are not to sit in stately grandeur, and see the people perish, nor, indeed, are they ever to forget that they hold their power and their possessions upon the understanding that they administer both more of the good of the people at large, than the people would do, if they had the administration of both themselves.[30]

Steeped in the agrarian flavor of Tory paternalism, *Blackwood's* was particularly critical of landholders who neglected their social responsibilities. Reproving them for their extravagant and self-indulgent displays of wealth and grandeur, the magazine suggested that the money spent on one night's lavish entertainment would be sufficient to provide a small plot of land and a cow for some of the needy poor in their districts.[31] In his management of St Giles House, the new Earl of Shaftesbury personally reflected these ideals in making changes to better the lives of his estate's labourers. Whereas his father had presided over the laborers' poor working conditions on the premises, Shaftesbury saw to it that, under his oversight, the workers would enjoy decidedly more comfortable conditions. The paternalist philosophy of *Blackwood's* thus found practical expression in Shaftesbury's superintendence of St Giles.

29. McDowell, *British Conservatism 1832–1914*, 14–15. William Blackwood founded the *Blackwood's Magazine* in 1817 as a counterpoint to the Whig-dominated *Edinburgh Review* which espoused liberal views sympathetic to political economy.

30. William Johnstone, "Our Domestic Policy, No. 1," *Blackwood's* 26 (1829); 768.

31. Ibid., 768.

Complementing *Blackwood's*, the *Quarterly Review* represented a similarly vocal advocate for the paternalist cause and the very periodical in which Southey and Ashley each found a firm voice.[32] With the *Quarterly* characterized as "proud, aristocratic, pontifical, conservative and stern," it was determined to promote a paternalist society that was "hierarchic, authoritarian and organic."[33] Appreciating Southey's conservative and paternalist credentials, the *Quarterly* soon invited the Lake poet to become one of its regular contributors. Between 1809 and 1839, Southey penned nearly one hundred articles for the journal and thus reinforced its paternalist disposition.[34] In his contributions, Southey nailed his high Toryism to the mast by defending the Established Church and condemning Catholic Emancipation. At the same time, he also exhibited his paternalism by denouncing Smith's *Wealth of Nations*, Malthus' *Essay on the Principle of Population* and the deleterious effects of the manufacturing system on the working classes. Proposing paternalist state intervention measures as an antidote, Southey proposed public works to alleviate unemployment and pauperism. Southey's paternalist voice in the *Quarterly* was echoed by his younger friend, Ashley, who expressed similar grievances. In an article for the review in 1840, he despaired at the plight of infants working fourteen-to-fifteen hours a day in some textile mills and reminded parliament of its duty to protect the weak.[35] Again, in an article on London's common lodging houses in 1847, Ashley invoked the creed of *noblesse oblige* to urge persons of "all ranks and professions" and "every holder of property" to consider the appalling living conditions of these houses' occupants.[36]

The attitude of the new Tory paternalists towards the state

By focusing on the new paternal responsibilities of government and parliament, the early nineteenth-century Tory paternalists sought to adapt to the changing social and political climate seen as necessitating a broader scale of superintendence. In the tradition of protectionism, they looked to the state for solutions to social as well as economic problems. To this end, the Tory

32. George Canning launched the *Quarterly Review* in 1808, also as an antidote to the *Edinburgh Review*.

33. Roberts, "The Social Conscience of Tory Periodicals," 158, 164.

34. Speck, "Robert Southey's Contribution," in Cutmore (ed.), *Conservatism and the Quarterly Review*, 166.

35. Ashley, "Infant Labour," *The Quarterly Review* 67:133 (December 1840), 171, 173–81.

36. Ashley, "Lodging-Houses," *The Quarterly Review* 82:163 (December 1847), 152.

paternalists were committed to proposing a national system of education as a means of seeking to integrate traditional paternal values into the new industrial order. Designed to inculcate notions of civic duty and reinforce deferential attitudes among the lower orders, these educational schemes, according to Lawes, generally had more to do with social unity than individual improvement.[37] Like the principles of balance and harmony, the paternalist approach to education reflected the conservative belief in an ordered, hierarchical chain of human relationships as articulated by Burke in his *Reflections*.[38] Foreshadowing Shaftesbury's support for the construction of adequate housing to accommodate working-class families in the 1870s, other initiatives proposed by the Tory reviewers included the construction of cottages and gardens for the rural laborer and home colonies established on wastelands for the industrial unemployed. Such objectives, whilst progressive, nonetheless rested on classic Tory paternalist principles.

Accordingly, the new Tory agitators' demands for a more active social and protective role for the state represented a departure from the *laissez-faire* philosophy underpinning the new economic doctrine of the nineteenth century. The aggressive competitiveness and self-interest underlying the commercial spirit, the driving force of the manufacturing system, was felt by these social commentators to be the root of all social and economic evils.[39] In particular, it was blamed for its effect in disrupting established social ties and causing misery amongst the urban, industrial poor.[40] While questioning the economists' preoccupation with commerce and material progress, as well as repeatedly voicing concerns about the impact of industrialization upon the laboring classes, the paternalists were not necessarily seeking to turn the clock back to restore England to some kind of pre-industrial, pre-modern rural utopia. Although this may have been the vision of such idealists as the Young England Movement, which flourished briefly in the 1830s and 1840s, the main body of paternalists accepted the modern reality of industrialization and thereby sought to restore a balance between the interests of the old agrarian order of landed property and the new world of manufacturing and commerce.[41] Southey, for example, had entertained faith in economic progress and anticipated that the spread of industrial machinery would be beneficial.[42]

37. Lawes, *Paternalism and Politics*, 7–8.
38. Finlayson, *Citizen, State and Social Welfare*, 51.
39. Finlayson, *Citizen, State and Social Welfare*, 51.
40. Kirby, *Child Labour in Britain*, 97.
41. Speck, "Robert Southey, Benjamin Disraeli," 197.
42. Hilton, "Sardonic Grins and Paranoid Politics," in Cutmore, *Conservatism and*

While leading figures such as Sadler, Robinson, and Ashley himself, each favored a greater degree of state intervention to ameliorate poverty and other social ills, the general attitudes of Tory paternalists towards government were ambivalent and somewhat paradoxical. On the one hand, paternalists traditionally regarded private institutions such as the landowner, the family, the church, charities, and voluntary associations as the primary agents for discharging paternal duties; whilst, on the other hand, paternalists came increasingly to view the state as potentially exercising a legitimate function as guardian and protector of the people.[43] With a rapidly industrializing society giving rise to new social needs, paternalists, who had hitherto desired government to be of a modest size, conceded that a paternal government might go some way to compensating for the failings of property and the deficiencies of the church in grappling with the problems of modern urban life in the early nineteenth century. Proponents of a paternalist state contended that it was demanded by the moral and physical condition of the people, whereby citizens entertained a right to expect amelioration and justice from the government to which they were subject.

Ashley's attitude to the state

Although a rural-landowning paternalist of the old school who esteemed landed property and the Established Church as the natural pillars of paternal order, Lord Ashley was receptive enough, as a parliamentarian at the coalface of government, also to envision a protective role for the state. Moved by the helpless and pathetic plight of enslaved factory children, Ashley called for the state to "accomplish her frequent boast and show herself a faithful and pious parent."[44] One of the chief grounds upon which Ashley supported the Ten Hours Factory Bill was the principle that "the State has an interest and a right to watch over, and provide for, the moral and physical wellbeing of her people."[45] Ashley entertained a similarly paternal notion of government with respect to the treatment of lunacy patients. His work to relieve the afflictions of lunacy patients languishing in public asylums was propelled by his conviction that the state stood in the position of *loco parentis* to this vulnerable and needy class of persons. As a responsible guardian,

---

the *Quarterly Review*, 54.

43. Roberts, *Paternalism in Early Victorian England*, 187.

44. Ashley, "Employment of Children in Calico Print Works," HC Debates, *Hansard*, 18 February 1845, Vol. 77, c. 655–56.

45. Ashley, "Hours of Labour in Factories," HC Debates, *Hansard*, 15 March 1844, Vol. 73, c. 1076.

the state was thereby morally obliged to intervene and remove many of the discomforts and cruelties to which these patients were subject. This was certainly the objective behind Ashley's chairing of the Metropolitan Commission on Lunacy in 1833, following his seconding of a parliamentary motion in 1828 for new legislation "to amend the defects of existing lunacy laws."[46]

In his paternalism, Ashley represented something of a bridge between the old paternalists, who looked to landed property and the church as the sources of paternal care, and the newer generation of paternalists, who turned to government as one of the principal paternal organs in society. Ashley's scope for paternal government was comprehensive but nonetheless circumspect. As a Tory, his support for government intervention was tempered by the concern of vesting too much power in the state. Ashley did not share the optimism of the socialist who proposed that a more active, central government with more departments, inspectors, and laws could remedy society's basic ills. For Ashley, the Evangelical Protestant, the fundamental and ultimate cure for such ills was to be found in the Christian gospel which promised personal salvation and moral regeneration to the individual. The transformation of such individuals, according to Ashley, would lead to the gradual reformation of society and the amelioration of social ills. Given that the propagation of the gospel was regarded as the prerogative of the Church, Ashley placed great store by the churches, especially the Established Church, as the proper agents for not only disseminating the gospel but for rendering the core paternal duties of poor relief, education and moral guidance through church-based schools, charities, and voluntary organizations.

Given his abiding faith in such bodies to provide welfare, the socialist allure of an all-encompassing welfare state entertained little appeal for Ashley who essentially rejected the utopian socialism of the Owenites as an acceptable panacea to social disadvantage. Owing to his support for extensive factory reform legislation, seen retrospectively as laying the foundations for the modern welfare state, the Victorian social reformer has been erroneously regarded by the eminent jurist Albert V. Dicey as a harbinger of modern socialism.[47] For Ashley, however, the state *alone* could not be the appropriate organ for organizing and regulating the whole of society. It was the view of Ashley, and Victorian Evangelicals at large, that government monopoly within the welfare sector was to be avoided since this would be seen to diminish the responsibilities of individuals to provide for those in

---

46. Bewley, "Shaftesbury," 1.

47. Dicey, *Lectures on the Relation*, 240. Here, for example, Dicey contended that the Ashley-supported Factory Acts "gave authority, not only in the world of labour, but in many other spheres of life, to beliefs which, if not exactly socialistic, yet tended towards socialism or collectivism."

need. Hence Ashley was an advocate of moderate state intervention, whereby the government had a responsibility proactively to ameliorate the living and working conditions of the poor, but never to the extent of inducing welfare dependency or usurping the vital charitable function of churches and voluntary associations in British life.

Justifying a prudent approach to state intervention, Ashley defended government legislation in cases where it was deemed capable of providing effective justice and redress to vulnerable classes of persons, particularly child and female factory laborers. Like the Tory agitators of the 1820s and 30s, Ashley eschewed the views of *laissez-faire* Tories who frequently regarded state intervention in the labor force as unnecessary at best and evil at worst. In a speech defending the Factories Bill (Health of Women, etc.) before the House of Lords in 1874, Shaftesbury questioned the notion that all the hard-won gains for factory workers could have been realized without legislation and proceeded to give credit to previous parliamentary reforms:

> It has been said, too, my Lords, that, after all, the whole of this great benefit would have been effected without legislation. Possibly it might have been so, but, as legislation has done the work, let legislation for the present have all the glory. By legislation you have removed manifold and oppressive obstacles that stood in the way of the working-man's comfort, progress and honour. By legislation you have ordained justice, and exhibited sympathy with the best interests of the labourers, the surest and happiest mode of all government. By legislation you have given to the working classes the full power to exercise, for themselves and for the public welfare, all the physical and moral energies that God has bestowed on them.[48]

Thus, the purpose behind the state acting was not so much to amass power for its own sake and aggrandizement as ultimately to empower the people to exercise their own talents and energies.

As with paternal rule generally, the chief end of state intervention for Ashley was not to circumscribe the freedom and autonomy of individuals but, on the contrary, to enlarge these for their benefit and enjoyment. Explaining how the state should go about discharging this paternal duty, Ashley had articulated his vision in 1843 in a Speech to the Commons on the Moral and Religious Education of the working classes:

> Now, if it be true, as most undoubtedly it is, that the State has a deep interest in the moral and physical prosperity of all her

---

48. Lord Shaftesbury, Factories (Health of Women) Bill (No 143), Second Reading, HL Debates, *Hansard*, 9 July 1874, Vol. 220, cc. 1338–1339.

children, she must not terminate her care with the years of infancy, but extend her control and providence over many other circumstances that affect the working-man's life. . . . I speak not now of laws and regulations to abridge, but to enlarge his freedom; not to limit his rights, but to multiply his opportunities of enjoying them; laws and regulations which . . . shall place him, in many aspects of health, happiness, and possibilities of virtue, in that position of independence and security, from which, under the present state of things, he is too often excluded.[49]

Such a vision rested on the premise that in a polity, such as Victorian England, where the rights and freedoms of individual workers were all too frequently trammeled by the harsh vicissitudes of industrial life, the state could intervene as a liberating force providing it did not over-reach its proper ambit. This contrasted with the *laissez-faire*, liberal Tory outlook which conceived of State powers in almost purely constraining, restrictive terms.

The Romantic Lake Poets and the contribution of Robert Southey to Ashley's political thought

Robert Southey (1774–1843) belonged to the romantic school of Lake poets who contributed to the revival and popularization of paternalist ideals in the immediate pre-Victorian age. Hailing from the Lake District of North West England, William Wordsworth, Samuel Taylor Coleridge, and Robert Southey, were largely radicals-turned-Tories repelled by not only the Enlightenment-rationalist outcomes of the French Revolution but also by the rapid transformations in English life wrought by the Industrial Revolution.[50] Associated with the burgeoning anti-modern romantic movement of the early nineteenth century, the Lake poets decried the advent of urbanization, large-scale industrialization and modern commercialism which they portrayed as severing the ancient, feudal link between close-knit rural communities and the land. Extolling the medieval era as a lost golden-age of simplicity and virtue, Southey and the Lake poets nostalgically harked back to an earlier rural life of close attachment to the land. When unfavorably comparing modern social conditions to those of the Middle Ages, they felt that something of value had been lost with the disappearance of feudalism.[51] In particular, they lamented the loss of the landed estate as a

---

49. Lord Ashley, Condition and Education of the Poor, HC Debates, *Hansard*, 28 February 1843, Vol. 67, c. 76.

50. Day, *Romanticism*, 150–54.

51. Cobban, *Edmund Burke and the Revolt*, 197.

universally stabilizing influence on society and the erosion of harmonious personal relations between master and servant. Building on the Tory tradition of Burke from the previous century, they frequently invoked what they esteemed as the patrician virtues of landed-property, aristocracy, harmonious class relations and education, all existing under the tutelage of the Established Church. Such themes, in turn, would feature prominently in the political outlook of Ashley who consolidated the Tory paternalist tradition of Southey.

From the 1830s, Ashley cultivated a warm friendship with Robert Southey whose influence upon the young aristocrat was pre-eminent amongst the Lake poets. Finlayson duly acknowledged the poet "as an exponent of the Tory paternalist school of thought," however he did not discuss Southey's "school of thought" in any detail.[52] Moreover, though Finlayson appreciated the contribution of Southey's thought to Ashley's own political outlook, his assessment of Southey's influence, whilst insightful and accurate, was somewhat limited. Finlayson recognized that Ashley's correspondence with Southey exposed him to the basic tenets of Tory paternalist thought. These ideas included a distrust of changes in the political structure, the ideal of a stable and hierarchical society bound together by mutual obligations between rich and poor, and the belief that only by showing care and concern for the poor could the rich hope to survive.[53] Thus, with Finlayson's observations serving as a valuable starting point, this section will examine the essence of Southey's paternalist philosophy and further discuss the considerable extent to which it informed the paternalism of Ashley.

Initially a radical in his youth who sided with the Jacobins in the French Revolution, Southey became increasingly conservative throughout the 1820s as he grew alarmed at what he saw as the liberal orientation of the Liverpool and Wellington administrations. Like most English Tories, Southey's supreme confidence was in the Church of England which he treasured as a bulwark against what he saw as the social deprivation and degenerating public morality of the age.[54] Despite sharing Ashley's reverence for the Established Church, the Lake poet did not assent to his Evangelical tradition of Anglicanism, claiming in 1812 that he could never have subscribed to the 39 Articles with their affirmation of a moderately Calvinist theology.[55] As a romantic high Tory, however, he defended the Church of England in his *Book of the Church* (1824) as indispensable to "the stability and security of

52. Finlayson, *Seventh Earl of Shaftesbury*, 74.
53. Ibid., 76.
54. Andrews, *Robert Southey*, xii.
55. Ibid.

the State."[56] For Southey, the Church had rescued England from "heathenism," "papal idolatry," and "despotism"; as such, it represented a "constituent and necessary part" in the "goodly fabric of that Constitution."[57]

The primacy of the British constitution and its perennial nature was a message consistently articulated by paternalists such as Southey, Sadler, and Ashley. Edmund Burke had asserted in 1790 that "it has been the uniform policy of our Constitution to claim and assert our liberties as an entailed inheritance derived to us from our forefathers and to be transmitted to our posterity."[58] David Eastwood astutely recognized that Southey's defense of the British Constitution in 1816 was positively Burkean.[59] Like the eighteenth-century statesman, Southey lauded the constitution as a permanent compact which evolved with society itself from one generation to the next and revered it as "our Ark of the Covenant." Southey's reverence for the constitution was, in turn, impressed upon Ashley who exhorted his audience in 1845 to preserve the great principles of the constitution: "I decide at once that you will avow, and will maintain, the great principles of the Constitution in Church and State, the Crown, the Bishops, the House of Lords and Commons, and every institution ecclesiastical and civil."[60]

While much of Southey's political thought drew from Burkean conservatism, it also contained paternalist strands of thinking not necessarily characteristic of Burke. Although Southey's paternalism, with respect to the historic roles of the constitution, the Church and the aristocracy stood firmly in the Burkean tradition, his *economic* paternalism represented a departure from Burke's outlook. In contrast to Burke who sympathized with political economy and thereby dismissed the need for public charity and ameliorative state intervention, Southey detested the *laissez-faire* views of the classical economists and called for greater expenditure on public relief.[61] Aware that the Industrial Revolution had brought a new industrial working class into existence, Southey believed that the social upheavals of unemployment and pauperism associated with this transition warranted state intervention.[62] Foreshadowing Ashley's campaigns and initiatives, Southey welcomed the interposition of the state to ameliorate the excesses of the factory system and supported the introduction of public schemes to

---

56. Southey, *Book of the Church*, 490.
57. Ibid., 490.
58. Burke, *Reflections on the Revolution*, 206.
59. Eastwood, "Robert Southey," 309.
60. Lord Ashley, "Social Condition of the Labouring Classes" (1845).
61. Eastwood, "Robert Southey," 315–16.
62. Speck, "Robert Southey, Benjamin Disraeli," 202–3.

help combat pauperism.⁶³ Crowning the existing paternalist functions of the Church, the aristocracy, and private individuals, Southey envisioned a strong paternalist state acting benevolently to remedy economic hardship. Appreciating this critical dimension to Southey's paternalist thought is thus fundamental to understanding Ashley's own evolving paternalism and his support for comparable government measures and reforms.

As early as 1828, Ashley made no secret of his admiration for the romantic poet when he launched a financial appeal for Southey. Lauding the poet as "the most distinguished man of his day for learning and acquirements," he boldly predicted that his writings would become "true national Treasures, so long as there shall be wisdom, morality and religion among the inhabitants of our country."⁶⁴ The first literature of Southey's that Ashley is recorded to have consulted were his two-volume *Colloquies* published in 1829.⁶⁵ That same year, Ashley noted he had been "lately reading Southey's Colloquies" adding "they are replete with learning and thought."⁶⁶ In this series of imagined exchanges between the Tudor-era statesman and writer, Sir Thomas More, and the contemporary Montesinos, a figurative *persona* of Southey himself, Southey's paternalist philosophy and critique of early nineteenth-century British society surfaced throughout the dialogue. Praising medieval society for its "system of superintendence everywhere," Southey suggested that this universal paternalist paradigm no longer held sway in modern Britain. The increasing complexity of society meant that new classes of people often escaped the watchful oversight of a paternal figure and were thereby consigned to a fate of "wretchedness."⁶⁷ To fill these new "gaps" in the superintendence, Southey believed that the interposition of a benevolent state to help remedy the afflictions of such vulnerable classes as factory children and agricultural paupers was called for.⁶⁸

In the midst of tumultuous social change accompanying industrialization, Southey called for the revival of a benign paternalism, initially at an individual level, to bring peace and happiness to society. In "this transitory state of existence" he argued that the object of a "good and wise man" would be to fulfill what was an avowedly paternalist calling:

---

63. Eastwood, "Robert Southey," 320.

64. Lord Ashley (1828) quoted by Finlayson, *Seventh Earl of Shaftesbury*, 74–75.

65. Southey, *Sir Thomas More: Or Colloquies on the Progress and Prospects of Society*, Vols. I & II.

66. Lord Ashley, Diary Entry (2 July, 1829), in Hodder, *Life and Work of the Seventh Earl*, Vol. I, 111–12.

67. Southey, *Colloquies*, Vol. I, 93–94.

68. Southey, *Colloquies*, Vol. II, 78.

> ... to do his duty first to his family, then to his neighbours, lastly to his country and his kind; to promote the welfare of those who are in a degree dependent upon him, or whom he has the means of assisting, and never wantonly to injure the meanest thing that lives; to encourage, as far as he may have the power, whatever is useful and ornamental in society, whatever tends to revive and elevate humanity....[69]

By fostering a paternalist ethos amongst private individuals, the poet hoped that the state would replicate this at large. Beyond exercising a merely administrative function, Southey believed that it was the "first great duty" of government to advance "the moral improvement of the people."[70] In so doing, the state would assume the eminently paternalist duty of "guiding" or "instructing" its subjects, particularly in the habits and virtues of religion. Accordingly, Southey urged the state not to abrogate its duty of ensuring "that the people be trained up in the way they should go."[71] The desired course for the people was to be inculcated with the precepts of religion. By "religion," Southey was speaking of Anglican Christianity in a very general sense as being morally conducive to the welfare of the people and the security of the state. In common with his fellow romantic paternalists, who were generally less concerned with the specifics of Church dogma, Southey primarily valued the Church for its moral utility in reinforcing his paternalist ethics of service, duty, care, honor, and deference.

Despite Ashley's Evangelicalism differing from Southey's 'non-doctrinal Anglicanism," he evidently imbibed the ideas articulated in Southey's *Colloquies*, not least his call for both individuals and the state to embrace a benign and practical paternalism. Echoing Southey's call for "good and wise men" to discharge their duties in all spheres "to elevate humanity," Ashley similarly called on the rising generation in 1844 to formulate and execute a robust paternalism:

> We must have nobler, deeper, and sterner stuff, less of refinement and more of truth; more of the inward, not so much of the outward, gentlemen; a rigid sense of duty, not a "delicate sense of honour," a just estimate of rank and property, not as matters of personal enjoyment and display, but as gifts from God, bringing with them serious responsibilities, and involving a fearful account; a contempt for ridicule, not a dread of it; a desire and

---

69. Southey, *Colloquies*, Vol. I, 165.
70. Southey, *Colloquies*, Vol. II, 424–25.
71. Southey, *Colloquies*, Vol. II, 48.

a courage to live for the service of God and the best interests of mankind....[72]

Conscious that practices such as landlord absenteeism and the truck-system were rife throughout Dorset and the rest of the country during the 1840s, Ashley attempted to cut through the pretentious façade of the country-squire gentlemen to demand a paternalism that was authentic, practical, and non-self-seeking. In so doing, he sought to apply something of Southey's ethic to his own class of rural landholders which had hitherto exhibited a ceremonial, tokenistic paternalism at best. Sharing Southey's concern that the Industrial Revolution had given rise to new classes of people deemed to be in need of paternalist superintendence, Ashley also appealed for the state to fulfill paternalist obligations, particularly that of "protection." Writing for the *Quarterly Review* in 1840, Ashley urged the laws of parliament to "assume the proper functions of law" to "protect those for whom neither wealth, nor station, nor age, have raised a bulwark against tyranny."[73] Identifying the industrial child labourers as one such class which lacked these advantages, it was Ashley's vision that the state would stand in *loco parentis* to shield these children from the tyranny of oppressive working conditions. In so acting, the state would step into fill the cracks that had emerged in Southey's idealized paradigm of "superintendence everywhere."

After reading the *Colloquies*, Ashley was not only influenced by Southey's paternalist view of society but indeed cultivated a warm personal friendship with the poet until his death in 1843. Through an exchange of letters during the 1830s, the two men shared their musings on contemporary political affairs and offered mutual encouragement, even where their positions did not always concur. Although Southey had vocally opposed Catholic Emancipation on the high Tory ground that it would weaken the constitutional hegemony of the Established Church, he acknowledged that Ashley's pragmatic support for the Catholic Relief Act of 1829 was done with "a pure motive."[74] On the question of factory reform, however, the two paternalist thinkers were essentially of the same mind and motive. Southey encouraged his friend to pursue the cause in parliament, "noting that the people of England will be with you." Appreciating the importance for the aristocracy to model paternalist leadership, Southey added that "it is indeed most desirable that it [factory reform] be taken up by one of your station."[75]

---

72. Ashley, Diary Entry (November 21, 1844), Hodder, *Life and Work of the Seventh Earl*, Vol. II, 77

73. Ashley, "Infant Labour," *The Quarterly Review* 67 (December 1840), 181.

74. Robert Southey to Lord Ashley, Keswick (May 28, 1832).

75. Robert Southey to Lord Ashley, Keswick (February 6, 1833).

Like Ashley's speeches in parliament, Southey's letters drew attention to the deleterious consequences of the existing factory system, particularly its tendency to "deaden and destroy all the better feelings" of human beings.[76] The system's effect of degrading, rather than edifying, the moral state of the industrial working class had grated against the paternalist instincts of Southey and Ashley who each stressed that the state had a duty to elevate the moral state of humanity.

As Ashley read draft copies of the romantic poet's writings that he sent to him with his letters,[77] he reiterated his appreciation for Southey's literature.

> I have derived the greatest benefit from the study of your works, and I think that the world also is largely indebted to your genius and industry. . . . I am fully convinced that a young man imbued with your principles, and instructed by your learning, will prove a public servant such as we need to superintend the immediate comforts, and gradually to promote the civilisation of India. . . . [I]t is due to a man who has done so much by his writings to extend the knowledge of true philosophy, and impress upon the world the consolation and practice of religion.[78]

At this early stage of his career in 1830, Ashley's parliamentary work had been chiefly preoccupied with two matters: namely, British colonial rule in India with his appointment to the India Board in 1828 and the plight of lunacy patients with his appointment as chair of a new Lunacy Commission in 1829. In each of these two affairs, he regarded Southey's principles of superintending the vulnerable to be directly applicable to ensure both the wellbeing of Indian colonial subjects and the humane treatment of lunacy patients. Ashley was convinced that Southey's principles and ideals would stand him in good stead as he furthered his campaigns in parliament for a paternalist government to "superintend the immediate comforts" of the vulnerable.

As Ashley's parliamentary career branched out into new areas, particularly the factory reform movement, the influence of Southey's thoughts and writings became even more apparent. If Southey had used his *Colloquies* to articulate paternalist principles, his other significant work, *Essays Moral and Political* (1832), succeeded in giving these thoughts more concrete expression. In his *Essays*, Southey proposed various schemes and policy measures

---

76. Robert Southey to Lord Ashley, Keswick (May 11, 1833).

77. Southey sent Ashley four volumes of his draft essays. Robert Southey to Lord Ashley, Keswick (January 1832).

78. Lord Ashley to Robert Southey, St Giles (September 12, 1830).

to give practical effect to his paternalist ideals, many of which were subsequently effectuated by Ashley. From factory-labor reform through to assisted emigration, public education and the relief of the poor, the genesis of such programs could be found in Southey's pages. To a greater degree than any other Lake poet, Southey represented the great architect of Victorian-era, Tory paternalist schemes and policies sponsored by Ashley. Thus, Geoffrey Carnell reflected that Southey, in many respects, "anticipated the Victorian social prophets, awakening the country's conscience to intolerable social evils, condemning the cold philosophy of selfishness which condoned those evils."[79] Carnell observed that if Southey "was a conservative, he was of the same school as Sadler, Oastler, and Lord Ashley."[80]

Examining Southey's influence on Ashley's campaign for factory reform first, it is evident that Southey's principal concern in his *Essays* had also been the condition of the factory worker. Like Ashley himself, Southey had read Michael Sadler's sobering report on the factory system and conceded that he had little conception of the evils associated with the system before discovering Sadler's findings. In contrast to the old agricultural order that had fostered close personal relations between workers, Southey chastised the new manufacturing system for its absence of community and of reciprocal obligation:

> The manufacturing poor have necessarily less of that attachment to their employers which arises from long connection, and the remembrance of kind offices received, and faithful services performed; an inheritance transmitted from parents to son: and being gathered together in herds from distant parts, they have no family character to support in the place to which they have been transplanted.[81]

Southey deplored the crude utilitarianism of the factory system as a disintegrating force in society. In his eyes, the entrepreneurial class associated with the factory system recognized no responsibility for their fellow compatriots who formed the working class; treating them worse than plantation slaves when there was work, and when there was none, neglecting them as though they were not human beings at all.

Like the new Tory agitators associated with *Blackwood's* and the *Quarterly Review*, Southey had little affection for the new class of entrepreneurial capitalist who were seen as the driving force of this oppressive manufacturing system. He attributed the impersonal and utilitarian nature of the

---

79. Carnell, *Robert Southey and his Age*, 193.
80. Ibid.
81. Southey, *Essays Moral and Political*, Vol. I, 113–14.

system to the individualistic, *liaises-faire* liberalism of Adam Smith and his philosophy of political economy:

> The manufacturing system has been carried among us to an extent unheard of in any former age or country. . . . Adam Smith's book is the code, or confession of faith, of this system; a tedious and hard-hearted book. . . . That book considers man as a manufacturing animal—not by duties to which he is called, not by the immortal destinies for which he is created; but by the gain which can be extracted from him.[82]

For Southey, the *laissez-faire* philosophy of liberal Toryism was bereft of any notion of social responsibility, and, as such, was anathema to his Tory paternalist sensibilities.

Deploring the appalling working conditions of factory life and the deleterious physical and moral effect this was having on the people, Southey publicly pleaded for a reform of the factory system. In an article for the *Quarterly Review* in 1834, he emphasized the contrast between the capitalists and their work-people, returning to a theme which he had first elaborated in *Letters from England* over a quarter of century before. The manufacturing system, according to Southey, had raised armies of miserably poor people who knew that their condition was worse than it needed to be. Breeding such popular discontent, the system had the potential to cause a social cataclysm if it made no attempts to ameliorate the condition of the poor:

> A manufacturing poor is more easily instigated to revolt. They have no local attachments; the persons to whom they look up for support they regard more with envy than respect, as men who grow rich by their labour; . . . If the manufacturing system continues to be extended, increasing, as it necessarily does increase, the number, the misery, and the depravity of the poor, I believe that revolution inevitably must come, and in its most fearful shape.[83]

In one sense, Southey was certainly a reformer in calling for necessary changes to be made to the existing factory system, but, in so doing, he was also displaying his conservative instincts. For, although some legislative adjustments to the existing factory labor regime would amount to change, they would have the desired effect of staving off a far greater change in the form of a revolution by the manufacturing poor, a prospect he truly dreaded. Like

---

82. Ibid., 111–12.
83. Ibid., 117–18.

Burke, he believed that society needed to possess the means of change in order to ensure its own preservation.

Sharing Southey's suspicion of the new manufacturing class and the horrors of the factory system, Ashley was similarly resolved to bring his Tory aristocratic principles to bear on humanizing the factory system. Thus began his long and arduous legislative campaign to make the long-held aspirations of factory-labor reform a reality. In an 1844 address to a committee aligned with the reform movement, Ashley enunciated his rationale and objectives for embarking on industrial labor reform, once again making it clear that he did not oppose the factory system *per se* but rather its negative effects which he was determined to mitigate:

> Now it would be almost equally foolish and wicked in me were I to call myself the enemy of the factory system. . . . No, gentleman, I am only the enemy of its abuses; and those abuses we seek to remedy. Let us but shorten the term of daily labour, giving, thereby, to those employed the means of enjoying their inalienable right of time for self-improvement and domestic life, and I believe that, in the present state of the country, the factory system might thus be made the channel of comforts and even blessings to this large community.[84]

Just as the MP saw the factory system in its present form as adversely affecting the whole of life, he desired that his legislative remedies correspondingly bring benefits and advances to all aspects of life, including workplace relations, the home environment, health, education, and leisure. His vision was truly that of the Tory paternalist who looked to the restoration of social order, the enhancement of hierarchical labor relations and the buttressing of traditional domestic roles as the chief ends of factory reform.

In addition to factory reform, Southey propounded a variety of other social reform schemes in his *Essays*. These included a system of national education with "wholesome training for the children of poverty,"[85] the diffusion of cheap and wholesome literature,[86] an organized system of emigration to the colonies,[87] allotments for laborers,[88] employment for agricultural paupers in cultivating wastelands,[89] the establishment of parochial schools,[90]

---

84. Ashley, *Legislation for the Labouring Classes* (1844).
85. Southey, *Essays Moral and Political*, Vol. I, 149.
86. Ibid., 295–96.
87. Ibid., 154–55.
88. Ibid., 197.
89. Ibid., 197–98.
90. Ibid., 243.

the abolition of bull-baiting and cock-fighting,[91] improvements in prison conditions[92] and phasing out the exploitation of juvenile chimney-sweeps.[93] Notwithstanding Southey's horror and indignation at what he had read of Sadler's reports, Southey counseled his younger friend not to occupy himself exclusively with the factory system, lest he wear himself out as Thomas Clarkson did over the slave trade. Despite consuming much of his early parliamentary career on the very issue of factory reform, Ashley appeared to have heeded his mentor's advice as he turned his attention to a myriad of other causes including the more humane treatment of lunacy patients, the education of the poor, the abolition of child-chimney sweeps as well as various sanitary and housing reforms.

Closely related to his revulsion against the modern factory system was Southey's disgust at the practice of employing child chimney-sweeps, a demeaning trade fraught with grave dangers to life and limb. Often known as "climbing boys," these juvenile chimney-sweeps would be forced by their masters to climb through chimneys to clean the inside despite their likely exposure to harmful fumes and risk of entrapment. Like the harsh conditions of the factory system, this trade had deleterious repercussions extending well into the young laborer's adulthood. Southey excoriated the trade for its cruelties in his *Essays*, calling for its abolition by legislation.

> It may be feared that we have carried it to a more brutal extent than any other nation; for, half a century ago, girls were employed in this disgusting and cruel occupation. This certainly would not be tolerated now by popular feeling; nor ought the trade itself to be tolerated longer.... An Act of parliament ought to be passed for abolishing the present trade; and public benevolence would, beyond all doubt, find suitable provision for the little slaves who would thus be emancipated.[94]

Both inside and outside of parliament, Ashley endeavored to give effect to Southey's plea for the trade to be outlawed. The MP strongly supported an act passed in 1834 with stricter clauses ensuring that no apprentices less than ten years old would be employed.[95] Speaking on a subsequent act in 1840 that introduced fines for anybody "who should compel, or knowingly allow, anyone under the age of twenty-one years to descend a chimney, or enter a flue [sic], for the purpose of sweeping or cleaning it," Ashley re-

91. Ibid., 219–20.
92. Ibid., 237.
93. Ibid., 225–26.
94. Ibid., 225–26.
95. Hodder, *Life and Work of the Seventh Earl*, Vol. I, 171.

marked that while the House had been benevolent to child factory laborers, it needed to extend the same mercies to juvenile chimney-sweepers.[96] As part of testing the effectiveness of the new laws, the MP visited climbing boys at their workplace, confronted the masters, ascertained the feeling of employers, and took legal proceedings at his own expense as "test cases."[97] After two successful proceedings, Ashley reflected:

> Succeeded in both my [law] suits. I undertook them in a spirit of justice. I constituted myself, no doubt, a defender of the poor, to see that the poor and miserable had their rights; . . . I have advanced the cause, done individual justice, anticipated many calamities by this forced intervention, and soothed, I hope, many angry, discontented Chartist spirits by showing them that men of rank and property can, and do, care for the rights and feelings of all their brethren.[98]

By publicly agitating on behalf of this oppressed class of laborers, Ashley expressed his hope that he could give the aristocracy a more human face. With Chartists and other English progressives frequently chastising the aristocracy for its prevailing preoccupation with wealth and cool indifference to the sufferings of the poor, the new wave of Tory paternalists sought to overturn this perception by appealing to a revival of the old rural paternal values as a compelling impetus for relieving the afflictions of the poor. Resolved to carry through this mission, the MP's sustained campaign against the child chimney-sweep trade culminated in the passing of the Chimney Sweepers Regulation Act of 1864, which made it "unlawful for a chimney sweeper to take into a house with him any assistant under sixteen years of age." The Act also increased penalties for offenders, empowering magistrates to impose imprisonment with hard labor *in lieu* of a fine.[99]

Once various forms of child labor had been ameliorated, if not abolished, Southey turned to the education of the people, particularly the poor, as one of the supreme paternal objectives to be realized. Second only to the family unit, the school was the principal organ through which the paternal duties of religious teaching, moral instruction, intellectual enrichment, and training in various vocations would be exercised for the nourishment and betterment of the rising generation. Southey appreciated that if this paternal

---

96. Ibid.

97. Ibid., 172.

98. Lord Ashley, Diary Entry (August 24, 1840), in *Life and Work of the Seventh Earl*, Vol. I, 173.

99. Hodder, Commentary, *Life and Work of the Seventh Earl*, Vol. III, 83–84.

objective of education was to be fully realized, it must be aided by the framework of a national scheme:

> The greatest boon which could be conferred upon Britain is a system of national education. . . . Lay but this foundation, poverty will be diminished, and want will disappear in proportion as the lower classes are instructed in their duties, for then only will they understand their true interests. . . . Let there be a system of parochial schools, connected with the church establishment, where every child may receive the rudiments of necessary knowledge, and be well instructed in his moral and religious duties.[100]

Like his fellow Lake poet Coleridge, Southey regarded the religious foundation of such a system as indispensable and envisaged that it would function as an arm of the Established Church to train up the next generation "in the way that it should go."

Ashley wholeheartedly concurred with Southey's agitation for education, even though he believed that the Lake poet's vision for the establishment of a national education scheme was unattainable during the earlier phase of his political career. In a speech to his new constituency of Bath in 1845, Ashley expressed his doubts about the practicality of setting up an educational scheme of the kind initially proposed by Peel's Home Secretary, James Graham, in his 1843 Factory Bill,[101] remarking, "I do not say that a scheme of national education is within our reach—it is in fact, beyond our reach."[102] While Ashley had been committed, in principle, to the introduction of an educational scheme under Graham's 1843 legislation, he appreciated that the polarity of opinion amongst the churches rendered it effectively impossible to obtain unanimity on the appropriate form of religious instruction to be delivered through the scheme. Many Anglicans, on the one hand, were dissatisfied that there would be no doctrinal interpretation attached to the daily reading of the Bible, whilst on the other, Nonconformist churches expressed concern that the clerical trustees of the schools might require the schoolmaster to teach the *Book of Common Prayer*.[103] In

---

100. Southey, *Essays Moral and Political*, 147, 149, & 244.

101. In his Factory Bill, reintroduced on 7 March 1843, Graham included an education clause whereby children aged between 8 and 13 would receive 3.5 hours of education a day in conjunction with 6.5 hours of work.

102. Lord Ashley, *Social Condition of the Labouring Classes*, Bath, Tuesday, May 25, 1845.

103. Finlayson, *Seventh Earl of Shaftesbury*, 191.

a subsequent speech to the Commons in 1848, Ashley gave voice to these difficulties frustrating the establishment of a national education scheme:

> I have heard it said, in the first place, that schools should be erected, and some system introduced of national education. But this cannot be undertaken, because the very instant any one proposes such a measure, the *vexeta quaestio* is raised, as to how children should be trained—whether by a secular or a religious education, and, if by a religious education, what sort of religion; whether that of the Church of England or of a mixed character.[104]

For this reason, Ashley accepted that Graham's decision to finally drop the education clauses from the 1843 Factory bill was practical politics in the existing circumstances,[105] even though he had personally supported the Anglican position for biblical instruction in schools to be accompanied by doctrinal explanation.[106]

Notwithstanding the fact that Ashley's skepticism about Southey's national education scheme was informed essentially by political pragmatism, the impulse and vision that would underpin his particular education strategy were essentially the same. He similarly viewed education, together with the family, as the essential channel through which moral values were inculcated and duties imparted to the rising generation:

> I do not mean to say that education is a panacea for all the evils. No; that education which we should all desire for the children of this realm is most admirably described in the language of our catechism. "To learn and labour truly to get my own living, and to do my duty in the station to which it has pleased God to call me." Reflect, and you will see that education is a much wider thing than the mere lessons and lectures of the school room; it ought to be connected with the discipline of the parent and the whole domestic system.[107]

Viewing proposals for a national scheme as beset by too many vexing questions that made any consensus unlikely, Ashley instead turned to enhancing existing voluntary education movements, namely the new "Ragged Schools," founded by Thomas Guthrie of Edinburgh. To facilitate the further

---

104. Lord Ashley, "Juvenile Population," HC Debates, *Hansard*, 6 June 1848, Vol. 99, c. 443.
105. Finlayson, *Seventh Earl of Shaftesbury*, 193.
106. Finlayson, *Seventh Earl of Shaftesbury*, 192.
107. Ashley, "Social Condition of the Labouring Classes" (1845).

establishment of such schools, throughout London in particular, Ashley founded the Ragged School Union (RSU) in 1844. To him, the Union would be the best means of advancing the Tory paternal project of education, particularly among the poorer classes. Ashley discussed the basis and objectives of the RSU in the education of its pupils:

> The children are taught to read, write, and cast accounts, and are carefully trained in the great precepts and doctrines of Christianity.... These schools are conducted altogether on a very wide basis: the teachers consist of various denominations of Dissenters, as well as the Church of England; and upon the committees Dissenting ministers and clergyman of the Established Church unite in the most hearty cooperation.... We must take good care, in whatever we do for the advancement of this system, to do nothing that shall dampen or discourage the voluntary principle.[108]

Ashley's decision to invest heavily in the nascent Ragged School movement rather than store hope in a future state education system reflected his conservative sensibilities. Undoubtedly it was driven by pragmatic considerations of urgency to deliver education without unnecessary delay, but, also, it was borne of his instinct that citizen-initiated, voluntary organizations, such as the RSUs, were preferable to state institutions in the provision of essential services to the underprivileged. Rejecting three alternative education proposals, with each relying upon some measure of state agency, Ashley's preference for the Ragged Schools stressed not only the value of volunteerism but the importance of education conforming to a sure notion of discipline and, moreover, his vision that formal education complement rather than replace the vital educating function of the family.[109]

By the 1870s, however, the conservative but realist Shaftesbury would not comprehensively oppose the establishment of a national education system despite voicing doubts about it previously. Maintaining the educational importance of the family and church-based organizations, he nonetheless cautioned that a national education scheme could not be regarded as the alpha and omega of all education:

> We have entered on a system of national education: this is good; but there are many things that may be taught, external to the school and its secular accomplishments: principally, the

---

108. Ashley, "Juvenile Population," HC Debates, *Hansard*, 6 June 1848, Vol. 99, c. 446.

109. Ashley, "Juvenile Population," HC Debates, *Hansard*, 6 June 1848, Vol. 99, c. 444.

> children may be trained in habits of economy; and as extravagance is a besetting sin in all of our populations, thrift, founded on sobriety, may be instituted as its cure. High wages will then be a blessing, instead of a curse.[110]

He was also determined to ensure that such a system had a solid religious grounding like that of the RSUs: "Our business is with one great principle—the great principle involved in the question whether the children of this country under a system of national education shall or shall not receive the Bible and religious teaching."[111]

Shaftesbury's concession to a national system of education in 1870 had in no way diminished his devotion and affection for the continuing Ragged Schools. For him, the passage of time had merely vindicated the success of these institutions in not only developing the intellectual faculties of their pupils but radically transforming their life and character.

> Let no one omit to call to mind what these children were, whence they came, and whither they are going, without this merciful intervention. They would have been added to the perilous swarms of the wild, the lawless, the wretched, and the ignorant, instead of being, as by God's blessing they are, decent and comfortable, earning an honest livelihood, and adorning the community to which they belong.[112]

Defending the Ragged Schools in the face of arguments that the establishment of a national education system had rendered them somewhat obsolete, Shaftesbury esteemed the RSUs as institutions of enduring value. By training up working-class children according to the precepts of Christianity together with the principles of personal responsibility and public duty, the defining educational aspirations articulated by Southey and the Tory paternalists could go some way to being realized. Thus, in one sense, ragged schools represented a project to export the Tory paternal values of the elite privileged classes to the laboring classes.

Lying at the root of Southey's schemes proposed in his *Essays*, particularly those of child labor reform and education, was the overriding objective to improve the condition of the poor. For Southey, and also Ashley, this was energized by the parlous plight of England's homeless and destitute in the wake of the Industrial Revolution together with a sense that the privileged classes had hitherto neglected their obligations to help the poor. Thus,

---

110. Shaftesbury, "Preface," to *The Agricultural Labourer*, ix.
111. Shaftesbury, *National Education Union* (1870), 5.
112. Shaftesbury, *The London Times*, November 13, 1871.

urgent, proactive strategies to address the needs of the poor were welcomed as timely and morally becoming. Deeply impressed with this calling to act, Southey wrote:

> Meantime it is the truest policy and the highest duty to improve the condition of the poor. The better the people are instructed, the happier and the better they will become; the happier they are, the more they will multiply, the greater will be the wealth, and strength, and security of the state; and these maxims are as certain as the laws of nature and of God.[113]

In accordance with his Tory instincts, Southey believed that initiatives to help the poor needed to start with individuals rather than the State: "So far as the further increase of pauperism can be prevented, and the poor-rates diminished, by improving the condition of the present generation of the poor, more may be done by benevolent individuals, and by making parishes sensible of their true interest, than by any parliamentary interference."[114] This, however, of course did not mean that he was opposed to state agency *per se* as evidenced in his campaigns for factory labor reform and national education. Rather, he meant that individuals and voluntary organizations would play a lead role in ameliorating poverty while government, at the same time, appropriately intervened to bring an end to practices exploiting and oppressing the poor.

Reflecting Southey's underlying sympathies, Ashley cited his duty to the poor as one of the motivating factors behind his involvement in the factory labor reform campaign. When requested in 1833 to take over the reins of the factory reform movement from outgoing MP, Michael Sadler, Ashley remarked that "I believe it is my duty to God and the poor" to do so.[115] The Dorset MP shared the conviction of the new Tory paternalists that the privileged classes needed to do more to seek the welfare of the poor. In 1843, he told the House of Commons that "we owe them, too, the debt of kinder language, and more frequent intercourse."[116] As an aristocrat himself, Ashley felt some weight of responsibility for the previous neglect of the poor exhibited by much of his own class including, not least, his own father in his superintendence of St Giles. The English nobility's indulgent preoccupation with its own wealth at the expense of the poor, throughout the Regency era, did not quite square with the lofty aristocratic ideals of *noblesse oblige* in-

---

113. Southey, *Essays Moral and Political*, Vol. I, 247.
114. Ibid., 212.
115. Turnbull, *Shaftesbury*, 76.
116. Ashley, "Condition and Education of the Poor," HC Debates, *Hansard*, 28 February 1843, Vol. 67, c. 74.

voked by contemporary paternalists such as Southey. Ashley felt powerfully convinced that he was responsible to do all within in his power to arrest this pattern of neglect and conscientiously discharge his paternal duties to the vulnerable. Accordingly, he viewed his agitation for factory labor reform, his involvement with the ragged schools and all his other parliamentary projects as the visible and practical exercise of these charges. Feeling deeply indebted to the influence of his poet friend, Ashley paid tribute to Southey after his death in 1843: "He was essentially the friend of the poor, the young, and the defenseless, no one so true, so eloquent, and so powerful."[117] Essentially for Ashley, Southey had furnished his early Toryism with a paternalist social conscience from the 1830s.

Paternalism in parliament: The continuity of Tory paternalist thought between Sadler and Ashley

At the same time Ashley was digesting the thoughts and proposals of his mentor Southey, the MP's political outlook was also being formed by yet another paternalist, Michael Thomas Sadler (1780–1835). As an MP between 1829 and 1832, the high Tory Sadler represented the immediate parliamentary successor to Ashley as the standard-bearer for paternalist causes such as factory reform. Like Ashley, he was naturally held in very high regard by Southey who despaired at the loss of his seat in 1832.[118] Acquainted with the plight of the urban poor in his home city of Leeds, Sadler attributed the human cost of economic distress to the exercise of liberal economic policies. A sworn enemy of political economy, Sadler had denounced the Malthusian "Law of Population," the new Poor Law, usury, free-trade and competition.[119] Highly suspicious of the doctrines propagated by Adam Smith, David Ricardo, and Thomas Malthus, Sadler began to formulate a coherent social and political philosophy in the 1820s to counter the prevailing *laissez faire* orthodoxy. Informed primarily by traditional high Tory politics, Sadler's political thought, like that of Southey, was inherently neopaternalist. Sharing both the romantic poet's distaste of political economy and the reckless manner in which the landed classes at large had abrogated their paternalist responsibilities, Sadler preached a similarly paternalist gospel of protection and dependence.[120] Together with Southey, he advocated

117. Lord Ashley, Diary Entry (March 14, 1843), in Hodder, *Life and Work of the Seventh Earl*, Vol. I, 262.
118. Speck, "Robert Southey," 203.
119. Hilton, *Age of Atonement*, 95.
120. Lawes, *Paternalism and Politics*, 45.

a more active social role for the government which became explicit in his pioneering parliamentary campaign for factory reform.

At first glance, the urban middle-class linen merchant of Leeds would seem like an unlikely forerunner to the aristocrat of Dorset. Despite their differing backgrounds and stations, however, the two men imbibed a markedly similar paternalist philosophy. Sadler had primarily imbibed his paternalism through his first-hand witness of urban pauperism in Leeds, whilst Ashley arrived at his paternalism by absorbing the ideals of Southey together with a conscientious resolve to correct the abuses in his father's stewardship of St Giles. Although Sadler was not a landowner himself, he was acutely aware of the vulnerable state of agricultural laborers across Britain and Ireland, many of whom were left to the mercy of either abusive or neglectful landholders. Sadler's appeal for a return to paternalist ethics in the agricultural context obviously resonated with Ashley who was privy to similar malpractices in his own county and on his own estate. In his work on *Ireland; Its Evils and Their Remedies*, Sadler chronicled the adverse effects of landlord absenteeism and the "depopulation of estates" on the agricultural laborers of Ireland.[121]

Like Southey and Ashley, Sadler lamented the breaking of the "sacred bond" between the landlord and the tenant which he attributed to the curse of absenteeism.[122] The remaining mercenary connections, divorced from the paternalist relationship, thus became devoid of any sense of filial responsibility or moral accountability on the part of the landholder. To arrest this erosion of paternalist ethics, Sadler called on absentee landlords to "reside in the country—to enrich it with their fortunes, ornament it with their taste, improve the morals of the people by their example, refine them by their politeness, and protect them by their authority."[123] Far from being mere administrators of the land, Sadler desired landholders to discharge a comprehensive set of paternalist duties that not only ensured the economic livelihood of their employees but also their moral nourishment and protection from harm and exploitation. It was a similarly broad paternalist philosophy to that which Ashley expressed in his 1843 Sturnminster speech when he called upon the estate owners of Dorset to "begin a more frequent and friendly intercourse with the laboring man." Thus, like Sadler, he encouraged landholders to cultivate relationships with their tenants which were not only mercenary but personal and eminently paternalistic.

---

121. Michael T. Sadler, *Ireland; Its Evils and their Remedies*.
122. Ibid., 55–56.
123. Ibid., 52.

Like Southey, Sadler extrapolated his paternalist philosophy to the operation of the state which he regarded as standing in *loco parentis* to its subjects, particularly those deemed most vulnerable such as juvenile factory workers. Introducing his 1832 Bill to regulate the labor of children in British mills and factories, Sadler told the House of Commons that it was its duty to protect factory children from "that system of cruelty and oppression."[124] Reminding the House that the first law officer of the Crown represented the guardian of all children, he maintained that it was consistent with the conventions of British justice for Parliament similarly to view itself as the guardian of the factory children and thereby intervene to rescue "these innocent victims" of the existing factory system.[125] Whilst the law ordinarily recognized parents to be the natural guardians of children, a prerogative Sadler and his fellow paternalists never had any intention of overriding, there were cases where the state could assume this responsibility if it was deemed to be beyond the capacity of the parents. Sadler viewed the factory children of the 1830s as falling under this category since their parents were left helpless to resist a system which forced them to surrender their children to the factories.[126] The meager wages offered for factory labor were often the only provision that could save such families from starvation and destitution. Thus Sadler demanded the superintendence of the state to protect factory children subject to the exploitation and abuses of the system

Succeeding Sadler as parliamentary leader of the Short Time Movement for factory reform in 1833, Ashley wholly embraced, and indeed expanded, his predecessor's doctrine of paternalist state intervention. In the early 1840s, Ashley initiated a parliamentary campaign to investigate the condition of children in not only factories but other theatres of industrial employment such as mines and collieries.[127] This resulted in the establishment of the Children's Employment Commission in 1842 and the introduction of a bill that year to extend protective measures to vulnerable workers in mine and collieries. Introducing this bill to regulate the employment of women and children in mines and collieries, Ashley justified this latest attempt of the legislature to afford protection: ". . . to remove or even to mitigate, these sad evils requires the vigorous and immediate interposition of the Legislature. That interposition is demanded by public reason, by public

---

124. Sadler, "Factories Regulation Bill," HC Debates, *Hansard*, 16 March 1832, Vol. 11, c. 345.

125. Ibid., c. 347–48.

126. Henriques, *Before the Welfare State*, 75.

127. Ibid., 108.

virtue, by the public honour, by the public character, and I rejoice to add by the public sympathy...."[128]

For Ashley, the doctrine of paternalist state intervention was not limited to vulnerable industrial workers but was applicable also to persons afflicted by mental illness. Speaking on the treatment of insane persons in England and Wales in 1845, he told parliament that "as an assembly of educated, humane and Christian men," it had a "duty of coming forward to the aid and protection of this utterly helpless class, who, under the marked visitation of a wise though inscrutable providence, demand an unusual measure of our sympathy."[129] Whilst Ashley's program of interventionist measures proved more expansive than that of Sadler, owing largely to his considerably lengthier parliamentary career, he never lost sight of Sadler's pioneering role in persuading the legislature of its paternalist obligations to intervene on behalf of the poor and vulnerable. Praising Sadler in 1874 as a "marvelous man of his generation," Shaftesbury conceded that without the preceding labors of the Newark MP, nothing could have been achieved by himself or others in terms of successfully carrying socially ameliorative legislation such as the successive Factory Acts.[130]

---

128. Ashley, "Employment of Women and Children in Mines and Collieries," HC Debates, *Hansard*, 7 June 1842, Vol. 63, c. 1336.

129. Ashley, "Treatment of Insane Persons in England and Wales," HC Debates, *Hansard*, 6 June 1845, Vol. 81, c. 194.

130. Shaftesbury, "Factories (Health of Women and Children) Bill," HL Debates, *Hansard*, 9 July 1874, Vol. 220, c. 1334.

5

The Place of Ashley's Paternalism within the Tory and Whig Traditions

A Tory among Victorian Tories?

Considering his parliamentary track-record of being able to implement a considerable number of the high Tory paternalist ideas and proposals articulated by the *Quarterly Review*, Southey and Sadler, Ashley's Toryism was manifest. Upon entering parliament in 1826 as the Tory MP for the pocket borough of Woodstock, Ashley's first parliamentary mentor was the Duke of Wellington who led a Tory administration from 1828 to 1830 and, again, in 1834, for a very brief interregnum. As a former field marshal and country landowner, the Duke initially commanded the warm affection of Ashley who admired him for his virtues of muscular patriotism, martial valor, and statesmanship.[1] For Ashley, Wellington thus represented the consummate British Tory hero with whom he cultivated a personal friendship in the early years of his political career. Ashley's friendship and loyalty to the duke was rewarded with Wellington appointing Ashley as a Commissioner to the Indian Board of Control in 1828. Whilst eager to cooperate with the duke initially, political differences soon surfaced over social reform as Ashley's penchant for paternalist state intervention clashed with Wellington's preference for parliamentary non-interference in the interests of fostering

---

1. Hodder, *Life and Work of the Seventh Earl*, Vol. I, 59.

private self-help.² Disillusioned with Wellington's seeming disinterest in social reform, Ashley turned to his newfound friend, Southey, a decidedly different caste of Tory, for political inspiration and philosophical nourishment during the 1830s.

Although Ashley remained a member of the Tory party, the relatively minimal party discipline of British parliamentary politics in the nineteenth century afforded MPs considerably more flexibility to vote either according to their personal consciences or the wishes of their respective constituencies. As early as 1829, Ashley departed from high Tory opinion, including that of Southey and Sadler, by voting in favor of the Catholic Relief Act. Similarly, in 1846, he broke ranks with many of his agrarian Tory colleagues by supporting the repeal of the Corn Laws. The paradox of Ashley's stance on the Corn Laws was that he supported a liberal, free trade measure as a strategy to aid his paternalist agenda of ensuring the eventual passage of the ten-hour bill. Without the necessity of adhering to a strict party line on legislation and policy matters, therefore, Ashley had the latitude to apply his deep-seated Tory paternalist principles to the legislative questions of the day without fearing the repercussions of disciplinary action from his own party. As Geoffrey Best correctly observed, Ashley soon "ceased to be the good party man he had begun as, and became a sort of free-lance Tory."³ The independent-minded Tory therefore entertained few qualms about breaking ranks with fellow Tories, or siding with Whig and Radical MPs, if it meant the successful passage of social reform legislation. Indeed, the most vocal support for Ashley's bill to protect cotton mill workers from exploitation came not from the parliamentary Tories, but from Radicals such as John Fielden, or from Whigs such as Thomas Attwood.⁴

Having established the authentic Tory credentials of Ashley, where did his conservatism stand within the British Tory party at large during the nineteenth century? Best appreciated that the "Toryism of his political apprenticeship stuck,"⁵ however he did not discuss this within the context of evolving developments within the Tory Party. In passing, Turnbull cited the relevance of high Toryism to the formation of Ashley's political outlook in the 1820s but did not explain this in detail or, indeed, its implications for Ashley's future relationships within the party.⁶ In a general sense, the

---

2. Finlayson, "Wellington, the Constitution," in Gash (ed.), *Wellington: Studies*, 198–99.
3. Best, *A Biography of AA Cooper*, 22.
4. Roberts, "Tory Paternalism," 325.
5. Best, *Biography of AA Cooper*, 22.
6. Turnbull, *Shaftesbury*, 33.

Tory party at large viewed itself as the legatee of Edmund Burke whom George Canning cited as "the manual of my political philosophy."[7] Burkean ideals including reverence for the Crown, the Constitution, the Established Church and the aristocracy; the primacy of landed property, patriotism, imperialism, and the preservation of an ordered, hierarchical society were accepted by all Tories as non-negotiable articles of faith.

In addition to sharing these conservative fundamentals, the Tory party, at least in the early stages of the nineteenth century, was heavily comprised of parliamentarians hailing from the wealthy landowning class of rural gentry before the gradual infiltration of a new industrial-based generation that included figures such as Peel who was the son of a master cotton-spinner.[8] Sufficiently removed from the new commercial dynamics of urban life in the wake of the Industrial Revolution, this class of landowners, and hence the Tory party at large, felt ostensibly freer than the more urban-based Whigs from the clutches of mercantile interests and the doctrines of political economy.[9] Owing to the more paternalistic instincts of their traditional landholding base, it was, ironically, the rural conservatives who felt more attuned to the moral and social conditions of the urban working classes, seen to be crying out for greater care and protection. With their party holding a majority in the House of Commons, it would appear that Tory paternalists wielded the potential leverage to make their creed an effective answer to the social hardships besetting a rapidly industrializing society. The two most acute social afflictions identified by Ashley and other Tory paternalists were the exploitation of women and children in the coal mines and the primitive treatment of the insane in private and country asylums.[10]

Although Tory party MPs such as Sadler and Ashley were determined to translate Tory paternalist concerns into concrete policy measures, the greatest obstacles to social reform often came from within the party itself. Indeed, as Roberts acknowledged, legislation proposed in 1833 to end the exploitation of children and adults in the cotton mills of England failed to win support from the bulk of the Tory Party's 150 MPs in the House of Commons and their leaders.[11] It was thus unsurprising that Tory parliamentarians represented some of the fiercest opponents of legislative interference in the economy, such as the coal miner Lord Londonderry, who persuaded his

---

7. Hilton, *A Mad, Bad and Dangerous People*, 315.
8. Adelman, *Peel and the Conservative Party*, 54.
9. Roberts, *Victorian Origins*, 59.
10. Ibid.
11. Roberts, "Tory Paternalism," 325.

friend Benjamin Disraeli to attack the mine reform bills.[12] Despite embracing a common set of conservative fundamentals, palpable differences within the Tory party began to surface over its attitude to state intervention and economic philosophy. This led to a rift between the "old guard" agrarian-based Tories who favored protection and the new urban-based Tories who supported free-trade. The decision of Sir Robert Peel to repeal the Corn Laws in 1846 only exacerbated the existing tensions between the Peelite free-traders and the protectionists.[13] Much of this division was attributable to the forgoing infiltration of more urban-based liberal Tories into the party whose affinity with the new mercantile, capitalist class brought a different perspective to bear on public policy to that of the paternalist Tories attached to the land. The party leadership eventually reflected this trend with the mercantilist Peel succeeding the aristocratic Duke of Wellington as Prime Minister in December 1834.[14] Almost immediately, Peel had placed his new stamp on the party with the issue of the Tamworth Manifesto on 18 December, 1834. Accepting the 1832 Reform Act as settled and promising the "redress of real grievances," such as relief for Nonconformists' disabilities, the Manifesto envisioned a modernized Tory party capable of harnessing the energy, influence and abilities of the new middle class.[15]

As an alternative pathway to that of the Peelite free-traders and their largely middle-class constituency, the protectionist and paternalist-minded Tories within the party aspired to a kind of Christian social order underpinned by sympathy for the poor with a practical interest in their moral and material welfare.[16] Such a society would aim to give effect to the vision articulated by Southey in the early 1830s:

> Let us hope that the time is not far distant, when the first object of every Christian government will be to better the condition of the people, and remove as many as possible of the factitious evils which flesh is heir to. The first great and indispensable measure is to provide for the instruction of the people, by training up the children in the way they should go.[17]

---

12. Coleman, *Conservatism and the Conservative Party*, 125.

13. Norton (ed.), *The Conservative Party*, 23. Although Ashley supported the repeal of the Corn Laws for a combination of pragmatic and humanitarian reasons, he largely identified with the protectionist wing of the Tory party, sharing many of its grievances with the policy directions taken by the Peelites.

14. Norton, *Conservative Party*, 21.

15. Adelman, *Peel and the Conservative Party*, 11.

16. Smith, *Disraelian Conservatism*, 7.

17. Southey, *Essays Moral and Political*, 227.

The Place of Ashley's Paternalism within the Tory and Whig Traditions 131

Imbued with a sense of *noblesse oblige* and a deep concern for the poor, the young Ashley naturally associated himself with this limb of the Tory Party as he embarked on his parliamentary career. Vehemently critical of industrial capitalism, to whose deification of self-interest and denial of social responsibility the evils of the towns were ascribed, this strand of Toryism saw it as the duty and mission of the party not to associate itself with the interests and ideology of the urban industrial class. Rather it sought to re-proclaim the paternalist concept of society, in the name of which the social wants of the people might be met by positive action.[18] This Toryism surfaced largely in the manufacturing districts of Yorkshire and Lancashire, where Oastler, Sadler, Stephens, Bull, Wood and Ferrand led the factory movement and the opposition to the new poor law.[19] In the press, Southey, Alison, Lockhart, and Giffard tried to recall Toryism to a sense of the importance of the social question and the necessity of reform.[20] Standing in this tradition of Tory agitators, Ashley applied his paternalist principles to the factory movement where he campaigned for the ten-hour movement and other reforms to better the conditions of factory workers. The paternalist approach to social questions was generally based on a sense of duty to the poor stemming from a Christian conscience.[21] This was coupled with ordinary humanitarianism and, critically, a mindfulness of social obligation which conservatives liked to think characterized the hierarchical rural world where most of them, including Lord Ashley, still had their roots.

With the Tory paternalist Ashley pitted against the large faction of liberal Tory MPs, his support for moderately interventionist legislation on factory labor and other matters encountered regular internal opposition. In campaigning for the ten-hour day, Ashley fought his own party with opposition from Gladstone and the Tory peers. Prime Minister Peel and fellow Conservative MPs denounced Ashley's measure as an invasion of the rights of property.[22] Ashley's bill to limit the labor of women and young people in factories to ten hours was defeated by three votes. Deserted by his party, Ashley turned to the removal of another social grievance, the cruel treat-

---

18. Smith, *Disraelian Conservatism*, 8.

19. Stewart, *Foundation of the Conservative Party*, 166. Together with Richard Oastler and Michael Sadler, Joseph Raynor Stephens, George Stringer Bull, John Wood, and William Busfeild Ferrand were active supporters of the factory reform movement in the 1830s and 1840s.

20. Smith, *Disraelian Conservatism*, 8.

21. Roberts, *Paternalism*, 47. Robert Southey said that "the object of all Christians was to promote the welfare and happiness of those who are in any way dependent upon him."

22. Roberts, "Tory Paternalism," 154–55.

ment of the insane. The MP's interest in the care of the insane began in 1828 when he spoke for the bill establishing the Metropolitan Commissioners in Lunacy. He subsequently became a commissioner himself, visiting asylums, inspecting patients, studying the newest methods of treatment, and writing official reports.

The ideal of a strong government protecting the weak and ameliorating abuses did not inspire leading Tories such as Peel, Graham, or Gladstone with quite the fervor it did with Ashley.[23] Gladstone distinguished himself at the Board of Trade more for his sympathy with the proprietors of mines, factories, and railways than by a paternalist concern for the laboring classes. His background, like Peel's, was mercantile, and he was a believer in free-trade and political economy.[24] Although Disraeli, like Ashley, espoused Southey-inspired Tory paternalist ideals, especially in his literary works,[25] the future Prime Minister shared little of Ashley's practical interest in the construction of a benevolent state.[26] This was evidenced in Disraeli's voting record on social reform measures, whereby he had voted against the Education Order of 1839, against the Public Health Act of 1848, against the Mining Act of 1850, and against the General Board of Health Act in 1854.[27] Shaftesbury himself regarded Disraeli as a politician bereft of principle, remarking in 1868 that "he is a leper, without principle, without feeling, without regard to anything, human or divine, beyond his personal ambition."[28] Thus, during the early Victorian period, Ashley stood as one of the most authentic practitioners of paternalism within the Tory Party.

The political significance of Ashley's Whig connections

Having discussed the place of Ashley's paternalism within the British Tory party, it would be remiss to overlook its relationship with nineteenth-century Whiggism, not least because of Ashley's close personal ties with the prominent Cowper and Palmerston Whig dynasties. The Tory Ashley entered a mixed marriage of sorts in 1829 when he married Emily Cowper, the daughter of

---

23. Roberts, *Victorian Origins*, 63.

24. Ibid.

25. Speck, "Robert Southey, Benjamin Disraeli," 204. Speck argued that "Southey's views could be detected behind a famous passage from *Sybil*," one of Disraeli's major novels published in 1845.

26. Roberts, "Tory Paternalism," 331.

27. Ibid., 332.

28. Lord Shaftesbury, Diary Entry (March 5, 1868), in Hodder, *Life and Work of the Seventh Earl*, Vol. III, 234.

Whig aristocrats and the future step-daughter of Viscount Palmerston who would become Prime Minister. Initially these connections perturbed the piously conservative Ashley who had described the Cowper family as tending to "confuse the distinctions between right and wrong."[29] Despite these early misgivings about his wife's background, however, Ashley's marriage proved an eminently fruitful one and he developed a deep and affectionate relationship with his parents-in-law, Lord and Lady Palmerston.[30] During his Prime Ministership, Palmerston regarded his son-in-law as a confidante and frequently deferred to him on ecclesiastical matters, particularly with respect to the process of appointing bishops to the Established Church. According to Palmerston's colleague, Lord Granville, Ashley took full advantage of family ties to impress his reform proposals on Palmerston.[31]

Despite Palmerston's Whig politics and nominal Anglicanism differing considerably from Ashley's own political and religious temperament, the two men were not without obvious similarities; finding common ground across a range of fronts. First, Palmerston and Ashley had each imbibed the *noblesse oblige* ethic of landed property ownership as the basis for performing paternalist duties.[32] Moreover, both men affirmed the paternalist conviction common to Tories and Whigs that religion represented the primary mainstay of a strong and ordered society. Like his Whig predecessor, Lord John Russell, who preached the importance of the Christian religion as the foundation of public spirit, good order, and virtuous government,[33] Palmerston was committed to upholding the influence of Christianity as a basis for social and national cohesion.[34] Despite supporting Catholic Emancipation in 1829, he remained, like Ashley, a firm advocate of the establishment of the Church of England in the midst of constitutional change.[35] Thus with a shared vision to buttress the Established Church as a guardian of social order and general tranquility, Ashley and Palmerston worked cooperatively to appoint to Anglican sees new bishops whom they regarded as suitable candidates for furthering this vision.

On the project of establishing an Anglican-Lutheran bishopric in Jerusalem, Ashley found Palmerston to be similarly amenable. Although Palmerston did not necessarily share Ashley's religious motives and premillennial

29. Best, *Biography of AA Cooper*, 25.
30. Scotland, *"Good and Proper Men,"* i.
31. Brown, *Palmerston: A Biography*, 372–73.
32. Roberts, *Social Conscience of the Early Victorians*, 446.
33. Brent, *Liberal Anglican Politics*, 57.
34. Wolffe, "Lord Palmerston and Religion," 907.
35. Ibid., 910.

zeal for establishing the new bishopric in the heart of the ancient Jewish homeland, he concurred with Ashley on the importance of this venture to strengthen British influence in the region.[36] Like Ashley, Palmerston desired a strong and paternalist British empire to make its civilizing presence felt in every region of the world. On the broader issue of paternalist state intervention, Ashley also found an ally in his father-in-law. During his tenure at the Home Office in the early 1850s, Palmerston oversaw the introduction of the Factory Act of 1853 which rectified some loopholes existing in the earlier forms of legislation.[37] Whilst the measure was not as far-reaching as his son-in-law had anticipated, the new Earl of Shaftesbury told Palmerston he nonetheless "rejoiced to see that the factory-bill has escaped all the quick-sands. That is remarkable; for this very same proposition, when made by myself in the H of Commons was stoutly resisted by Sir G Grey & Bright, and afterwards by Derby and Walpole."[38] Resolved to abolish the truck-system abhorred by Shaftesbury, Palmerston successfully passed the Truck Act which prohibited the practice of landlords paying their laborers in goods instead of money, or forcing them to purchase goods from shops owned by their employers.[39]

In other socially ameliorative measures welcomed by Shaftesbury, Palmerston passed the Smoke Abatement Act in 1853 to reduce air pollution in urban centers and in 1854 reformed the General Board of Health, on which Shaftesbury served as a commissioner. The social reform measures of Palmerston could not only be attributed to the highly likely influence of his son-in-law but also to his own aristocratic background from which he arguably imbibed a Whig form of paternalism. Palmerston was born into a prosperous landowning family and inherited some 10 000 acres of land in Ireland alone.[40] In a remarkably similar fashion to Ashley, Palmerston swiftly discharged his paternalist obligations on his newly inherited estate in 1808 by ordering cottages, roads, and piers to be built, the schools to be repaired and staffed, and for the middle-men to be abolished.[41] Performing his duties in the public sphere, Palmerston had sought to improve the condition of society, both morally and environmentally, and thereby complemented Ashley's Tory-inspired sense of public duty to seek the welfare of the people.

36. Ibid., 911.
37. Brown, *Palmerston*, 343.
38. Shaftesbury to Palmerston (August 23, 1853).
39. Shaftesbury to Palmerston (August 23, 1853).
40. Roberts, *Paternalism*, 230.
41. Roberts, *Paternalism*, 230.

Ashley's affinity with Whig politics, particularly in the area of social reform, could not wholly be explained by his close personal friendship with Palmerston, as significant as this was, but also reflected the broader realignments occurring in British political life during the 1840s. During this period, paternalists, such as Ashley, increasingly vested greater faith in the Whigs rather than the Tories to make paternalist state intervention a political reality. Like many Tory Evangelical paternalists, Ashley had entertained high hopes that the return of the Tories to government under Peel in 1841 might have facilitated the progress of social reform legislation such as the Factory Acts.[42] His faith in Peel's administration, however, steadily crumbled with its seeming inaction on the factory question. In 1844, Ashley's Tory colleagues frustrated the passage of his Ten Hour bill for factory labor.[43] In other areas, the ruling Peelite-Tories disappointed with their threat in the House of Lords to block Ashley's bill to protect chimney sweeps. Added to this were their failures to make substantial advances in public education, to bring order to the chaos of railway construction, to end notorious evils in the merchant marine, and to promote urgently needed sanitary reforms.[44] Despairing that Peel had been led away from the path of social reform into the great morass which ultimately overwhelmed his party, Ashley remarked that "All Peel's affinities are towards wealth and capital. His heart is manifestly towards the mill-owners; his lips occasionally for the operatives." On Peel, he asked, "What has he ever done or proposed for the working classes?"[45] Ashley's damning verdict on the Peel administration was that "this government is ten times more hostile to my views than the Whigs."[46] The disillusioned Tory thus welcomed the return of a Whig administration in 1846 as an opportunity to revive his social reform agenda. With the resurrection of the Ten Hours Bill in 1847, Ashley found Russell to be "decided and firm" in his sympathy for the measure in stark contrast to his Tory predecessor, Peel.[47]

The receptivity of the Whig Party to Ashley's policies of ameliorative state intervention bore fruit as the Russell administration of 1846–52 oversaw the expansion of public aid to church schools of all denominations, the passage of the Ten Hours Act of 1847, the Public Health Act of 1848,

---

42. Lewis, *Lighten Their Darkness*, 87; Mandler, *Aristocratic Government*, 205–6.

43. Roberts, "Tory Paternalism," 329.

44. Ibid., 330.

45. Ashley, Diary Entry (February 24, 1842), in Hodder, *Life and Work of the Seventh Earl*, Vol. I, 407.

46. Ashley, Diary Entry (July 3, 1843). [Broadlands Archives SHA/PD/2-3]

47. Ashley, Diary Entry (February 11, 1847). [Broadlands Archives SHA/PD/4]

and the Mining and Merchant Marine Acts of 1850—all of which increased the paternalistic role of the government.[48] To be sure, British Whiggery in the early Victorian period undeniably contained a *laissez-faire* school of thought informed by political economy, as exemplified by liberal voices such as the *Edinburgh Review*. Nevertheless, many Whigs were also imbued with a "sense of aristocratic responsibility" that tended to favor state intervention measures of the kind pursued by the Russell administration.[49] This paternalist tradition accordingly surfaced conspicuously in the pronouncements of Russell who talked openly of a "Condition of England [Question]" strategy to advance social reform.[50] In 1844, Russell told the House of Commons that "the government should interfere wherever beneficial and wherever calculated to do good."[51] Addressing an assembly of electors in London in 1846, Russell told his audience that "great social improvements were required" in the areas of public education, the treatment of criminals and the sanitary conditions of urban centers.[52] In executing its social reform program, Russell's administration not only passed Ashley's Ten Hours Act but appointed him as a commissioner to the General Board of Health in 1848, a public body established under the Public Health Act to plan and administer the provision of sanitary works across the country.[53] With Whig leaders justifying such reforms on the basis that "*laissez-faire* and free contract" *alone* could not secure the moral and physical welfare of the people, thereby requiring the interposition of the legislature,[54] the chasm between this tradition of Whiggism and the Tory paternalism espoused by the *Quarterly Review* and Southey was certainly not that great. As such, it enabled the Tory paternalist Ashley to forge a working alliance with the Russell-led Whigs, a feat he proved largely incapable of accomplishing with the Peelite Tories.

48. Roberts, "Tory Paternalism," 331.
49. Mandler, "Cain and Abel," 97.
50. Mandler, *Aristocratic Government*, 223.
51. Lord John Russell, HC Debates, *Hansard*, 1844, Vol. 74, c. 658, in Roberts, *Social Conscience of the Victorians*, 447.
52. Lord John Russell, "Address to the Electors of the City of London" (July 1846), in Mandler, *Aristocratic Government*, 239.
53. Mandler, *Aristocratic Government*, 260.
54. Lord John Russell, HL Debates, *Hansard*, March 25, 1844, cc. 1509–10.

Paternalism in the name "of the people"

The reality that paternalism was such a potent driving-force behind Ashley's life and parliamentary activity has warranted its thoroughgoing examination as a tradition and political philosophy, without which, the impetus behind this Victorian social reformer would be impossible to wholly appreciate. Ashley's enduring paternalism was animated by a combination of his domestic circumstances, his friendship with Southey and his key relationship with figures such as Palmerston. Importantly, the expression of Ashley's paternalism was both *reactive* and *affirmative*. On the one hand, his desire to exercise the more benign paternalist duties of filial care, succor, and protection, especially within the domestic context, were driven by his determination to demonstrate a radically different pattern of stewardship to that of his father over the St Giles estate. He envisioned that his renovation of the workers' cottages and cultivation of a more personalized culture on the estate would serve as a deliberate contrast to the perfunctory and detached approach of the Sixth Earl.

On the other hand, Ashley's paternalism was not merely the product of what his father's paternalism was *not*, but also a positive affirmation of the paternalist ideals espoused by Southey, Sadler, and the Tory reviewers. Growing disenchanted with the bland Tory pragmatism of his old friend, Wellington, Ashley saw his new friend Southey as offering an alternative political vision that he esteemed as beneficent, compassionate and edifying for the nation. With Ashley's deprived and traumatic childhood imbuing him with a social conscience to advance the dignity of the poor and underprivileged, Southey and Sadler's appeals for paternalist state intervention in the 1820s–30s to remedy the afflictions of child labor and pauperism resonated with his instincts. Accordingly, Ashley was resolved to give effect to their paternalist principles by devoting much of his political career to such causes as factory reform and the humane treatment of lunacy patients.

With Ashley's exposure to a spectrum of figures and influential movements over the course of his career, the other noteworthy feature of his paternalism was its *catholicity*. As Roberts appreciated, paternalism remained a very broad, complex and amorphous concept in the early Victorian context,[55] and, to a large degree, Ashley's paternalist philosophy, with its many strands, reflected this property. Through both his friendship with Robert Southey and his quest, as a landowning peer from 1851, to model paternalist virtues in contradistinction to his father, Ashley exhibited a paternalism that was romantic, classically agrarian and ecclesiastic. In an

---

55. Roberts, *Paternalism*, 242.

age where the ascendency of industrial capitalism was seen to erode the old ties between worker and master, his paternalist thought never ceased to be influenced by Southey's romantic ideal of intimate and personalized interclass relationships, whether it was in the context of the traditional country estate or the modern factory. Despite supporting measures unpopular amongst country landholders, such as the 1846 repeal of the Corn Laws, Ashley shared the view of the country squires that landed property remained the essential basis for performing the paternalist duties of protection, succor and guidance, a principle he manifested in his management of St Giles. In the meantime, his emerging Evangelical Anglicanism lent force to his paternalist conviction that one of the chief purposes of the Established Church was to edify the people through moral and spiritual instruction.

Whilst the fundamentals of Ashley's paternalist thought were derived primarily from Southey's high Tory tradition with its emphases on ancient filial bonds, the sanctity of landed property and the primacy of the English Church, it was also informed, particularly in Shaftesbury's middle years, by a Whig tradition of paternalism represented by leaders such as Russell and Palmerston. As Jon Lawrence appreciated, together with Brent, Mandler, and Roberts, a strong current of paternalism ran through the Whig party which largely accounted for its support of state intervention initiatives in the name of "the people."[56] Through his family ties with Palmerston, together with his unhappy experience of struggling to enlist Tory party support for his social reform bills, Ashley seamlessly embraced this Whig tradition. Although such Whigs had shared neither his high Tory precepts, nor his Evangelical religiosity, Ashley appreciated that their motives for passing measures such as the Factory and Public Health Acts were perfectly legitimate. Accordingly, like Russell and Palmerston, he was happy to invoke the classically Whig objective "to improve the social, moral and material wellbeing of society" as justification for advancing his paternalist social reform agenda. Traces of Whig paternalist influence were evident also in Ashley's practical strategies, especially his utilization of government commissions to further the causes of mental health, factory, and sanitary reform. The capacity for Ashley's paternalism to evolve and accommodate a combination of strands across both the Tory and Whig traditions attested to its innately fluid and multifarious character.

---

56. Lawrence, "Paternalism, Class and the British Path," 148.

Part III

Ashley and the Emerging Synthesis of Evangelicalism and Tory Paternalism

6

A Convergence of Tory Paternalism and Early Victorian Evangelicalism

In an 1884 letter to Canon Wilberforce, Shaftesbury reflected that the key movements of his public life were undertaken with "a desire to show that independence in position and fortune, possessing, as they do, social privileges, brought with them: corresponding Christian obligations."[1] Towards the end of his life, the champion of factory reform was able to acknowledge the marriage of patrician social privileges with Christian obligations as the inspiration for his reforms. Having discussed Evangelicalism and Tory paternalism each as two distinct tributaries contributing to the philosophical outlook of Ashley, this third part will examine the confluence of these tributaries into a discernible "Evangelical-Tory" channel of thought which Ashley came to personify.

Certainly, amongst the broader array of ideological currents contributing to social reform in Victorian Britain (particularly those of Evangelical Protestantism, Benthamite utilitarianism, Foxite Whiggism, paternalism and working-class Radicalism) a working alliance between an emerging Evangelical Anglican school of political thought and a Tory paternalist philosophy could be discerned. According to Boyd Hilton, the earlier Anglican Evangelical generation of Wilberforce and the Clapham Sect, together with the evangelical Presbyterian Thomas Chalmers, had been broadly

---

1. Shaftesbury to Canon Wilberforce, November 10, 1884, in Hodder, *Life and Work of the Seventh Earl*, Vol. III, 268. The Grandson of William Wilberforce, Albert Basil Orme Wilberforce (1841–1916) served as an Honorary Canon of Winchester from 1871 to 1894.

sympathetic to political economy and thus shied away from pursuing paternalist policies of state intervention.[2] On the other hand, the succeeding Anglican Evangelical generation of Lord Ashley, Michael Sadler, and other leaders of the factory reform movement expressly supported ameliorative state intervention.[3] Essentially, this generation of high Tory-disposed Evangelicals came to appreciate in the 1830s–40s that their religious premise of a world ruled by a universal, fatherly deity was not wholly incompatible with their temporal aims, as committed paternalists, to cultivate a moderately interventionist state that would exercise a benevolent superintendence over its citizens. Accordingly this third part will discuss the origins, forms, and implications of this convergence in the broader religious and political milieus of pre and early Victorian society as well as in the personal philosophy of Lord Ashley.

After explaining the intrinsic reasons why such an alliance between Evangelicalism and Tory paternalism was able to be forged in the pre and early Victorian period, this chapter will discuss the importance of appreciating the Established Church as a spiritual incubator for Tory paternalist thought. This is borne out by the way in which Tory paternalists such as Sadler and Ashley maintained a firm spiritual footing in the Anglican domain of Evangelicalism. Appreciating the reality, however, that some Anglican proponents of Tory paternalism, including Southey and Coleridge, did not share Ashley's Low Church loyalties, discussion will focus specifically on how Evangelicals within the Church, such as Edward Bickersteth, embraced high Tory paternalist ideals of the kind espoused by the High Church Southey. Turning to the broader political and economic contexts, this part will explore how the transition of the Evangelical movement from the generation of Wilberforce and Chalmers to that of Sadler and Oastler had implications for how the movement envisaged the role of the state, for the new Evangelical generation moved closer towards the paternalist and interventionist stance of the high Tories in the 1830s and 1840s.

In addition, the constitutional reforms of 1828–29 and the lingering anxieties about their implications for the future status of the Established Church brought the Recordite Evangelicals into an alliance with the High Tory paternalists to defend England's Protestant Constitution. In terms of defining religious trends, it will be explained how the Recordite generation's embrace of a premillennial eschatology gave Evangelicals such as Bickersteth and Ashley a new theological impetus to champion paternalist social

---

2. Boyd Hilton, "The Role of Providence," in Beales and Best (eds), *History, Society and the Churches*, 218; Hilton, *Age of Atonement*, 16.

3. Ibid., 15, 94–95.

reform. With this forgoing convergence of Evangelical and high Tory paternalist interests, the ground was fertile for "Evangelical Tory" writers such as Robert Benton Seeley and Charlotte Elizabeth Tonna to publish blueprints for paternalist social reform of the kind pursued by Ashley in parliament. This chapter will also survey the larger social context of Evangelicalism by showing how it enjoyed some degree of success in permeating the ranks of the aristocracy. In many instances, vital religion reinforced the paternalist philosophy of the patrician classes giving rise to a sizeable number of landowning Evangelicals entering parliament in the 1830s.

Given that the Ten Hours factory legislation represented the defining social reform of Ashley and his immediate Evangelical Tory forerunners, it was noteworthy that the factory reform movement marked the culmination of the alliance between Evangelicalism and high Tory paternalism. Notwithstanding the significant input of popular Radicals such as William Cobbett, the leading figures of the factory reform movement, including George S. Bull, Richard Oastler, Michael Sadler, and Lord Ashley, evidently exhibited a mixture of Evangelical and high Tory paternalist assumptions. By examining each of these protagonists, chapter seven will proceed to discuss the significance of the factory reform movement as a tangible outworking of the synthesis between Evangelicalism and high Tory paternalism. In doing so, however, it will also appreciate the validity of earlier historical interpretations that variously regarded the reform movement as a reaction by landowning patricians against the industrial class, a transitional phase in the evolution of the modern interventionist state, and as the first stirrings of working-class consciousness. Chapter eight will conclude by focusing more specifically on how Ashley personified this convergence of Evangelical and paternalist interests in his own thinking, an outlook that became manifest in his recommendation of Anglican bishops during the premiership of Lord Palmerston in the 1850s–60s.

The basis for a working alliance between Evangelicalism and Tory paternalism

Given the potential for points of conflict between the two belief systems: for example, the tension between Evangelical teaching that individuals under God were responsible for their own moral improvement and the paternalist assumption that external intervention was warranted to realize the same outcome, how was it possible for Evangelicalism and paternalism to have forged such a considerable degree of common ground in the thought of Ashley? From the outset, it is important to be reacquainted with the reality that Evangelicalism and paternalism were each very diffuse and fluid schools of thought capable of absorbing multiple influences from the surrounding cultural milieu of pre and early Victorian Britain. Hence it was eminently plausible for these somewhat disparate traditions to adopt the traits of each other.

With respect to Evangelicalism, Bebbington appreciated that this religious movement had proved "remarkably adaptable to a wide range of diverse societies, taking up aspects of their ways of life and merging them with the distinctive features of the faith."[4] Thus, with this adaptive faculty, British Evangelicalism was seamlessly able to embrace the precepts of political economy in the late 1700s and early 1800s—this while also proving capable of adopting paternalist notions of state intervention from the 1820s–1840s without compromising its core doctrinal tenets. Meanwhile, with regards to paternalism, Roberts made the critically pertinent observation that "the strands of paternalism were . . . almost always intermingled with strands from other social outlooks," noting that "for each person the proportions of paternalist and non-paternalist strands differed."[5] Hence paternalism had the capacity to embrace either the high Anglican assumptions of the Church posited in the romantic literature of Southey, S. T. Coleridge, and Wordsworth, the utilitarian ideals of centralized administration in the case of Edwin Chadwick or, indeed, the Evangelical rationales for social reform espoused by Sadler and Ashley. Thus paternalism, at once, could complement the non-doctrinal, "constitutional" Churchmanship of Southey and the radically different, Evangelical form of Anglicanism found in Ashley and his co-religionists.

The Established Church as a spiritual nursery for Tory paternalism

To understand this confluence of Evangelicalism with Tory paternalism in the early Victorian era, it is first necessary to appreciate the close institutional and spiritual affinity existing between Tory paternalist thought and the Established Church of England from which Evangelicalism originally sprung. As evident from the philosophy of the High Church Lake poets, Tory paternalism not only esteemed the Established Church as an institutional pillar of society but embraced that Church's belief in an all-sovereign and beneficent God who was to be honored and obeyed as the paternal ruler

---

4. Bebbington, "Evangelicalism and Cultural Diffusion," in Smith (ed.), *British Evangelical Identities*, 18.

5. Roberts, *Paternalism*, 8.

of the universe. For Anglican divines and conservative patricians alike, this God embodied the paternal attributes of authority, care, protection, moral guidance, and fatherly discipline. As such, He represented the source of all paternal duties and obligations to be performed. Accordingly, God's dominion over the world represented the "gold-standard" by which earthly leaders were to govern their subjects. As an essential check on human pride and unfettered power, Tory paternalists such as Southey maintained that, just as every subject was accountable to their ruler, each ruler in turn would be called to account by the Supreme Being for their conduct. Such an attitude undoubtedly had its origins in the historic traditions and catechism of the Anglican Church imbibed by Southey and his coreligionists.

To be sure, however, the Tory paternalist notion of hierarchy was not wholly ecclesiastical in origin but rather a pre-Christian concept with roots in ancient Greece. According to ancient Greek philosophy, persons at the top of the hierarchy were deemed "noble," while those at the bottom were considered "base."[6] English Tory paternalists appropriated this basic worldview to determine a person's "pecking order" in society by associating their social position with a calculus of property, privilege, dress, education, honor, obligation, residence, occupation, friendship, beauty, strength, and wisdom.[7] Although this concept predated Christendom, much of the English Church accepted it as congruent with a perceived providential order of creation. Reflecting this outlook, the Anglican Bishop of Lincoln, George Pretyman, explained how "God himself makes one man to differ from another"; consequently, "the distinctions of high and low, rich and poor, are the appointments of divine providence, and are made the sources of various duties, the bonds of mutual affection."[8] Pretyman contended that a gradation of ranks in society was a necessary precondition to practicing the Christian virtues of compassion, gratitude and humility. Accordingly, it was hoped that society's consciousness of certain classes of people existing in positions of vulnerability and dependency, such as the poor, sick, and very young, would engender attitudes of humility and deference amongst the poor and disenfranchised corresponding with a renewed spirit of compassion and duty on the part of the more wealthy and powerful classes. The cultivation of the latter attitudes would provide fertile ground for well-heeled Evangelicals, such as Ashley, to articulate and practice conservative patrician values.

Owing to both its privileged status within the English polity and also its hierarchical, episcopal structure of internal governance, the Established

6. Clark, *English Society 1660–1832*, 166.
7. Ibid.
8. Pretyman, *Charge Delivered to the Clergy*, 21.

Church, of all Christian denominations, could be regarded as the spiritual nursery of Tory paternalism.[9] Conscious of the power and privilege which Establishment status conferred, Church clergy espoused an ecclesiastical form of *noblesse oblige*. Just as the more scrupulous landholders believed that the prestige and privilege associated with property ownership imported a moral obligation to serve the needs of the poorer classes, various Anglican clergy felt the Church had a similar duty to show compassion to the poor in its midst. This was articulated in 1845 by the Bishop of Salisbury, Edward Denison, who stated that the rich face great dangers in the future world since "they have the deep responsibility of God's stewardship."[10] Meanwhile, the Church's tradition of episcopal governance did much to foster a paternalist culture within the church, whereby local parish clergy would defer to a bishop appointed by the Crown. At enthronement ceremonies, a newly appointed bishop would be presented with a shepherd's staff symbolizing a paternal, shepherd-like stewardship over the parishes within his diocese. In turn, the local parish priest would be exhorted to perform similar duties as pastor to the parishioners of his congregation. This distinguished the Church of England from many of the less hierarchical Dissenting churches where clergy derived their authority not from a bishop above, but rather from the elders or rank-and-file members of a given congregation. Given the Established Church's favorable disposition towards the notion of a hierarchical society, Anglican intellectuals gave more, not less, weight to the idea of rank and its attendant duties.

The Evangelical Anglican embrace of Tory paternalism

If Ashley was able to harmonize the two traditions of Evangelicalism and paternalism, were other Evangelical Anglicans able to achieve a similar synthesis in pre and early Victorian society at large? Whilst Evangelicals in the Established Churches of England and Scotland appeared happy to adopt paternalist ideals within the *ecclesiastical* realm, the relationship existing between Evangelicalism and paternalism at the *state level* was infinitely more complex. This was due to the fact that both Evangelicalism and paternalism represented such broad and varied schools of thought, that they could give rise to not only potential points of agreement but areas of profound difference. Accordingly, the extent of consensus reached on a given issue, such as poor relief, would often be contingent upon the particular traditions of Evangelicalism, or forms of paternalism, engaged on that particular

9. Stewart, *Foundation of the Conservative Party*, 166.
10. Denison, *Charge to the Clergy*, in Roberts, *Paternalism*, 151.

A Convergence of Tory Paternalism and Early Victorian Evangelicalism   147

question. Appreciating this heterogeneity, Hilton explored the attitudes of both the Claphamite and Recordite schools of British Evangelicals towards various political philosophies embodying varying degrees and forms of paternalism, namely those of the liberal Tories, the high Tories and the Whigs. Receptive to the nuances evident in the prevailing currents of political and religious thought shaping government policy between 1785 and 1865, Hilton's historically grounded analysis studiously avoided oversimplified generalizations about the political and economic outlooks of pre and early Victorian Evangelicalism. Essentially accepting Bebbington's premise that Evangelicalism was malleable and thereby capable of adapting its core doctrines to changing political and economic paradigms, Hilton concluded that the Recordite generation became decidedly more attached to the notion of a paternalist state than their Claphamite predecessors. This thesis of Hilton is singularly beneficial to understanding how this broader shift in Evangelical political thought historically corresponded with Ashley's own conscious assent to a paternalist philosophy in the 1830s.

According to Hilton, the Claphamite Evangelicals and Thomas Chalmers remained wedded to the philosophy of political economy.[11] As such, they favored free-trade over protectionism, limited government over state intervention and thereby eschewed all forms of economic paternalism.[12] In terms of party allegiance, Chalmers and the Claphamites were drawn to liberal Tories such as the Second Earl of Liverpool, George Canning and Peel who proposed "deterrence-based" poor laws and self-help initiatives, rather than ameliorative social intervention, as the best means to addressing social disadvantage.[13] Hence Southey and Sadler's conception of a paternalist state enacting ameliorative legislation and social welfare measures was decidedly absent from their Evangelical worldview. Hilton starkly contrasted this posture of the Claphamites with that of the Recordite Evangelicals "whose views were diametrically opposed." Whilst similarly fired by an Evangelical ethos, Evangelicals such as Henry Drummond, Bickersteth, Oastler, Bull, Sadler, and Ashley himself strongly supported state intervention with generous welfare payments to the poor.[14] Repudiating the political economy and self-help individualism of the Claphamites, this generation of Evangelicals was chiefly drawn to the high and radical Tories[15] and, to a lesser extent, social reform-minded Whigs. For both envisioned a paternalist mandate for

11. Hilton, "Role of Providence," 218.
12. Ibid.
13. Hilton, *A Mad, Bad and Dangerous People*, 341; Hilton, *Age of Atonement*, 219.
14. Hilton, *A Mad, Bad and Dangerous People*, 407.
15. Ibid., 342.

the state to intervene proactively and ameliorate the afflictions plaguing the poorer laboring classes. The stark juxtaposition in the political outlook of the two Evangelical schools was captured in an exchange between Chalmers and Oastler, with the Scottish theologian opposed to the Ten Hours bill on the basis that it was inimical to free trade principles while the Yorkshire activist supported it as a necessary measure of state intervention.[16] Thus, as Hilton revealed, paternalism, at the state level, really only became a bedfellow of the Recordite and radical Tory generation of Evangelicals.

Although Hilton made references to Ashley in his discussion of the changing political and economic outlook amongst nineteenth-century evangelicals, he did not specifically discuss Ashley's marriage of paternalist principles with his Evangelical convictions. What Hilton's account did reveal, however, was that the synthesis between Evangelicalism and paternalism did not exist as a natural "given" which Ashley would have automatically imbibed upon his spiritual conversion. On the contrary, it was an alliance forged only after some decades of Evangelical introspection on the role of providence and its implications for the role of the state. From this speculation on the superintendence of the Almighty, the Recordite generation emerged with a radically different interpretation of providence to their Claphamite predecessors.

The generation of Wilberforce and Chalmers had understood providence to operate generally and predictably through natural and fixed laws of cause and effect. Unlike the Deists, they maintained belief in a personal and relational Deity; however, they held providence to be basically neutral and non-interventionist. Accordingly, with respect to the state, these Evangelicals maintained that temporal government should refrain from interfering with the "natural laws" of providence, and where possible, repeal interventionist laws.[17]

On the other hand, the Recordite generation entertained an interventionist view of providence which saw God as constantly directing earthly affairs by special warnings and judgments. To emulate the role of providence, therefore, it behooved earthly governments to take an interventionist approach to social and economic problems.[18] With such Evangelicals embracing this interventionist role of government, they found the High Tory paternalist ideals of Southey and the *Quarterly Review* eminently more compatible with their theological convictions than an earlier generation of Evangelicals. With transitional Evangelicals, such as Bickersteth, beginning

---

16. Hilton, "Role of Providence," 215.
17. Hilton, *Age of Atonement*, 16.
18. Ibid., 15.

to appreciate the merits of ameliorative state intervention from the 1830s, this paved the way for Evangelicals such as Sadler and Ashley similarly to reconcile their paternalist philosophy to their Evangelical worldview.

Edward Bickersteth's adoption of high Tory paternalism

Given the pre-eminent influence of Bickersteth on the formation of Ashley's religiosity, it would be beneficial further to probe how this Anglican clergyman integrated his evolving paternalism with his Evangelicalism, and how he, like Southey, encouraged his protégé to pursue paternalist social reforms in parliament. Hilton's comprehensive accounts of Recordite Evangelical support for interventionist government from the 1830s mentioned Bickersteth, but offered no examination of his emerging paternalism and its broader significance. Meanwhile, Gareth Atkins' recent study of Bickersteth usefully discussed his assent to premillennial eschatology in the early 1830s,[19] his staunch opposition to Tractarianism and Roman Catholicism[20] and his role in "steadying Anglican Evangelicals during a period of flux"[21]—though not his avowed support for social reform measures such as the factory acts. Atkins made a reference to Bickersteth's "premillennial paternalism,"[22] but did not spell out the practical implications of this for his political and economic outlook nor the probable bearing this had on the thought of his younger friend, Ashley. Despite imbibing the Claphamite Evangelicalism of Wilberforce and Simeon in his early life, Bickersteth's religiosity absorbed Recordite characteristics during the 1830s with his conversion to premillennialism and adoption of new beliefs in an interventionist providence. Characteristic of the emerging Recordite and radical Tory generation of Evangelicals, Bickersteth eschewed the liberal, *laissez-faire* political outlook of the Claphamites in favor of a decidedly more paternalist approach entailing benign state intervention.

The roots of Bickersteth's paternalist ethic could be found in his interpretation of prophecy. Convinced that providence had bestowed the blessings of wealth and power upon Britain, Bickersteth was convinced that the maladies of pauperism, lawlessness, and vice besetting the nation in the early 1840s were "punishments" for its sins of selfishness, greed, and idolatry.[23] Whilst the charitable initiatives of individuals were to be wel-

19. Atkins, "Anglican Evangelical Theology," 8.
20. Ibid. 11–13.
21. Ibid., 18.
22. Ibid., 15.
23. Bickersteth, *Divine Warning,* xiii.

comed, Bicksteth ultimately believed, like the high Tory paternalists, that a collective national response led by the government was also needed to remedy these afflictions plaguing early Victorian society. In addition to his preference for interventionist government, Bickersteth's evolving paternalism was evident in his attitude to property. On this issue he approvingly quoted Sydney Herbert, the Secretary for the Admiralty, who noted that neither the government nor opposition "feel sufficiently the responsibility of wealth and the duties which the possession of property entails on them."[24] Reconciling this paternalist conception of property with his Evangelical understanding that the "Lord of Hosts" declared himself the owner of all wealth, Bickersteth asked of property: "Is it spent for God's glory; first in providing for the necessities of the temporary owner, according to our station, and then is the remainder spent for God's direct service, in the highest good of our fellow-men?"[25] Although Bickersteth was no landowning peer, he nonetheless grasped hold of the paternalist obligations attending to the possession of property and wealth. Chiefly for this reason, he shared Ashley's abhorrence of the truck system used by some unscrupulous landowners, denouncing it as an "organized fraud" on the wages of the poor.[26]

Bickersteth brought his paternalism to bear in his blistering critique of the prevailing factory system. Quoting the romantic paternalist S. T. Coleridge, Bickersteth wrote in 1845 that in the manufacturing districts, "the mass of the population is mechanized [sic] into engines for the manufactory of new rich men; yea the machinery of the wealth of the nation is made up of the wretchedness, disease, and depravity of those who should constitute the strength of the nation!"[27] In a previous rebuke of the factory system, Bickersteth chastised "the worldly selfishness of those who have been amassing riches in trades, manufactures, and commerce, or by other means, without any regard to the spiritual or even temporal welfare of those who have toiled for them."[28] In sentiments echoing the high Tory Southey, Bickersteth argued that this exploitation led to not only the oppression of the poor, but the alienation of the lower classes from the higher.[29] The clergyman insisted that Britain sorely needed "the expression of more sympathy between the rich and the poor' with 'more personal communication

---

24. Sydney Herbert quoted by Bickersteth, *Divine Warning*, 264.
25. Bickersteth, *Signs of the Times*, 235.
26. Ibid., 336.
27. Ibid., 83.
28. Bickersteth, *Divine Warning*, xiii.
29. Bickersteth, *Signs of the Times*, 344.

[between] them."[30] Like Southey and the *Quarterly Review*, Bickersteth cherished the paternalist virtue of cultivating harmonious class relations, believing this to be critical to preserving the hierarchical structure and good order of society. In common with paternalist thinking, Bickersteth believed that placating the grievances of the working classes was critical if Britain was to escape the fate of other European nations, wherein class enmity and warfare had given rise to revolution and lawlessness.[31] Ashley expressed similar concerns in 1840 about working class disaffection when he warned of the "demons of socialism and Chartism stalking the land" and thus the urgent need for paternalist state intervention to assuage the discontent of the laboring classes.[32] Sharing Bickersteth's prophecy that the neglect of the laboring poor would incur the wrath of God, Ashley called for the industrial system to revive the "mutual sympathies of master and servant, landlord and tenant, employer and employed."[33]

Regarding the oppression, misery, and squalor of the poorer classes as not merely individual afflictions but rather as a collective, nationwide malaise, Bickersteth accordingly believed that a coordinated national response by the state was warranted. Again, appealing to his understanding of prophecy as the guiding rationale for government intervention, Bickersteth wrote that "Parliaments, Senates, and Statesman" of nations such as Britain "have a Supreme Governor, who will shortly summon all to his bar of judgment, and all their measures, laws and statutes, will be revised at his judgment seat."[34] Thus, according to Bickersteth, it was "the very design of law and government to correct what is wrong, and to protect the weak and helpless"[35] if they were to be found blameless on the Day of Judgment. Bickersteth's paternalist conception of law and government differed radically from that of Chalmers and the Claphamites who did not see it as the government's prerogative to help the poor and vulnerable. To such Evangelicals, this was misguided paternalism since it was the proper responsibility of individuals, churches, and private charities to ameliorate human suffering.

Thus, on the factory reform debate, Bickersteth's views predictably concurred with those of Oastler rather than Chalmers. Like the Tory Evangelical factory campaigner, Bickersteth regarded the Ten Hours Bill as an

30. Bickersteth, *Divine Warning*, 265.
31. Bickersteth, *Signs of the Times*, xiv.
32. Ashley, "Infant Labour," in *The Quarterly Review* 67:133 (December 1840): 180.
33. Ibid., 180.
34. Bickersteth, *Signs of the Times*, 309.
35. Ibid., 343.

imperative government measure to protect the wellbeing of vulnerable workers. Sharing the same frustrations as his protégé with the Peel administration's lack of resolve to carry the bill, Bickersteth condemned all the forgoing obstructions to its passage as "a national sin."[36]

Accordingly, for the paternalist and Evangelical Bickersteth, "sin" was not simply a matter of an individual's transgression against God but also one of the state refusing to honor what he regarded as its divine duty to protect the poor from oppression. Owing to the influence of paternalism and its emphasis on societal obligations, Evangelicals such as Bickersteth, Sadler, Oastler, and Ashley were more inclined to conceive the doctrine of sin in *collectivist* terms as well as the traditionally individualist ones.

The shift in Evangelical attitudes towards economic policy and the role of the state

Bickersteth's attraction to paternalistic state intervention in the 1830s was by no means atypical of the emerging generation of Recordite and radical Tory Evangelicals. Hilton attributed this shift in Evangelical thought primarily to a new understanding of the role of providence and explained how this precipitated a rethink in Evangelical attitudes to the proper function of the state. While Hilton shed light on the key theological developments accounting for the Evangelical embrace of paternalist ideals, Douglas Holladay and Donald Lewis each discussed the practical manifestations of this new paternalist mindset in Evangelical circles. In his account of Evangelical social and political activism in the crucial decades between 1830 and 1850, Holladay similarly exposed the political and economic fault lines dividing the Chalmers and Oastler school of Evangelicals but, to a greater extent than Hilton, he explained the practical implications of this for Evangelical approaches to both philanthropy and social reform. According to Holladay, the "Chalmers" school continued to invest in individual and church-initiated philanthropy, together with self-help enterprises, as the primary means by which social disadvantage could be addressed. The "Oastler" school, by contrast, maintained that private charity needed to be substantially supplemented with paternalist, social reform legislation.[37] Like Holladay, Lewis also discussed the differing attitudes between the two Evangelical schools across a similar time-frame, noting the "wide divergence of opinion within Evangelicalism both as to the analysis of social problems and on the political

---

36. Ibid., 343.
37. Holladay, "19th Century Evangelical Activism," 60–66.

solutions required."[38] Together with Hilton, the accounts of Holladay and Lewis assisted in shedding light on the broader Evangelical background to the convergence of Ashley's Evangelical beliefs and high Tory inspired paternalist attitudes.

Concurring with Hilton's thesis that it was really only the latter school of Evangelicals such as Bickersteth, Oastler, Sadler and Ashley that came to embrace Tory paternalist state intervention by the time of Victoria's reign, Holladay and Lewis revealed the extent of the preceding generation's lack of enthusiasm for such measures. In the pre Victorian period, Wilberforce and the Clapham Evangelicals were on the record as clearly favoring free trade and limited government. The *Christian Observer* had defended free trade as a "truly Christian system of intercourse," warmly applauding the "liberal Tory" tariff reforms of William Huskisson and Frederick Robinson after 1823.[39] While not oblivious to the realities of human suffering in their midst, these Evangelicals favored private acts of mercy and alms-giving, rather than large-scale programs of state intervention, as the appropriate response to alleviating temporal hardship. This preference could be attributed not only to their non-interventionist doctrine of providence, as highlighted by Hilton, but also their belief that this form of poor relief was more heartfelt, personalized, and respectful to the human dignity of the persons requiring aid.

Chalmers had typified this outlook by opposing the idea of a right to statutory poor relief whilst enthusiastically supporting voluntary, church-administered charity aimed to foster self-help.[40] Writing for the *Edinburgh Review*, Chalmers asked whether a needy family would rather be attended to by the "visit of an affectionate neighbor" who knew their misfortunes and their worth, or whether they would prefer to "troop around Public Benevolence" for a weekly allowance?[41] Chalmers feared that money given to the poor via the state would "lose its original character of a free-will offering" and, instead, assume "the shape of an extorted right from the wealthier to the humbler classes of the community."[42] So long as an active army of laity could attend to the poor at a personalized, grassroots level, Evangelicals of Chalmers' political persuasion entertained few ethical or theological

---

38. Lewis, *Lighten their Darkness*, 164.

39. *Christian Observer*, XVIII (1823), 131, cited in Lewis, *Lighten their Darkness*, 164.

40. Lewis, *Lighten their Darkness*, 60.

41. Chalmers, "Causes and Cure of Pauperism," 13.

42. Ibid., 16.

qualms about a *laissez-faire state* affording free reign to the market forces of the economy.

The advent of overt, large-scale poverty in the burgeoning industrial cities of England engendered a shift in thinking towards state intervention amongst some Tories and Whigs in political circles. This same phenomenon precipitated an analogous shake-up of attitudes in the Evangelical world, thus bringing some Evangelicals to form an unlikely working coalition with utilitarian free-thinkers in projects aimed at addressing urban pauperism. At the same time that high Tories and Benthamite Whigs were beginning to propose state intervention measures as a timely response to the Condition of England Question, Evangelicals were also starting to ponder the merits of state intervention as they experienced shocking first-hand encounters with urban poverty and squalor resulting from mass industrialization.[43] Like Sadler, whose witness of urban pauperism in Leeds had impelled him to support the factory reform campaign in parliament, Ashley was another Evangelical spurred into action after observing the horrors of slum-life. In 1851, he attested to the effect of first-hand experience with the conditions of the poor:

> No person who has perambulated these districts—who has dived into the cellars or mounted into the garrets—who has gone into the houses right and left—who has given but one day to the inspection of this . . . can have the slightest doubt of what I assert—that the condition of the dwellings of the people lies at the very root of one half of the social, physical and moral mischief that besets our population.[44]

Thus, for Evangelicals, such as Ashley, the evil of poverty lay in not only the discomfort and misery it visibly inflicted on the life of the poor but also in its perceived function as a reservoir for breeding all manner of vice and delinquency. In this vein, at least, Ashley entertained a not too dissimilar view on the effects of poverty to that of Benthamite utilitarians such as Edwin Chadwick.[45] Whilst not denying the reality of Original Sin, Ashley agreed with the Benthamites that the curse of material poverty impaired the flourishing of private and public virtue leading to human happiness. This understanding of poverty would serve to strengthen the conviction of Evangelicals and Benthamites alike that paternalist state intervention, in the form of factory legislation, public sanitation, and housing provision, was

---

43. Holladay, "19th Century Evangelical Activism," 61.

44. Earl of Shaftesbury, "Seventh Annual Meeting," in *The Labourer's Friend*, 98–99.

45. MacDonagh, *Early Victorian Government*, 7.

A Convergence of Tory Paternalism and Early Victorian Evangelicalism 155

necessary to bring not only practical relief to the poor but also to strike at the root of much immorality and social dysfunction.[46]

Ashley himself concurred with the earlier Evangelical mindset that there was some providential purpose behind the permanent existence of a poorer class in society. He did not, however, believe that this necessarily validated the continued indifference of fellow citizens and the non-intervention of the state; particularly given that the poor's parlous condition of living imperiled their very livelihood. As he noted in his diary in 1843, the underprivileged still had the right to basic human dignity and the enjoyment of acceptable living standards:

> The poor shall never cease out of the land. That we know, for God has said it. But the poor of London are very different from the poor of Scripture. God has ordained that there should be poor, but He has not ordained that, in a Christian land, there should be an overwhelming mass of foul, helpless poverty.[47]

Contrasting the helpless and oppressed poor of early Victorian London with the poor of Scripture, whom he understood to be relatively self-sufficient and self-respecting, Ashley was far from convinced that contemporary Evangelicals could still invoke the Bible to justify the present condition of Britain's urban poor. Rather, it behooved all Evangelicals who honored the Bible to work towards the elevation of this poorer class to a level where they could enjoy the right to basic comfort and security. Thus, for Shaftesbury, remedial legislative action was called for not *despite* the Scriptures, but *because* of the Scriptures.

With Evangelicals such as Chalmers and the Clapham Sect hitherto placing greatest store on private charity by individuals and voluntary associations as the appropriate means to address human suffering, broader Evangelical support for state intervention on *social issues* was initially cautious.[48] Evangelicals had traditionally supported state intervention as a conventional means to regulate *moral behavior*, as evidenced by their sponsorship of the Royal Proclamation "for the encouragement of piety and virtue," but rejected it as a mechanism for addressing social disadvantage. By the 1830s, however, Evangelicals gradually came to recognize the inadequacy of private volunteerism and hence the broader merits of state intervention, particularly in the vital purpose government legislation could serve as a check on unfettered commercial greed and exploitation. According to Lewis, a major

46. Hilton, *Age of Atonement*, 268.
47. Shaftesbury, Diary Entry (December 30, 1853), in Hodder, *Life and Work of the Seventh Earl*, Vol. II, 409.
48. Holladay, "19th Century Evangelical Activism," 66.

catalyst for this Evangelical reappraisal of private charity's sufficiency to address social disadvantage was the low-profile but highly effective Christian Influence Society (CIS). Founded in 1832 by a small coterie of Anglican clergy and laity, the CIS styled itself as an Evangelical pressure group with the objective of influencing the parliament, the Established Church and the press.[49] The leading figures of the society included the wealthy philanthropist Robert Gordon and the Evangelical authors Robert Benton Seeley and Charlotte Elizabeth Tonna. Through its publishing organ, *The Churchman's Monthly Review*, the Society made its paternalist views known about what it regarded as the detrimental effects of political economy on the poor and the inadequacy of Chalmers' favored "private philanthropy" approach to remedying poverty.

Both Seeley and Ashley typified the attitudes of the new Evangelical generation which recognized the high Tory paternalist ethic of state intervention as augmenting, rather than detracting from, their forgoing Evangelical convictions. From bodies such as the Christian Influence Society, and individual social reformers such as Sadler and Ashley, Evangelical support for government intervention eventually extended to the *Record* newspaper. Despite having been mildly disposed to political economy in its early days, the publication appreciated the need for legislative action by the 1840s with its appeal for the House of Commons to remove the "palpable moral evil" of child labor in factories.[50] Ashley proved receptive to the CIS's appeal for state intervention in his support for the prudent regulation of the labor force, particularly with respect to humanizing working conditions in the nation's factories, mines and collieries. Concurring with Seeley that voluntary efforts needed to be augmented by legislation, Ashley asserted that with respect to eradicating the causes of crime and mischief amongst the poorer classes:

> Private duty will do a great deal towards the removal of them, but legislation will do a great deal more, by directing and stimulating our lagging efforts. But these things must not remain as they are, if we have the slightest regard for the welfare of our country.[51]

Hence the enactment of appropriate legislation would provide much needed direction and clout in the quest for social reform. As evidenced by his continuing involvement with voluntary organizations, not least the RSU,

---

49. Lewis, *Lighten their Darkness*, 154.
50. Editorial, *The Record*, March 25, 1844, 4.
51. Ashley, "Social Condition of the Labouring Classes," 195.

Ashley's support for state intervention, however, was never intended to replace existing charitable schemes but, rather, to supplement these private enterprises with beneficent legislative measures. Later Evangelicals deemed state intervention necessary because the existing exercise of social responsibility at the personal level was too weak to overcome the present obstacles of social disadvantage.[52] In Ashley's strategy to improve the condition of the poor, such action on the part of the state would serve to provide initial relief and long-term empowerment. This would be complemented with legislation which would afford overarching legal protection to the laboring classes from any further exploitation and degradation.

The Evangelicals' embrace of state intervention was impelled by a perception that, with the proliferation of poverty and dislocation in urban centers, unbridled industrial capitalism and its creed of political economy had been tried and found palpably wanting. Evangelicals such as Sadler, Seeley, and Ashley concluded that the teachings of political economy, together with the population theories of Thomas Malthus, were largely responsible for many of the abuses of the factory system. Political economy held economic gain and competition as its primary goals, irrespective of their adverse effects on unprotected workers. Hence, in an economic order of unrestrained competition, the poor and weak would be the inevitable losers.[53] Whereas the romantic Lake poets had decried the new industrial economic paradigm as the great destroyer of the traditional rural life and community they had cherished and sought to revive, the Evangelicals primarily denounced its utilitarian presuppositions as repugnant to the teachings of Christian scripture.[54]

Grounding their critique of political economy in their understanding of the Bible, they scorned a philosophy perceived as worldly, selfish, and devoid of moral content. For these socially awakened Evangelicals, political economy was based on atheistic precepts rather than biblical principles. Seeley thus stressed the incompatibility of political economy with Christianity:

> We aver, that in God's word . . . there are given doctrines, and reproofs, and instructions in righteousness, for legislators, for statesman, and for men of wealth and influence; and the general tenor of these is directly opposed to what a set of philosophers, "falsely so called," of our own times, have conspired to dignify with the name of "political economy." And accordingly, and very

---

52. Holladay, "19th Century Evangelical Activism," 65.
53. Ibid., 68.
54. Lewis, *Lighten their Darkness*, 155.

naturally, as the Bible and they are at variance, they agree to lay the Bible on the shelf . . . .[55]

Evangelicals maintained that political economists had "served notice on God" that his ethic of love and charity was no longer to govern men in their economic relations, and that the ruler of the universe had no business to interfere. Essentially, it was this shift of economic thinking amongst Evangelicals that brought them into robust agreement with the high Anglican Lake poets and the emerging generation of Tory paternalist agitators. Whilst their grounds for opposing political economy may have differed in some areas, Evangelicals and traditional high Tories concurred that unfettered industrial capitalism was an affront to the human dignity of the laboring classes and that state intervention was necessary to curb the abuses of market power and protect workers from exploitation. Accordingly, Evangelicals, such as Seeley and Ashley, invoked "fatherhood of God" terminology common to both Evangelical piety and Tory paternalism to articulate their case for state intervention. Seeley spoke of the idea that God's agents, in the form of the Christian state and the Christian magistrate, should interfere on his behalf to provide fatherly protection to the poor as the Scriptures commanded.

Throughout his public life, Ashley regarded the notion of a non-interventionist, *laissez-faire* state as morally untenable and unbecoming for what he regarded as a Christian nation. Whilst the most vulnerable classes of people were being oppressed and exploited by an essentially unchecked industrial labor regime, it seemed simply unconscionable for the state to remain as a passive and indifferent bystander. With Ashley regarding the state as both the paternal guardian of the people and the instrument of God to effect righteousness and punish wickedness, it was axiomatic for the state to play an active, but by no means overbearing or excessive role in the spiritual, moral, and economic affairs of the country. Viewing the oppressive effects of the factory system as a moral stain upon the nation to be erased, Ashley implored the legislature in 1842 to act accordingly: "Now, Sir, to remove or even to mitigate, these sad evils requires the vigorous and immediate interposition of the Legislature. That interposition is demanded by public reason, by public virtue, by the public honor, by the public character, and I rejoice to add by the public sympathy."[56] With every valid justification, the state for Ashley thereby had a paternalist and Evangelical mandate to mitigate oppression and injustice by enacting such measures as the factory

---

55. Seeley, *Remedies*, 51.

56. Ashley, "Employment of Women and Children in Mines and Collieries," HC Debates, *Hansard*, 7 June 1842, Vol. 63, c. 1336.

reform legislation and regulations to humanize the treatment of mentally ill patients.

A shared communitarian vision of society also united Evangelicals and Tory paternalists in their campaign against political economy. Both Evangelicals and Tory paternalists alike deplored the aggressive individualism of political economy and what they perceived to be its socially disintegrating effect on local communities and the nation at large. Whilst Evangelical piety always had a strongly individualist strain, with special focus on the *individual's* personal salvation, holiness, and communion with God, there was also a firm emphasis on corporate fellowship and community, particularly within the contexts of the family and the church. Evangelicalism essentially viewed human beings not as isolated individuals, but rather as interdependent members of families, churches, communities, nations, and, indeed, the wider human family existing under the one, sovereign God. Thus, within such spheres, there was typically an emphasis on the responsibilities and obligations of sharing, caring, serving, leading, and obeying.

This conception of society squared well with the philosophy of Tory paternalism that similarly stressed the intrinsic value of community. Reinforced by writers such as Southey and Wordsworth, Tory paternalists extolled the virtues of an organic society which concerned itself with the community as a whole, and was bound together by natural bonds of tradition, loyalty, religion, duty, and obligation, rather than by the market relations of "self-interest."[57]

Both Evangelicals and Tory paternalists esteemed the primacy of religion as a moral and spiritual unifier, guaranteeing the stability and continuity of the nation. For Evangelicals and Tory paternalists, the individualistic thrust of rampant industrial capitalism, on the other hand, was seen to weaken these communal bonds. The impersonal nature of the factory system diminished the age-old bond between employer and employee, whilst the demands of inordinately long working days detracted from family time, church fellowship and participation in community life. Such outcomes were seen to represent an affront to the closely-knit, communal ideals shared by both traditions.

Nourished by a vibrant Anglican Evangelical spirituality, together with the high Tory paternalist ideals of Southey's works, Ashley exemplified this distaste for atomistic individualism perpetuated by political economy and the modern industrial system. In its obituary for the Earl in 1885, the *Times* observed that, with respect to *laissez-faire* liberalism, "Lord Shaftesbury would have none of it" and credited the Earl for having "retarded the

---

57. Holladay, "19th Century Evangelical Activism," 75–76.

advance of social dissolution" in Victorian Britain.[58] Throughout his life, he had yearned for a renewal of the old kinships and human bonds that hitherto defined society as a web of interconnected and interdependent individuals. Addressing his fellow Lords during a debate on the Representation of the People Bill in 1867, Shaftesbury expressed his regret at how recent demographic trends in industrial centers were severing traditional bonds:

> ... in the manufacturing towns—in Manchester, Huddersfield, and others I could name. The same complaint is made everywhere—that the people of property and station are leaving the towns and are removing themselves from the working classes, and that a "hard and fast line" is being drawn between employer and employed, between persons of influence and those who ought to be subject to it.[59]

A greater sense of mutual acquaintance and cordial relations amongst the people, according to Shaftesbury, would be the key to fostering a greater sense of accountability and responsibility to one another. For a Tory and an Evangelical, this outcome was eminently desirable as it would auger well for the vitality of community life and the flourishing of its institutions, particularly families, churches, schools, voluntary associations and local businesses. If, however, a spirit of rampant individualism was allowed to fester unchallenged, than communities would further fragment with the disintegration of basic communal bonds. With the social fabric of society already tested by the industrial system, Ashley was anxious to avoid the consequences of relative social cohesion and stability giving way to class tension and civil unrest.

As well as decrying the perceived moral deficiencies of *laissez-faire* political economy, both Tory paternalism and Evangelicalism shared an inherent distaste for the utopian socialist doctrines propounded by Robert Owen (1771–1858) and his disciples. High Tory paternalists regarded socialist ideals of class equality and wealth redistribution by the state as grave threats to the hierarchical order of society while Evangelicals were suspicious of socialism's message which they saw as directly subversive of orthodox Christian attitudes.[60] Bickersteth was an outspoken opponent of socialism and perceived its presence in somewhat apocalyptic terms. Emerging as a leading writer on biblical prophecy, Bickersteth used his premillennial views to account for the 'mushroom growth' of socialism, denouncing it in 1842 as a manifestation of the "Spirit of Infidelity" to be discerned by the propheti-

---

58. "Death of Lord Shaftesbury," *The Times*, October 2, 1885, 11.

59. Shaftesbury, "Parliamentary Reform—Representation of the People Bill," HL Debates, *Hansard*, 23 July 1867, Vol. 188, cc. 1930–31.

60. Davidoff and Hall, *Family Fortunes*, 94.

A Convergence of Tory Paternalism and Early Victorian Evangelicalism 161

cally aware. Bickersteth pinpointed socialism as the working of the "unclean spirit from the mouth of the dragon" portrayed by scripture in chapter 12 of the book of Revelation.[61]

As an Anglican Evangelical himself, Ashley's attitudes to socialism ordinarily concurred with those of Bickersteth. Socialism was anathema to both his aristocratic Tory background and Evangelical convictions. In 1840, he wrote alarmingly of socialism's influence in the nation along with that of Chartism:

> The two great demons in morals and politics, socialism and Chartism, are stalking through the land; yet they are but symptoms of a universal disease, spread throughout vast masses of the people, who, so far from concurring in the attitudes [sic] suppose that anything must be better than their present condition.[62]

Ashley's protestations reflected the mission of Evangelicals in the 1830s and 1840s "to counter the spread of socialist and infidel ideas among the working classes."[63] Whilst Ashley was disturbed by the apparent rise of socialism, he was convinced its popular allure laid not so much in its intrinsic merit but rather in the widespread disenchantment with modern capitalism that had prompted many to consider alternative systems. Although rejecting the socialist remedy, he noted in his diary in 1840 that the prevailing system of industrial capitalism left much to be desired, essentially empathizing with the grievances of its dissidents.

> No wonder that thousands of hearts should be against a system which establishes the relations, without calling forth the mutual sympathies, of master and servant, landlord and tenant, employer and employed.... [T]he rich and the poor are antagonist parties, each wanting an opportunity to gain an advantage over the other. Sickness has no claim on the capitalist; a day's absence, however necessary, is a day's loss to the workman ....[64]

Thus, if modern capitalism could recover some of the old paternalist virtues of harmonious class relations, fair working conditions, and just remuneration for employers, Ashley believed that any threat of socialism or radicalism

---

61. Bickersteth, *Divine Warning*, 9.

62. Ashley, Diary Entry (1840), in Hodder, *Life and Work of the Seventh Earl*, Vol. I, 322.

63. Davidoff and Hall, *Family Fortunes*, 94.

64. Lord Ashley, Diary Entry (1840), in Hodder, *Life and Work of the Seventh Earl*, Vol. I, 322.

could be abated as the common people once again accepted the prevailing economic order. For the Tory Ashley, ameliorating problems within the familiar system of capitalism was vastly preferable to the wholesale adoption of a new socialist order deemed alien to traditional British values. A radical system he detested for its overly bold faith in the goodness of the state at the expense of traditional organs such as the church, the family, and the voluntary society.

Profoundly distrustful of radical politics, Evangelical mouth-pieces such as the *Christian Observer* and the *Record* initially identified themselves closely with the Tory party, and once Peel became prime minister, it was not unknown for Evangelicals to flex their influence amongst the faithful on behalf of the Tory government.[65] Seeley, an associate of both Sadler and Ashley, became an important figure in Tory party circles around London. The Tory networker would lobby politicians such as Ashley on issues that might jeopardize the standing of Peel's government, the survival of which was seen to be in the Evangelicals' best interests.[66] Whilst deeply sympathetic to the plight of factory laborers, Seeley was concerned in 1841 that Ashley's pursuit of his Factory Bill might be injurious to Peel's administration in the longer term.

The initial goodwill of Evangelicals towards the Tory Party, however, evaporated steadily as their lofty expectations were left unfulfilled by the record of the Peelite Tories in office. The long-awaited church extension proposals were finally introduced, but the final measures were seen as so compromised that it was hardly an auspicious moment.[67] In other Tory policies which disappointed Evangelicals, Peel's government had introduced the Dissenters' Chapels Bills that allowed ex-Presbyterian Unitarians to retain their properties and endowment funds, whilst, at the same time, making the annual grant to the Roman Catholic College in Maynooth, Ireland, permanent.[68] Evangelicals were appalled by the Tory party's patronage of these non-Evangelical faith groups, with the *Record* declaring that the party had "departed from the principles of our Christian and Protestant Constitution" in "an amount of evil incomparably greater than the Whigs could accomplish."[69] In spite of this disillusionment with contemporary Tory politics in the 1840s, Evangelicals such as Bickersteth, Oastler, Seeley, Sadler, and Ashley remained wedded to classic high Tory paternalist ideals,

---

65. Lewis, *Lighten their Darkness*, 83.
66. Ibid.
67. Ibid., 86.
68. Ibid., 90.
69. *The Record*, February 6, 1845, 3.

even where these had been abandoned by Peel's predominantly liberal Tory administration.

Constitutional Protestantism: A rallying point for Anglican Evangelicals and high Tory paternalists

In addition to embracing the paternalist paradigm of an interventionist state, the new Evangelical generation of Ashley and the Recordites found common cause with high Tory paternalists in the defense of the Church Establishment as the mainstay of England's Protestant constitution. Whilst the preceding Clapham Evangelicals had been similarly committed to the Establishment, the forgoing campaign by Nonconformists in the 1820s for the Church of England to be supported by voluntary means, rather than by the state, galvanized Evangelical forces to defend the Church of England fearing that its disestablishment would ultimately lead to a secular, nonconfessional state.[70] With the repeal of the Test and Corporation Acts in 1828 and the passage of the Catholic Relief Act in 1829 breaking the constitutional monopoly of the Church of England, the institution's survival was brought into even sharper focus for both high Tories and Evangelicals.

As Robert Hole correctly observed, the 1828–29 constitutional reforms and the accompanying debates had both an ideological and theological dimension.[71] For high Tory paternalists such as Southey and Coleridge, the Established Church represented the ancient, institutional linchpin of a hierarchical and organic society. In his *Book of the Church* (1824) Southey had mounted a powerful defense of the Church of England's hegemony within an essentially confessional state. Accordingly, he railed against Catholic Emancipation in both his *Colloquies* and his contributions to the *Quarterly Review*. With the admission of Roman Catholics to public office, Southey and other high Tories feared that "the vital interests of England would be seriously endangered" because the authoritarian nature of the Roman Catholic Church would disturb the religious liberty of England.[72]

Meanwhile, for Evangelicals such as Bickersteth and Ashley, the Established Church represented a historic repository of sound Protestant doctrine and a practical apparatus by which to disseminate the Christian gospel across the nation. By preserving the pre-eminence of the Established Church, Evangelicals had hoped to infuse the institution with "Reformation religion" which, in turn, would shape the religious character of the nation.

70. Lewis, *Lighten their Darkness*, 17.
71. Hole, *Pulpits, Politics and Public Order*, 233.
72. David Eastwood, "Robert Southey," 310.

Bickersteth articulated this Evangelical form of Protestant constitutionalism when he wrote that "the absolute duty of monarchs and nations to give their royal and national support to the truth," as revealed in "the word of God," was "the very foundation of the British Constitution, fully laid at the glorious Reformation."[73] Protestant constitutionalism also permeated the pages of the *Record* which denounced the forces of democracy, Popery, and Dissent for endangering "our glorious Constitution in Church and State."[74] Indeed, the *Record* and its constitutionalist stance was instrumental in "leading a large segment of Evangelicalism in the direction of conservatism in politics."[75] As John Wolffe appreciated, the anti-Catholic sentiment common to both high Tory and Evangelical guardians of the Protestant constitution was significant "because of the ideological convergence between Toryism and Evangelicalism which was particularly evident in the mid-1830s."[76] In addition to Ashley himself, figures such as the Evangelical Hugh McNeile (later appointed Dean of Ripon in 1868), and the third Earl of Roden, Robert Jocelyn, evidently "had feet in both camps."[77]

The Tory disposition of the Recordite Evangelicals and their robust defense of the Church Establishment distinguished them, however, from their Nonconformist co-religionists. Evangelical Nonconformists were somewhat skeptical that a state institution such as the Church of England could be infused with gospel principles.[78] Indeed, they were convinced that Anglican disestablishment would allow the movement of evangelicalism, as a whole, to flourish without the handicap of an institutional barrier dividing Church from Dissent. Given that the Whigs had historically favored disestablishment, Nonconformist evangelicals tended to be Whiggish rather than Tory in their political disposition. Electoral documents revealed that Nonconformist ministers voted overwhelmingly for Whig or liberal candidates at elections, while Nonconformist publications, such as the *Patriot* and *Nonconformist*, supported the Whig-Liberal-Radical wing of the House of Commons.[79] On the other hand, almost no Dissenting MP ever ran as a Tory.

Like general Whig support for economic liberalism and free-trade, Nonconformists supported an analogous "free-trade" ethic in religion

---

73. Bickersteth, *Signs of the Times*, 312.
74. Lewis, *Lighten their Darkness*, 83.
75. Ibid., 17.
76. Wolffe, *Protestant Crusade*, 300.
77. Ibid.
78. Lewis, *Lighten their Darkness*, 26.
79. Timothy, *Friends of Religious Equality*, 37.

A Convergence of Tory Paternalism and Early Victorian Evangelicalism 165

where church establishments and state restrictions on religious liberty represented undesirable forms of protectionism.[80] Accordingly, they found the liberal politics of the anti-Establishment Whigs decidedly more congenial to their religious sympathies than that of the pro-Establishment high Tories much favored by the Recordite school of Anglican Evangelicals in the 1830s. Meanwhile, sandwiched between the Tory-disposed Anglicans and the Whig-leaning Nonconformists, the Wesleyan Methodists constituted a third slice of the evangelical constituency. Owing to their Anglican heritage in John Wesley, however, politically conservative Wesleyans such as Jabez Bunting (1779–1858) generally felt more comfortable with the existing relationships between Church and state than their Dissenting co-religionists.[81] Thus with this broad spectrum of political views across Anglican, Wesleyan, and Nonconformist evangelicals, it was virtually impossible for evangelicals *at large* really to forge a "concerted social or political theory."[82]

Given the dual input of the high Tory paternalist Southey and the Evangelical Bickersteth, it was no surprise that Ashley emerged as a staunch Protestant constitutionalist. Opposing the Reform Bill of 1832, he pledged himself to "defend those great principles which inspire and regulate our glorious constitution in Church and State."[83] Concurring with the sentiments of the *Record*, Ashley praised the coronation rite for reinforcing the constitutional primacy of the Established Church. Reflecting on the coronation service for Queen Victoria in July 1838, he remarked how the ceremony made the "Church everything" and "secular greatness" nothing.[84] Despite having earlier voted for the Catholic Relief Act in 1829,[85] largely on the grounds of political expediency, Ashley remained committed to defending the constitutional hegemony of the Established Church. This was particularly evident in his opposition to the Peel administration's Maynooth grant of 1845, with the fear that this endowment of a Roman Catholic seminary in Ireland would pave the way for "the concurrent existence of two Established Churches" in Ireland.[86] Notwithstanding his close collaboration with Nonconformists through pan-Evangelical ventures such as the BFBS and LCM,

---

80. Ibid., 118, 121.

81. Wolffe, *God and Greater Britain*, 40.

82. Bebbington, "Response," in Haykin and Stewart (eds.), *Emergence of Evangelicalism*, 429.

83. Hodder, *Life and Work of the Seventh Earl*, Vol. I, 125.

84. Ashley, Diary Entry (July 2, 1838), in Hodder, *Life and Work of the Seventh Earl*, Vol. I, 239.

85. Hodder, *Life and Work of the Seventh Earl*, Vol. I, 85.

86. Ashley, Diary Entry (April 7–8, 1845), in Hodder, *Life and Work of the Seventh Earl*, Vol. II, 101.

Ashley was decidedly in favor of protecting the privileges of the Established Church against the encroachments of not only Catholics but Nonconformists.[87] Although Ashley's religiosity impelled him, at the *grassroots* level, to forge working coalitions with Nonconformist evangelicals on common Protestant causes such as Bible distribution, evangelism, and mission, his avowed Tory paternalism, at the *governmental* level, made him wary of relinquishing Church monopoly over public institutions for fear of disturbing the constitutional settlement in place since 1688.

The link between Evangelical premillennial eschatology and Tory paternalism

Importantly, the Evangelical embrace of Tory paternalist ideals in the 1830s was reinforced by a new historicist premillennial eschatology that had gained traction amongst the post-Clapham generation of Evangelicals since the mid-1820s.[88] Believing that the return of Christ would precede the "millennium," the premillennial outlook of these Evangelicals was closely intertwined with their *interventionist* doctrine of providence which saw God as constantly directing earthly affairs by special warnings and judgments.[89] Essentially adopting the classic Old Testament paradigm of divine intervention, Martin Spence observed that premillennial eschatology conspicuously invoked Old Testament prophecy during the 1830s.[90] In this vein, premillennial Evangelicals such as Seeley, Tonna, and Ashley frequently sought to apply Old Testament teachings and notions of justice to the afflictions of the present day. For earthly governments best to reflect the interventionist God of ancient Israel, premillennial Evangelicals argued it was axiomatic for such governments to take a similarly interventionist approach to contemporary social and economic problems.[91] Owing to the inherent resemblance of this view to the forgoing Tory paternalist theory of government, the confluence of Evangelicalism and Tory paternalism which had occurred in many spheres during the 1820s and 30s became particularly evident in this strand of eschatology.

Appropriately, Hilton identified Bickersteth as a lightening-rod for this convergence, noting that Ashley's mentor had assented to premillennial eschatology at the same time he keenly endorsed his protégé's parliamentary

---

87. Larsen, *Friends of Religious Equality*, 5.
88. Bebbington, *Evangelicalism in Modern Britain*, 84.
89. Hilton, *Age of Atonement*, 15.
90. Spence, "Renewal of Time and Space," 267.
91. Ibid.

campaigns.[92] According to his biographer, Bickersteth embraced premillennialism in 1832 when he was "led to believe that the second coming of Christ would preceded the Millennium; that the first resurrection is literal, and that Christ will establish a glorious kingdom of righteousness on earth at His return, before the resurrection of the wicked, and their final judgment."[93] Sharing the common high Tory and Evangelical commitment to defending the role and status of the Established Church, premillennialists such as Bickersteth and Seeley maintained that the Church, also, must champion the doctrine of national responsibility which lay at the heart of divine prophecy and its relationship to historical events.[94] In this capacity, the Church would act as the conscience of the nation on moral and spiritual matters to prophesy what it saw as the will of God in daily national life, particularly with respect to the preservation of "Protestant truth" and care for the poor.[95]

For Bickersteth, the implications of the Second Advent extended from the Church to the nation at large when he wrote that "The second coming of Christ is not merely a doctrine needful and profitable for our personal edification as private Christians, but it has also a most important connexion with the duties of nations at large."[96] Hence, for Bickersteth, premillennialism was not an invitation to indulge in mere introspection and escapist pietism but rather a compelling rationale for Christian believers to attend to the national duties of delivering "righteous laws,"[97] poor relief,[98] and factory reform.[99] On such causes, the social reform agenda of premillennial Evangelicals evidently converged with that of the high Tory paternalists associated with *Blackwood's* and the *Quarterly Review*.

Despite offering a different explanation for post-Clapham Evangelical social activism from Hilton, Ralph Brown agreed in a general sense that premillennial eschatology was one of the motivating factors for Evangelical support of paternalist state intervention. Whereas Hilton had argued that Evangelical social reformers of Ashley's generation had sought to "protect" the socially vulnerable "from the stormy blasts" believed to precede the Second Coming, Brown contended that these Evangelicals were impelled by the

92. Hilton, *Age of Atonement*, 96.
93. Birks, *Memoir of the Rev Edward Bickerseth*, Vol. II, 25.
94. Brown, "Evangelical Social Thought," 131.
95. Bickersteth, *Signs of the Times*, 263, 346.
96. Ibid., 309.
97. Ibid., 317–22.
98. Ibid., 331–33.
99. Ibid., 333–35.

concept of a "covenanted nation and national religion" and thus regarded the Established Church as instrumental to improving the moral welfare of the population.[100] The explanation offered by Brown for premillennial activism helps to account for the Evangelical championing of Protestant Constitutionalism in the 1830s.

Whatever their precise motivations, Evangelicals such as Bickersteth, Sadler and Ashley all tended to view the maladies of early Victorian society through a Tory paternalist prism. According to Brown, these Evangelicals believed that, whilst social reforms were indeed necessary to ameliorate incidences of evil and injustice, they could not come at the cost of disturbing the divinely ordained social hierarchy.[101] The presence of social inequalities was seen as ordained by God in order to try human virtues. Thus, rather than necessitating a "leveling" state program such as socialism to eradicate such class disparity, the presence of inequality necessitated a degree of paternalistic charity, on the part of the wealthy, to ensure that poverty did not rise to unacceptable levels.[102] Moreover, state intervention, although welcome, needed to be restrained to ensure that idleness was not encouraged. The social reform impulses of Adventist premillennialism were, therefore, somewhat tempered by its conservatism stemming from the infusion of high Tory paternalist values.

'Evangelical-Tory' manifestos for social reform: Robert Benton Seeley and Charlotte Elizabeth Tonna

Fuelled by a resurgent Protestant constitutionalism and premillennial eschatology, the convergence of post-Clapham Evangelicalism with high Tory paternalism, particularly on the question of the state's proper role in society, gave rise to the articulation of a distinctive blueprint for social reform in the early Victorian period. In spheres such as the Christian Influence Society, the lead writers, R. B. Seeley and C. E. Tonna, each penned a treatise diagnosing the maladies afflicting Britain in the early 1840s and proposed what they believed to be the appropriate remedies.[103] Infused with an ample dose of both premillennial Evangelicalism and Southey-inspired Tory paternal-

---

100. Brown, "Victorian Anglican Evangelicalism," 687.

101. Ibid., 686.

102. Ibid., 686.

103. Tonna, *Perils of the Nation*. C. E. Tonna actually published this work in the name of her friend and associate, Robert Benton Seeley, believing that a male author's name would give the work greater credence. This was followed by Robert Benton Seeley's sequel, *Remedies*.

ism, Seeley and Tonna each proposed a pathway of government intervention which would ameliorate the harsh working conditions of factory laborers, relieve the distress of the rural poor, expand educational opportunities and facilitate the harmonization of class relations. In their vision for reform, Seeley and Tonna were impelled by a combination of paternalist antipathy towards the political economy of liberal Toryism and a premillennial sense of "apocalyptic urgency" to see ameliorative legislation enacted.[104] With *Perils of the Nation* and *Remedies* providing much of the immediate inspiration behind Ashley's social reforms, such as the Ten Hours Act, a careful examination of these treatises is warranted.

Robert Benton Seeley (1798–1886)

Given that Seeley was a close associate of Ashley within CIS circles[105] as well as being one of the lead authors espousing "Tory Evangelical" ideals in the 1830s and 1840s, it is surprising that he and his influential writings have received very scant attention in the biographies of Ashley to date. The various studies of Turnbull, Best, Battiscombe and the Hammonds made no mention of him at all. Even in the more extensive biographical works of Hodder and Finlayson,[106] together with Hilton's volume on Evangelical political and economic thought, his name was mentioned only in passing.[107] With this dearth of commentary on Seeley and the influence of his literature on Ashley, Lewis gave some welcome attention to this relatively neglected figure in *Lighten their Darkness*.[108] His discussion of Seeley primarily established the writer's link with Ashley as well as providing an outline of Seeley's Evangelical paternalist philosophy which denounced political economy and advocated humanitarian state intervention to relieve the afflictions of the poor. Although Lewis helpfully delineated the contours of Seeley's thought, he did not proceed to discuss its relationship to the specific policy objectives of Ashley. Accordingly, the materialization of Seeley's guiding biblical premises and paternalist propositions in Ashley's own social reform agenda will be examined.

---

104. Dzelzainis, "Charlotte Elizabeth Tonna," 181–82; Gleadle, "Charlotte Elizabeth Tonna," 100.

105. Lewis, *Lighten their Darkness*, 154.

106. Hodder, *Life and Work of the Seventh Earl*, Vol. II, 135–36; Finlayson, *Seventh Earl of Shaftesbury*, 145.

107. Hilton, *Age of Atonement*, 271–72.

108. Lewis, *Lighten their Darkness*, 83, 154–56, 158.

As an active author and publisher, Seeley became the literary driving force behind the early political career of Ashley. Closely associated with the lay activity behind the *Record*, he strongly supported its policy of Protestant constitutionalism and became an outspoken opponent of the Malthusian economics and *laissez-faire* policies supported by Evangelicals such as Chalmers and John Bird Sumner.[109] The blueprint for society he frequently espoused in his works represented a thoroughgoing synthesis of both high Tory paternalism and the premillennial Evangelicalism of the post-Clapham generation. Accordingly, he gave voice to their shared antipathy towards political economy and appeals to a more communitarian direction for society aided by the benign intervention of the state. In his *Remedies*, Seeley explicitly endorsed Ashley's campaign for education to cultivate the morality of working-class children and quoted extracts from his 1843 Sturminster speech.[110] On the issue of impoverished agricultural laborers, Seeley once again referred to Ashley, citing a piece of correspondence which alerted the then Dorset MP to the destitute state of farm employees in his own county.

Elsewhere in *Remedies*, Seeley continued to decry what he regarded as the dehumanizing ethic of political economy, whereby workers of the laboring class were demeaned as mere machines for creating wealth for those "above them."[111] Seeley maintained that this materialistic and utilitarian view of human worth was contrary to the Old Testament principles of Moses who had exhorted the authorities to afford special protection to the poor. He thus urged the "Christian" legislators of his day to uphold these principles: "If we turn to the general tenor of the enactments of Moses (Levit. xxv, Deut xv.), we find their main object to be, the protection of the poor; and that, not against violence, but against the exactions and oppressions of the rich. This ought, in fact, to be ever a chief business of all Christian legislators."[112]

In his invocation of Old Testament ethics, he cited the law of the Sabbath as being the most "wise and merciful provision."[113] As with Ashley, Seeley's defense of the Sabbath stemmed from a combination of Evangelical and conservative sensibilities. As well as being seen as an exercise of piety and faithful obedience to the scriptures, Sunday observance was esteemed as conducive to nature, reason, and the good order of society. Recognizing the Sabbath as self-authenticating, Ashley praised "the wonderful adaption of this institution to the social, physical and religious wants of man,"

109. Rennie and Lewis, "Seeley, Robert Benton," 993.
110. Seeley, *Remedies*, 271–72.
111. Ibid., 36.
112. Ibid., 120.
113. Ibid., 124.

A Convergence of Tory Paternalism and Early Victorian Evangelicalism 171

arguing that this, if nothing else, attested to "the divine character of the institution."[114]

In the Old Testament scriptures, it was the character of Job whom Seeley appreciated as the supreme exemplar of a "rich man rightly fulfilling his functions," thereby providing a golden template for the modern leader to emulate. A landholder initially blessed with a large tract of land and abundant livestock before natural calamity intervened radically to deplete his fortunes, the biblical Job shared much in common with the classic Tory paternalist conception of the English landholder frequently eulogized in the romantic prose of the Lake poets. Like the romanticized country squire imbibed with a spirit of *noblesse oblige*, a latter-day "Job" would similarly use the blessings of privilege and wealth to uplift the poor. In the Old Testament book attributed to Job, the landholder was recorded as saying:

> When the ear heard me; and when the eye saw me, it gave witness to me: Because I delivered the poor that cried, and the fatherless, and him that had none to help him. The blessing of him that was ready to perish came upon me; and I caused the widow's heart to sing for joy. I was eyes to the blind, and feet was I to the lame. I was a father to the poor; and the cause which I knew not I searched out. And I brake the jaws of the wicked, and plucked the spoil out of his teeth.[115]

Musing on these reflections of Job, Seeley could see stark parallels between the plight of the poor in ancient Israel and the parlous condition of Britain's working poor on the cusp of the Victorian age. Thus if God had raised up people such as Job to fend for the poor in Old Testament times, than surely the time was ripe again for leaders to take up the cause of the poor factory worker oppressed by an unjust industrial labor regime. To this end, he prosecuted the case for factory and agricultural labor reform.

As heir to the St Giles estate, Ashley entertained the conviction that he was raised up by God to be one such latter-day Job, entrusted by the Almighty with the gifts of privilege and wealth to bless the poor in his midst. Speaking on the condition of the laboring population, many of whom languished beneath the poverty line, Ashley enunciated the responsibilities and duties stemming from high birth and privilege.

> But let us draw our resolutions from a higher source, recollecting that all wealth, talent, rank, and power, are given by God for his own service, not for our luxury; for the benefit of others, not

---

114. Ashley, "Post Office," HC Debates, *Hansard*, 30 May 1850, Vol. 111, c. 472.
115. Job 29:11–17, quoted by Seeley, *Remedies*, 126.

> for the pride of ourselves; and that we must render an account of privileges misused, of means perverted, of opportunities thrown away. Employ them aright, and they sanctify the possession of property, bless its use, and grace its enjoyment—accomplishing still higher and better ends by leading the poor, who experience their value, to thoughts of piety and peace; and, in their heart and prayer, to bless almighty God that such men (and such we all must become), are invested with station and leisure, and property and power.[116]

Ashley's appeal to a "higher source" reflected his Evangelical beliefs that the rank, wealth and power he inherited at birth were not simply the accretion of assets and privileges from the hands of his forebears but, rather, gifts from God to be used for what were understood to be his purposes. Like Job of the Old Testament, Ashley grasped these "divine purposes" to be about leading the poor not only to greater material comfort and well-being but also to a knowledge and delight in their God. Accordingly, the Dorset MP's use of his own privileged station to agitate for the improved working conditions of labourers was about both ameliorating the material afflictions of the poorer classes and affording them greater opportunities for education and spiritual nourishment.

Ashley's "Evangelical-Tory" conception of *noblesse oblige* could thus be distinguished from more secular Tory concepts of the creed which tended to stress that the rationales for sharing one's wealth and talents were often about affording due recognition to the enterprise and ingenuity of one's ancestors, bringing public esteem to the "family name" and perpetuating the honor and prestige of the landed elite. Notwithstanding a difference in some motives, however, the Evangelical Ashley and Tory paternalism at large agreed that the defining essence of *noblesse oblige* was the use of privilege to advance the common good.

As both an Evangelical and conservative paternalist, Seeley's push for social reform was impelled not only by biblical ethics but also by a desire to revive the old virtues of a lost "golden-age." Like the Lake poets, Seeley romanticized the labor relations of the pre-industrial age, lauding these as decidedly more personalized and benevolent than those existing in the detached workplace of the modern day.

> In the days of our forefathers, the farmer kept a major part of his workmen under his own roof, finding them a comfortable home and abundant food, for the whole year. But now

---

116. Ashley, *Condition of the Labouring Population*, 90.

the farm-laborers are banished with one consent to miserable hovels, and employed irregularly, and merely when it suits the farmer.[117]

Seeley attributed much of this deterioration in working conditions to an "overstocked" labor force that had absorbed large numbers of women and young children. Accordingly, he called for the "clearing of all young children" from the mills and the mines and for working women (particularly mothers) to be "sent home to their families" as remedies to an overcrowded labor market.[118] In addition, he desired to limit the hours of labor to a "fair day's work" of ten hours and for landholders to employ the number of laborers duly proportionate to the maintenance of the land. Defending these objectives against charges of "interference between employer and workman," Seeley called on the parliament swiftly to legislate these measures so as to advance the happiness and tranquility of the working classes.[119] Such motives for furthering working-class wellbeing were intrinsically conservative, with the aim of ensuring order, stability, and continuity in the longer term. Like Ashley and the *Quarterly Review*, Seeley believed that an oppressed working class could pose a potential threat to established institutions. Embittered against their employers and "those above them," it was feared that the simmering discontent of an aggrieved working class could boil over into insurrection and revolution against the established order. Despite his later displeasure with Ashley's decision in 1846 to support the Peel administration's repeal of the Corn Laws, Seeley's writings did much to reinforce the high Tory and Evangelical strands of Ashley's thought.

Charlotte Elizabeth Tonna (1790–1846)

A close friend and associate of Seeley, C. E Tonna emerged as a fellow Tory-Evangelical agitator and author. Like Seeley and his Christian Influence Society, she was closely associated with Ashley in his parliamentary campaign for the Ten Hours legislation.[120] Given her influence and collaboration with Ashley on such a significant Victorian social reform, together with the striking similarity of her political and religious thought to that of the parliamentary social reformer, it is again surprising that Tonna's role in her own right, and her connection to Ashley, have rated little or no mention

---

117. Seeley, *Remedies*, 190.
118. Ibid.
119. Ibid.
120. Dzelzainis, "Charlotte Elizabeth Tonna," 181.

in the biographical studies produced to date.[121] To compensate for not only her invisibility in the Ashley biographies, but also her absence or, at best, her peripheral place in the forgoing narratives discussing Evangelical inspired social reform,[122] Ella Dzelzainis, Kathryn Gleadle, and Monica C. Fryckstedt produced a set of welcome studies that sought to give due attention and contextualization to this much neglected Evangelical writer and paternalist social reformer.

Dzelzainis made the critical observation that Tonna, like Ashley, was a premillennial Evangelical "whose religious-inspired social paternalism" led her "to advocate a Ten Hours Bill."[123] Appreciating the interwoven threads of Evangelicalism and high Tory paternalism underpinning the factory reform campaign of Tonna and Ashley, Dzelzainis noted that "the congruity of rhetorical and structural detail between Tonna's fiction and Ashley's [parliamentary] speech suggests that she had a more extensive role in the development of his campaign strategy than has been recognized."[124] Gleadle similarly discussed the significance of Tonna as an Evangelical standard-bearer for Tory paternalist social reform, but did not closely examine her links with Ashley.[125] Fryckstedt, meanwhile, discussed the major social reform themes in Tonna's literature and made reference to her "support of Lord Ashley's campaign for renewed factory legislation" through publications such as the *Christian Lady's Magazine* founded in 1834 and *Helen Fleetwood* (1841).[126] The contribution of these studies on Tonna to remedying the lacuna in the biographical works and relevant historical narratives has been appreciable; nonetheless, a fuller comprehension of the fundamental ideas informing Ashley's social reforms would be aided by a more detailed analysis of Tonna's works, particularly her *Perils of the Nation*.

Tonna's great admiration for Ashley and his parliamentary campaign for the Ten Hours legislation manifested itself in her novel, *Helen Fleetwood*.

---

121. Hodder, *Life and Work of the Seventh Earl*, Vol. I, 392–93. Hodder cited a brief letter from C. E. Tonna to Ashley (December 1841) where she warmly commended the social reformer for his determined stance against Tractarian "Puseyism" in the Established Church. Aside from quoting this extract, Hodder did not discuss Tonna's thought and influence on Ashley. Subsequent biographical works, including that of Finlayson, made no mention of C. E. Tonna.

122. Hilton, *Age of Atonement*, 97. Hilton credited C. E. Tonna's literature as "powerful propaganda for the Ten Hours Movement," but did not examine it further.

123. Dzelzainis, "Charlotte Elizabeth Tonna," 182.

124. Ibid., 188–89.

125. Gleadle, "Charlotte Elizabeth Tonna," 100. At 102, Gleadle did make reference to Ashley's assistance of Tonna's parliamentary research for one her novels, *Michael Armstrong* (1839–40).

126. Frysckstedt, "Charlotte Elizabeth Tonna," 196.

In this fictional story of a family bearing the hardships of an insufficiently regulated factory system, a physician, claiming to be a friend of Lord Ashley, remarked how he "proceeded on Christian principles" steadily to keep in view "the declared object of his compassionate efforts—an amelioration of bodily suffering to the factory children."[127] Moreover, in Tonna's autobiographical *Personal Recollections* (1841), the anonymous editor to a subsequent edition of the work paid tribute to "the noble efforts of Tonna's kind Christian friend, Lord Ashley, on behalf of the labouring classes."[128] The editor also testified to the immediate impact of Tonna's *Perils of the Nation* on social reform legislators such as Ashley. According to the editor, Tonna's prequel to Seeley's *Remedies* was "quoted on platforms and discussed in private circles," thereby having "a marked and decided influence, not only on the tone of public feeling, but directly on the Legislature."[129] In so doing, *Perils* was believed to have "aided the passing of the Mines and Collieries' Bill, and the Ten Hours Bill, and in bringing forward the Health of Towns Bill."[130] Thus, as Hilton appreciated, her writings of urban despair and degradation were, as she intended, powerful ammunition for the Sadler-Ashley-led Ten Hours movement.[131] Whatever the actual extent of influence the *Perils* may have exerted on early Victorian social reform legislation, the ideas proposed in the treatise were certainly pertinent and are worthy of closer examination.

Publishing *Perils* at a time when there was growing unease amongst both high Tory paternalists and premillennial Evangelicals over the Peel administration's seemingly inadequate response to social and economic upheaval,[132] Tonna sought to fill the perceived policy vacuum created by liberal Toryism. Accordingly, she provided not only general guidelines for how Evangelicals should engage politically, but how Evangelicals in public office should respond paternalistically to some of the specific issues of the *present day*, namely the plight of manufacturers, miners, workshop laborers and the agricultural poor, together with the dearth of adequate formal education. Tonna's appeals in her treatise for a national system of religious-based education, for legislative intervention in the labor force to protect vulnerable workers, and for holders of high office to govern benevolently resonated

127. Tonna, *Helen Fleetwood*, 385.

128. Editor of "Concluding Remarks" to Tonna, *Personal Recollections*, 373. In this 1854 edition following Tonna's death in 1846, the anonymous editor wrote an epilogue entitled "Concluding Remarks," 358–93.

129. Tonna, *Personal Recollections*, 375.

130. Ibid.

131. Hilton, *Age of Atonement*, 97.

132. Gleadle, "Charlotte Elizabeth Tonna," 100.

with conservative patricians and Evangelicals alike. With sustained public demand, *Perils* was soon re-released in second and third editions.[133] Its momentum was such that it was credited for spawning three new societies; the Society for Improving the Conditions of the Laboring Classes, the Church Extension Fund and the Clerical Education Fund. Invoking a combination of paternalist and Evangelical motifs, Tonna's *Perils* essentially appealed to the ruling groups not to permit the growing misery and oppression to imperil the social order and warned that divine retribution was certain to descend upon those who failed to heed the frequent signs of imminent danger.[134]

As to the notion of public duty advanced in *Perils*, Tonna shared the same presuppositions as Sadler, Southey and the *Quarterly Review* that this was a noble calling especially assigned to the aristocratic class. Owing to the powerful influence they possessed within the body-politic, Tonna insisted that this privileged class had a responsibility to use such influence for the advancement and edification of the whole nation. Accordingly, she posed these questions:

> Who can look upon the splendid assemblage of England's aristocracy on the one hand, and on the other her independent gentlemen, convened for the dispatch of public business, without being forcibly struck by the enormous amount of INFLUENCE possessed by them, apart from their senatorial functions? Who can doubt that if each among them resolved to exert his portion of that influence, comprising wealth, authority, talent, eloquence, and example; to stem the tide of demoralization, and to lighten the pressure of distress, and to elevate the national character . . . the introduction of so vast a portion of wholesome leaven, in so many quarters, would rapidly work for the transformation of the whole mass?[135]

In contrast to more modern moral reform movements, which stressed that effective change or renewal had to emanate from the "grassroots," Tonna remained wedded to the Burkean notion that the real agents for change existed in high places. Rather than simply deferring to the will of the common people, it was principally the prerogative of the governing classes to set forth the moral tone of the nation. Hence aristocrats and political leaders, such as Ashley, did not necessarily share the modern view that reform legislation was more a product of the electorate's prevailing attitudes than a vehicle

---

133. Fryckstedt, "Charlotte Elizabeth Tonna," 98.
134. Ibid.
135. Tonna, *Perils of the Nation*, 280.

A Convergence of Tory Paternalism and Early Victorian Evangelicalism 177

for transforming public opinion. This accounted for why Ashley placed so much faith in parliamentary legislation as the means to transform and humanize the workplace culture of Britain's mills, factories, and mines.

On the issue of state intervention, Tonna advocated a paternalistic approach, which, in her words, would be "guided by the true pole-star, the word of God."[136] Hence, where any enactment on the statute-book was deemed to be "opposed to the will of the Most High," legislators were bound to "labor for its erasure." Drawing from the Old Testament ethic of each master ensuring that their hirelings were not oppressed in wages, Tonna claimed that the legislature held a "guard over the poor man's hard-earned wages."[137] This protective rationale thereby warranted the intervention of the legislature in instances where labourers did not receive due remuneration for their exertions. Acutely sensing the injustice suffered by child factory workers, Tonna concluded that "The state must legislate for the factories: pity, reason, justice, common prudence all demand it."[138] For Tonna, nowhere was the case for state intervention more compelling than in circumstances where the poor were oppressed by the rich. "We repeat that to lighten this merciless pressure of the rich upon the poor, is part of the sworn duty of a British legislator."[139] From Tonna's commentary on the factory system, it was evident this "merciless pressure of the rich" referred to some of the factory owners' treatment of their employees which could not continue unabated. Sharing Tonna's guiding philosophy and impetus for state intervention, Sadler and Ashley each attended to the poor plight of the child labourer in their respective parliamentary campaigns for factory reform.

A further key plank of Tonna's paternalist platform was a national system of education. Tonna argued that the legislature must provide for a "far more extensive and efficient system of national education than has ever yet been proposed." The objectives were again paternalist and Evangelical. In a similar vein to Southey, Tonna believed an organized system of national education would provide the primary mechanism through which the state could exercise its paternal duties to the rising generation. In addition to acting as a vital functionary of the paternalist state, Tonna anticipated that the education system would serve as an invaluable channel through which to infuse the next generation with Christianity. The method of Christian instruction through these schools would be characteristically paternalist and not merely didactic. By doing this, Tonna hoped that the "seed of

---

136. Ibid.
137. Ibid., 277.
138. Ibid., 273.
139. Ibid., 269.

faith" prudently cultivated in each child would be hardy and not "rudely-broken."[140] Of broad educational objectives, Tonna stated: "We want for the rising generation of England, not the power to read obscene books, and to pen seditious placards, but instruction in those Holy Scriptures which are able to make them wise unto salvation, through faith which is in Christ Jesus."[141]

Herein, Tonna's overriding vision for national education was to impart paternalist virtue together with Evangelical instruction. This essentially entailed the promulgation of deference to authority, habits of industry, cleanliness, moral respectability, and an abiding faith in Christianity, all of which Tonna viewed as imperative to advancing British civilization. Given her encounters with Hannah More in the 1820s which had encouraged her in her enterprise of instructing hearing impaired children,[142] Tonna's abiding faith in the reformatory value of a Christian education for young minds owed just as much to the paternalist Southey as it did to the Evangelical More.

Despite Ashley expressing his reservations in 1848 about the national scheme of education favored by Tonna and earlier proposed by Graham's Factory Bill,[143] his RSU project otherwise mirrored Tonna's paternalist and Evangelical ideals for education. From his initial acquaintance with the Field Lane School in 1843, Ashley envisaged the mission of the Ragged Schools to be always two-fold and ensured that this was demonstrably executed by the various schools in his capacity as RSU Chair from 1844. Firstly, the Ragged Schools would fulfill the paternalist function of receiving children from impoverished backgrounds and training them to cultivate habits of cleanliness, respectability and sobriety as well as proficiency in basic literacy, arithmetic and practical life skills. Second, the Ragged Schools would offer this training and instruction within an overtly religious framework enmeshed with scriptural precepts and teachings which, in Tonna's and also Ashley's words, would make the children "wise unto salvation," thereby accomplishing the Evangelical limb of the mission. Commending the work of the Ragged Schools to parliament, Ashley reiterated the findings of an 1847 Committee Report cataloguing the schools' desirable effects on children and the community: "In every point of view, social, moral and religious, they are deserving of countenance; they relieve the wants of the children of destitution—and, above all, they train these destitute ones to habits of

---

140. Ibid., 234.

141. Ibid., 224.

142. Fryckstedt, "Charlotte Elizabeth Tonna," 85.

143. Ashley, "Juvenile Population," HC Debates, *Hansard*, 6 June 1848, Vol. 99, c. 443.

A Convergence of Tory Paternalism and Early Victorian Evangelicalism 179

decency and order, and inculcate that knowledge which, with the blessing of God, maketh wise unto salvation."[144]

With such a positive endorsement of the Ragged Schools, Ashley would have felt vindicated in his judgment that Tonna's approach of combining paternalist training with Evangelical instruction was a winning formula for educating the poorer classes. For Ashley, it seemed apparent that the RSUs were beginning to yield the very fruits of moral refinement and spiritual maturity that Tonna had hoped for in her manifesto.

Tonna's conception of sound governance was indebted to both Tory paternalist and Evangelical notions of leadership. In the tradition of both Burke and Wilberforce, Tonna reminded leaders of their accountability to a higher authority:

> By whatever steps you attained your present eminence, the hand that placed you on it was the hand of God; and to Him must you render an account of your mighty stewardship. For "the Most High ruleth in the kingdom of men, and giveth it to whomsoever He will." He has, for the time being, committed a Kingdom to your guidance, and it is required of you, that you be found faithful.[145]

Tonna urged ministers of the Crown to recover the notion that their career was a divine vocation and not simply a temporal affair; whereby such leaders are not merely elected or appointed but "called by providence to exercise authority as responsible ministers of the crown."[146] This conception of leadership combined classic paternalist emphases on orderly, responsible and accountable government with core Evangelical doctrines of obedience to God and fidelity to the Bible. For Seeley and other Tory Evangelicals such as Oastler, Sadler, and Ashley, these two schools of thought were eminently compatible and mutually reinforcing. Whether specifically Tory paternalist or Evangelical, the desired outcomes of sound governance were typically the same; namely, the realization of a hierarchical but just society characterized by "ordered liberty."

---

144. Ashley, "Employment of Children," HC Sitting, *Hansard*, 6 June 1848, Vol. 99, c. 453–54.

145. Tonna, *Perils of the Nation*, 303.

146. Ibid.

Evangelizing in high places

While Evangelical thinkers and writers commended Tory paternalist values as timely remedies for society's ills in the pre and early Victorian period, the other trend which helped account for the convergence of Evangelical Protestantism with Tory paternalism was the gradual permeation of Evangelical attitudes and habits through the upper echelons of British society. This phenomenon, however, had deeper historical roots dating back to the evangelistic activity of the Clapham Sect amongst the British establishment in the latter half of the eighteenth century. Observing that the late eighteenth-century Regency era aristocracy had been generally permissive in lifestyle and poorly disposed towards Evangelical ideals, David Spring credited the endeavors of the Clapham Sect with the spread of Evangelical Christianity amongst the upper classes of wealthy urban professionals and rural landowners.[147] In particular, Nigel Scotland singled out Hannah More, Thomas Gisborne and William Wilberforce as figures whose writings "each gave strong impetus and encouragement to the higher orders of society" to bring Evangelical principles to bear on national life.[148] In his *Enquiry into the Duties of Men in the Higher and Middle Classes* (1794), Gisborne reminded Evangelicals serving in the House of Lords of what he regarded as their duties to advance religion and morality. Gisborne maintained that the nation would look to the peers "for plans for the elucidation of the Scriptures, the amendment of morals, and the suppression of seminaries of vice; for the establishment of new institutions for the instruction of the poor, and the improvement of those already existing for the rich."[149] Similarly eager to call Evangelicals of the upper class to their public responsibilities, Hannah More used her *Christian Morals* (1813) rhetorically to ask whether influential persons had used their power in "discouraging injustice, in promoting particular as well as general good; in countenancing religious as well as charitable institutions; in protecting the pious, as well as in assisting the indigent?"[150]

The impression of such duties on Evangelicals of the upper echelons resulted in an emerging generation of aristocrats in the early Victorian period who displayed more religiosity in their attitudes and daily habits (i.e., church-going and prayer) than their forbears. Most relevantly, Ashley would exemplify this new, more religious aristocratic generation. Typifying the Evangelical conception of property and privilege as divine blessings, Ashley

---

147. Spring, "Aristocracy, Social Structure and Religion," 265.
148. Scotland, *Evangelical Anglicans*, 51.
149. Gisborne, *An Enquiry into the Duties*, 153.
150. More, *Christian Morals*, 86.

reflected in 1844 that members of his class ought to have "a just estimation of rank and property, not as matters of personal enjoyment and display, but as gifts from God, bringing with them serious responsibilities, and involving a fearful account."[151] By the early Victorian era, these sentiments resonated with many aristocratic families of his generation as they abandoned the more "worldly" pursuits characteristic of aristocratic life such as art patronage, balls, horse races, and theatre-going in favor of regular church attendance, philanthropic service, education, and missionary work.[152] Spring and other historians have identified the Clapham Sect as one of the prime conduits by which Evangelical ideals were transmitted to the upper classes. It was, ultimately, the persuasive and unremitting advocacy of the Claphamites that yielded success in spreading evangelicalism amongst the aristocracy.

The proponents and messengers of Evangelicalism amongst the upper classes did not so much make Christians out of pagans. Rather, they introduced this more overt and public form of Christianity to large numbers of aristocratic families already reared in what William J. Conybeare had identified as the "High and Dry" school of Anglicanism—noteworthy for its affluence and lukewarm temperament.[153] This was certainly the case with Ashley whose own assent to vital religion was attributable not to the formalistic Anglican tradition of his immediate family but, rather, the Anglican Evangelicalism of his nursemaid Maria Millis who had belonged to an Evangelical parish of Woodstock. Other aristocratic heirs similarly touched by Evangelicalism during the early nineteenth century included the Duchess of Beaufort who converted to "vital religion" in 1814 and Lady Olivia Sparrow, who had earlier acquaintances with Wilberforce and Hannah More.[154] Given the preponderance of wealthy landholders in the British parliament, the permeation of Evangelicalism through the aristocracy had positive ramifications for Evangelical representation in both Houses. Bradley noted that, by the 1830s, fourteen Evangelical MPs in the House of Commons were Tories of prosperous landowning families.[155] These included Captain James Gordon (Tory, Dundalk 1831–32), Antony Lefroy (Tory, Longford 1830–32), George Viscount Mandeville (Tory, Huntingdon

---

151. Ashley, Diary Entry (November 21, 1844), Hodder, *Life and Work of the Seventh Earl*, Vol. II, 77.

152. Spring, "Aristocracy, Social Structure and Religion," 268.

153. Spring, "Aristocracy, Social Structure and Religion," 278; Conybeare, "Church Parties," 326, 328.

154. Spring, "Aristocracy, Social Structure and Religion," 278.

155. Ian Bradley, "The Politics of Godliness," 66.

1826–33), Granville D Ryder (Tory, Tiverton 1830–32), Sir Frederick Shaw (Tory, Dublin 1830–32), and Spencer Percival (Tory, Newport 1827–31).[156]

Even where there was no family background of "vital religion," such Tory landholding MPs had found Evangelicalism to be somewhat congenial to their ingrained conservatism. As avowed Protestant constitutionalists, they appreciated the Evangelical emphasis on preserving this settlement and also recognized this form of Anglicanism as providing a solid theological undergirding to their values of social order, deference, duty, and obligation.[157] By the early Victorian period, Evangelicalism, according to Bebbington, was "well-staffed by the aristocracy and gentry," with Victorian subscription lists including sizeable numbers of peers and wealthy landowners.[158] Evangelical landholders could act as catalysts for the dissemination of new ideas and practices amongst their own tenants and employees.[159] Certainly, this was evidently the case at St Giles after 1851 where the new Earl of Shaftesbury had sought to impress his Evangelical habits on the day-to-day operation of the estate. Hodder noted that the new owner appointed a scripture-reader for the district of Horton, planned new schools for Hinton Martell and Woodlands, as well as transforming the parish chapel of St Giles from the appearance of "an old ball room" to an actual "church."[160]

---

156. Rennie, "Evangelicalism and English Public Life," 127; Bradley, "The Politics of Godliness," 280.

157. Rennie, "Evangelicalism and English Public Life," 127–30.

158. Bebbington, "Evangelicalism and Cultural Diffusion," 28.

159. Ibid.

160. Hodder, *Life and Work of the Seventh Earl*, Vol. II, 367, 370.

7

Ashley and the Factory Reform Movement

Considering that the grim plight of oppressed factory children offended the sensibilities of Evangelicals and high Tories alike, the factory reform movement provided an eminently practical outlet for these interests to converge and articulate a shared vision for benign state intervention. Owing to the indebtedness of his philosophical outlook to both these traditions, Lord Ashley was able to advance this cause to considerable effect, with the passage of the Ten Hours Bill in 1847 arguably representing his defining social reform achievement. Accordingly, his parliamentary contribution to the nineteenth-century factory reform movement has justifiably received considerable attention in the biographical studies. Whilst the majority of biographers rightly attribute the humanitarian thrust of the factory reform legislation to Ashley's *personal* Evangelical religiosity or paternalist instincts, discussion of the *broader* radical Tory and Evangelical impulses of the factory reform movement, together with the input from Radical figures such as John Fielden, is somewhat limited. The biographies generally recognize the pioneering role of Michael Sadler, the "behind the scenes" agitation of Richard Oastler and the overtures made by George S. Bull encouraging Ashley to pursue the cause in parliament.[1] However, they do not discuss, nor contextualize in any great depth, the religious convictions and political ideals which animated the parliamentary and extra-parliamentary leaders

---

1. Best, *Biography of A. A. Cooper*, 82; Battiscombe, *Shaftesbury: A Biography*, 70–72; Finlayson, *Seventh Earl of Shaftesbury*, 72–73, 76; Pollock, *Shaftesbury: The Reformer*, 43–45; Turnbull, *Shaftesbury*, 75–77.

of the reform movement. The critically significant figures of Oastler, Bull, and Sadler thus remain relatively obscure with little insight shed on the ideals that they actually espoused and impressed upon Ashley. It was, however, apparent that even before their personal acquaintance with Ashley, the "radical Tory" creed of these factory reformers closely resembled the personal philosophy of the Dorset aristocrat. James Sack defined their Tory radicalism as being based on "normal Christian humanitarianism, on *noblesse oblige* ideals endemic to the traditions of powerful monarchies" and on opposition to "anti- monarchical and anti-clerical" forces.[2]

Turning to the general studies on Victorian era factory reform, John T. Ward primarily understood the factory reform movement as an attempt by the landed gentry to act as a counterweight to industrial capital.[3] By agitating for legislative curbs on unbridled industrial capitalism, rural patricians hoped to infuse a paternalist ethic of social responsibility which was informed by both Evangelical and high Tory principles. In a more recent study, Robert Gray similarly appreciated the Tory-Evangelical influences, but understood factory reform to be more of an episode in the evolution of the working class and a transitional phase in the formation of the early and mid-Victorian "liberal state."[4] In light of these themes, this section will examine each of the factory reform leaders connected with Ashley which included the radical Tory and Evangelical identities of Oastler, Bull, and Sadler. In so doing, it will explore the extent to which their pronouncements revealed not only their Tory and Evangelical sensibilities but also their premises about the role of the landed gentry, their conceptions of the working class and their visions for an interventionist state.

Popularizing factory reform: The Yorkshire Evangelical Tory radicals

As Gray noted, the early Ten Hours movement was heavily infused with the values of "domestic patriarchy, evangelical religion and patrician philanthropy."[5] The key progenitors of such values were the new Yorkshire generation of radical Tories steeped in Anglican Evangelicalism. While Evangelicalism had gradually infiltrated the ranks of the aristocratic classes, a kind of inverse phenomenon also took place, whereby the aristocratic creed of high Tory paternalism began to seep through the middle classes of

---

2. Sack, *From Jacobite to Conservative,* 157.
3. Ward, *The Factory Reform Movement.*
4. Gray, *The Factory Question,* 7–9.
5. Ibid., 22.

British Evangelicalism between the 1820s–40s. In part, this trend was aided by the growing disaffection of middle class Evangelicals from the prevailing liberal Toryism of the day and its seemingly cold-hearted stolidity in regards to the festering problems of poverty and injustice plaguing early Victorian Britain. It was in the West Riding district of Yorkshire, with its combination of Evangelical heritage and textile industry, that the new Evangelical embrace of high Toryism, or "radical Toryism," as it became known in its Yorkshire context, was most evident. Since the missionary exploits of Wesley in the eighteenth century, this region of England had represented something of an evangelical stronghold with large numbers of Anglican and Methodist converts erecting parish churches and chapels throughout the county.[6] Thus, at the time that cities such as Leeds, Halifax, Huddersfield, and Sheffield emerged as burgeoning industrial centers in the early nineteenth century, a thriving Evangelical community still existed in many parts of the county.[7] For this reason, the Yorkshire Evangelicals in many cases were confronted with the harsh realities of industrial life at an earlier stage and perhaps to a greater degree than Evangelicals in other parts of Britain.[8]

Significant numbers of Evangelicals, both clerical and lay, worked amongst these industrial centers and witnessed first-hand the afflictions of the working classes engaged in factories and mills.[9] The dominant social concern of Evangelical preaching seems to have been the inculcation of a "mutual obligation" ethic within a hierarchical order and "the duties of charity incumbent upon the wealthy."[10] Arguably, Evangelical parsons, farmers, artisans, and small-business people felt impelled by a paternalist calling to seek the wellbeing of the working classes in their midst. In this vein, West Riding activists sought to expand their local campaigns for more humane conditions by mobilizing masses of factory and handicraft workers through demonstrations, petitions, election campaigns, and community meetings.[11] Eventually this led to the formation of what became known as "Short Time Committees" in industrial cities across Lancashire and West Riding, thereby

---

6. Bebbington, *Evangelicalism in Modern Britain*, 26. Bebbington noted that in their evangelistic outreach, Wesley and his co-religionists deliberately targeted the growing industrial centres of Yorkshire. These densely populated regions proved to be fertile soil for the cultivation of 'vital religion'; Atkins, "Wilberforce and his Milieux," 33.

7. Rennie, "Evangelicalism and English Public Life," 384–85.

8. Ibid., 378–79.

9. Ibid., 393.

10. Gray, *Factory Question*, 111.

11. Creighton, "Richard Oastler, Factory Legislation," 297.

giving the factory reform movement the popular momentum needed for it to have legislative clout.

The central campaign message of activist leaders such as Bull, Oastler, and Sadler was for a more humane and interventionist state to interpose on behalf of the factory children. Like Southey and the high Tory reviewers, they came to despise political economy and attacked the liberal Toryism of Peel and Huskisson as "earthly, selfish and devilish."[12] Repulsed by the individualist creed of "atomistic" liberalism on both religious and humanitarian grounds, these Yorkshire Evangelicals inclined towards the high Tory paternalism associated with the romantics, ecclesiastics and country squires.[13] In contrast to *laissez-faire* liberal ideology, which defended the rights of industrial employers to employ child labor at their whim and was generally content to allow the excesses of industrial capitalism to go unfettered, Bull, Oastler, and Sadler each welcomed high Tory paternalism as a political philosophy with a conscience. Without resorting to the unacceptable remedies of socialism or Chartism, its appeals for a more controlled and balanced form of industrial development would help mitigate the brute force of unfettered market capitalism.[14] By embracing this creed, they felt it was possible to be less inhibited than the liberal Tories in their advocacy for the industrial working class and the rural poor, yet still be faithful to the traditional social order.[15] Indeed the factory reform activists, like Ashley, viewed the aristocracy and the underprivileged as "natural allies."[16]

With the welfare of the working classes emerging as a common objective for high Tories and popular radicals alike, independent radicals such as John Fielden were able to join forces with the Tory radicals in their advocacy for the Ten Hours bill.[17] Indeed, as critical as the contributions were of Bull, Oastler, Sadler and Ashley to the advance of the factory reform movement in parliament; its success was also indebted to reformist agitators outside the "Tory Evangelical" sphere. As Stewart Weaver recognized, the "justifiably pre-eminent position" within the factory movement of two Tory Evangelicals, "Richard Oastler and Lord Ashley," has "obscured the vital contribution of popular radicals" including William Cobbett, Thomas Duncombe and John Fielden.[18] A Unitarian and a member of the House of

---

12. Ward, *Factory Movement*, 31.
13. Roberts, *Paternalism*, 212–29.
14. Creighton, *Richard Oastler, Evangelicalism*.
15. Henriques, *Before the Welfare State*, 73.
16. Gill, *Parson Bull of Byerley*, 72.
17. Gray, *The Factory Question*, 7; Hilton, *A Mad, Bad and Dangerous People*, 585.
18. Weaver, *John Fielden*, 267.

Commons between 1832 and 1847, Fielden frequently gave voice to the factory reform interests of his Lancashire constituency and his piloting of the Ten Hours Bill through parliament in 1847 represented the culmination of his political career. Like the Yorkshire Tory radicals, Fielden and his popular radicals sought to alleviate the distress of the working classes through the enactment of legislative restrictions on the length of the working day.[19] Unlike the Tory radicals, however, who primarily represented paternalist and Evangelical interests, the popular radicals encompassed an eclectic mixture of farmers, industrialists, Nonconformists, Owenite socialists, and Chartists supporting ameliorative state intervention in the factory system.[20] In this vein, the factory reform movement was not only the manifestation of Tory paternalist reaction or Evangelical social concern but also the first stirrings of working class consciousness and welfare democracy.[21]

Blazing the trail for Evangelical Tory activism: George Stringer Bull

As the first of these Yorkshire Tory radicals, the extra-parliamentary campaigner, George S. Bull (1799–1865), represented something of a trailblazer for Evangelical-Tory activism, particularly in his resolve publicly to plead the cause of the oppressed factory worker. In this capacity, he foreshadowed the work of Ashley whose sustained parliamentary advocacy for factory legislation brought progressive legal protection and relief to this exploited class. Indeed, without his critical conscience-raising role of publicizing the oppressive plight of factory children, it is doubtful the ensuing parliamentary campaign of Sadler and Ashley to ameliorate their condition would have gained quite the same traction. For this reason, he is viewed as being one of the leading lights of the factory reform movement. As an Evangelical Anglican parson, Bull had a vision of transplanting the paternal ideals of his local parish church to the realm of England's factory system. With his track-record of early study at the CMS Missionary House and his commitment to the temperance movement and his Sunday school teaching activity, Bull's Evangelical Anglican credentials were fairly well-established.[22] The parson had built a school, organized temperance lectures, encouraged benefit soci-

19. Ibid., 2.
20. Ibid., 3.
21. Ibid., 267.
22. Scotland, "Bull, George (Stringer)," 162–63; Gill, *The Ten Hours Parson*, 2, 4, & 31. At p. 2, Gill introduced Bull as "an Evangelical clergyman who worked in Bowling and Bradford for fourteen crucial years."

eties and visited the poor before joining fellow-reformer, Richard Oastler, to campaign for the Ten Hours Act.[23]

This foregoing Tory-Evangelical activity thus seasoned him for the arduous crusade against the injustices of the prevailing factory system. Reflecting Tory and Evangelical concerns, Bull published a pamphlet entitled "A Respectful and Faithful Appeal on behalf of the Factory Children" which catalogued the evils of the modern factory system. These included its prevention of education and religious instruction, its detrimental effect on home life and morals and the tyranny it afforded many masters. Of the system, he wrote, "the possession of power, without sufficient responsibility or control, is enough to make any man a despot or extortioner." Bull was enthusiastic about the potential for the Ten Hour movement to remedy many of these foregoing ills, lauding its policy objective as a "God-like" measure.

By immersing himself in the campaign for factory reform, Bull had the opportunity to give full expression to both his Evangelical and conservative patrician sympathies, citing these as his two motiving impulses to alleviate human suffering:

> Of course it is my continual desire and object as a minister of Christ, and as a friend of the social order to soften all such impressions as these, and to endeavour to encourage kindly feelings and feelings of contentment; but I am sure I find it very difficult under present circumstances to make that impression upon their minds in this respect which I could wish, for they immediately refer me to the increasing duration of their labour and its decreasing remuneration; the only salve that I can apply to such a wound is to hope that their condition will be ameliorated.[24]

Viewing his newfound responsibility to reform the factory system as inseparable from his existing parish responsibilities, Bull addressed a pro-factory reform mass meeting in 1832 with this declaration of support:

> I beg leave to support this resolution. As I entered this room, I heard a person say, "What have the parsons to do with it?" Sire [sic], they have a good deal to do with it; and I conceive that a most fearful responsibility rests upon those Ministers of the Gospel to oppose all the influences they possess against any system which tends to prevent the moral improvement and religious advance of the people....[25]

23. Gill, *Ten Hours Parson*, 21.
24. Bull quoted in Gill, *Ten Hours Parson*, 64.
25. Leeds papers for first days of January 1832 cited in Gill, *Ten Hours Parson*, 20.

Although a member of parliament and not a cleric, Ashley equally shared Bull's conviction that the public responsibility to seek the welfare of the working classes was inextricably bound up with one's personal religious piety. For both men, it seemed profoundly incongruous to be worshipping a God who exhorted his people to fend for the cause of the fatherless, the widow and the poor; whilst at the same time, displaying a rank indifference to the human suffering in their midst. Accordingly, the incidence of child laborers groaning under the weight of an unchecked industrial system rendered any Christian defense of *laissez-faire* political economy to be morally untenable.

Following Sadler's loss of his parliamentary seat of Leeds in the December 1832 general election, Bull was eager to seek out a suitable successor for the parliamentary factory reform campaign. Desiring to recruit somebody in his own image, Bull sought a candidate who was a Tory *and* an Evangelical.[26] The candidate was to be an authentic Tory paternalist who recognized the moral blight of the modern factory system upon the traditional social fabric of England. Tory leadership of the campaign was deemed essential because, without it, the movement could easily be made to appear but one aspect of radical agitation. As a staunch Tory, the last thing Bull desired was any association with the socialist or Chartist movements. In addition, this Tory candidate was to be a deeply pious individual whom like, Sadler, was convinced of the righteousness of the cause before God.[27]

With these criteria, it was hardly surprising Ashley emerged as the natural successor to Sadler, with Bull lauding his prospective candidate as "noble, benevolent and resolute in mind."[28] In his 1833 letter to the Ten Hours' Bill Committees, Bull did not elaborate on Ashley's Evangelical convictions, which were then still taking shape, but was satisfied nonetheless with Ashley's express undertaking that it was "his duty to God and the poor" to lead the parliamentary campaign.[29] Finally accepting Bull's offer to succeed Sadler after much prayer and deliberation, Ashley invariably viewed the factory reform issue in religious terms: "It was a great religious

---

26. Gill, *Ten Hour Parson*, 81. Bull stressed that "Only in the Tory party" could the factory reformers "hope to find a leader whose outlook resembled theirs."

27. Ibid., Initially, Bull considered approaching the Evangelical MP, Sir Andrew Agnew, but his individualistic Whig tendencies rendered him less than suitable. Agnew then suggested to Bull that Lord Ashley might undertake the task of leading the factory reform campaign; hence Bull sought out Ashley who finally agreed.

28. *Correspondence of the Rev George Stringer Bull to Short-Time Committees*, London, February 6, 1833, in Oastler, *Fleet Papers*, 214.

29. Ashley quoted in Oastler, *Fleet Papers*, 214.

question; for it involved the means to thousands and tens of thousands of beings brought up in the faith and fear of the God who created them."[30]

As with Bull, he viewed the factory children as created in God's image and, as such, were endowed by their creator with innate physical, intellectual, and spiritual faculties in need of nurture and development. Whilst the factory system could be credited for providing children with the opportunity to work and utilize their physical capabilities, the excessively long shifts it demanded came at the detriment of nourishing their more intellectual and spiritual lives through both the family home and an adequate system of education offering Christian instruction. Alluding to the deleterious effects of long work hours on the emerging behavioral patterns of children, Ashley expressed his concerns to the House of Commons in 1840:

> Now let the House hear the consequences of this defect of education—the result of this overwork in the first years of life:—They leave their homes at an early age, and they spend the surplus of their wages in smoking, drinking and quarrelling. Boys of thirteen will not unfrequently [sic] boast that they have taken to smoking before they are twelve. Early marriages are very frequent. They take their wives from the coke hearths, the mine, and coal-yard, having had no opportunities of acquiring any better principles or improved habits of domestic economy.[31]

Thus it was only by curtailing the daily hours of toil that sufficient time could then be allocated to the socialization, education and spiritual nourishment of children in accordance with what appeared to him to be God's purpose to bless and equip each succeeding generation.

While Bull and Ashley both affirmed that the paternal responsibilities of the Evangelical extended beyond the church walls to the whole of society, they had each arrived at this position through somewhat different pathways. As a parson charged with the pastoral responsibilities of teaching and tending to the welfare of his working-class congregation, the paternal mindset was almost second nature to Bull. Like Wesley, he had ministered amongst the working poor in his curacy at Byerley and came to see his parish as extending to the community at large. Given that the people to whom he personally ministered were suffering at the hands of the industrial system, he believed that it was his responsibility to mitigate this system's harmful effects despite the source of his people's grief lying outside the ambit of his church. For this reason, Bull believed that, if the welfare of all people, both

---

30. Ashley quoted in Gill, *Ten Hour Parson*, 82.

31. Lord Ashley, "Employment of Children," HC Debates, *Hansard*, 4 August 1840, Vol. 55, c. 1264.

within and outside the church, was to be advanced; he had the responsibility to be a paternalist agent for change within the wider world.

Ashley, on the other hand, had been a lifelong layman with none of Bull's experience as a pastor. As a keen student of Southey's romantic literature in his late twenties and early thirties, Ashley had imbibed the poet's idealized philosophy of a benign and solicitous paternalism that contrasted starkly with the form of paternalism practiced by his father. It was from his gradual assent to Evangelical Protestantism as a young adult, however, that this abiding sense of public duty acquired a distinctively religious flavor. Accordingly, he believed that, whilst his *raison d'être* of life had always been to further the common good, this was to be done in a way that accorded with what he understood to be the will and purposes of his God. Thus, in short, Bull, the Evangelical parson, had added Tory paternalism to his outlook; whilst Ashley, the Tory patrician, had added Evangelicalism to his philosophy, thereby bringing the two men into fraternal agreement.

Reconciling Evangelical faith with Tory politics: Richard Oastler

Converted to the factory reform cause in 1830 through his encounter with the Bradford-based worsted spinner and Evangelical Tory, John Wood,[32] Richard Oastler (1789–1861) similarly personified the newfound coalescence of high Tory paternalist and Evangelical interests, thereby representing a natural forerunner to Ashley. Applauding Ashley's attributes of "rank, character, talents, industry and influence," Oastler regarded the parliamentary successor to Sadler in the Ten Hours cause as an indispensable asset that Peel and his new administration would be foolish to reject.[33] Born to devout Wesleyan Methodist parents and educated in a Moravian school, Oastler drank from a similar well of evangelical spirituality and practiced the evangelical habits of prayer, public worship, and Bible reading. As a young man, he became a local preacher for the Methodists and a visitor for the Bible Society.[34] Recognizing the more hierarchical and traditional nature of the Established Church as being in greater alignment with his emerging high Toryism, Oastler eventually became an Anglican Evangelical by the close of the 1820s.[35]

---

32. Hargreaves "Richard Oastler and Yorkshire Slavery," in Hargreaves and Haigh (eds), *Slavery in Yorkshire*, 5.
33. Oastler, *Fleet Papers*, Vol. I (September 18, 1841), 302.
34. Driver, *Tory Radical*, 5, 16–17, & 21.
35. Rose, "Oastler, Richard," 839–40.

Part III: Ashley and the Emerging Synthesis

For Oastler, the belief systems of high Tory paternalism and Evangelical Christianity were eminently compatible:

> I am a Tory of the old school. I despise the term 'Conservative'. It is only a dilution of a pure principle. A Tory must be a Conservative.... He would destroy all oppression, cruelty, tyranny and Malthusianism and have a sound and Christian legislation based upon that old-fashioned book, the Bible.[36]

In disowning the more general "Conservative" label in 1842, this Evangelical consciously identified himself with the high Tory paternalist limb of English conservatism, thereby dissociating himself from the more economically liberal, Peelite tradition of the Tory Party which was less than partial to the question of factory reform and other similarly interventionist measures to ameliorate economic injustice. Accordingly, Oastler developed a personal social philosophy, which had much in common with Southey's defense of traditional society and its pillars of the Crown, the Church, and the aristocracy. In 1841, Oastler sought to dispel conceptions that his factory reform agitation was a threat to the established order by boasting that "there is no man living who has more sincerely and disinterestedly defended the rights of the aristocracy than myself."[37] Like Southey, Oastler desired greater harmony and intercourse between social classes and thereby called on the "nobles" to follow Ashley's example and "freely mix with the working men."[38] Affirming his high Tory convictions, he called for "modern wiseacres" to "take lessons from our ancient sages" and to "above all, and before all," restore the national Church to its "pristine purity and consequent utility."[39]

Although Oastler did not hail from quite the same landed aristocratic background as Ashley, his affinity with country life was no less great. As in the case of Ashley, his attachment to the countryside had inescapable repercussions on his emerging political outlook. Observing the stately manors and carefully manicured lawns of rural Yorkshire, Oastler perceived a keen sense of the continuity of life and of institutions.[40] Moving into the estate of Fixby Hall in 1820, Oastler soon assumed the typical responsibilities of a landowner, managing a vast tract of land encompassing multiple

---

36. Oastler, *Fleet Papers*, Vol. II (March 26, 1842), 102.
37. Oastler, *Fleet Papers*, Vol. I (January 14, 1841), 30.
38. Oastler, *Fleet Papers*, Vol. I (August 14, 1841), 264.
39 Oastler, *Fleet Papers*, Vol. I (January 23, 1841), 32.
40. Driver, *Tory Radical*, 27.

cottages, farms, collieries, quarries, and turnpike investments.[41] Regarded as the "surrogate squire of Fixby" on account of its absentee landlord, Thomas W. Thornhill, Oastler drifted from the urban Whiggism of his youth and embraced the high Toryism of the country squires. In the very conception of "gentleman" he saw a wealth of significance. It connoted ancient ideals and the security of accepted ways; it implied duties and responsibilities and leadership; it involved, in fact, the whole matrix of personal relationships that composed the pyramid of society.[42] To the proud new landowner, all these intangibles seemed to find their manifestation in the bucolic surrounds of Fixby. With Oastler positioning himself as a simple English country-squire, Gray appreciated his "contribution to the construction of Tory paternalism."[43] In assenting to these ideals, Oastler was resolved to live them out as the steward of his estate. Accordingly, he revived the old landholding customs just as the new Earl of Shaftesbury would do upon inheriting his St Giles estate. Affirming the traditional paternal duties of the squire, both men sought to befriend their cottagers and each ensured that they received adequate provisions.

For Oastler and Ashley, the obligation of the aristocracy to protect the rights of the poor and needy was a non-negotiable article in their creed of Tory paternalism. Articulating his political philosophy to his *Fleet Papers* readership in 1841, Oastler explained accordingly:

> A Tory is one who, believing that the institutions of this country are calculated, as they were intended, to secure the prosperity and happiness of every class of society, wishes to maintain them in their original beauty, simplicity and integrity. He is tenacious of the rights of all, but most of the poor and needy, because they require the shelter of the constitution and the laws more than the other classes.[44]

In a blunt warning to the aristocracy, Oastler reminded them that "only while they respect the rights of others, can they expect their own to be maintained. If they persist in robbing the poor, they must expect retaliation and revenge."[45] The belief that the poor and needy required the most protection impelled both Oastler and Ashley not only to remind the aristocracy of it moral duties but also to campaign for greater state intervention in the industrial labor force. For each of these men, the most poor and needy per-

41. Hargreaves, "Richard Oastler and Yorkshire Slavery," 1–2.
42. Driver, *Tory Radical*, 27.
43. Gray, *Factory Question*, 53.
44. Oastler, *Fleet Papers*, Vol. I (January 30, 1841), 39.
45. Oastler, *Fleet Papers*, Vol. I (January 14, 1841), 30.

sons were the vulnerable and much exploited child laborers. Whether they were toiling away on the factory floor, or down the mine, or inside the colliery or outside on the brickfield or the farm, this laboring class of children desperately needed the state to interpose on their behalf to afford relief and legal protection from unscrupulous employers. For these Tory Evangelicals, the purposes of such intervention were not merely to "sanctify" the industrial system in accordance with biblical principles and to demonstrate basic human decency and compassion to an oppressed class of people—as important as these two objectives were; but, in addition, they sought to ensure the material wellbeing and contented state of the working class. Oastler warned the aristocracy that "if they persist in robbing the poor, they must expect retaliation and revenge."[46] Thus, by securing the happiness of the poorer classes, the institutions of the country would be deemed to have served their proper purpose, thereby negating the plea of more radical voices for their change or removal.

As a life-long Evangelical, Oastler encountered little difficulty in reconciling his newfound Tory paternalism with his existing religious beliefs. Viewing the archetypal Tory as also a Christian, he explained in his *Fleet Papers* of 1841 how both belief systems affirmed social order and interdependency within society:

> A Tory is a staunch friend of order for the sake of liberty; and knowing that all our institutions are founded upon Christianity, he is of course a Christian, believing with St Paul that each order of society is mutually dependent on the others for peace and prosperity, and that although there "are many members, yet there is but one body" ... Sir, I am just such a Tory ....[47]

Moreover, he saw both traditions as accepting the sovereign will of God and stressing dutiful deference to a Supreme Being. Evangelicals and high Tories alike believed in the doctrine of "one's assigned station and its attendant duties," obliging an individual to make a contribution to society commensurate with their talents and endowments. As an Evangelical of the Established Church, Oastler's integration of his Tory paternalism was aided by the fact that a longstanding alliance between Toryism and the Church of England had existed since the seventeenth-century. Despite the grievances of Recordite Evangelicals and high Tories over the recent concessions granted to Nonconformists and Roman Catholics, the historic rapport between the Established Church and the Tory party had largely withstood the recent 1828–29 constitutional reforms of Wellington's Tory administration.

46. Oastler, *Fleet Papers*, Vol. I (January 14, 1841), 31.
47. Oastler, *Fleet Papers*, Vol. I (January 30, 1841), 39.

Dissenting forms of evangelicalism, on the other hand, did not enjoy the same historic affinity with Toryism and tended to align themselves with Whiggery.⁴⁸ The Church of England's pre-eminent status within the British polity, together with its hierarchical structure and corporate style of worship, tended to lend itself better to Tory values than the somewhat more egalitarian and individualistic-minded Nonconformist churches. With high Tory paternalism augmenting his Anglican Evangelical tradition, Oastler felt repelled by the aggressive individualism espoused by the new mercantile capitalist class presiding over the modern industrial system.

Accordingly the conflict between the high Tory landowners and the Whig industrialists had not only a conspicuous class dimension but also a sectarian element of antipathy between Church and Dissent. As Ursula Henriques noted, the fact that many of these mill-owning capitalists in the West Riding and Lancashire identified as Noncomformists accounted for the "tinge of Anglican intolerance" in the rhetoric of Oastler and the broader Short Time Movement for factory reform.⁴⁹ In his crusade against the factory system, Oastler's invective was directed not only against "Whigs" but also the "sleek, pious, holy and devout Dissenters."⁵⁰ Similarly, Gray observed that attitudes to the factory question were affected by religious and denominational affiliation.⁵¹ Given the dominance of "Old Dissent" in the new industrial class of factory entrepreneurs, Nonconformist ministers from the denominations of Old Dissent were rarely to be seen joining Anglicans and Methodists on Ten Hours platforms.⁵² Where Anglican Evangelicals such as Oastler, Sadler, and Ashley could be associated with paternalism and traditional social institutions, evangelical Dissenters, on the other hand, could be linked to commerce, industry, social, and moral progress.⁵³ Like the Clapham generation of Anglican Evangelicals, Nonconformists were generally wary of government intervention in the economy, believing that the injustices of the factory system could be best remedied by prudent self-regulation.⁵⁴ Thus high Tory Evangelical Anglicans such as Oastler often tended to view *laissez-faire* liberal individualism and Protestant Nonconformity as two sides of the same coin.

48. Larsen, *Friends of Religious Equality*, 37.
49. Henriques, *Before the Welfare State*, 74.
50. Driver, *Tory Radical*, 299.
51. Gray, *Factory Question*, 52.
52. Ibid. 'Old Dissent' referred to the English Nonconformists including Congregationalists, Baptists and Independents who had generally parted from the Established Church after the Restoration of 1660.
53. Gray, *Factory Question*, 114.
54. Hoppen, *The Mid-Victorian Generation*, 96.

In common with Ashley, Oastler believed it was possible to mitigate this individualism by injecting the traditional paternalist ethic of social obligation, deriving from rank and station, into the modern factory system.[55] It was hoped that a renewed sense of social obligation would awaken factory managers to put an end to many of the abuses afflicting juvenile employees, particularly the regimen of inordinately long work hours. In contrast to the *laissez-faire* policy underpinning the existing factory system, Oastler and his fellow campaigners stood for a revivified high Toryism which conceived of a society where the interests of no single class should be allowed to dominate the rest.[56] With respect to the factory system, this meant that the profiteering interests of the capitalist factory owners ought not to overrule the interests of the working classes, particularly the category of vulnerable child labourers for whose welfare it was necessary to enlarge opportunities for leisure, recreation, education, and spiritual nourishment. Dismissing Whiggery as only likely further to entrench the power of the capitalist operatives, Oastler believed that a rejuvenated high Toryism was the only suitable remedy for correcting abuses in the factory system.[57] In this vein, Oastler's rhetoric appeared evidently to conform to Ward's classic interpretation of the factory reform movement as a concerted effort by the landed gentry to act as a counterweight to industrial capital by reviving the high Tory paternalist ethic of "social responsibility."[58] Like Southey, *Blackwood's* and the *Quarterly Review*, campaigners such as Oastler bewailed the passing of the paternal relationship between the upper and lower orders and thereby sought to give it a new birth in the industrial context.[59]

Accompanying his attachment to Tory paternalism and Evangelical Protestantism was Oastler's profound antipathy towards *laissez-faire* political economy. Like Seeley and Tonna, Oastler regarded this system, with its perceived idolization of wealth and capital detracting from human wellbeing as wholly incompatible with not only traditional high Tory precepts but Christianity. In the postscript to his *Eight Letters to the Duke of Wellington* (1835), Oastler had excoriated political economy's liberal philosophy: "The Demon called Liberalism who is now stalking through the land scattering absolute want in the richest cornfields, and the deepest distress amongst the bustling rattling of our looms . . . this Demon will be found to have been the

---

55. Driver, *Tory Radical*, 112.
56. Ibid., 203.
57. Ibid., 204.
58. Gray, *Factory Question*, 7.
59. Henriques, *Before the Welfare State*, 8.

enemy of true religion and the prosperity and well-being of man."[60] Under the system of *laissez-faire*, Oastler could see the evils of ignorance, intemperance and frustration exacting their terrible toll on society unchecked.[61] Unless the state could interpose by enacting humane legislation, such maladies would only multiply and fester. Accordingly, Oastler appealed for the re-establishment of a regulatory system grounded firmly upon the welfare of the working classes. Invoking a combination of Evangelical and Tory paternalist motifs, Oastler enunciated his philosophy of the proper role for civil government and its duties:

> God has appointed the proper stations and ranks for each. ... Why, then, should any starve who are surrounded by such means of acquiring plenty? It is solely, Sir, because the duty of our Governors is neglected ... they entirely neglect the great object for which they are appointed—to take supervision of the wants of the people, and the best means of providing for their comforts and necessities.[62]

Thus for society truly to reflect what he deemed to be God's order and purpose, Oastler maintained it was necessary for government to fulfill its objective of taking supervision of the wants of the people. In practice, this would entail the intervention of the state in the industrial system to provide opportunities for the working classes to pursue their desires for greater leisure, education and spiritual nourishment.

Pursuing his grand project of factory reform through parliament, Ashley shared Oastler's keen awareness that his combination of Tory paternalist and Evangelical objectives were set for a direct collision course with the agenda of political economy.

> I had to break every political connection, to encounter a most formidable array of capitalists, millowners, doctrinaires, and men, who, by natural impulse, hate all "humanity-mongers." They easily influence the ignorant, the timid, and the indifferent; and my strength lay at first ("tell it not in Gath!") among the Radicals, the Irishmen, and a few sincere Whigs and Conservatives.[63]

By alluding to the derisive term "humanity-mongers," Ashley deliberately sought to highlight the disdain many political economists felt towards

60. Richard Oastler, *Eight Letters to the Duke of Wellington*, 173.
61. Driver, *Tory Radical*, 297.
62. Oastler quoted in Driver, *Tory Radical*, 427.
63. Shaftesbury, quoted in Nash, "Sixty Years of Empire," 3.

reformers like himself who desired to humanize the industrial system. The term itself belied a sneering contempt for those who accorded priority to the wellbeing of humanity over and above the more materialistic and utilitarian considerations of efficiency, productivity, profit, and capital. It was this very attitude of the political economists that Ashley sought to expose as the "repulsive mindset" standing in the way of just and humane state intervention. Given the traditional preference of the landed gentry for *localized* paternalism, the calls of Oastler and Ashley for a paternalist approach by *government* demonstrated that the factory reform movement was more than simply a revolt by the landowning class against industrial capitalism. Rather, as Gray recognized, it was a critical phase in the evolution of the Victorian "liberal state."[64] The agitation for factory legislation in the 1830s and 1840s was really the early sign of more state interventionist measures to follow. The Whig administrations of Russell and Palmerston introduced significant reforms in factory regulation, public health, and sanitation which gave added substance to the Victorian liberal state.[65] Although Oastler remained primarily a provincial figure, whose activity was chiefly confined to his home county of Yorkshire, John Hargreaves was nonetheless correct in his assessment that Oastler and his factory reform campaign had "a far-reaching impact on the social history of nineteenth century Britain."[66]

Michael T. Sadler: Towards an "Evangelical" doctrine of state interventionism

Michael Sadler was not only a key figure behind the formation of Ashley's high Tory paternalist philosophy but also a pioneering parliamentary leader of the pre and early Victorian factory reform movement. As Kim Lawes recognized, Sadler's brief but significant parliamentary contribution to the factory reform movement "has largely been overshadowed by the prominence given to Lord Ashley."[67] Although Sadler's Ten Hours Bill differed little in substance from John Hobhouse's 1831 act, his avowedly paternalist and Evangelical rationales for pursuing the factory reform measure resonated with Ashley and are thus worthy of examination. Whereas fellow Tory-Evangelical figures such as Bull, Oastler, Seeley and Tonna had each played a critical part in formulating a social ethic equally indebted

---

64. Gray, *Factory Question*, 9.

65. Roberts, *Tory Paternalism and Social Reform*, 332 ; Brown, *Palmerston*, 343–47; Mandler, *Aristocratic Government*, 236–70.

66. Hargreaves, "Richard Oastler and Yorkshire Slavery," 21.

67. Lawes, *Paternalism and Politics*, 150.

to conservative patrician values and Evangelical ideals, Sadler was the first such figure to enter parliament. Thereby he was in a position to bring his distinctive worldview directly to bear on the legislation and policy of the day. Elected to the House of Commons in 1829, Sadler was able to voice the concerns of the Tory-Evangelicals on the floor of parliament, the chief of these being the need for the state to interpose on behalf of the poor and helpless child laborers. To this end, Sadler was largely responsible for tabling the landmark *Report of the Select Committee on the Bill for the Regulation of Factories* (1832).[68] In its macabre exposé of the existing factory system, the *Report* served as a catalyst for the ensuing parliamentary campaign to introduce factory legislation.

Spearheading this reform, Sadler was the first parliamentarian not simply to articulate but *exercise* the new Evangelical doctrine of state interventionism advocated by Bull and Oastler in their respective community campaigns, and subsequently expounded by Seeley and Tonna in their publications of the early 1840s. Rooted in the soil of Evangelical social ethics, particularly Old Testament precepts, this doctrine of state interventionism was essentially guided by the Tory paternalist objectives of affording guidance and protection to society's needy, together with the amelioration of prevailing physical and social ills. Accordingly, as the practitioner of this doctrine, Sadler appealed to what he regarded as the Evangelical principles of justice and mercy as the great inspiration and justification for legislating to afford necessary protections to factory labourers. As Sadler's successor in the parliament, Ashley continued to exercise this doctrine of state intervention with speeches in support of paternalist legislation typically drawing upon biblical injunctions to defend the poor and helpless.

Sadler's attachment to the Tory cause was longstanding; as a young man he became a frequent contributor to the *Leeds Intelligencer*, the leading paper in Yorkshire for the Tory party.[69] In 1807, he also assisted the Tory-aligned Wilberforce in his bid to represent the constituency of York.[70] As both a Tory and Evangelical, he was an ardent Protestant constitutionalist. In one of his early speeches in Leeds on the vexing issue of Catholic Emancipation in 1813, Sadler declared:

> Sir, the Protestant cause has long been identified with that of the British nation. May they never be separated! But we are firmly convinced, that to concede to its great adversary the power it seeks to recover . . . would be to dilapidate the venerable fabric

---

68. Nardinelli, "Child Labour and the Factory Acts," 739–40.
69. Seeley, *Michael Thomas Sadler*, 15.
70. Ibid., 16.

> of that happy constitution erected by the wisdom and cemented by the blood of our ancestors; would shake the very pillars on which the Protestant throne of these realms is founded; would invalidate the title of the present Protestant royal family; would threaten the existence of the Protestant establishment; would change many of our laws and subvert many of our sacred institutions[71]

Thus, Sadler was impelled to defend traditional values and institutions because he was a conservative who felt the need to maintain them purely for the sake of order, continuity, and stability; but as an Evangelical, too, he saw their preservation as critical owing to their inherently *Protestant* identity. As a loyal Church of England Evangelical, Sadler powerfully combined Southey's "Church and Constitution" Toryism with the "national Protestantism" of the Recordite Evangelicals," whereby the Protestant character of the nation would need to be robustly asserted in order to stave off the perceived threats of either a resurgent Roman Catholicism or a "creeping Infidelity." During the 1820s, Sadler gradually integrated his Evangelical philanthropy with his Tory paternalist political ideology. As Sadler's successor, Ashley was committed to this same conservative creed of national Protestantism, even going so far as to view Protestantism and conservatism as two sides of the same coin. Expressing disillusionment at the direction of some of his Tory party colleagues, whom he regarded as forsaking many of the traditional paternalist ideals that had hitherto defined an authentic conservative, Ashley affirmed that "the only conservative principle is the Protestant religion as embodied in the doctrines and framework of the Church of England."[72]

As with Oastler, Bull, and Ashley, Sadler's hue of Toryism was avowedly paternalist and of the non-liberal variety. His friend and biographer, R. B. Seeley, described its leading objectives as being "to foster, protect, cherish, encourage and promote," while "presenting to human beings the motives of benevolence and hope."[73] Seeley encapsulated Sadler's somewhat lofty conception of paternalist rule with this closing exhortation:

> In short, deal paternally with your people, and they will repay your care. Feel for them; supply those wants which they cannot supply for themselves; guard them from the oppression of those

---

71. Sadler quoted in Seeley, *Michael Thomas Sadler*, 19.

72. Lord Ashley, Diary Entry (23 January, 1840), in Hodder, *Life and Work of the Seventh Earl*, Vol. I, 166.

73. Seeley, *Michael Thomas Sadler*, 33.

who would "make haste to be rich," and you will reap an abundant harvest of internal strength and permanent tranquillity.[74]

It was to these ends that Sadler's reform campaigns were essentially directed. In contrast to the creed of self-reliance preached by the political economists, his outlook rested on the paternalist premise that vulnerable classes of persons simply did not possess the wherewithal to look after themselves and thus required the state to interpose on their behalf. As Gray appreciated, the factory acts supported by Sadler constituted "a classic case-study in state intervention in the framework of economic and political liberalism" during the 1830s and 1840s.[75]

Throughout his career, Ashley made similar appeals to the parliament to discharge its paternalist obligations, particularly to those classes of people who were deemed helpless. On this occasion, pleading for the cause of the chimney-sweep children in the 1860s, Shaftesbury entreated his parliamentary colleagues: "I appeal to you now on behalf of another class of weak and suffering humanity. I ask you to protect, not adults, who can take care of themselves, but the helpless young, many of them orphans, and some the offspring of cruel and unnatural parents."[76] Shaftesbury thus viewed this vulnerable class of chimney-sweepers as not merely materially poor, but poor in the sense that they lacked a strong and dependable family background. Esteeming the family as the mainstay of social stability and prosperity, the absence of this vital support unit rendered these children to be acutely helpless, thereby attracting the *loco parentis* jurisdiction of the state.

Together with his Evangelicalism, Sadler's paternalism impelled him to adopt the cause of the factory children whom he viewed as a particularly vulnerable class of subjects in need of legislative protection. Speaking on an 1832 Bill "for regulating the labor of children and young persons in the Mills and Factories of this country," Sadler told the House of Commons:

> I have prepared the way for the conclusion, that children, at all events, are not to be regarded as free labourers; and that it is the duty of this House to protect them from that system of cruelty and oppression to which I shall presently advert. . . . The protection of poor children and young persons form those hardships and cruelties to which their age and condition have always

---

74. Ibid., 621.

75. Gray, *Factory Question*, 5.

76. Lord Shaftesbury, "Chimney-Sweepers and Chimneys Regulation Bill (No. 76)," Committee, HL Debates, *Hansard*, 3 June 1864, Vol. 175, c. 1132.

rendered them peculiarly liable, has ever been held one of the first and most important duties of every Christian legislature.[77]

This contrasted sharply with *laissez-faire* voices who argued that factory children, or at the very least their parents, were free and autonomous agents possessing an unfettered right to work without undue encumbrances from the state. Political economy generally regarded state intervention in the labor force as not only an unwarranted impediment to individual freedom, but also as a handicap to the realization of maximum productivity and prosperity in the national economy.

While not opposed to free enterprise, Sadler and Ashley were convinced that political economy's overriding focus on material aggrandizement tended to eclipse less material considerations pertaining to the social and moral wellbeing of workers.[78] For the two reformers, it was all very well for factory children to be earning a wage, but at what cost to their spiritual nourishment, intellectual development, family life, recreational opportunities and leisure time? The two men were essentially convinced that the philosophy of political economy was found wanting in its failure holistically to address the human needs of workers, particularly those of children employed in factories and mines. With the contemporary factory system representing one of its chief manifestations, political economy was seen to foster a cold and detached indifference, devoid of any protective instinct or paternal care towards the wellbeing of factory children.

Whilst still in parliament, Sadler was conscious of a kindred spirit in Ashley whom Bull entrusted with the leadership of the parliamentary factory reform campaign after 1832. Ashley embodied both Sadler's "vital religion" and Tory paternalism, thereby representing his natural successor. As was the experience with Ashley, Seeley observed that Sadler's "first steps, in early life, were taken in the safest of all paths, reverence for, and implicit belief in God's word; and pity for the poor."[79] With their Evangelical social concern attended to by an innate conservatism, each man felt a profound attachment to the old English system of care for the poor, that benevolent paternalism of the country landholder much romanticized by Southey and the Lake poets. This corresponded with a thorough detestation of the modern opponents and detractors of that system; namely, the Malthuses,

---

77. Michael Sadler, "Factories' Regulation Bill," HC Debates, *Hansard*, 16 March 1832, Vol. 11, cc. 345 and 349.

78. Lawes, *Paternalism and Politics*, 110.

79. Seeley, *Michael Thomas Sadler*, 568.

Martineaus, Marcets and others associated with the school of political economy seen to be propelling the new factory system.[80]

Accordingly, the sympathies of both men lay with the plight of agricultural laborers as well as that of the urban factory children toiling under the yoke of industrialization. So overt was the problem of agrarian poverty for Sadler, particularly in Ireland, that he remarked it was "scarcely possible for any one thing to be made more clear and indubitable, than is the way in which our agricultural poor may be raised from their present too general depression."[81] As with ameliorating the hardships of the factory children, Sadler added that legislative interference was "absolutely essential." Although Ashley may not have had quite the same exposure to rural destitution as Sadler who had spent his earlier years among the agricultural poor, his suspicion of agricultural malpractices, such as the truck system on Dorset properties (including his own father's estate), ensured that the plight of farm laborers did not escape his attention. After campaigning for children employed in factories, mines and collieries, Ashley shifted his focus towards the plight of children employed in agricultural gangs, and to this end, supported remedial legislation.[82]

80. Ibid.
81. Ibid., 584.
82. Lord Shaftesbury, "Agricultural Gangs," Motion for Address, HL Debates, *Hansard*, 12 May 1865, Vol. 179, cc. 174–77.

8

"Something Admirably Patrician in His Estimation of Christianity"

Continuing Sadler's factory reform campaign in the Commons for the legislation of the "ten-hour day," Lord Ashley emerged as his natural heir in both policy objective and philosophical temperament. Like Sadler and his fellow travelers, he personified the confluence of Evangelical and high Tory paternalist interests that had occurred over the preceding decade or so in British life and was determined to perpetuate its influence in public policy for as long as he remained active in parliament. Ashley had a vision to reform along Tory Evangelical principles, not only the industrial workplaces of factories, mills, mines, collieries, and brickfields, but also the mode of education; the weekly pattern of work and rest; the residential environment of working-class families; the medical treatment of mentally insane patients and even the treatment of animals.

To this end he embarked on an ambitious reform agenda which oversaw the eventual enactment of the "ten-hour" working day: the proscription of children under the age of thirteen from employment in factories and other industries; the steady expansion of "Ragged Schools" to educate poor and destitute children; the construction of cottages to house working class families in relatively salubrious conditions; the provision of adequate sanitation for urban communities; the introduction of more humane treatment and rehabilitation for mentally ill patients; and the outlawing of animal vivisection. If these facets of daily life in Victorian Britain could be reformed to reflect what he believed to be the loving fatherhood of God and the redemptive power of Christ—together with one's duty to protect the weak, fend for the poor, and nurture the young—Ashley would consider his life-mission a success. Also appreciating the link between Ashley's Evangelicalism and Tory paternalism, Michael Roberts reflected that "It was this class and religion-tinged sense of chivalry which was to drive many an individual paternalist—Lord Ashley most notably of all—into the campaign for state regulation of child and female labor."[1]

It was not only Ashley's policy agenda inside the parliament, but also his philanthropic activity outside of it, which typified this fusion of Evangelicalism and high Tory paternalism. Ashley's Evangelical sense of providence instilled a paternalistic obligation to provide protection and care for the weak which, in turn, gave birth to philanthropic activity. In conjunction with his parliamentary efforts to ameliorate the working conditions of workers, Ashley patronized the Labourers' Friends Society and subsequently assisted in founding the Society for Improving the Condition of the Labouring Classes (SICLC). In 1858, the Seventh Earl articulated the guiding purpose behind his philanthropic endeavors:

> All society can do it ought to do to remove difficulties and impediments; to give every man, to the extent of our power, a full, fair and free opportunity so to exercise all his moral, intellectual, physical and spiritual energies, that he may, without let or hindrance, be able to do his duty in the state of life to which it has pleased God to call him.[2]

As the above philosophy revealed, Shaftesbury did not so much view philanthropy as a mere "hand-out" and an "end in itself," but, rather, more as a means to enable individuals to be self-sufficient and become positive contributors to society themselves.[3] Here, the Earl espoused the perennially conservative ideals of self-reliance and mutual obligation within an overarching framework of the individual's calling by God to work and serve in accordance with His purposes.

Conforming the episcopate to his own image: Shaftesbury's appointment of bishops

In ecclesiastical affairs, also, the combination of Evangelicalism and Tory paternalism in the outlook and approach of Lord Shaftesbury was palpable, particularly in his role as "bishop maker" during the Palmerston years.

---

1. Roberts, *Making English Morals*, 155.
2. Shaftesbury, *Addresses of the Earl of Shaftesbury and the Hon W. F. Cowper*, 9–10.
3. Finlayson, *Citizen, State, and Social Welfare*, 90.

Given the Earl's responsibility in the 1850s for providing counsel to his father-in-law, Lord Palmerston, on the appointment of new bishops to the Church of England, it was of no coincidence that a large proportion of the episcopal appointees reflected a similar combination of Evangelicalism and paternalism to the figure who had recommended their promotion. With the Prime Minister, Palmerston, entrusting Shaftesbury with the task of recommending episcopal appointments to him, primarily on the basis that he regarded his more devoutly Anglican son-in-law as possessing a superior grasp of ecclesiastical affairs,[4] Shaftesbury arguably viewed this as a timely opportunity to impress both his Evangelicalism and paternalism on the character of the English episcopate. Whilst Palmerston did not share his son-in-law's ardent Evangelicalism, he nonetheless had a decided preference for the Low Church party accompanied with a suspicion of Tractarian ritualism.[5] Thus, Shaftesbury found Palmerston's ecclesiastical policy generally amenable to his own preference for proposing Evangelical candidates to episcopal vacancies. As to the Evangelical credentials of these new appointments, Shaftesbury recalled in 1865 that:

> the first bishops were decidedly of the Evangelical School; and my recommendations were made with that intention. . . . I was resolved to put forward men who would preach the truth, be active in their dioceses, be acceptable to working people, and not offensive to the Nonconformists. He [Palmerston] accepted my suggestions on these very grounds, and heartily approved of them.[6]

In accordance with the pan-evangelical vision he imbibed from Bickersteth, Shaftesbury desired Anglican prelates who would work constructively with Nonconformist leaders in the furtherance of the broader evangelical cause. As Nigel Scotland acknowledged, however, not all of Palmerston's appointees were Evangelicals, with only eight out of fourteen belonging to this school of Churchmanship.[7]

Constituting a majority of the new appointments, nonetheless, the Evangelical bishops represented a visible presence in the Anglican hierarchy during the 1850s and 60s. Given that their selection was largely determined by Shaftesbury, it was telling that this cohort of new Evangelical prelates similarly embodied a combination of Claphamite and Recordite

---

4. Scotland, "*Good and Proper Men*," 5.

5. Ibid., 21, 25–26.

6. Lord Shaftesbury, Diary Entry (1865), cited in Hodder, *Life and Work of the Seventh Earl*, Vol. III, 196.

7. Scotland, "*Good and Proper Men*," 51.

characteristics. Two of the new bishops, W. Thomson and F. Jeune, were drawn from the older, moderate Claphamite tradition, which was less adventist and more measured in tone than the Recordites. For Shaftesbury, these two bishops would continue the Clapham approach of providing a respectable, reasoned and credible Evangelical apologetic to the educated and professional classes. To complement these appointments, six other bishops including H. M. Villiers, C. Baring, R. Bickersteth, S. Waldegrave, J. T. Pelham, and J. C. Wigram, were selected from the Recordite school. With the ascendency of the Tractarian movement and a resurgent Roman Catholicism posing new challenges for Evangelicals, Shaftesbury believed that the forthright and uncompromising Protestantism of the Recordites was needed effectively to neutralize the influence of "ritualism" within the Church hierarchy.

One of these Recordite appointees, Robert Bickersteth, was in fact the nephew of Edward Bickersteth, one of Shaftesbury's great mentors and confidantes. Like that of his uncle, Bickersteth's Evangelicalism was unequivocal with his support for Evangelical societies and mission agencies, his staunch adherence to the authority of scripture and his antipathy to both Anglican ritualism and Roman Catholicism.[8] In recommending such an appointment, it was highly plausible that Shaftesbury regarded R. Bickersteth to be the most apt and natural successor to the elder Bickersteth, the very figure to whom Shaftesbury attributed much of his own Evangelicalism. Thus, by elevating Bickersteth to the episcopate, he had sought to align the theological disposition of the Anglican hierarchy a little closer to his own.

Palmerston's new cohort of bishops was distinctive for not only the preponderance of Evangelicals but also the large number of prelates who exhibited distinctively *paternalist* traits. From the various profiles of the new appointees, it was evident that Shaftesbury's ideal candidate for the episcopate was somebody who reflected the Evangelical priorities of biblical preaching, mission, and evangelism *together* with the paternalist hallmarks of filial responsibility and concern for the welfare of the vulnerable. Desiring to inject his paternalist ideals into the Church hierarchy, Shaftesbury encouraged Palmerston to appoint bishops who would be familiar with the plight of the poor and willing to render ameliorative pastoral care. Palmerston appointed bishops who recognized the need for bold initiatives that would engage with the poor, elevate them from their condition and, where possible, provide them with education and a spiritual framework for their lives.[9] Thus Bishop Robert Bickersteth recognized the urgent need to estab-

8. Ibid., 53.
9. Ibid., 61.

lish facilities for the education of the poor,[10] while Bishop Jeune expressed his grave concern that a number of schools in the diocese were left "in a lamentable state as to discipline and attainment."[11] Like the country landowners who had neglected the upkeep of their estates and the wellbeing of their workers, previous church leaders had abandoned their paternalist duties. Seeking to emulate in his diocese some of the social schemes proposed by the *Blackwood's* paternalists, Bishop Charles J. Ellicott encouraged his clergy to provide allotment land and to establish friendly societies and working-men's clubs for the rural poor.[12]

As Scotland recognized, the prevailing philosophy of the bishops was generally one of paternalist rule rather than liberal self-help. In contrast to Church leaders such as Chalmers, who had encouraged individual parishioners to initiate charitable enterprise,[13] Palmerston's Anglican bishops saw it as their prerogative to provide aid and poor relief "from above." This was reflected in the pronouncements of bishops, such as Harold Browne, who were inclined to take it upon themselves to improve the condition of the poor without giving the laborers the wherewithal to accomplish this task themselves.[14] Thus, the interventionist nature of such episcopal oversight bore decidedly closer resemblance to the Tory paternalism of Southey and the *Quarterly Review* than the liberal Toryism of Chalmers

In the oversight of their dioceses, Palmerston's bishops sought to reinvigorate the paternalist culture of Anglicanism with its intrinsically hierarchical paradigm and priestly tradition of shepherd-like stewardship. In common with Tory paternalists such as Southey, Sadler, and Ashley, the bishops were concerned that the classic paternalist duties of filial responsibility, guidance, and training had been neglected by a previous generation of leaders. Within the ecclesiastical context, they were therefore resolved to oversee the expansion of paternalist initiatives such as education and poor relief. Moreover, the paternalist outlook of the bishops could be attributable to the fact that a large number of them hailed from aristocratic families like Ashley and Palmerston. Scotland appreciated the significance that four

---

10. Bickersteth, *A Sketch of the Life*, 231

11. Jeune, *Charge delivered to the Clergy*, 12, in Scotland, "Good and Proper Men," 64.

12. Ellicott, *The Church and the Rural Poor*, 14–15, in Scotland, "Good and Proper Men," 69.

13. Chalmers, "Causes and Cure of Pauperism," 20. Chalmers urged individuals to save themselves from the condition of pauperism 'by the exertions of their own industry, and the frugality of their own management'.

14. Browne, *The Clergyman in Social Life*, 12, in Scotland, "Good and Proper Men," 71.

of Palmerston's Evangelical bishops—namely Villiers, Baring, Pelham, and Waldegrave—were from aristocratic Whig families with several of the other appointees coming from influential, landed families.[15] Whilst there was nothing historically unusual about Anglican prelates hailing from the upper echelons of society, it was telling that most of Palmerston's appointees had actually had first-hand experience of working in parishes largely consisting of poorer, working-class people.

In contrast to earlier bishops such as Howley, Hinds, and Blomfield, who had remained typically within the scholarly circles of the elite, this new breed of aristocratic prelates had ventured across the class divide.[16] This resembled not only an outworking of their Evangelical, missionary strategy to reach new people groups with the gospel, but also their paternalist impulse to intervene in the affairs of the working classes. This enmeshment of Evangelical and paternalist objectives in Palmerston's bishops visibly reflected the Evangelical and aristocratic impulses of Shaftesbury. On the one hand, Shaftesbury had been a zealous supporter of evangelistic outreach to the working classes through initiatives such as the RSUs and London City Mission whilst, on the other hand, his paternalism had impelled him to foster more personal and filial ties between the classes. Once again, it was evident that Shaftesbury in the 1850s sought the opportunity to align the English episcopacy closer to his own Evangelical and paternalist sympathies.

Making Evangelicalism a patrician creed

As well as building upon the forgoing convergence of Evangelical principles and Tory paternalist attitudes that culminated in the factory reform campaign, it would be reasonable to deduce that Ashley's robust and enduring Tory Evangelicalism owed much to the formative influences of his personal life. While it was evident that his determination to cultivate a radically different form of paternalist leadership from his father, together with the influence of the high Tory Southey, imbued him with lifelong conservative patrician attitudes, how was it that he not only became an Evangelical, but indeed remained an Evangelical *and* a Tory? It has already being established that Ashley's Evangelicalism was indebted to the early influence of his nursemaid, Maria Millis, with this nascent "seed of faith" subsequently nourished by the theological works of Doddridge and Scott in Ashley's twenties, followed by the input of Bickersteth from his mid-thirties. With this firm grounding in vital religion, however, Ashley remained firmly wedded to

15. Scotland, *Good and Proper Men*, 37.
16. Ibid., 60–61.

the Tory paternalist principles of the kind propounded by non-Evangelicals such as Southey and Coleridge.

Like fellow Evangelicals Seeley and Sadler, Ashley appreciated the complementarity between high Tory paternalist principles and Evangelical social teaching, particularly in their calls for the greater care of the poor and protection for the weak. Ashley's amalgamation of Evangelicalism and Tory paternalism was certainly made easier by the example of his mentor, Bickersteth, who emerged as a conspicuous Evangelical voice for advocating high Tory paternalist ideals. Mirroring the approach of Southey and the Tory reviewers, Bickersteth used his publications in the 1830s and 1840s to denounce the "avarice" and "selfishness" of political economy whilst calling for ameliorative state intervention, factory reform, and the restoration of harmonious relations between the upper and lower orders of society.

In addition, Ashley's capacity to synthesize these two traditions in the 1830s and 1840s was no doubt aided by the broader political and religious realignments taking place on the cusp of the Victorian age. The evolution of his political and religious outlook coincided with the period in which the post-Clapham generation of Evangelicals and Southey's high Tory paternalists were beginning to forge common ground on such issues as the ethical soundness or otherwise of political economy, the appropriate treatment of the poor, the defense of the Protestant Constitution, the necessity of factory reform and the merits of an interventionist state. The high Tory-inspired ideals of a constitutionally supreme Church of England, a benign interventionist state and a social paradigm of filial class relations largely stemmed from the pens of romantic writers such as Southey and Coleridge. Consequently, the explicit appropriation of these paternalist motifs by key Evangelicals such as Bickersteth, Oastler, Sadler, and Ashley essentially reflected what Bebbington diagnosed as the "inflow of the Romantic movement into Evangelicalism."[17]

Thus, with his own personal combination of Evangelicalism and high Tory paternalism, Ashley had the benefit of being able to exploit this "romantic inflow" to advance his social reform agenda. His ability to add a distinctively patrician quality to Evangelicalism was recognized by one of his contemporaries who penned a letter to the Earl in 1882:

> You have not only elevated the Christian faith in the eyes of the multitude, and in the judgment of its not too friendly critics. You have given to that particular school of Christian doctrine with which you are identified a certain aristocratic *cachet*. You have made Evangelicalism a popular and even patrician creed[;]

---

17. Bebbington, *Evangelicalism in Modern Britain*, 84.

> . . . you have done a great deal to convince the governing classes in England that they have more to hope than to fear from the influence of Christian teaching on the multitude. There is something admirably patrician in your estimate of Christianity. You would not for one moment admit that it was in its inception, a levelling, or anything else but a well-born and well-bred, movement.[18]

With this evolving paternalist character of nineteenth-century Evangelicalism representing the consequence of wider trends and phenomena in both religious and political thought, it could not possibly be attributed to Ashley alone. Nevertheless, it underscored the extent to which Ashley was perceived by some observers to be the epitome of an emerging paternalist-infused Evangelicalism in the Victorian era.

18. Kosmos, "Letters to Eminent Persons," 5.

Part IV

Ashley and the Milieu of Victorian Evangelicalism

9

Locating Ashley's Place within the Victorian Evangelical Terrain

Ashley, together with Bickerseth, was essentially a "transitional" Anglican Evangelical who combined characteristics of both the older Claphamite and newer Recordite generations. As such, where did he fit within the landscape of Victorian Anglican Evangelicalism and to what extent did the Victorian Ashley represent the tendencies and preoccupations of the religious movement? In the world of Anglican Evangelicalism, the early Victorian era witnessed the eclipse of the dominant Clapham or *Christian Observer* "school" of Evangelicals by a cluster of new Evangelical groups that emerged in the 1830s. Whilst the Victorian heirs to the Claphamites did not altogether fade (as instanced by the elevation of Evangelical moderates such as William Thomson and Francis Jeune to the episcopate under Palmerston)[1] their prominence was nonetheless overshadowed by new arrivals on the Evangelical stage. These included Recordites such as Haldane and Seeley, the Yorkshire radical Tory Evangelicals Bull, Oastler and Sadler,[2] and on the fringes of the movement, the small prophetic 'Albury circle' of Edward Irving and Henry Drummond's radical premillennialists.[3]

Whilst these subgroups of Victorian Evangelicalism differed in their internal cultures, practical strategies and approaches to doctrinal matters, such as the precise mode of premillennial eschatology, they were together responsible for giving Evangelicalism a more aggressively Protestant and

---

1. Scotland, *"Good and Proper Men,"* 52.
2. Scotland, *Evangelical Anglicans*, 63–66.
3. Carter, *Anglican Evangelicals*, 158–59.

conservative disposition at the onset of the Victorian age. As Bebbington appreciated, this ensuing tone of Victorian Evangelical religion marked an appreciable departure from the cautious pragmatism and reasoned moderation of the Clapham "Saints."[4] In contrast to the Claphamite generation who were influenced by the assumptions of the Enlightenment, particularly with respect to their views on the "natural" laws of economics, the succeeding generation largely drank from the cistern of romanticism which was manifest in both their premillennial eschatology and romantic Tory conception of church and state.

Given his own immersion in the high Tory romantic thought of Southey and his evolving friendship with the Recordite Haldane, Ashley was ideally placed to identify closely with the temperament and preoccupations of Anglican Evangelicalism in the Victorian age. The interests of this religious movement were indeed manifold, and not every one of these can be catalogued apropos of Ashley but the extent to which he embodied the more salient of these will be surveyed. Navigating the terrain of Evangelicalism in their specialized studies of the faith in the Victorian age, Hylson-Smith and Scotland identified some of its defining contours, all of which occupied a conspicuous place in the thought and activity of Ashley. These included the complex relationship between Evangelical Anglicans and Nonconformist evangelicals,[5] the prominence of the "Recordite school,"[6] the circulation of premillennial eschatology,[7] the connection between mission and the British imperial enterprise,[8] the impulses of Jewish mission and Christian Zionism,[9] the struggle for the soul of the Established Church amid the challenges of Roman Catholic resurgence, Tractarian advance, and rationalist influence,[10] the Victorian cult of domesticity,[11] the championing of the "Victorian Sunday,"[12] and the continued cultivation of "the voluntary society" as a vehicle for philanthropy, mission, and evangelism.[13]

4. Bebbington, *Evangelicalism in Modern Britain*, 75.

5. Hylson-Smith, *Evangelicals in the Church of England*, 177–79.

6. Hylson-Smith, *Evangelicals in the Church of England*, 96, 102; Scotland, *Evangelical Anglicans*, 53, 134.

7. Scotland, *Evangelical Anglicans*, 172–80.

8. Ibid., 292–96.

9. Ibid., 173–77.

10. Scotland, *Evangelical Anglicans*, 139–45, 315–40; Hylson-Smith, *Evangelicals in the Church of England*, 111–21, 133–41.

11. Hylson-Smith, *Evangelicals in the Church of England*, 105–6; Scotland, *Evangelical Anglicans*, 404.

12. Scotland, *Evangelical Anglicans*, 181–204.

13. Ibid., 83–84.

In their respective surveys of Victorian Evangelical traits, however, references to Ashley (later Shaftesbury) are typically limited with minimal discussion about his personal position on a given issue. Although Hylson-Smith did assign a portion of his chapter on "Evangelicals in Action" to "Lord Shaftesbury,"[14] it focused chiefly on his contribution to factory reform and philanthropy but not his attitudes on such questions as imperialism, Jewish emancipation or the status of women. In a similar vein, Scotland provided a subsection on the social reformer appraising his factory reform achievements, activity on the General Board of Health and political party allegiance[15] but, again, did not provide comprehensive insight into the thinking of Ashley across the broad spectrum of issues eliciting the attention of Victorian Evangelicals. This paucity of analysis on the social reformer's religious, political, and social perspectives, however, is by no means confined to the general narratives of Victorian Evangelicalism such as those of Hylson-Smith and Scotland. With the exception of Donald Lewis' study on Christian Zionism,[16] the specialized studies to date on relevant Victorian themes such as the Sabbath, imperialism, race, domesticity, and gender featured little or no commentary on Ashley and his views.[17]

Accordingly, the purpose of this part is to take the defining preoccupations of Victorian Evangelicals and then interpret the original sources of Ashley/Shaftesbury to explore critically his mindset on each of these matters. By analyzing each of these themes in turn, this section will gauge the extent to which Ashley's pronouncements and activities represented the prevailing culture and disposition of Victorian Evangelicalism. It will become apparent that on some issues, such as domesticity and philanthropy, the approach of Ashley and his co-religionists accorded with the earlier Clapham tradition; whilst, on other matters, such as premillennial eschatology and anti-Catholicism, Ashley's posture resembled that of his Recordite contemporaries. The section will thus conclude that, despite its enduring continuity with the earlier Clapham school of Evangelicalism in some critical areas, Ashley's Anglican Evangelicalism was largely a reflection of

---

14. Hylson-Smith, *Evangelicals in the Church of England*, 196–201.

15. Scotland, *Evangelical Anglicans*, 74–82.

16. Lewis, *Origins of Christian Zionism*, 107–24, 146–72. Lewis, in particular, discussed the evolving attitudes and pronouncements of Ashley on Jewish affairs.

17. For example, Wigley in *Rise and Fall of the Victorian Sunday* made brief references to Shaftesbury's advisory role in Palmerston's appointment of bishops at 93 & 113, but made no mention of his personal pronouncements on the Sabbath. Davidoff and Hall in *Family Fortunes* made only a brief reference at 84 to Ashley's status as stepson-in-law to Palmerston, but not to his outlook on gender and family issues.

its contemporary Victorian context, with its hallmarks chiefly resembling those of the Recordites.

Ecclesiastical foes or gospel brethren? Ashley and relations between Anglican and Nonconformists evangelicals

While discussion of Ashley's Evangelicalism in the Victorian age will primarily be within the context of his own Anglican sphere, it is important at the outset to examine the extent to which his Evangelicalism bore similarities and differences to that of Victorian Nonconformity. To appreciate this comparison, it is first necessary to explore Ashley's evolving personal views on Nonconformity. Recognizing he was conscious of his Anglican identity long before he also considered himself an Evangelical, Ashley acknowledged that his early views of Nonconformists typified the thinking of Churchmen at the beginning of the nineteenth century when the Anglican and Protestant Constitution of England was still assured. In a conversation with his biographer, Hodder, he recalled that "he was brought up in the old high-and-dry school [of the Church of England], and believed it was a meritorious thing to hate Dissenters."[18] While it has already been appreciated that the Anglicanism of Ashley's upbringing was far from deeply pious, it was nonetheless zealous to maintain the constitutional union of church and state and, accordingly, regarded Nonconformity as a threat to this settlement. Impressed with this mindset, the young Ashley was inclined to distrust interdenominational bodies such as the Bible Society that were seen as "evil and revolutionary institutions" opposed to "Church and State."[19]

With the first stirrings of Evangelical faith in his mid-twenties, however, his opposition to Nonconformity began to soften as he appraised the merits of Nonconformist leaders and writers such as the Congregationalist, Philip Doddridge.[20] After reading the Bible commentaries by the Anglican Thomas Scott, who wrote of his sympathy and admiration for Doddridge, he soon learned that there was another Anglican school of thought that held Nonconformists in high esteem, particularly those of the evangelical variety. In contrast to the "high and dry" Anglicanism Ashley had been accustomed to as a child, Scott's avowedly Evangelical Anglican tradition recognized many Nonconformists who shared the same commitment to evangelical

---

18. Hodder, *Life and Work of the Seventh Earl*, Vol. I, 44.
19. Ibid.
20. Ibid.

Protestant orthodoxy as "brethren." Ashley's awakening to the alternative outlook of Scott served to dispel his early assumption that Nonconformists were incapable of "doing any good in the world."

As Ashley's Evangelical views matured under the tutelage of Bickersteth, he came to warmly regard Nonconformist evangelicals as brethren and vital partners in the endeavors of Christian education, Bible dissemination, urban outreach, philanthropy, and overseas mission. As will become apparent, this attitude accounted for his strong support of the Evangelical Alliance and other ventures fostering pan-evangelical unity. At the same time, however, Ashley's enduring high Tory paternalism brought him into disagreement with his Nonconformist co-religionists, particularly on the issue of church establishment. Whilst welcoming the growth of evangelicalism in other denominations, Ashley remained fiercely committed to the primacy of the Established Church as both a repository of sound Protestant doctrine and an institutional bulwark of the confessional Christian state. In that respect, his romantic high Toryism differed from the typical liberal Whig philosophy of Nonconformists who favored disestablishment and ecclesiastical equality. In contrast to the traditional Established Church order favored by Tory Evangelical Churchmen such as Ashley, Nonconformists believed that a plurality of free churches existing in a free state was most conducive to the flourishing of religion and morality.

Both Ashley's similarities and differences with Evangelical Nonconformity in the Victorian age were nowhere better encapsulated than in his friendship with the Baptist preacher, Charles Haddon Spurgeon (1834–92). On matters of theology, the Anglican aristocrat and Reformed Baptist pastor were soul-mates in their unshakeable fidelity to the supreme authority of the scriptures, their distaste for doctrinal modernism, and even their philanthropic activity.[21] In political temperament, however, the differences between the two practitioners of vital religion were stark. In contrast to the Tory-aligned Ashley, Spurgeon detested the Tory party and the values it stood for. His antipathy towards Tory politics was expressed in the midst of Benjamin Disraeli's campaign for re-election in 1880:

> Are we to have another six years of Tory rule? . . . Are we to go on slaughtering and invading in order to obtain a scientific frontier and feeble neighbours? How many wars may we reckon on between now and 1886? . . . Let those who rejoice in war vote for the Tories. . . . Shall all great questions of reform and progress

---

21. Turnbull, *Shaftesbury*, 199–200.

be utterly neglected for years to come? They will be, unless true liberals come to the front.[22]

This scathing denunciation of what he regarded as the Disraeli administration's bellicosity in foreign policy revealed Spurgeon's chronic opposition to Toryism and its imperialistic spirit. According to David Smith, he remained an implacable enemy of British imperialism and jingoism all his life and resisted the growing trend towards a civil religion given respectability by its association with Christian symbolism.[23] To be sure, Ashley was also critical of British imperial policy on occasions, but he generally maintained faith in the potential goodness of the Empire as an instrument for advancing Christianity and civilization.

With the election of an avowed atheist to public office in 1880, the differing reactions of Shaftesbury and Spurgeon were also telling. Whilst Shaftesbury decried the election as unbecoming of Britain's profession to be a Christian country and a sad departure from religious convention, Spurgeon welcomed it as a "blessing" in that it demonstrated modern Britain's religious toleration—a liberty previously denied to Spurgeon's own denomination.[24] For Shaftesbury the Churchman, the preservation of Christian institutions and traditions was obviously paramount, whilst for Spurgeon the Nonconformist, it was the realization of religious freedom that was of prime importance. In so expressing their positions, each man succeeded in typifying the prevailing outlook of his own tradition within Victorian pan-evangelicalism.

To what extent, then, did Shaftesbury's relationship with Spurgeon typify that between Evangelical Anglicanism and Nonconformity at large in the Victorian age? On the basis of existing historical accounts, the case study of Ashley and Spurgeon by no means appeared to be atypical of the general relationship between the two limbs of Victorian evangelicalism. Leonore Davidoff and Catherine Hall observed that, like Ashley, "Anglicans and Nonconformists found much to agree on and large areas within which, despite other agreements, they were fully able to co-operate."[25] Their shared belief system entailed the conviction of original sin, the possibility of re-

---

22. Spurgeon quoted in Smith, *Transforming the World*, 55.

23. Ibid., 56.

24. Correspondence between C. H. Spurgeon and Shaftesbury, 1876–84. Neither Spurgeon or Shaftesbury revealed the identity of this elected 'atheist'. It is quite possible they may have been referring to Charles Bradlaugh (1833–91) who was elected to the House of Commons as the Member for Northampton in 1880. A member of the Liberal Party, Bradlaugh had founded the National Secular Society in 1866 and was reputedly one of the most well-known English atheists of the nineteenth century.

25. Davidoff and Hall, *Family Fortunes*, 87.

demption through the divine mission of Christ, the central importance of the family and the call to live a holy life of prayer and good deeds.[26] In enterprises such as the RSUs, the BFBS, the LCM, and the EA, Evangelicals and Nonconformists found themselves working side-by-side. Despite sharing an evangelical canon of doctrinal fundamentals, together with the common objectives of evangelism, mission, and philanthropy, the repeal of the Test and Corporations Acts and the granting of Catholic Emancipation served to sharpen political differences between Anglican and Nonconformists from the 1830s.[27]

In contrast to Tory Evangelical Anglicans such as Bickersteth, Seeley, Tonna, Oastler, Sadler, and Ashley, who supported the Establishment, paternalist state intervention and economic protectionism, Nonconformist Victorian evangelicals rallied around the causes of disestablishment, religious equality, *laissez-faire* economics, and free trade.[28] In his excoriation of the Establishment in 1833, the Congregationalist leader Thomas Binney described the Established Church "as a great national evil" and an "obstacle to the progress of truth and godliness in the land."[29] Thus, while Anglican Evangelicals esteemed the Establishment as an instrument for cultivating the gospel, Dissenters, on the other hand, saw it as the supreme obstacle to the advance of the Kingdom of Christ.[30] Unlike Evangelical Churchmen who feared that Jewish Emancipation would deliver yet another blow to the confessional state, Nonconformists welcomed the 1858 reform as an affirmation of religious equality. As Timothy Larsen noted, the differing political approaches of each side were aptly summed up by Disraeli who recognized the Anglicans as motivated by "defending the principle of religious truth" and Nonconformists as impelled by "promoting the principle of religious liberty."[31]

Differences between Anglican and Dissenting evangelicals in the Victorian age were socio-economic as well as political. While Anglican Evangelicalism appealed to "those who count" and attracted growing numbers of the aristocracy, Dissenting evangelicalism offered a "place to feel at home" to the newly affluent, and the urban working classes were left to conclude that, however much they might be attracted to Jesus, these churches had

26. Ibid., 74, 87.
27. Ibid., 98.
28. Larsen, *Friends of Religious Equality*, 118.
29. Smith, *Transforming the World*, 30.
30. Ibid.
31. Larsen, *Friends of Religious Equality*, 130.

little to offer them.[32] The Nonconformist, Edward Miall, realized that the association between institutional Evangelical religion and the "aristocratic sentiment" led to the alienation from the churches of masses of people for whom elite culture was both foreign and despised because it was recognized as a badge of those responsible for the oppression of the poor.[33] Characteristically, the Nonconformist Spurgeon distanced himself from the symbols of elite culture in an attempt to communicate with ordinary people.

Across the denominational divide, Ashley was all too aware of this alienation and this impelled his efforts to make Anglican Church services more working-class friendly. Accordingly, Shaftesbury issued this blunt message in 1857 to the Established Church in the House of Lords:

> . . . the working-classes, when they attend the services of the Establishment, generally find the churches pewed up in the very aisles—that they are shut out from places where they can hear and be well accommodated, and not placed on a footing of equality with the rest of the congregation. . . . Unless, therefore, you show them proper respect . . . the vast proportion of the labouring population in London, will never be brought to attend the worship of the Establishment.[34]

Whilst remaining a creature of the Anglican-dominated aristocracy, Shaftesbury was eager to bring the British working classes within the Evangelical fold. For his Evangelicalism to remain a potent force he desired not only doctrinal uniformity but also class harmony. A spiritually disenfranchised working class, after all, would pose a threat to the hegemony of the Established Church and the traditional social order. The best way to neutralize such a threat, therefore, was not only to bring the working classes within the reach of evangelical Protestantism generally, but specifically within the churches of Anglican Evangelicalism. Evidently, the relationship between Ashley's Anglican Evangelicalism and Victorian evangelical Nonconformity was underpinned by a complex amalgam of ecclesiastical, political and class interests that both converged and conflicted, but nevertheless allowed for sustained cooperation.

---

32. Smith, *Transforming the World*, 31.

33. Ibid., 37.

34. Shaftesbury, Religious Worship Act Amendment Bill, Second Reading, HL Debates, *Hansard*, 8 December 1857, Vol. 148, c. 329.

Identifying with *The Record*: Ashley's friendship with Haldane

With the onset of the Victorian age, Ashley's maturing Evangelicalism owed much to his evolving friendship with Alexander Haldane (1800–1882), the Scottish-born Anglican proprietor and unofficial editor of the influential *Record* newspaper. Trained as a barrister in Edinburgh, he was originally associated with the 'Albury circle' of radical premillennialists which included Edward Irving and Henry Drummond.[35] Haldane, however, later came to adopt the more outward-focused and activist premillennialism of the Anglican Evangelicals as he distanced himself from the pessimistic fatalism of the "Irvingite" school. Combative in temperament, robustly Calvinist, politically conservative, prophetic, premillennial, anti-rationalist, anti-Catholic and uncompromisingly Protestant, the Anglican Haldane came to typify the emergent generation of Anglican Evangelicals in the pre and early Victorian age. His *Record* publication would become the mouthpiece of the new Anglican Evangelicals, just as the *Christian Observer* represented the organ of the old Clapham-generation of Anglican Evangelicals. Accordingly, the *Record*'s aggressive tone and militant Protestantism contrasted with the *Observer*'s somewhat more moderate and conciliatory tenor.

Attuned to the dominant concerns expressed by Ashley and other Anglican Evangelicals of the Victorian age, the *Record* campaigned vocally against Roman Catholicism, Tractarianism, and rationalism whilst stoutly defending biblical orthodoxy, championing the English (Protestant) Constitution beloved of Tories and promoting pan-evangelical unity.[36] Despite his claim that the *Record* "represented only a narrow spectrum of evangelical religion," Frank Turner acknowledged that it "achieved influence far beyond evangelical circles by virtue of its high circulation of four thousand copies."[37] Even within the Evangelical realm, W. J. Clyde Ervine argued that the *Record*, of all publications, represented the stance of most Anglican Evangelicals.[38] In its ability to amplify the politically and theologically conservative sentiments of Victorian Anglican Evangelicals, the *Record* became synonymous with this religious movement, where "for many people, Evangelicalism

---

35. Corsbie, *Biographical Sketch of Alexander Haldane*, 12. Led by Edward Irving and comprised largely of Scottish and Ulster premillennialists of the 'introversionist' school, the 'Albury circle' convened annually for a series of prophetic conferences staged at the Albury Park estate of Henry Drummond.

36 Altholz, "Alexander Haldane," 23–31.

37. Turner, *John Henry Newman*, 40.

38. Ervine, "Doctrine and Diplomacy," in Lewis, *Lighten their Darkness*, 17.

meant the *Record*."³⁹ Ian Rennie claimed that the *Record* may well have been "considered the most important single influence on the Evangelical party in the Victorian age."⁴⁰

Initially critical of the *Record* for what he saw as its abrasive and graceless tenor, Ashley came to appreciate this bold new mouthpiece of Evangelicalism as a kindred spirit and ally in his own crusade for Protestant truth, thus a friendship ensued between the parliamentary social reformer and the *Record* proprietor.⁴¹ Although Haldane initially had little interest in the humanitarian legislation of Ashley, their shared opposition to Tractarianism in the 1850s brought the two men closer together as strong friends and co-religionists.⁴² After the death of Bickersteth in 1850, Haldane took his place as Ashley's principal "counselor and friend."⁴³ The two stalwarts of Victorian Evangelicalism collaborated together in the campaign against rationalism and the *Record* proprietor became a useful "sounding board" for Shaftesbury in the 1850s and 60s after he was delegated responsibility for appointing bishops under the premiership of Palmerston.⁴⁴ With Haldane's death in 1882 marking the end of a thirty-five year friendship, Shaftesbury paid tribute to his spiritual soul-mate:

> He [Haldane] believed intensely in the Lord Jesus, His power, His office, His work. He intensely loved Him, and ever talked with a holy relish and a full desire for the Second Advent. A long life, one less of personal activity than of religious intellectualism, was devoted to the advancement of Christ's Kingdom and to the temporal and eternal welfare of the human race. His sole hope was in the all-atoning blood of our blessed Saviour; any approach to a doctrine of works was his abhorrence . . . .⁴⁵

In an age where he saw Victorian society increasingly turning away from the "old paths" of Evangelicalism with the advance of naturalistic science and reason, together with the ascendency of higher biblical criticism in ecclesiastical ranks, it was Haldane's steadfast and robust Evangelical Protestantism that Shaftesbury found most appealing.

39. Altholz, "Alexander Haldane," 26.
40. Rennie, "Evangelicalism and English Public Life," 77.
41. Finlayson, *Seventh Earl of Shaftesbury*, 102–5, 160–61.
42. Ian S Rennie, "Haldane, Alexander," 500.
43. Altholz, "Alexander Haldane," 28.
44. Turnbull, *Shaftesbury*, 176.
45. Shaftesbury, Diary Entry (July 20, 1882), in Hodder, *Life and Work of the Seventh Earl*, Vol. III, 449–50.

In the continued evolution of Ashley's Evangelicalism, the significance of this close, enduring friendship spanning over half of the Victorian era should not be understated. While Haldane simply reinforced attitudes which Ashley had long held and could hardly be said to have revolutionized his general religious outlook, he nonetheless helped to shift Ashley's Evangelicalism towards a more strident, uncompromising, and combative disposition.[46] Just as Ashley's friendship earlier with Bickersteth was instrumental in the formation of his premillennialism and missiology, his later personal bond with Haldane was profoundly influential in giving his Evangelicalism a more pronounced conservative flavor. A Tory as well as a theological conservative, Haldane found the political creed of liberalism simply unpalatable to the Christian conscience because it was perceived to substitute the "will of autonomous man" for the "revealed will of God" as the ultimate standard for the State.[47] An avowed Evangelical Tory in the mold of Sadler and Oastler, Haldane's politics of Protestant nationalism, anti-socialism, and anti-Chartism was congenial to Ashley's own sympathies. Whereas Ashley's Evangelicalism had always been noteworthy for the doctrines it stood *for* and affirmed, it began also to acquire a reputation for the beliefs and practices it stood *against* and opposed: namely those of Roman Catholicism, Tractarian ritualism, and theologically progressive rationalism.

This typified the shift in emphasis of Anglican Evangelicalism from the affirmative approach of the *Christian Observer* to the defensive slant of the *Record*. Although it had always been a religious movement of a conservative cast, particularly on doctrinal matters concerning the Bible, its *principal* focus had shifted from affirming the need for spiritual and moral reform in the late eighteenth and early nineteenth centuries to defending traditional doctrines and paradigms in the Victorian period. In addition to reflecting the influence of historicist premillennial eschatology, this reorientation was a reaction to the rise of competing movements perceived as inimical to Evangelical Protestantism. Thus it was Shaftesbury's ensuing crusades against Romanism, ritualism, and rationalism, in concert with Haldane's *Record*, which would come to define the strongly conservative essence of his personal faith and that of Victorian Anglican Evangelicalism during the 1850s and 60s.

---

46. Finlayson, *Seventh Earl of Shaftesbury*, 320.
47. Rennie, "Evangelicalism and English Public Life," 132.

10

Premillennialism
Thy Kingdom Come, Thy Will Be Done

As Nigel Scotland observed, the nineteenth century witnessed considerable developments in Evangelical eschatology.[1] Prior to the 1820s, most Evangelicals probably shared the postmillennial outlook of the Clapham Sect and the *Christian Observer*.[2] The advent of tumultuous upheavals such as rapid industrialization and constitutional reform, however, provoked a feeling amongst Evangelicals from the 1820s and 30s that the tribulations of the present age might be the prologue to a new age previously unimagined.[3] According to Carter this new outlook drove considerable numbers of Evangelicals towards a premillennial understanding of the "end-times."[4] In forging the activist temperament and outlook of Victorian Evangelicals such as Ashley, Oastler, Sadler, Seeley, Tonna, and Haldane, the adoption of this premillennial eschatology amongst the emergent generation was fundamentally critical.[5] Although Scotland rightly cited Evangelical "support for Jewish projects" as a key outworking of premillennialism,[6] he did not discuss the extent to which this new eschatology contributed to the social reform impulses of Ashley and similarly activist Victorian Evangelicals. Meanwhile, Bebbington had appreciated the link between premillennialism

1. Scotland, *Evangelical Anglicans*, 172.
2. Carter, *Anglican Evangelicals*, 155.
3. Ibid., 153.
4. Ibid.
5. Brown, *Providence and Empire*, 74.
6. Scotland, *Evangelical Anglicans*, 173.

and anti-Catholicism in Victorian Evangelical circles,[7] but in his discussion of historicist premillennialism, he did not elaborate on its significance as a stimulant for Evangelical social action.[8] Considering the conventional understanding that a premillennial outlook invariably accounted for a pessimistic view of human progress and thus a retreat from efforts to improve the word before the return of Christ,[9] it is perhaps not surprising that neither Scotland or Bebbington would necessarily attribute the ameliorative work of Ashley and other Evangelical social reformers to a premillennial eschatology.

The adoption of a distinctively activist premillennialism by Victorian Evangelicals

Recent scholarship from Ralph Brown and Martin Spence, however, revealed that premillennialism, at least in some forms, could indeed be regarded as a motiving factor for Ashley and fellow Evangelicals engaged in social reform, humanitarian activism, and mission during the Victorian age. Far from universally fostering a pietistic withdrawal from the world and its affairs, this new eschatology prompted Evangelicals to assess one's place in the temporal world and the social responsibilities that laid before ordinary Christian believers who dwelt in the 'here and now' awaiting the return of Christ. With premillennialists believing the Second Coming of Christ to be nigh, were believers supposed to withdraw from the world as if it were a "sinking ship," only to leave its ultimate fate to the return and judgment of Christ? Or, on the contrary, were such believers impelled to do as much as they could, in the limited time available, to redeem the world and its souls before the Second Advent? The answer to such questions largely depended upon the *form* of premillennialism embraced in the 1830s. Appreciating the nuances within early Victorian premillennial eschatology, Brown posited that premillennialism was adopted within differing theological frameworks and this resulted in two markedly different ways of looking at the world, at society and at the role and responsibility of both individuals and of churches.[10]

Dispelling the common assumption that premillennialism uniformly lulled believers into a despondent withdrawal from society, Brown distinguished between the two dominant strands of this eschatology. The *futurist*

7. Bebbington, *Evangelicalism in Modern Britain*, 103.
8. Ibid., 85.
9. Brown, *Providence and Empire*, 71.
10. Brown, "Evangelical Social Thought," 127.

form of premillennialism, on the one hand, was essentially 'introversionist' in nature and thus disposed to withdraw rather than engage with society and public life. Typically associated with a high Calvinist emphasis on double predestination, it inclined towards a separatist theory of the "gathered" church of the elect. Possessing a fatalistic outlook, it saw the world as inexorably spiralling towards a hopeless state of degeneration, thereby rendering any attempt at ameliorative or redemptive social reforms as practically futile.[11] This premillennial school acquired currency chiefly in non-Anglican circles, popularized by radical Scottish and Ulster Protestants such as Edward Irving, Henry Drummond, and, initially, Alexander Haldane.[12]

The alternative *historicist* school of premillennialism, by contrast, was decidedly this-worldly in focus and proactive in spirit. Although sharing the fatalistic view of all premillennialists that human society was ultimately doomed to face divine judgment, these adventists saw this pending judgment as providing every reason to intensify their efforts to awaken a sinful society to the perils it faced.[13] Indeed, they were proactive in mission and social reform *because* of their despair at the prospects of a sinful nation, and not despite it, as was commonly perceived. Inspired by biblical prophecy, they were determined to triumph against the odds with the abiding hope that their seemingly futile efforts at reform and redemption would ultimately prove victorious with the return of the Messiah vindicating his followers and destroying the enemy. Unlike the premillennialism of Irving and Drummond, this tradition of eschatology was primarily incubated in the Evangelical wing of the Established Church and propagated by Anglican leaders such as Thomas R. Birks, R. B. Seeley, C. E. Tonna, and Bickersteth.[14] Evangelicals from other denominations, particularly the Church of Scotland, also identified with this historicist premillennial strand.

Given that Ashley's Evangelicalism was nurtured in the Anglican tradition, it is not surprising that his brand of premillennialism palpably resembled that of the historicist school. From his zeal for evangelism and mission, to his focus on redeeming both the body and the soul, to his social reform endeavors, Ashley's religion bore all the hallmarks of this Anglican premillennial tradition. Thus, by examining the various impulses of this premillennialism, the theological roots of Ashley's Victorian Evangelical activism can be that much better appreciated. Arguably, the most defining

11. Ibid.

12. While associating himself with the 'Albury Circle' of futurist premillennialism in the early days, Haldane gravitated towards the more activist and interventionist school of historicist premillennialism.

13. Brown, "Victorian Anglican Evangelicalism," 689.

14. Brown, "Evangelical Social Thought," 128.

feature of this Anglican premillennialism was its robust missionary impulse. Conscious of the imminent judgment, Anglican adventists were eager to call sinners to repentance before the "open door" to salvation slammed shut, hence they invested heavily in domestic and overseas mission to ensure that as many souls as possible could respond to the gospel before it was deemed too late. Typifying this missionary imperative, Bickersteth compared the salvation of souls to the rescue of human bodies trapped on a burning ship. Of mission, he declared that "we have a yet more important work to accomplish—to save immortal souls from a more terrific fire which will one day be kindled for the wicked, and which, when kindled, leaves no way of escape!"[15] Aroused to act, Anglican adventists embarked on mission with a mixture of optimism and pessimism, hoping that multitudes of souls would be saved but despairing for the fate of the "lost."

Concurring with Brown's thesis that the historicist premillennialism adopted by Victorian Anglican Evangelicals served as a critical impetus for their social activism, Martin Spence added that their premillennial preoccupation with temporal affairs could be explained not only by a sense of urgency before the return of Christ but also by their conviction of *physical continuity* between this world and the next.[16] Spence argued that one of the hallmarks of the Anglican premillennialists was their affirmation of the material world.[17] According to Spence, Anglican premillennialists believed in the "restitution of all things," both temporal and spiritual, before the "materiality" of the future life.[18] Hence, if the material world were to continue in perpetuity, then seeking the material wellbeing of the earth in the present age through philanthropy and social reform was a worthwhile and purposeful enterprise. For Anglican premillennialists, the ultimate proof of God's concern with the material world was the incarnation in that he elected to reveal his Son in earthly flesh and blood.[19]

Importantly, Spence pointed out that the concern for the material world was not just with individuals but also with communities. Habitually turning to Old Testament prophecies which spoke of a promised earthly Kingdom, premillennial Evangelicals emphasized a sense of God's concern with corporate, temporal structures and thus the need to "redeem" these before the Second Coming.[20] Given that their notion of temporal restitution

---

15. Brown, "Victorian Anglican Evangelicalism," 691.
16. Spence, "Renewal of Time and Space," 101.
17. Spence, "Renewal of Time and Space," 94; Spence, *Heaven on Earth*, 166.
18. Spence, "Renewal of Time and Space," 91–93.
19. Ibid., 96.
20. Ibid., 97.

was universal, these premillennialists focused on reforming nations and communities as well as individuals. With the belief that salvation should work itself out on earth, within temporal structures, Anglican premillennialists such as Seeley criticized other evangelical and eschatological traditions for regarding "the Bible as merely a guide to heaven, and as having very little bearing upon the things of this sublunary earth."[21] Identifying evil as a problem to be dealt with in not only the hearts of individuals but also in the conditions of society, Seeley and Tonna campaigned for wide-scale social reforms that included humanizing the factory system, the provision of public housing and sanitation, improving the quality of public health, furthering opportunities for education and promoting the institution of the Sabbath. For these premillennialists, the amelioration of the material world, through social reforms in the present age, was regarded as part of a divine master-plan which Christ would return to complete and fulfill.

The evolution and outworking of Ashley's premillennialism

Assenting to Anglican premillennialism in the mid-1830s under the influence of his mentor Bickersteth and subsequently forging a close friendship with the similarly premillennial Alexander Haldane, Ashley came to imbibe the characteristic traits of this eschatological thinking discussed by Brown and Spence. Eagerly awaiting and longing for the return of Christ, his simple daily prayer became "Even so, come Lord Jesus," a motto he would inscribe in the original Greek upon the flaps of his daily envelopes.[22] Embracing the premillennial missionary hope of bringing the gospel to the entire world in anticipation of the Second Advent, Shaftesbury wrote in 1852: "I see it, surely I see it; the Gospel will be offered where, in truth, it has never yet been fairly offered, in China and Japan; it will then have been preached for a witness to all nations," and then will 'the end come!' Come, Lord Jesus, come quickly."[23]

Desiring to make this universal reach of the gospel a reality in his lifetime, Shaftesbury supported the deployment of missionaries across the British Empire and the world through Evangelical bodies such as the CMS and the BFBS. Whilst eagerly anticipating the return of Christ, Shaftesbury conceded his immediate focus was on the "interval" of the present age:

21. Seeley, *Remedies*, 108, in Spence, "Renewal of Time and Space," 97.
22. Hodder, *Life and Work of the Seventh Earl*, Vol. III, 10.
23. Shaftesbury, Diary Entry (September 3, 1852), in Hodder, *Life and Work of the Seventh Earl*, Vol. II, 440.

> I am now looking, not to the great end, but to the interval. I know, my friends, how great and glorious that end will be; but while I find so many persons looking to no end, and others rejoicing in that great end, and thinking nothing about the interval. I confess that my own sympathies and fears dwell much with what must take place before that great consummation.[24]

Thus, for Shaftesbury, there was a pressing agenda of evangelism, mission, and social reform to be executed before he could even contemplate basking in the glory of the "great consummation." His acute preoccupation with the needs of the present age before the return of Christ essentially typified the activist outlook of the historicist school of premillennialism identified by Brown.

Although the premillennial Ashley interpreted historical events, such as the laying down of the Atlantic cable in 1858, as "signs" of the Second Advent,[25] he did not necessarily concern himself with the specifics of how the "end times" would unfold and made no attempt to forecast or even to speculate about the actual time at which this was likely to occur:

> The Second Advent, as an all sufficient remedy, should be prayed for; and, as a promise, should be looked for. The mode, form, and manner of that event are not revealed, and therefore are no business of ours. The whole will become intelligible only by the issue, but we have enough to rouse and guide us in St Paul's First Epistle to the Thessalonians, and in the words of our Lord Himself at the close of Revelations, Surely I come quickly.[26]

His stance on the Advent was characteristic of Anglican Evangelical premillennialists in the Victorian age who generally frowned upon human attempts to determine the mode and date of the Second Coming, viewing such forecasts as an unwarranted addition to what was already recorded in scripture. Moreover, it was doubtful that Ashley's premillennialism insisted on a literal one thousand year period of Christ's reign on earth. According to Georgina Battiscombe, it was probable that Ashley shared Bickersteth's "dread" of "attempting to fix the exact time" of Christ's earthly reign.[27]

In the tradition of Seeley and Tonna, Ashley's social and political activism was arguably galvanized by Anglican premillennialism in the 1840s. Relying upon Seeley for advice and deferring to his older friend, Bickersteth,

24. Ashley quoted in Turnbull, "Eschatology and the Social Order," 1–4.

25. Battiscombe, *Shaftesbury: A Biography*, 103.

26. Shaftesbury, Letter to Dr Angus (January 27, 1870), in Hodder, *Life and Work of the Seventh Earl*, Vol. III, 261.

27. Battiscombe, *Shaftesbury: A Biography*, 101.

who, in turn, was influenced by Tonna, Ashley's acceptance of Christ's return before the millennium gave an added layer of spiritual urgency to his support for social reforms such as the Ten Hours Bill.[28] Ashley and his fellow premillennialists had interpreted industrial unrest in the early 1840s as signs of God's displeasure at the neglect of the industrial masses with the Chartist riots erupting in August 1842. Thus in efforts to avert God's impending wrath, urgent action was needed to ameliorate the dire conditions of factory workers by way of sponsoring the Ten Hours Bill. Reflecting on the protests of the industrial classes, Ashley observed: "They [the working classes] see in their rulers no interest or care, and they will, therefore, feel no confidence. 'Had we,' said the Chartists of Leeds to me, 'a few more to speak to us as you have done, we should never again speak of the Charter.'"[29]

By listening and responding to the grievances of the working classes, Ashley was acting true to both his conservative instincts and premillennial disposition. First he had the Tory objective of desiring to forestall any industrial disturbance to the traditional social order, and, secondly, he felt impelled to allay God's anger and judgment by doing something proactive about the neglect of the industrial masses. As well as averting the "coming wrath," Ashley's social reform was also about redeeming the body as well as the soul before the coming of Christ. Thus, while evangelistic mission and Christian education had the salvation of people's souls as their guiding rationale, social reforms such as the provision of sanitation, the construction of adequate housing and the humane treatment of the mentally ill had the restitution of the human body as its purpose. With Shaftesbury viewing the body as created by the same God who also made the soul, he remarked that "in our pursuits, the moral and physical elements are closely, intricately, and inseparably combined."[30] Ashley's focus on redeeming the "body" was characteristic of what Spence identified as the premillennial affirmation of the material world and its mission to seek the "restitution of all things"

---

28 Dzelzainis, "Charlotte Elizabeth Tonna," 183.

29. Shaftesbury Diary Entry (August 18, 1842), in Hodder, *Life and Work of the Seventh Earl*, Vol. II, 434.

30. Shaftesbury, "Legislation on Social Subjects," Address to Open the Social Science Congress of 1866, in *Speeches of the Earl*, 360.

11

Desire for the Nations

Ashley and Victorian Evangelical attitudes towards empire and race

With premillennialism constituting the principal driving force behind the missionary impulses of Ashley and the Victorian Evangelicals, this stream of eschatology had implications for their attitudes towards the British Empire.[1] This was particularly so, given that overseas missionary enterprise and imperial expansion were often closely intertwined in their common aspiration to reach the entire globe. To be sure, the Evangelical impulse for mission and empire long predated the Victorian era with the establishment of overseas Christian missions representing a central concern of the Clapham Sect.[2] As early as 1786, William Wilberforce and Henry Thornton persuaded the Pitt administration to appoint an Evangelical chaplain, Richard Johnson, to the new colony of New South Wales. In 1793 the chair of the British East India Company, Charles Grant, had sought to introduce into the Company's charter, measures for the gradual promotion of the religious and moral improvement of the inhabitants of India. This was followed by the establishment of the Church Missionary Society (CMS) in 1799 with Wilberforce, Grant and James Stephen serving as the inaugural vice-presidents. Sharing the vision of the Clapham "Saints" and the London Missionary Society founder who had asserted in 1812 that "This land seems

1. Spence, "Renewal of Time and Space," 96–101.
2. Hylson-Smith, *Evangelicals in the Church of England*, 87.

peculiarly destined to be the instrument . . . to carry His salvation into the ends of the earth," Victorian Evangelicals saw Britain's expanding global empire as providing an invaluable mechanism through which to export the gospel to the four corners of the earth.[3] Whatever ethical misgivings they may have entertained about the whole imperial project, the machinery of the empire was in place to be capitalized on for missionary purposes. Indeed, the Victorian Evangelical priority accorded to mission was such that Elisabeth Elbourne credited the Victorian missionary movement with being "a characteristic feature of modern British imperialism."[4]

While generally enthusiastic about the potential opportunities for Christian mission afforded by the British imperial enterprise, the broader perspective of Evangelicals on empire during the Victorian age was generally nuanced, appreciating the potential blessings of the imperial project but also awake to its limitations and prospective dangers. Unlike many Irish Catholics, the emerging Owenite socialists and other British radicals, Anglican and, to a lesser extent, Nonconformist Victorian evangelicals generally supported the British Empire, viewing it as a valuable mechanism through which to diffuse the Christian gospel across other lands.[5] In addition, the Empire would aid the cultivation of British values and institutions seen to have a Christian basis, such as the rule of law and the education system, in countries such as India. Notwithstanding these manifold benefits, Victorian evangelicals were also aware of the tendency for unchecked power to corrupt and so warned against the excesses of imperial policy, particularly in cases where the rights of native peoples were impinged or overlooked in the unbridled quest for imperial aggrandizement. In instances where British commercial exploitation and military aggression abroad were evident, evangelicals, otherwise loyal to the imperial cause, would not hesitate publicly to upbraid the Empire for its misconduct.[6] In short, Victorian evangelicals desired to ameliorate empire rather than abolish it.[7] Despite the change in perspective from the Claphamite generation to the succeeding Recordite generation on a number theological, political, and economic matters, Hilton observed that the general evangelical perspective on British imperialism remained fairly consistent throughout the Victorian age.[8]

3. Haweis, *View of the Present State*, 13, 24.

4. Elbourne, "Religion in the British Empire," in Stockwell (ed.), *The British Empire*, 138.

5. Brown, *Providence and Empire*, 195.

6. Thorne, *Congregational Missions*, 8.

7. Elbourne, *Blood Ground*, 15.

8. Hilton, *Age of Atonement*, 10–11, 205–13.

Within the spectrum of Victorian evangelical thought on British imperialism, there were discernible differences between the outlooks of various Anglican and Nonconformist evangelicals. Wedded to the Tory paternalist view, popularized by Southey and the romantic Lake poets, that the Church of England represented the spiritual conscience of Britain and its Empire, Anglican Evangelicals generally saw the mission of their Church as inextricably intertwined with the broader imperial project of propagating Christianity and civilization. For Ashley and other Anglican Evangelicals, the Established Church represented the anchor of the colonies in its promotion of monarchy, faith, duty, and social order.[9]

A sizeable proportion of Nonconformist evangelicals, on the other hand, tended to regard the Church and State as two rather separate entities and hence viewed the imperial enterprise in more secular terms. The mission of the Church was to preach the gospel and win converts whilst the overtly imperial objectives of expanding overseas trade and commerce, acquiring fresh territories and settling new colonies were seen primarily as the business of the state. For Nonconformist evangelicals such as Spurgeon, it was accordingly not axiomatic for *all* missionary-minded evangelicals necessarily to endorse the imperial cause. Indeed, as Andrew Porter noted, "religion and Empire frequently mingled, but were as likely to undermine each other as they were to provide mutual support."[10] Reflecting this disconnect between evangelicalism and Empire, Spurgeon, as mentioned earlier, remained an implacable enemy of British imperialism and jingoism all his life.[11] Unlike the Tory, Anglican Ashley who maintained faith in the potential goodness of the enterprise, the anti-Tory, Nonconformist Spurgeon chided the Empire for its belligerence and avarice, viewing little of it as befitting the Christian ideals of "peace and justice."[12] As well as embracing a separation of Church and state paradigm, significant numbers of Nonconformist Evangelicals tended towards political radicalism in contrast to the Tory-leaning Anglican Evangelicals, and this, too, accounted for their questioning of the imperial enterprise.[13]

As one of the pre-eminent evangelical Protestants of the Victorian age, Shaftesbury and his personal perspectives were particularly noteworthy and warrant further analysis, with his pronouncements typifying the foregoing

9. Johnson, *British Imperialism*, 100.
10. Porter, "Religion, Missionary Enthusiasm and Empire," in Porter (ed.), *British Empire*, 245.
11. Smith, *Transforming the World*, 55.
12. Spurgeon (1880), quoted in Smith, *Transforming the World*, 55.
13. Johnson, *British Imperialism*, 100.

evangelical mindset on imperial issues. Stemming from the Tory traditions of his aristocratic upbringing in rural Dorset, together with his assent to Anglican Evangelical Christianity as a young adult, Shaftesbury's personal values of patriotism, conservatism, paternalism, hierarchy, moral order, and Christian missionary zeal aligned with much of the philosophy behind British imperialism. Accordingly, he spoke enthusiastically about the potential of the empire to elevate the morality, religion, and civilization of colonized peoples, particularly those on the Indian subcontinent. Like Southey, Ashley held to the romantic Tory construct of the Church of England as the soul and conscience of the British nation. As such, Shaftesbury told the House of Lords in 1867 that he envisaged the Established Church as "being powerful and beneficent" in "the East and in the West, in the North and in the South and in all the regions of the earth, wherever the English name is heard."[14] For Ashley, the potential religious, cultural and political positives of the imperial project were seemingly endless, providing it could be executed along just and humane principles. If such principles, however, were seen to be compromised or jettisoned in the imperial scramble for power and prestige, then Ashley felt little compunction in making these transgressions publicly known.

Of particular relevance to molding Ashley's outlook on empire were the attitudes of Bickersteth. Conscious of the imminent judgment attending the return of Christ, Bickersteth and his fellow premillennial Anglicans were eager to call sinners to repentance before the "open-door" to salvation slammed shut. In consequence, they invested heavily in domestic and overseas mission to ensure that as many souls as possible could respond to the gospel before it was deemed "too late." Typifying this missionary imperative, Bickersteth compared the salvation of souls to the rescue of human bodies trapped on a burning ship.[15] For Bickersteth and Ashley, this evangelical missionary resolve to reach the entire globe with the Bible corresponded with, and reinforced, the analogous imperial ambition to unfurl the Union Jack on every continent. At the same time as reviving enthusiasm for the British Empire, however, premillennialism also prompted Bickersteth and like-minded evangelicals soberly to reflect on its ethical shortcomings. Prophesying that the Second Coming of Christ was imminent, Bickersteth felt it timely to offer some critical self-examination of Britain's spiritual and moral course as a nation and empire in the early Victorian period. In his reflections, Bickersteth drew on the familiar Evangelical belief that the

---

14. Shaftesbury, "Clerical Vestments (No 2) Bill," Second Reading, HL Debates, *Hansard*, 14 May 1867, Vol. 187, c. 501.

15. Brown, "Victorian Anglican Evangelicalism," 691.

continual amassing of power tended to corrupt the soul. Applying this to Britain, he cautioned in 1845 that imperial success could all too easily descend into a destructive national pride. "We are proud and vainglorious; we are lifted up with our victories, and our subjugated countries, and our widespread dominions. Conquest is as dangerous as it is alluring."[16] Bickersteth further warned that Britain's "position as a civilised and powerful and military nation, bordering in our colonies everywhere on uncivilised, weak, and helpless nations, is a fearful snare to us."[17] Indeed a snare to which Ashley would come to regard Britain as having fatally succumbed, particularly in its opium trade with China and approach to Indian affairs.

Despite Bickersteth's grim assessment of imperial Britain's ethical disposition, he nonetheless shared the prevailing Evangelical optimism that the British Empire had the potential to be a force for good: "But among all the nations of the earth, there is not one that has the immense power to do good that Great Britain has. Its political power, its vast colonial empire in all parts of the earth, its commerce with all lands, its accumulated wealth, its ships sailing over every ocean, and visiting every region."[18] In extolling the Empire's positive potential, Bickersteth reflected the British exceptionalism of the Clapham generation which would typify much of Ashley's own attitudes to British imperialism. Owing to a combination of fortuitous national circumstances, many of which Bickersteth referred to above, coupled with an avowedly Protestant national identity, Ashley and his fellow Victorian Evangelicals believed providence had especially assigned Britain with an imperial mission that it, alone, was deemed equipped to carry forth. As will become evident, however, this by no means implied that Victorian Evangelicals saw every deed of the British Empire as providentially sanctioned. On the contrary, ethical misdeeds in trade, commerce and administration were deplored as grave betrayals of the Empire's providential purpose to spread abroad British civilization and Christianity.

Sharing Bickersteth's providential view of empire, Ashley was quick to denounce any imperial conduct deemed as unbefitting for Britain's role as a beneficent and responsible custodian. Thus his general affection for the empire was frequently punctuated by protestations against the greed, injustice and oppression on the part of the Empire in cases where he felt it betrayed its paternal duties to its subjects. In 1845 he penned this damning assessment of Britain's failure to act honorably in its colonial dealings: "We cover the world with our colonies, and yet we have not, or practice not, one

16. Bickersteth, *Signs of the Times*, 324.
17. Ibid., 330.
18. Ibid., 394.

single healthy principle of colonisation! This last was the best imagined of all. Religion went hand-in-hand with political government, and we have, nevertheless fallen short of the mark."[19] As a zealous Evangelical Anglican, Ashley felt that imperial Britain's propensity towards greed, exploitation, aggression and oppression stood in stark contrast to what he saw as the Christian values of mercy, justice, and generosity. Believing as he did that Britain was a Christian country, he found this behavior not only disturbing but unbecoming of the nation's professed religious identity.

Shaftesbury was particularly affronted by Britain's unscrupulous role in the opium trade with China during the 1840s.[20] Maintaining in 1843 that "opium and the Bible could never enter China together," he explained how inconsistent the imperial practice of drug dealing was with that other imperial objective of inculcating religion and morality:

> It will seem scarcely credible that in the nineteenth century, while British missionaries were preaching the Gospel in every quarter of the globe, and while British philanthropists were combating almost every known phase of evil under the sun, British statesmen could be found capable of defending, for the sake of the revenue, a system which has been again and again conclusively proved to be fraught with misery and ruin to tens of thousands of the Chinese people[21]

Whilst Britain claimed no direct colonial sovereignty over China, with the exception of annexing Hong Kong Island under the 1842 Treaty of Nanking, its exploitative behavior nonetheless amounted to an abuse of its international obligations as a global empire to be an arbiter of fair trade. Shaftesbury's revulsion at the opium trade was echoed by other Victorian evangelical voices. The *Wesleyan Methodist Magazine* in 1856 claimed that the unethical nature of the trade was being "held up to the confusion of our Missionaries when they attempt to glory in the cross of Christ." The English Nonconformist clergyman John Angell James concurred, asserting that "every chest of opium that is smuggled into China is a stone of stumbling thrown in the missionary's path."[22]

---

19. Ashley, Diary Entry (June 26, 1845) in Hodder, *Life and Work of the Seventh Earl*, Vol. II, 140.

20. Finlayson, *Seventh Earl of Shaftesbury*, 174.

21. Ashley, Diary Entry (February 13, 1843) in Hodder, *Life and Work of the Seventh Earl*, Vol. I, 463.

22. Stanley, "British Evangelicals," in Wolffe (ed.), *Evangelical Faith and Public Zeal*, 108.

Reflecting the dominant evangelical conviction that the Bible spoke of a common origin of all races and people groups,[23] Ashley also believed that the native inhabitants of colonies were no less entitled to the same benefits and protections afforded to the British people themselves. Sharing the anti-racist outlook of the Aborigines Protection Society, a humanitarian organization founded by Evangelicals in 1837, Ashley accepted the premise in the book of Acts that God had made all the peoples of the earth "of one blood." Accordingly, he agitated for Indian factory children to receive the same rights and safeguards as their British co-labourers had done from the passage of key Factory Reform Acts in the 1840s. Speaking on an 1879 Bill to regulate child labor in India, Shaftesbury told the House of Lords: "Creed and colour, latitude and longitude, make no difference in the essential nature of man.... The Hindoo children are surely entitled to the same protection as afforded to 'young persons' in the United Kingdom."[24] Shaftesbury saw the humane treatment of native peoples as not only the outworking of a Christian conscience but also as wise imperial policy in Britain's longer-term interests. By treating the Indian people well, it was hoped the native people of such colonies would look favorably upon Britain to "daily rise up and call her blessed."[25]

Ashley and the Victorian Evangelical stance on the 'Jewish question'

The Victorian era represented a watershed for the centuries-old Jewish-Gentile relationship which, throughout much of Europe's history, had been highly vexed and troubled with a long catalog of anti-Semitic prejudice, discrimination and violence against the Jewish people. The reign of Victoria witnessed the passage of Jewish Emancipation in 1858 when Lord Derby's administration finally succeeded in repealing discriminatory laws that had precluded Jewish citizens from full participation in British public life. The Zionist movement to establish a tangible and permanent Jewish homeland in what was then Palestine also had its origins in the Victorian age. In these two nineteenth-century developments, the attitudes of Victorian Evangelicals, such as Ashley, were eminently pertinent. According to Donald Lewis, philosemitism and Christian Zionism by the mid-nineteenth century had

---

23. Larsen, "Book of Acts," 35–36.

24. Shaftesbury, Speech to the House of Lords, 4 April 1879, Parliamentary Debates, Lords, 3rd ser., Vol. 245 (1879), col. 351.

25. Shaftesbury, Speech to the House of Lords, 3 April 1876, Parliamentary Debates, Lords, 3rd ser., Vol. 228 (1876), col. 1047.

become important "identity markers" for large numbers of Evangelicals, particularly those aligned with the Recordite school.[26] Jewish affairs featured conspicuously in the thinking and activity of Victorian Recordite Evangelicals for two primary reasons, the first being that their theology of a richly Calvinist Protestantism identified itself closely with its Old Testament, Jewish roots, and, second, their mission to restore the Jewish people to their ancient homeland represented a practical corollary of their premillennialism. With Ashley frequently giving voice to the prevailing views of Victorian Evangelicals on what became known as the "Jewish Question," the broader context and thinking behind his pronouncements merit close evaluation.

Engraved on the gold ring of Ashley was the psalmist's petition to "Pray for the Peace of Jerusalem."[27] To Ashley, this was not only a simple prayer but a clarion call to act for the Jewish cause in whatever capacity he felt able. As both an Evangelical Anglican and a Tory politician committed to the British Empire, Ashley managed to link his religious ideals to the Victorian political project of procuring a Jewish home-state in the land of Palestine. With an Evangelical faith steeped in the Hebrew Scriptures, Ashley imbibed an abiding affection for the Jewish people whom he revered as modern-day heirs of Old Testament Israel. As Lewis demonstrated, Ashley's affection for the Jewish people and support for their restoration evidently reflected the Victorian Evangelical *zeitgeist*. Along with biblical literalism, anti-rationalism and anti-Catholicism, Lewis noted that philosemitism came to represent a defining characteristic of Evangelical culture in Victorian Britain.[28]

Whilst the thinking of the Victorian Recordite Evangelicals departed from that of their Clapham predecessors in a number of areas, they retained, and indeed intensified, the philosemetic and pro-Zionist outlook of Claphamites such as Charles Simeon. The principal organ through which Ashley and the Victorian Evangelicals promulgated their philosemitism and Christian Zionist agenda, the London Society for Promoting Christianity amongst the Jews (LSPCJ), had been largely a Clapham Sect initiative. Although the inception of the Society in 1809 was the direct product of the growing influence of Lutheran pietism in the English-speaking world,[29] the LSPCJ attracted considerable patronage from the Claphamite circle in its

---

26. Lewis, *Origins of Christian Zionism*, 10.

27. Hodder, *Life and Work of the Seventh Earl*, Vol. II, 477. The petition "Pray for the peace of Jerusalem" appears in Psalm 122:6.

28. Hempton, "Evangelicalism and Eschatology," 180.

29. Lewis, *Origins of Christian Zionism*, 50.

founding years. Together with Simeon of Cambridge, William Wilberforce, Robert Grant, and Thomas Babington featured as regular speakers for the Society.[30] Representing the latent bud of Victorian evangelical philosemitism, the LSPCJ had as its strategy the recruitment of converted Jews whose leadership provided a visible testimony to the conversionist cause and to evangelical perceptions of the Jews as a group with a biblically grounded national identity.[31] Like the Claphamites, the Victorian Evangelicals came to see the Jews in their midst as a living, tangible link to their biblical roots. In the Jewish street vendor, they saw not a "Christ-killer" but a living reminder of their special affinity with "God's ancient people" and the conversion of individual Jews became a vindication of their religious and cultural identity.[32]

Turning specifically to Ashley, what was the guiding inspiration behind his thinking on the Jewish question and how did this manifest itself in his speeches and public policy positions? As with most of his Evangelical attitudes, his esteem for the Jews was indebted to the influence of Bickersteth.[33] Inspired by Simeon's pioneering interest in missionary outreach to the Jews, Bickersteth became involved with the London Society for the Proclamation of Christianity amongst the Jews (LSPCJ) and preached sermons on their behalf in London, Edinburgh, and Dublin. Bickersteth articulated his affection for the Jews and his support for Jewish restoration in his volume, *The Restoration of the Jews to Their Own Land* (1841). Lauding the Jewish nation as "unquestionably" the "largest blessing to the human race," Bickersteth regarded the modern-day church as singularly indebted to this nation for its "daily spiritual food" and "richest inheritance of blessing."[34] Despite the present-day diaspora of the Jewish people, Bickersteth believed that God had "marvelously preserved their distinctiveness" in anticipation that they would be restored to their ancient homeland as a literal fulfillment of Old Testament prophecy.[35] The mission to restore the Jews, according to Bickersteth, was "clearly foretold in the word of God" and he submitted that it was also a "practical and seasonable doctrine for the edification of the church."[36] Appending a copy of Simeon's final address on the Jewish question to his *Restoration of the Jews*,[37] Bickersteth evidently saw himself as assuming the

30. Gidney, *History of the London Society*, 60.
31. Adler, *Restoring the Jews*, 140.
32. Lewis, *Origins of Christian Zionism*, 13.
33. Ibid., 120.
34. Bickersteth, *Restoration of the Jews*, vii.
35. Ibid., ix–x.
36. Ibid., v.
37. "The Rev C. Simeon's Address from his Death-bed" quoted in Bickersteth,

mantle of the Clapham-aligned clergyman in his philosemitism and mission for Jewish conversion and restoration. Despite his eschatology differing from the postmillennialism of Simeon and the Claphamites at large, Bickersteth played a key role in transmitting the philosemitic and Christian Zionist ideals of the Claphamites to Ashley and his generation of Victorian Evangelicals.

In 1835, the same year that Ashley first called on Bickersteth at his Watton rectory, Ashley's interest in the Jewish question became manifest when he accepted an invitation to become the Society's vice-president in 1835. Having found the ideal forum in which to advance his philosemitic views, Ashley became an active participant in the LSPCJ governing committee from 1840 and it was in this capacity that he became largely responsible for setting the tone of evangelical relations with the Jewish community in Britain and abroad through the Victorian age. In a keynote address to the Society in 1845, Ashley articulated Evangelical aspirations to embrace and convert the Jewish people:

> Our Church and our nation have been called to the glorious service of making known the Gospel of Christ to the many thousands of Israel. In whatever light I view this great question, whether I regard it as purely secular, whether I regard it as purely religious, or whether I regard it as partaking of both characters, I see no subject which can surpass, or even approach it, in magnitude and in all those attributes which feed the imagination and stir into life the warmest energies of the heart.[38]

The avowedly missionary tone of his address reflected the prevailing Victorian Evangelical conviction that the "people of Israel" were to be prioritized in the proclamation of the Christian gospel throughout the world. Importantly, he also implied that the project of making the gospel known amongst the Jews could represent the simultaneous outworking of both religious and political objectives. In the Victorian era, the quest to establish a Jewish homeland in the Near East was not only conceived in religious terms as a necessary precursor to converting the Jews to Christianity in preparation for the Second Advent, but also as a geopolitical strategy to bolster the British imperial presence in that region. With the Near East Ottoman Empire seriously endangered, imperial Britain recognized the Jews as potential pawns in a power struggle to buttress the rule of its Ottoman allies.[39] To

---

Restoration of the Jews, 291–293.
    38. Ashley, *Speech from the Chair of the London Society* (1845).
    39. Adler, *Restoring the Jews*, 133.

achieve this, it was accordingly proposed that a permanent Jewish settlement be established in Palestine.

As an active Anglican layman and Tory parliamentarian, Ashley was only too well aware of these dual motives and was thus ideally placed to capitalize on what seemed to him an auspicious confluence of heartfelt Evangelical aspiration and British imperial policy objective. With the interests of the "Bible and Flag" thereby seen as effectively interchangeable on the issue of a Palestinian Jewish homeland, Shaftesbury had the luxury of being able to advance this cause in either religious or political language to achieve essentially the same end. In the political milieu of the Palmerston administration, Shaftesbury thought it expedient to press the cause on "political, financial and commercial" grounds since this was the only motivation to which Palmerston seemed attuned.[40] Accordingly, the plan he submitted to Palmerston for the Jewish resettlement in Palestine merely pointed out that the resettling of Jews in Palestine was the "cheapest and safest mode of supplying the wastes of those depopulated regions."[41] Avoiding any biblical references or allusions to God and the Second Advent, Ashley used purely political terminology to advance a cause close to the hearts of Victorian Evangelicals.

For all his zeal, however, his relationship with the Jewish community was far from straightforward. At times, both parties failed to see eye-to-eye on key questions of religious identity and the extent to which the Victorian British polity was prepared to accommodate multi-faith communities such as that of the Jews. On the question of Jewish Emancipation, Shaftesbury had opposed legislation in the 1850s to admit Jews to Parliament, a stance which put him at odds even with the positions taken by fellow Evangelicals such as Sir Robert Grant and Nicholas Vansittart.[42] In the House of Lords, Shaftesbury defended his posture in 1853 on the grounds of his conscientious commitment to Britain as a "Christian nation." As such, he could not bring himself to consent to doing away with the office that required one to pledge loyalty "on the oath of a Christian."[43] He saw the issue not so much as one of extending justice to Jews but rather of maintaining Britain's Christian profession.

> We maintain, my Lords, that the words "on the true faith of a Christian" assert the authority, the growth, and the predominance of Christianity; that it ought to be, if it is not, the

---

40 Bar-Yosef, "Christian Zionism," 29.

41. Ibid.

42. Lewis, *Origins of Christian Zionism*, 148.

43. Ibid.

> governing rule and spirit of all our legislation; that it ought to be the professed belief of everyone who undertakes to legislate for this Christian country.[44]

As Stewart Brown noted, opponents of Jewish Emancipation feared that such measures would undermine the Christian basis of the British state.[45] Shaftesbury supported, on the other hand, the admission of Jews to other civil offices that did not compromise Britain's profession of Christianity. Thus, while Shaftesbury desired to advance the status of Jews in Britain, he was not prepared to do so if it came at the cost of compromising his much cherished Tory Evangelical ideal of a confessional Christian state with a Protestant constitution. At this point in time, it was Shaftesbury's Tory paternalist interests in maintaining traditional politico-religious paradigms, rather than his benevolent disposition towards the Jews, which overrode an otherwise logical inclination to support the measure.

Second, Shaftesbury was convinced that his advocacy for a Jewish homeland in Palestine accorded with Jewish public opinion. In 1876, he wrote in the *Palestine Exploration Fund Quarterly* that the existence of a "spirit" *for* the Palestinian project justified its execution by the British government:

> To England, then, naturally belongs the role of favouring the settlement of the Jews in Palestine. . . . The nationality of the Jews exists; the spirit is there and has been for three thousand years, but the external form, the crowning bond of union, is still wanting. A nation must have a country. The old land, the old people. This is not an artificial experiment; it is nature, it is history.[46]

Once again guided by his paternalist assumptions, Shaftesbury believed that the wishes and best interests of the Jewish people accorded with what he *assumed* were theirs. In fact, contrary to what the Earl had assumed, the vast majority of Western European Jews entertained no aspiration to return to Palestine.[47] It is possible Shaftesbury's misconceptions on this matter stemmed from his limited personal contacts with British Jews, other than those in the upper echelons of British life and those associated with the

---

44. Shaftesbury, "Jewish Disabilities Bill," HL Debates, *Hansard*, 29 April 1853, Vol. 126, c. 763.
45. Brown, *Providence and Empire*, 194.
46 Shaftesbury, "Notes and News," 107–19.
47. Lewis, *Origins of Christian Zionism*, 156–57.

LSPCJ.[48] With Shaftesbury and the Victorian Evangelicals obviously viewing their missionary overtures to the Jews as a well-meaning gesture, the Jewish community did not always see it in the same light.

There were suspicions that the Evangelicals' strategy, with conversion to Christianity as its chief end, was part of an attempt by Christian, Gentile society gradually to subsume Jewish identity into the dominant Christian identity. Although this approach differed greatly from the violent persecution and pogroms that had terrorized Jews in countries such as Russia and Poland, the proselytizing of Jews was nonetheless seen as an unwelcome invasion of their cultural and religious integrity. The Evangelical project to create a Jewish homeland was also received with reservation. Throughout the nineteenth century, most Western European Jews were strongly opposed to the idea of returning to Palestine. On the contrary, such Jews saw it as their vocation to maintain something of a visible Jewish presence in the midst of their respective new homelands as a way of asserting the universality of their culture and religion.[49]

It was this complex web of nineteenth-century Evangelical Protestant and Jewish relations which gave some fascinating insights into the still evolving notions of religious freedom and toleration in Victorian British society. Importantly, it revealed the innate tensions between Shaftesbury's high Tory paternalism and Evangelicalism which would often have the effect of pulling him in conflicting directions on this question. On the one hand, both his Evangelical Protestantism and conservative instincts impelled him to further Jewish interests. His love of the Hebrew Scriptures since early childhood imbued him with an enduring love and veneration of the Jews.[50] In this sense, his intense Evangelical interest in the Old Testament gave him a capacity to appreciate Judaism to an extent which would have been atypical of Victorian times when ancient anti-Jewish prejudices still lingered. His affection for the Jews was also reinforced by his conservative instinct to cherish the roots of enduring traditions, not least the Christian religion. In the same vein as Bickersteth,[51] Shaftesbury believed that the Hebrew genesis of Christianity was worth honoring and he felt no small gratitude to the Jewish race for the fact that Christianity owed so much to the imperishable treasures of Hebrew civilization. The notion of a loving and just God, the *Imago Dei* of all persons, the Decalogue of Moses, the

48. Ibid., 162.
49. Ibid., 161.
50. Hodder, *Life and Work of the Seventh Earl*, Vol. I, 87.
51. Bickersteth, *Restoration of the Jews*, vii. For Bickersteth, the arts, science, genius, eloquence, taste, wealth, and jurisprudence of modern civilization were pre-eminently the fruits of the Jewish nation.

'lively oracles' of Jehovah, and the wisdom literature of Solomon were just some of the riches Judaism had bequeathed to Christianity. After expressing his indebtedness to the Jews, he told parliament that "We owe them much, very much, for the wrongs they have endured, and much for the services they have performed; they ought to be 'beloved for their fathers' sakes.'"[52] In practical terms for Shaftesbury, this meant establishing a Jewish homeland in Palestine, befriending members of the Jewish community, and denouncing the persecution of their religious brethren in other lands.

Notwithstanding this pro-Jewish disposition, his very same Tory-Evangelical convictions had paradoxically acted as a handicap to advancing the status of Victorian Jews. While eventually accepting the admission of Jews to both houses of parliament, a view he expressed in correspondence to Prime Minister William Gladstone in 1868,[53] Shaftesbury had been a vocal opponent of Jewish Emancipation in the 1850s. As an Evangelical, he held fast to the exclusivist claims of the gospel which held salvation to be impossible for all outside of Christ. For Shaftesbury and his co-religionists, Jews could not be included in God's salvation plan because they refused to confess Christ as "Savior and Lord." Conflating the spiritual realm of Christianity with the temporal realm of the British body-politic, Shaftesbury concluded that the exclusion of professing Jews from the "Body of Christ" axiomatically necessitated their exclusion from the British legislature.[54] His conflation of the two spheres no doubt stemmed from his belief that they were inextricably linked by virtue of the Established Church existing as both a tangible form of the Body of Christ and an organ of the state.[55]

Unlike his Nonconformist brethren who appreciated the separate spheres of church and state, Shaftesbury failed to appreciate that it was possible for a polity such as Britain to admit adherents of other faiths to public office without this compromising, in any way, the integrity of the existing Body of Christ. In contrast to the resistance of such Anglican Evangelicals, Larsen has noted that Victorian Nonconformist Evangelicals were at the

---

52. Shaftesbury, "Oath of Abjuration (Jews) Bill," HL Debates, *Hansard*, 17 July 1851, Vol. 118, c. 886.

53. Shaftesbury, Letter to William Gladstone (December 22, 1868), in Hodder, *Life and Work of the Seventh Earl*, Vol. III, 240. Shaftesbury told Gladstone, "The Jewish question has now been settled. The Jews can sit in both Houses of Parliament. I, myself, resisted their admission, not because I was adverse to the descendant of Abraham . . . but because I objected to the mode in which the admission was to be effected. All that has passed away, and let us now avail ourselves of the opportunity to show regards to God's ancient people."

54. Shaftesbury, "Oath of Abjuration (Jews) Bill," HL Debates, *Hansard*, 17 July 1851, Vol. 118, c. 882–83.

55. Ibid.

vanguard of agitating for religious equality before the law, supporting the civil rights of Roman Catholics, Jews, and atheists.[56] Shaftesbury's insistence on maintaining a homogenously Christian British polity thus owed much to his Anglican high Tory paternalism in addition to mere Evangelical conviction. For high Tory paternalists of the Victorian era, defending the hegemony of the Established Church, the Protestant constitution and the "Christian profession" of the British state still represented non-negotiable articles of faith, which Shaftesbury, for one, seemed unwilling to relinquish.

---

56. Larsen, *Contested Christianity*, 5.

12

Repudiating "Romanism," "Ritualism," and "Rationalism"

Turning to the ecclesiastical sphere, the Evangelical Ashley found his religious creed continuously contested both inside and outside the Church of England. Although the Victorian age, in many respects, represented the high-noon of Evangelicalism, it was also a period which witnessed the more conspicuous presence of Roman Catholicism in "Protestant Britain" and the march of rationalism. As well as focusing on countering the external advances of Catholicism, Ashley found his own church pulled three ways by the competing forces of Low Church Evangelicalism, High Church Tractarianism (or Anglo-Catholicism), and Broad Church latitudinarianism (or theological liberalism). Whilst acknowledging that each of these 'parties' had 'always existed,' William J. Conybeare observed in 1853 that the contrast between these traditions became more sharply pronounced within the *Victorian* Church of England.[1] As a loyal Churchman, Ashley became deeply immersed in these internal machinations and was determined to put his Evangelical stamp on the Anglicanism of his day. Examining this context of Victorian Anglican church life is important as the unfolding of these internal tensions were seen to have the effect of intensifying Ashley's Evangelical convictions together with his long-held political and cultural conservatism.

---

1. Conybeare, "Church Parties," 273.

Repudiating Romanism

As an avowed Evangelical Churchman, Ashley reflected the widespread antipathy of Victorian evangelicals (both Anglican and Nonconformist) towards the Roman Catholicism of their day. The staunchly Protestant flavor of Ashley's Anglicanism has been widely appreciated,[2] but a closer examination of Ashley's attitudes to Catholicism is particularly apposite given Wolffe's observation that Victorian anti-Catholicism represented a significant sphere for the "ideological convergence between Toryism and Evangelicalism which was particularly evident in the mid-1830s."[3] Together with Ashley, Anglican anti-papists such as Hugh McNeile and Robert Jocelyn (later Lord Roden) had "feet in both camps" where their high Tory Protestant constitutionalism melded with their Evangelical Protestantism. Although British anti-Catholicism amongst Protestants had its roots in the English Reformation, where persecution under Queen Mary and the threat of Spanish invasion had combined with theological objections to fan Protestant sentiment, it experienced something of a resurgence in the Victorian era with a series of contemporaneous events and longer-term trends reviving old Protestant fears.[4] The growing presence of Irish Catholic immigrants in Britain, the passage of Catholic Emancipation in 1829, the "Papal Aggression" of 1850 and the Tractarians' gradual resuscitation of quasi-Catholic ritual within the Church of England all created the suspicion that Protestantism was increasingly under siege from "Popery."[5] This set the stage for an ensuing campaign against "Romanism" to which Ashley provided much reinforcement. Hodder observed that "the battle of the Reformation had to be fought over again, and Lord Ashley, for forty years, was one of the leaders in the fight."[6]

Wolffe's identification of a "hardening in anti-Catholicism among Evangelicals" was yet another trait which distinguished the Recordite Evangelicals from the previous Claphamite generation. Like their differences in political and economic outlook, their varying attitudes towards Catholicism were largely the product of external forces and developments. Early nineteenth-century Evangelicals such as Wilberforce and Chalmers had inhabited a world where the French Revolution was seen to diminish

---

2. Battiscombe, *Shaftesbury: A Biography*, 103; Best, *Biography of A. A. Cooper*, 60–61; Finlayson, *Seventh Earl of Shaftesbury*, 160; Turnbull, *Shaftesbury*, 107–8.

3. Wolffe, *Protestant Crusade*, 300.

4. Ibid., 8–9, 16–25.

5. Wolffe, *God and Greater Britain*, 45.

6. Hodder, *Life and Work of the Seventh Earl*, Vol. I, 387–88.

Catholicism as a serious challenge.[7] Accordingly, they tended to be moderate in their anti-Catholicism, believing that Catholics could be won from error with their Church likely to fade into obsolescence.[8] This contrasted with the mindset of the succeeding Evangelical generation who had witnessed the advent of Catholic Emancipation and a growing Catholic population in their midst. Perceiving these developments as threats to the Protestant ascendency, influential Recordites such as Robert and Alexander Haldane helped inject the Evangelical movement with a more militant, anti-Catholic spirit. Considering the indebtedness of Ashley's Evangelicalism to the stridently anti-Catholic Bickersteth and the fact that the great bulk of his public career coincided with the dominance of the Recordites, his hard-line attitudes to Catholicism generally typified those of the latter Evangelical generation.

The Evangelical crusade against Catholicism was waged in both the parliamentary and ecclesiastical spheres with the Catholic threat perceived as political as well as theological. Given Ashley's status as a parliamentarian and active Anglican laymen, he was ideally placed to fight the crusade on both fronts. In the political realm, Evangelical Anglicans saw the successful campaign for Catholic Emancipation and the willingness of a Tory-led government to fund Catholic institutions in Ireland as the principal manifestations of a resurgent Catholicism, the ascendency of which needed to be arrested lest the Church one-day succeed in attaining establishment status in Ireland.

Interestingly, on the question of Catholic Emancipation in 1829, Ashley supported the Catholic Relief Act in parliament and thereby broke ranks with some of his co-religionists who had urged opposition to this concession. Evangelicals, including Bickersteth, had resisted the measure on the ground that it was seen as affording undue legal legitimacy to a religious system they regarded as effectively apostate, with Bickersteth going so far as to denounce it as one of Britain's "national sins."[9] Ashley, on the other hand, took a somewhat more pragmatic approach to the question, adopting the view of Chalmers and the Claphamites that it was a purely "political" matter.[10] Whilst by no means desiring to elevate the status of the Catholic Church, he shared the view of the Wellington administration that, in order to prevent simmering Catholic grievances in Ireland from boiling over into

---

7. Wolffe, *Protestant Crusade*, 30.

8. Ibid., 30.

9. Bickersteth, Diary Entry (April 7, 1829), in Birks, *Edward Bickersteth*, Vol. I, 421.

10. Wolffe, *Protestant Crusade*, 45.

open insurrection, Catholic Emancipation needed to be conceded. Accordingly, he spoke of the measure's expediency:

> The Duke to my great joy, has resolved upon considering the expediency of Roman Catholic Disabilities removing all Catholic disabilities, and substituting in their stead other defences for Church and State. I have long and deeply desired this policy. . . . Nevertheless the measure, although pregnant with danger, is one of high expediency. I rejoice.[11]

Thus, in supporting Catholic Emancipation, Ashley not only voted in accordance with the will of his early parliamentary mentor, Wellington, but aligned himself more closely with the pro-Emancipation stance of the old Clapham "Saints."[12] With this issue surfacing early in Ashley's public career, it illustrated his still continuing affinity with the more moderate Evangelicalism of Wilberforce and the Clapham Sect before his gradual alignment with the emerging "Recordite" generation of Victorian Evangelicals through his ensuing friendships with Bickersteth and Haldane.

On the subsequent issue of publicly funding Catholic-run institutions, however, Ashley was decidedly less accommodating and joined his fellow Evangelicals in opposing such policies. In particular, Ashley campaigned vehemently against the Peel government's decision in 1845 to fund a Roman Catholic seminary in the Irish district of Maynooth. Known as the Maynooth grant, Ashley articulated the widely-held Protestant fear that this measure would irrevocably elevate the status of Roman Catholicism in the British realm and thereby diminish the existing Protestant ascendancy to the nation's great detriment.

> Maynooth will prove a stumbling-block. . . . What a strange ignorance, or haughty contempt for the deep, solemn Protestant feelings in the hearts of the British people! . . . I am resolved to oppose it on this ground: . . . This endowment leads necessarily to the endowment and elevation of the whole priesthood of Ireland you must, having raised them to a certain level, keep them there, and this can be effected by adequate endowment only. Thence the establishment by law of the Roman Catholic Church, and the concurrent existence of two Established Churches![13]

---

11. Ashley, Diary Entry (5 February, 1829), in Hodder, *Life and Work of the Seventh Earl*, Vol. I, 109–10.

12 William Wilberforce, Thomas Buxton, and eventually Charles Simeon, were all on the record as supporting Catholic Emancipation in the late 1820s.

13 Shaftesbury, Diary Entry (April 7–8, 1845), in Hodder, *Life and Work of the Seventh Earl*, Vol. II, 101.

Ashley defended his stance on Maynooth, essentially arguing that to free Roman Catholics from political oppression was one thing but to give them an undue ascension in the body-politic was quite another. Attempting to reconcile Ashley's hard-line position on Maynooth with his more liberal position on Catholic Emancipation sixteen years earlier, Hodder similarly maintained that Shaftesbury "drew a strong distinction between the *persecution* and the *patronage* of Roman Catholics."[14] He added that, of the latter, Ashley "was now and always, a consistent and determined opponent."[15] Thus, in essence, Ashley was happy for Roman Catholics to be accepted into the British polity providing they "kept their place" in the religious and ecclesiastical "pecking-order," with Protestants, particularly those of the Established Church, always in the ascendant. To exclude Catholics entirely, on the one hand, would be oppressive and unjust; but to elevate Catholics to any position of seniority in the nation, on the other hand, would imperil and subvert the nation's Protestant character which Ashley cherished as both an Evangelical and a high Tory.

In the ecclesiastical realm, Ashley was even more determined to counter the perceived threat of "Popery" and resolutely opposed any attempt by the Catholic Church to assert its authority or spread its influence. As important as the preservation of the nation's Protestant constitution was to the Tory Shaftesbury, the theological doctrines of the Evangelical Protestant religion represented matters of life or death with no room for compromise or appeasement to Roman Catholic interests. Wedded to an Evangelical tradition within the Church of England which stressed the supreme authority of the Bible, the simplicity of Christian worship and the rejection of any mediator between Christ and human beings, the Roman Catholic traditions of a sacrificial priesthood performing the "sacrifice of the mass," the need for a priestly mediator in confession, the invocation of the Virgin Mary and the saints in popular piety, together with the œcumenical supremacy of Rome were repugnant to his avowed Protestantism. As with his opposition to government patronage of Catholic institutions, Ashley's theological objections accorded with prevailing evangelical protestant sentiment, both inside and outside the Established Church. According to Robert Robson, Victorian Protestants typically regarded distinctive Roman Catholic doctrines and practices as superfluous, superstitious, fallacious and delusive.[16] They were widely perceived to be medieval corruptions and distortions of

---

14. Hodder, *Life and Work of the Seventh Earl*, Vol. II, 97.
15. Ibid.
16. Robson, "Popular Protestantism," in Robson (ed.), *Ideas and Institutions*, 118.

the Christian church from its original, apostolic, New Testament form of the first century.

With this widespread fear that Anglican worship and the Church of England, generally, could become subsumed into a resurgent Catholic Church, the advent of "Papal Aggression" in 1850 proved to be a rallying-point for such Evangelicals. In what would be popularly termed "Papal Aggression" in Evangelical Protestant circles, Pope Pius IX announced in September 1850 that for the first time since the Reformation, England and Wales would be made an ecclesiastical province of the Roman Catholic Church with an archbishop and twelve suffragans under the jurisdiction of the Pope.[17] Victorian Evangelicals instantly denounced this as a "Papist" encroachment upon the Established Church's territory and saw it as an attempt by Rome to re-foist the Catholic religion on what they defended as a Protestant land with a Protestant people. Addressing a public meeting in London packed with aggrieved Evangelical Protestants in December 1850, Ashley gave expression to their worst fears:

> A foreign priest and potentate, who misunderstands and misgoverns his own people . . . has presumed to treat this realm of England alike "to a tenement or paltry farm," part of its soil into provinces and dioceses, invest his nominees with titles of episcopal and territorial jurisdiction, and usurp the functions of our Royal Mistress. We protest against this as an act of monstrous audacity.[18]

Ashley dreaded not only the ecclesiastical power of Rome in the English realm but also the re-imposition of Catholic doctrines and practices that he and his co-religionists had long detested:

> But what are these to the great and master-temptation the manifest tendency in many of our clergy, in faith and practice, to the faith and practice of the Church of Rome. The numerous perversions of that unscriptural creed, the adoption of rites, ceremonies, and languages fitted only to a Popish meridian need.[19]

Herein, Ashley identified what he perceived to be one of the chief causes of this Catholic revival, namely, the steady drift of the Church of England itself towards a more sacerdotal orientation in doctrine and worship. Like Bickersteth in his *Divine Warning* of 1843,[20] he despaired at

17. Brown, *Providence and Empire*, 180.
18. Ashley, *Speech against Papal Aggression*, 7.
19. Ibid.
20. Bickersteth, *Divine Warning*, 170.

the introduction of auricular confession, a practice Victorian Protestants suspected as having the potential for presiding priests to probe and seduce unsuspecting penitents.[21] With the adoption of such practices, according to Ashley, was it "any wonder that the appetite of the Pope was whetted, that his eyes were blinded, and that he believed the time was come for once more subjecting this Protestant land to his odious dominion."[22] The *Record* concurred, claiming it was "too obvious to be denied that the ritualistic churches have been but nurseries of Popery."[23] These grievances brought into play the second front on which Ashley was fighting for the Protestant cause, the Evangelical crusade against Anglican 'ritualism,' or the 'enemy within.'

Repudiating ritualism

Ashley's opposition to Tractarian ritualism in the Established Church has been widely appreciated by the major biographical studies, which rightly attribute his anti-ritualist stance to his Protestant form of Anglicanism that emphasized the "priesthood of the laity."[24] What needs to be explored, however, are the following considerations: the place of Ashley's anti-Tractarian position within the broader context of ecclesiastical currents shaping Victorian Anglicanism in the 1840s and 50s; the reason why the high Tory Ashley could not countenance an ecclesiastical tradition similarly indebted to romantic Toryism; the specific doctrinal bases for Ashley's rejection of ritualism; and finally, the position of Ashley's Protestantism on the broad continuum of Anglican ecclesiology from Anglo-Catholicism to radical Puritanism.

The Victorian age witnessed the struggle between the Low-Church Evangelical party and the High-Church Tractarian party for the soul of the Established Church. The Evangelical movement emphasized the primacy of scripture and simplicity in church worship, whilst the Oxford-based Tractarian movement stressed the importance of church traditions such as the sacraments and tended towards more elaborate and sacerdotal forms of worship. Given that Ashley's personal Anglican piety was essentially forged through his longstanding friendship with the Evangelical Bickerseth and subsequently reinforced through an evolving friendship with another

21. Robson (ed.), *Ideas and Institutions*, 132–33.
22. Ashley, *Speech against Papal Aggression*, 7.
23. Editorial, *The Record*, May 17, 1867, 2.
24. Battiscombe, *Shaftesbury: A Biography*, 104; Best, *Biography of A. A. Cooper*, 62; Finlayson, *Seventh Earl of Shaftesbury*, 519; Turnbull, *Shaftesbury*, 189.

Evangelical firebrand, Alexander Haldane, the Anglican layman emerged as a warrior for the Evangelical cause in this ecclesiastical battle. In the early 1840s, Ashley's absorption of anti-ritualist Anglicanism from the pens of Bickersteth and Haldane followed closely behind the release of *Tracts for the Times*, the doctrinal blueprint for the Tractarian movement published between 1833 and 1841. With the subsequent appearance of Tractarian vestments such as the alb, chasuble, and stole in the 1850s, Shaftesbury used his parliamentary position in the 1860s to legislate against the use of such vestments and thereby restore the Protestant character of Anglican worship.[25]

Notwithstanding the sharp doctrinal disagreements between Tractarians and Evangelicals such as Bickersteth and Ashley, the Oxford Tractarian movement was largely indebted to the same romantic tradition of the high Tories.[26] In the same vein as Southey, Coleridge, and, indeed, Ashley himself, the over-arching aim of the Tractarians was to re-establish the universal respect for the Church of England as the national church.[27] Like the Victorian Evangelicals, they deplored the modern trends towards disestablishment and secularization. Despite their decidedly Catholic orientation, the Tractarians saw eye-to-eye with the Evangelicals in their mission to preserve the hegemony of the Established Church, and both parties believed that the Church's engagement with the working classes was critical if this was to be realized.[28]

Whilst pursing a common aim, Tractarians and Evangelicals profoundly disagreed with the doctrinal and ecclesiological means by which they sought to achieve that objective. While the Evangelicals believed in restoring the Church to its Protestant identity gifted by the English Reformation, the Tractarians were attracted to periods when they considered the Church of England had, through its ritual and episcopal government, witnessed to Catholic tradition—whether in the Middle Ages or the seventeenth century, the age of the Laudian ideal of promoting the "beauty of holiness." To this end, John Henry Newman, Edward Pusey, John Keble, and their Oxford associates published their *Tracts* which interpreted core Anglican doctrines in a more Catholic light.[29] It was contended that this decidedly Catholic construction of Church doctrine was truer to the original

25. Scotland, *Evangelical Anglicans*, 324.
26. Ibid., 316.
27. Ibid., 315.
28. Ibid., 316.
29. Parsons, *Volume I: Traditions* in *Religion,* 30. Comprised of ninety tracts published between 1833 and 1841, the *Tracts for the Times* series emphasized the place, role and importance of liturgy, sacraments, priesthood, apostolic descent and ecclesiastical continuity, as well as the authority of clergy and bishops within the Church of England.

form and nature of Anglicanism.[30] Evangelicals within the Church, however, countered that this represented a grave distortion of the Church's avowed Protestant identity, forged through the flames of the English Reformation and solidified by the Protestant Anglican martyrs, Thomas Cranmer, Hugh Latimer, and Nicholas Ridley.

As with Roman Catholic doctrine and worship, the Tractarian (or Puseyite) form of Anglicanism was distasteful to Ashley and his Evangelical co-religionists. In addition to undermining the Protestant foundations of the Established Church, Tractarian worship was seen to appeal to the more sensual and worldly instincts of the worshipping public. For Evangelicals in the English Church, worship was to be, ideally, plain and simple so that focus was not unduly diverted from Christ and the pure message of scripture by the interception of mere ceremony.[31] The superficially attractive nature of Puseyite, Catholic-style worship, with its elaborate vestments, chants, candles, incense, and ceremonial excess was seen to seduce the senses and lead astray "the unthinking, the disorientated and the lovers of pomp."[32] In 1866 Shaftesbury reflected these Evangelical misgivings about Tractarian worship with this detailed description of a recent visit to an Anglican parish church in London:

> Service intoned and sung, except the Lessons, by priests with white surplices and green stripe. . . . Then ensued such a scene of theatrical gymnastics, of singing, screaming, genuflections, such a series of strange movements of the priests, their backs almost always to the people, as I never saw before even in a Romish Temple. . . . Is our blessed Lord obeyed in such observances and ceremonials? Do we thus lead souls to Christ or Baal![33]

Surpassing even Roman Catholic worship in its ritual, Shaftesbury believed this was an affront to what he cherished as the historic Protestant tradition of the Anglican Church and was resolved to arrest its burgeoning influence.

To stem the tide of ritualism in the Established Church, Shaftesbury in the 1860s was proactive in supporting a number of parliamentary measures aimed at circumscribing the introduction of Tractarian rituals. Several years before introducing the bills, Ashley had warned his fellow Evangelicals of the spiritual and moral threats posed by "creeping Popery" within

---

30. Ibid., 31.

31. J.O.T Clericus, "On Tractarianism—Letter V," in *The Record*, January 15, 1844, 3.

32. Wolffe, *Protestant Crusade*, 118.

33. Shaftesbury, Diary Entry (July 23, 1866), in Hodder, *Life and Work of the Seventh Earl*, Vol. III, 213–14.

the Anglican Church. In his 1850 *Address to Lay Members of the Church of England*, Ashley appealed to his audience to: "let us turn our eyes to that [mischief] within -; from Popery in flower to Popery in the bud; from the open enemy to the concealed traitor; from the menace that is hurled at our Church to the doctrine that is preached from our pulpit; from the foreign assailant, to the foes of our own household."[34] As Nigel Scotland rightly observed, the restoration of the Roman Catholic hierarchy did much to exacerbate suspicion amongst Evangelicals of anything that even resembled Popery.[35] Determined to muzzle the 'foes' within the Anglican 'household,' Shaftesbury in 1867 moved the first of many anti-ritualist bills in the House of Lords, "An Act for the Further Regulation of the Rites, Ceremonies, and Ornaments used in the Churches or by the Ministers of the United Church of England and Ireland."[36] Whilst warmly welcomed by his fellow Evangelicals of the *Record*, it received little support within the parliament and from the Church of England hierarchy.[37]

Undeterred, Shaftesbury proceeded to introduce his "Clerical Vestments Bill" for the regulation of clerical dress in May 1867. Speaking to the House of Lords, he claimed that the use of "sacramental vestments" offended the country in an unusual degree. Drawing not only on his Protestant convictions but also his conservative instincts, Shaftesbury argued that there was nothing innovative about his bill. On the contrary, it was essentially a "preserving" measure designed to restore Anglican worship to what he understood to be its traditional, simplified form:

> Now, the remedy I wish to propose is not by introducing any innovation. What I maintain is, that these Ritualistic practices are a great innovation on the system and conduct of the Church. ... I wish to see the usage and practice of the Church ever since the period of the Reformation, which has been sanctioned by experience, which has given contentment and satisfaction to our forefathers, our fathers, and ourselves.[38]

Thus, for Shaftesbury, the Evangelical mission to rid the English Church of "Romish" ritualism was just as much a conservative campaign to restore and preserve for all time, the traditional Protestant character of Anglicanism.

---

34. Ashley, *Speech against Papal Aggression*, 7.
35. Scotland, *Evangelical Anglicans*, 332.
36. Whisenant, *Fragile Unity*, 79.
37. Ibid.
38. Shaftesbury, "Clerical Vestments (No 2) Bill," Second Reading, HL Debates, *Hansard*, 14 May 1867, Vol. 187, c. 479.

The antipathy of Shaftesbury towards Puseyism was echoed by lead Evangelical periodicals and Evangelical members of the Church hierarchy. The *Record* drew attention to what it perceived to be the sensual snares of ritualism, editorializing that it was often embraced at the expense of genuine theological conviction: ". . . there are a great number of educated people, rather fastidious and artistic in their natures, who, without much theological bias, like choral services and a richly dressed altar, and think that, as they have to go to church, they may as well go to a place where the service is tastefully conducted."[39] J. C. Ryle, the Evangelical Bishop of Liverpool from 1880–1900, warned that "church decorations, church music, and a semi-historic mode of going through Church worship might seem to have some appeal, but they were a threat to spiritual religion." Like Shaftesbury, he feared that they could introduce dangerous tendencies into otherwise Protestant parishes. Esteeming Evangelicalism as a heart-felt, muscular form of Christianity, Ryle concluded that "Processions, banners, flowers, crosses, music, beautiful vestments, etc. might please children and weak-minded people, but they would never help forward heart conversion or heart sanctification."[40]

For all his emphatic opposition to ritualism, however, it would be inaccurate to characterize Ashley as a Protestant in the radical Puritan mold who was emphatic about expunging every tradition with even the slightest hint of Catholicism. First of all, Ashley was well aware that a High Church tradition had always existed within the Church of England alongside his own Low Church party. He acknowledged that the High Church contained "many wise, good, and learned men."[41] Pointing out that the gulf between the existing Low and High Church parties themselves was in fact less than that between the old High Church and new Tractarians, he nonetheless saw the contemporary ritualist movement as a bridge too far, even for the relatively accommodating and heterogeneous Church of England.[42] Unlike the Puritan secessionists of the seventeenth century, Ashley was content to operate within the Church of England and therefore accepted he would be in communion with those who favored more elaborate forms of worship. Owing to his loyalty to the English Church, characteristic of Tories generally, he imbibed some church traditions that many Nonconformist or "Puritan-minded" Protestants would dismiss as not necessarily mandated by scrip-

---

39 *The Record*, quoted in *The Times*, 20 August, 1867.

40. J. C. Ryle quoted in *The Record*, 14 Oct 1867.

41. Shaftesbury, "Clerical Vestments (No. 2) Bill," Second Reading, *Hansard*, HL Debates 14 May 1867, Vol. 187, c. 498.

42. Ibid., c. 497–98.

ture. It appeared Ashley observed key "Holy Days" of the Church calendar including Ash Wednesday and Trinity Sunday. He "took the sacrament" on Trinity Sunday and defended his decision to decline an invitation to a party on Ash Wednesday, viewing such a celebration as unbefitting of that day's solemnity and traditional significance within the English Church.[43]

In contrast to the seventeenth-century Puritans, Ashley also regarded the crucifix as an acceptable part of personal piety and worship, even going so far as to praise its presence in the Catholic districts of Switzerland and to lament its absence from some Protestant churches in Scotland. On touring the Swiss countryside in 1833, he reflected:

> ... the ensign of the Cross, comely in its form and adapted to the scenery, places the humiliation and the power of God in wondrous juxtaposition. The use of the Cross has been superstitiously abused, and Protestant nations have therefore mostly abandoned it; but we suffer by the change. Such a memorial is necessary and ought to be pleasing.[44]

Accordingly, on a subsequent visit to Scotland in 1840, he noted with satisfaction, the decision of many Presbyterian Churches to re-adorn their steeples with a cross.[45] Ashley had even purchased a crucifix from Italy, esteeming it as a fitting memorial to the atonement of Christ but cautioning against its abuse as an "idol" to be worshipped.

> At Padua, bought a small crucifix. . . . The worship of the material or the mere representation, is senseless, wicked, and idolatrous, but to bear about a memorial of what God himself once exhibited to the world, does but simply recall His death and passion, and forces us, as Scripture has foretold, "to look on Him whom we pierced."[46]

This essentially encapsulated Ashley's Anglican Evangelical outlook which, on the one hand, denounced Roman Catholicism and Tractarianism for

---

43. Ashley, Diary Entries (June 6, 1841) and (Ash Wednesday February, 1850), in Hodder, *Life and Work of the Seventh Earl*, Vol. I, 337 and Vol. II, 312.

44. Ashley, Diary Entry (1833), in Hodder, *Life and Work of the Seventh Earl*, Vol. I, 173.

45. Ashley, Diary Entry (August 22, 1840), *Life and Work of the Seventh Earl*, Vol. I, 263–64. Ashley saw this trend of many Presbyterian Churches to re-surmount a steeple cross as "proof of the abatement of the bigoted ignorance and furious spirit of the Covenanters, and a practical advance towards the reasonable service of the Church of England."

46. Ashley, Diary Entry (1833), in Hodder, *Life and Work of the Seventh Earl*, Vol. I, 177–78.

what he saw as their excessive veneration of religious symbols such as the crucifix but, on the other hand, declined to follow the extreme Protestant tendency to dismiss such symbols altogether. Ashley's tone of Protestantism was thus determined and resolute, but by no means fanatical and iconoclastic. Repudiating the radicalism of Puseyism or Puritanism, the Earl's Anglican Evangelicalism remained eminently conservative in keeping with his innate Toryism.

Repudiating rationalism

The emergence of the liberal 'Broad Church' party in the Established Church from the 1850s and 60s had the effect of accentuating the defensive conservatism of Shaftesbury's Evangelicalism, making it more visibly characteristic of the Recordite school. In 1856 he wrote that the progress of rationalism was "rapid, fearful and resistless."[47] In the face of this challenge, Ashley stood firmly with the Recordites in their defiant stance on scriptural authority and their attainment of a *modus vivendi* with the Tractarians. During the Victorian era, the Church of England had not only been polarized by the opposing Tractarian and Evangelical movements, but pulled in yet another direction by the emerging rationalist or "Broad Church" movement in the 1840s and 50s. Unlike either the Tractarian or Evangelical movements, the Victorian Broad Churchmen did not bask in the perceived glories of the past, whether that was the early medieval period or the English Reformation. On the contrary, they were eager to modernize the Church of England and recalibrate its theology to reflect the insights and advances of the present age, particularly in the fields of natural science and anthropology.[48] The rationalists contended that the scriptures and other sacred texts of the Church needed to be reinterpreted in light of contemporary assumptions about the nature of humanity and the origins of the universe. For many of these Broad Churchmen, this entailed a questioning of the creation account in Genesis and the supernatural miracles of Christ recorded in the four Gospels through the lenses of a then radical hermeneutic known as "higher biblical criticism."[49]

Emanating chiefly from German academic circles, most notably the Tübingen School of theology, higher criticism sought a reappraisal of the biblical texts in their historical and cultural contexts.[50] The new rational-

---

47. Shaftesbury, Diary Entry (May 28, 1856). [Broadlands Archives SHA/PD/7]
48. Brown, *Providence and Empire*, 235.
49. Ibid., 228.
50. Brown, *Providence and Empire*, 228; Hylson-Smith, *Evangelicals in the Church*

ist perspectives were principally enunciated in the *Essays and Reviews* of 1860, followed by Bishop John William Colenso's work on *The Pentateuch and Book of Joshua Critically Examined* (1862–63) and John Robert Seeley's work, *Ecce Homo* (1866). While the majority of Evangelical Anglicans were uniformly critical of the new works for what they regarded as their departure from scriptural authority, Nigel Scotland discerned a difference in the *scale* of reaction between the Recordite Evangelicals and those that stood in the moderate tradition of Simeon and the Clapham Sect.[51] Holding to an unequivocal doctrine of "verbal inspiration" that regarded *all* parts of the Bible as *equally* inspired, the Recordites were singularly hostile in their response to the higher criticism. On the other hand, the moderates were prepared to recognize the validity of some of the points that the essayists had raised, most notably in matters of eschatology and the authorship of the Pentateuch.[52] While the Simeon moderates similarly held to the divine inspiration of scripture, they had recognized that not all scripture was equally inspired in the sense that some passages clearly provided divine and salvific revelation while others were merely historical narrative, poetry, or ceremonial law.[53] Despite his earlier indebtedness to Thomas Scott, whose own view of scripture had accorded with that of Simeon, Shaftesbury's doctrine of verbal inspiration in the 1860s resembled that of the Recordites. Like his friend Haldane, Shaftesbury insisted that the entire Bible must be accepted in its literal sense, lest its authority be shaken. He told the Church Pastoral Aid Society in 1862 that the "blessed old book is God's from the very first syllable to the very last."[54]

Together with the *Record*, Shaftesbury was committed to forging common ground with his Tractarian opponents on the issue of biblical orthodoxy. With Evangelicals and Tractarians each devoted to conserving the received traditions of the Established Church, albeit in markedly different ecclesiastical forms and often in bitterly conflicting ways, higher criticism was denounced by each of these parties as a radical subversion of historic Church teaching. So great was the chasm between the new modes of thinking and the old, that this unwittingly gave rise to an unlikely alliance between two old foes who now found themselves at war with a "common enemy" against a "common orthodoxy." Viewing themselves as newfound

---

of England, 135.

51. Scotland, *Evangelical Anglicans*, 139–40.
52. Ibid.
53. Ibid., 132.
54. Shaftesbury, Address to Church Pastoral Aid Society (1862) in Hodder, *Life and Work of the Seventh Earl*, Vol. III, 7.

co-belligerents in the fight against rationalism, Evangelicals and Tractarians temporarily suspended some of their old hostilities in a shared determination to defend what they each cherished as the doctrinal pillars of historic Christianity.[55] The common ground between the two parties was reinforced when the Judicial Committee of the Privy Council reversed a lower court decision against two of the authors of the *Essays and Reviews*.[56] In a letter to the *Record*, the lead Tractarian, Pusey, called for a united memorial repudiating the ideas advanced by the essayists. Pusey's initiative was warmly welcomed by most Victorian Evangelicals and strongly endorsed by the *Record*.[57] In an ensuing gesture of unity, a committee comprised of prominent Evangelical and Tractarian members drafted the "Oxford Declaration" in July 1864 affirming their shared commitment to Christian orthodoxy. Determined to buttress the supremacy of the Bible, the Declaration affirmed that "the Church of England . . . maintains, without reserve or qualification, the inspiration and Divine authority of the whole Canonical Scriptures as not only containing but being the Word of God."[58]

Like the *Record*, Shaftesbury saw eye-to-eye with his old Tractarian opponent Pusey on the perceived threat to Christian orthodoxy posed by rationalist theology. In the lead up to the 1864 Oxford Declaration, he wrote to his fellow alumnus of Christ Church, Oxford, pleading for a conservative show of solidarity between the Evangelical and the Tractarian in the common battle to defend the "faith once delivered."

> My Dear Pusey . . . Time, space, and divergent opinions have separated us for many years: but circumstances have arisen which must, if we desire combined action in the cause of our common Master, set at nought, time, space and divergent opinions. We will fight about those another day; in this we must contend earnestly for the faith once delivered to the saints; and it must be done together now. We have to struggle, not for Apostolic Succession or Baptismal Regeneration, but for the very Atonement itself, for the sole hope of fallen man, the vicarious sacrifice of the Cross.[59]

The Earl's desire for unity was reciprocated by the High Church party in 1864 with the Bishop of Oxford, Samuel Wilberforce, pledging cooperation

55. Hylson-Smith, *Evangelicals in the Church of England*, 137, 139.
56. Whisenant, *Fragile Unity*, 80.
57. Ibid.
58. Ibid.
59. Shaftesbury, letter to Dr Pusey (February 26, 1864) in Hodder, *Life and Work of the Seventh Earl*, Vol. III, 166.

with Shaftesbury in the defense of core Christian doctrines against the "tide of rationalism":

> It is my earnest desire that the terrible evil of this judgment should become the means of healing the wound which the separation of High and Low Church inflict upon us, by bringing together all who believe simply in the Bible and in the plain language of our creeds. I have no doubt that this is your wish, too, and I shall be heartily glad to co-operate with you, so far as you will allow, in resisting this flood of Rationalistic infidelity which is rising daily higher and higher.[60]

Notwithstanding his willingness to forge a constructive alliance with ritualism in the battle against rationalism, Shaftesbury was under no illusion that the remaining differences between his fellow Evangelicals and the Tractarians faded into insignificance. Such differences needed to be dealt with at an opportune time once the rationalist controversy had subsided. Indeed of ritualism and rationalism, he continued to perceive ritualism as the graver of the two challenges facing the institutional Church of England whilst viewing rationalism as by far the greatest threat to Christianity as a whole.[61]

For all his attachment to the Established Church, the survival of orthodox Christianity was Shaftesbury's pre-eminent concern, thereby necessitating the priority to combat rationalism ahead of all other challenges to Evangelical Christianity. Notwithstanding the advances of Victorian rationalism in ecclesiastical quarters, with the Society for the Promotion of Christian knowledge publishing Thomas G. Bonney's *A Manual of Geology* (1876),[62] Shaftesbury remained optimistic that classical Christianity would prevail.[63] Owing to his premillennial faith in the triumph of the Second Advent, the veteran Evangelical crusader defiantly shared with Bonney in 1878, his "ardent hope that this decline of true belief may be followed by a day more bright and glorious than England has yet known."[64] Unshaken in

60. Bishop Wilberforce, letter to Shaftesbury (February 29, 1864) in Hodder, *Life and Work of the Seventh Earl*, Vol. III, 168.

61. Shaftesbury, Diary Entry (May 26, 1864) in Hodder, *Life and Work of the Seventh Earl*, Vol. III, 164–65.

62. As a Church of England clergyman and geologist, Thomas G. Bonney (1833–1923) penned his *Manual of Geology* on the premise that claims of divine revelation ought to be subject to scientific and historical scrutiny. Evangelicals such as Shaftesbury rejected such propositions, claiming that they undermined the authority of scripture.

63. Shaftesbury, Diary Entry (February 16, 1878) in Hodder, *Life and Work of the Seventh Earl*, Vol. III, 385.

64. Shaftesbury, "Letter to the Rev T. G. Bonney," 18–19.

his belief in the historicity of the Pentateuch, he told Bonney that "a time is at hand when High Criticism will accept, with reverential joy, the 26th of Leviticus and the 28th of Deuteronomy and science will bow, in grateful amazement, before the superhuman truths of the first chapters of Genesis."[65] Despite a sense of resignation that the progress of higher criticism and scientific revelation in the 1870s had left him increasingly isolated in his essentially unchanged orthodoxy,[66] Shaftesbury's spirits were no doubt buoyed by the rise of later Victorian Evangelicals such as J. C. Ryle who championed the Recordite doctrine of "verbal inspiration" in *Knots United* (1874) and *The Authoritative Interpretation of Holy Scripture* (1877).[67]

Seeking pan-evangelical unity in the "faith once delivered"

With Victorian Evangelicalism encountering the twin challenges of "Romanism and ritualism" in the 1840s, prominent figures within the movement, including the clergyman Baptist Noel,[68] Edward Bickersteth, and Lord Ashley began to appreciate the need to build bridges with brethren outside the Established Church, especially Nonconformists, in a show of pan-evangelical solidarity. T. R. Birks, the biographer and son-in-law of Bickersteth, observed that the two principal factors driving pan-evangelical unity were "the growing conviction, in the minds of sincere Christians, belonging to different bodies, that their real union of heart and judgment was far greater than outward appearance," and secondly, the need for a pan-evangelical offensive to counter "the progress of Popery."[69] Wolffe added that the cause of pan-evangelical solidarity was bolstered by the Scottish Disruption of 1843 which inspired evangelicals to emulate the quest of Chalmers and his secessionists for a doctrinally purified, national church, together with the interdenominational Anti-Maynooth Conference of 1845 that mobilized Anglican and Nonconformist Evangelicals against Peel's decision to endow

---

65. Ibid.

66. Hodder, *Life and Work of the Seventh Earl*, 384.

67. Scotland, *Evangelical Anglicans*, 144–45.

68. In the Church of England, Baptist Noel served as minister of St John's Chapel, Bedford Row, London from 1827 to 1848. Afterwards, however, he switched his denominational allegiance to become the Baptist minister of John Street Baptist Church and eventually President of the Baptist Union.

69. Birks, *Edward Bickersteth*, Vol. II, 303, in Wolffe, "The Evangelical Alliance," 340.

an Irish Roman Catholic Seminary.[70] This new spirit of evangelical concord culminated in the formation of the Evangelical Alliance in August 1846, an initiative in which Bickersteth played a key role by agreeing to attend the inaugural Liverpool conference of the Alliance.[71] The *Record* was willing to support the Alliance,[72] having declared the previous year that "as at the Reformation, so unquestionably now, do we urgently stand in need of the union of all orthodox and evangelical Christians who hold the head according to the reformed faith."[73]

While the quest for pan-evangelical unity represented a noteworthy development in Victorian Evangelicalism, it was by no means embraced by the entirety of the movement.[74] As Wolffe appreciated, the establishment issue which had divided Church and Dissent still loomed large in the climate of the 1840s and thereby dampened much of the enthusiasm for unity. Evangelical Anglicans such as Hugh McNeile, together with the *Christian Observer*, maintained that anti-popery was an insufficiently cohesive force to bind Churchmen to Nonconformists who had attacked the Establishment and, on occasions, sided politically with Catholicism.[75] Amid this background, it was specific Evangelical leaders such as Bickersteth who inspired Ashley to continue the cause of pan-evangelical solidarity.

Desiring to replicate Bickersteth's support for trans-denominational Evangelical initiatives, Ashley was eager to work collaboratively with Nonconformists in a range of movements championing the broader evangelical cause. In addition to the Evangelical Alliance, Ashley worked through the BFBS, the LMS, and the RSU to foster pan-evangelical unity. Shaftesbury's appreciation of Nonconformist evangelicals was on display with his unveiling of a statue of the Congregationalist hymn-writer Isaac Watts in 1861[76] and in his close personal friendship with the Victorian Baptist preacher C. H. Spurgeon during the 1870s. Along with Ashley himself, Spurgeon was a key figure of Victorian evangelicalism with his uncompromising stance on the Bible's authority and his philanthropy demonstrated through his church-run orphanage. Ashley and Spurgeon found much evangelical common ground in their shared distaste for ostentatious worship and desire

70. Wolffe, "Evangelical Alliance," 336–38.

71. Brown, *Providence and Empire*, 128; Wolffe, "Evangelical Alliance," 339.

72. Wolffe, "Evangelical Alliance," 344.

73. Editorial, *The Record*, March 18, 1844, 4.

74. Wolffe, "Evangelical Alliance," 339. Wolffe noted that of the 216 delegates who attended the Liverpool conference of the Alliance, only 15 were members of the Church of England.

75. Ibid., 343–44.

76. Shaftesbury, *Inauguration of the Memorial Statue to Dr Isaac Watts*, 10.

for simple, informal worship. Despite Shaftesbury's aristocratic status, both were essentially "men of the people" determined to connect the church and its gospel message to the common folk. In attempts to bring the Established Church closer to the people, Shaftesbury energetically supported legislation to allow worship services to be conducted in nonconventional venues such as theatres and public halls. In so doing, he succeeded in reducing the gap between Anglican Evangelicals and Nonconformist evangelicals who had practised such services for years.

Indeed Shaftesbury regarded the traditional Anglican insistence on worship services in cathedrals, churches and chapels as one of the historic handicaps to closer collaboration between Anglicans and Nonconformists. This Anglican tradition appeared to perpetuate the perception amongst Dissenters that, like the Roman Catholics, Anglicans were unduly preoccupied with the outward forms of religious observance.[77] Accordingly, Shaftesbury appealed for the Church of England in 1860 to relax its ordinances regarding the venue for its worship services in the interests of not only drawing closer to the Dissenters but also attracting more people to the Church, particularly those of the working classes:

> Such are the classes whom I and my friends desire to soften and to render amenable to order and civilization. They must be won, and for that purpose resort must be had to everything that is true and legitimate. For this purpose I rejoice to say that many Churchmen and Nonconformists have joined together in a common effort. The question now is, shall these vast masses be left in ignorance, or shall they be brought in this way to a knowledge of the truth? Is the evil of thus opening the theatres comparable to the evil of abandoning the people to total darkness?[78]

Although the conduct of worship services in non-conventional places would signify a break with tradition and perhaps otherwise run counter to Shaftesbury's conservative instincts, it was vastly preferable to draw more people back to the "old paths" of the Evangelical faith than to cling to the old places of worship. If the increase of church attendance meant innovating worship services to cater to working-class sensibilities, than this was a change he was prepared to wear for the greater cause of reaching the working class.

---

77. Shaftesbury, Clerical Vestments (No 2) Bill, Second Reading, *HL Debates, Hansard,* 14 May 1867, Vol. 187, c. 489. Shaftesbury told the House of Lords that "Anglicans are reproached by [Dissenting] Protestants with their resemblance to Romans; they say a stranger entering into a church where ritual is carefully attended to might easily mistake it for a Roman Service."

78. Shaftesbury, "Divine Services in Theatres," HL Debates, *Hansard*, 24 February 1860, Vol. 156, c. 1676.

While enthusiastic about collaborating with Nonconformists in the pursuit of common evangelical ideals and eager for the gospel to transcend denominational boundaries, Shaftesbury's Churchmanship remained firm and his desire was always for the Church of England to maintain its ascendant status. Indeed, his campaign to reform worship services was not *despite* his attachment to Anglicanism, but precisely *because* of his attachment to the Church of England. Although his call to conduct worship services in theatres and halls was about partnering with Nonconformists for the sake of the gospel, there was also an element of rivalry as he told his fellow Lords in 1860 that he did not wish to see the Church of England cede this whole outreach strategy to the Nonconformist churches:

> I ask whether you are prepared, as members of the Church of England, to see the Church stand aloof, and the whole of this movement given up exclusively to the Dissenters? Will you say to these destitute and hungering men, we can do you no sort of good. Come, if you like, to Episcopal churches and chapels, and there you shall be preached to in a stiff, steady, buckram style.[79]

Thus, by urging the Established church to mutate to this new culture of worship, the Church of England would be able to survive as a key player in the contemporary Victorian evangelical scene. By stubbornly resisting such innovation, however, the Church was in danger of forfeiting its lead role and becoming an irrelevancy, a fate the Anglican Shaftesbury was studious to avoid. The quest by Shaftesbury and his Victorian co-religionists to claim the soul of the Church of England for the Evangelical cause underscored not only his Evangelical convictions but also his high Tory ideals, particularly those of patriotism and attachment to traditional paradigms. The Earl's crusade against Romanism was fueled not simply by reformed Evangelical theology but also by the romantic Tory tradition of Southey, espoused in his *Book of the Church*, to preserve what he cherished as Britain's political and cultural Protestant identity.

---

79. Shaftesbury, "Divine Services in Theatres, HL Debates, *Hansard*, 24 February 1860, Vol. 156, c. 1687.

13

Home and Hearth

The Victorian Evangelical idealization of family life

The basic conception of the family remained relatively unchanged between the late Hanoverian and Victorian generation of Evangelicals. Where matters such as eschatological doctrine and economic ideology had tended sharply to divide the Recordite generation of Evangelicals from the preceding Claphamites, a shared idealization of the family as the temporal microcosm of the "heavenly family" and the bosom of social virtue, on the other hand, had emerged as one of the constants bridging the two generations. Despite the aversion of the Claphamites to state paternalism, their conception of the family reflected innately paternalist assumptions which were of course shared by the Recordites. According to Davidoff and Hall, Victorian Christians of all denominations and dispositions envisioned the family as a hierarchical unit with its members discharging their duties according to their rank.[1] Within the family, it was natural that the husband should command and the wife, children and servants obey.[2]

For Recordite and Claphamite Evangelicals specifically, this patriarchal and paternalist family paradigm was seen to accord with the teachings of scripture, where in his Epistle to the Colossians, St Paul had exhorted "wives to submit yourselves unto your own husbands' and children to

---

1. Davidoff and Hall, *Family Fortunes*, 108.
2. Ibid.

'obey your parents in all things."³ Eager to impress the Pauline doctrine of family on the faithful, Evangelical collections of family prayers were fond of invoking this passage.⁴ Through the publication of tracts and treatises, Chaphamite Evangelicals including Henry Thornton, Hannah More, and Thomas Gisborne sought to inculcate their ideal of the family as a paternalist kinship sanctioned by scripture. As early as 1792, More opined in *Village Politics* that the landed gentleman was the head of his family, whose wife and children should obediently follow his judgment, whose faithful servants and labourers would value the kindness and consideration of their master.⁵ Gisborne took the view in 1796 that the duties of women were to care for their relatives, to improve their menfolk and to bring up their children on a Christian path.⁶

Building on the teachings of the Claphamite Evangelicals, Edward Bickersteth popularized the cult of domesticity for a new generation of Victorian Evangelicals, including his protégé, Ashley. Believing, like Thornton, that habitual devotions of family prayer and Bible reading were critical to the daily rhythm and wellbeing of the Evangelical household, Bickersteth published his own collection of *Family Prayers* in 1842. As well as aiming to provide spiritual "refreshment" and "strength" to family life, a couple of his composed prayers attempted to prescribe a distinctively paternalist pattern of family life for Victorian households. As petitions to God, these prayers asked that the Almighty fashion domestic life according to a hierarchical system of authority and headship complemented by obedience, submission and dependency.

Drawing on the paternalist assumption of the dependent party seeking direction and rule from its leader, Bickersteth's prayer "For persons dependent on us" reminded family-heads that God had entrusted them with a "solemn" responsibility over their children who looked up to them "for direction and government."⁷ Accordingly, the prayer asked God to help these heads of the family to use "so solemn and responsible a trust for the best good of those committed" to their charge.⁸ Invoking the paternalist motifs of duty, instruction and training, Bickersteth's "Prayer for [the] husband and wife to use together" petitioned God to help the spouses fulfill their

---

3. Colossians 3:18–22.

4. *Family Prayers for Everyday of the Week: Culled from the Bible for Morning and Evening* (1824) cited in Davidoff and Hall, *Family Fortunes*, 104.

5. Ibid., 168–69.

6. Gisborne, *Enquiry into the Duties*, 286.

7. Edward Bickersteth, *Family Prayers*, 379.

8. Ibid.

"family duties" and specifically requested help for the parents "to train up" their "children in the way they should go, commanding them to keep the way of the Lord, and continually instructing them in thy truth."[9] Unlike his premillennial eschatology or pro-state intervention posture, his ideal of the family did not mark a break from his Claphamite past. Whilst Bickersteth could not countenance the *laissez-faire* attitudes of the Claphamites, he happily imbibed their paternalist conception of the family. As Davidoff and Hall pointed out, the majority of classical liberal political economists, in any case, were comfortable "with a conventional view of the family," providing the paternalist paradigm of the private household was not extrapolated to the state.[10]

Ashley similarly embraced the Claphamite Evangelical philosophy of the family, thereby contributing to its perpetuation throughout the Victorian era. Although he never published any literature extolling the virtues of domestic life, his views on the subject were frequently and clearly expressed in parliamentary debates, particularly those on factory reform legislation. Despite having much to say about the significance of the family and its role in Victorian society, Ashley's views on the subject do not seem to have elicited a great deal of attention and analysis in the major biographical studies to date.[11] Even when focusing on Ashley's contribution to the factory reform debates, the principal context where his views on family and gender surfaced, the biographers made much of the social reformer's concern for the plight of factory children but little about his defense of domestic life as one of the guiding rationales behind his agitation for the cause.[12] Meanwhile, in their otherwise insightful discussion of Victorian Evangelical family life, Davidoff and Hall recognized the historical significance of Clapham figures such as Thornton and More, but did not touch upon Ashley and the extent to which his pronouncements typified Victorian Evangelical attitudes towards the family. Davidoff and Hall briefly quoted the factory reformer, G. S. Bull, in passing but made no mention of how he, and his fellow campaigners such

---

9. Ibid., 411.

10. Davidoff and Hall, *Family Fortunes*, 185.

11. The one exception is Edwin Hodder who quoted an extract from Ashley's reply (September 26, 1842) to the Address of the Central Short-Time Committee decrying the adverse effects of the factory system on family life. See Hodder, *Life and Work of the Seventh Earl*, Vol. I, 437.

12. Turnbull, *Shaftesbury*, 80–81. For example, Turnbull made due reference to Ashley's concern about the adverse effects of factory labor on the mental health and physique of children but not its ramifications for family life.

as Ashley, conspicuously saw the existing factory system as detrimental to family life.[13]

In the tradition of Bickersteth and the Claphamites, Ashley cherished what he regarded as the paternalist essence of the family unit. In a departure from the thinking of the Claphamites, however, he argued that it was not only essential for Evangelicals to cultivate this pattern of family life in their own households but also necessary for the state proactively to intervene and protect domestic life from the encroachments of the factory system. Accordingly, for Ashley, the principal objectives of factory reform legislation were the release of children from oppressive forms of industrial labor, the restoration of harmonious relations between employer and employee *and* the protection of the family which he saw as groaning under the weight of unregulated labor.[14] Responding to an 1842 Short-Time Committee, Ashley cataloged the deleterious social effects of the prevailing factory system:

> Domestic life and domestic discipline must soon be at an end; society will consist of individuals no longer grouped into families; so early is the separation of husband and wife, of parents and children. Thousands of young females of tender years are absorbed, day by day, in the factories and workshops; every hour is given to their toil, and that toil the most unsuited to their age and sex.[15]

Viewing families, rather than individuals, as constituting the basic units of society, Ashley was resolved to arrest this social disintegration by regulating factory labor in such a way as to preclude it from continually intruding upon family relationships. Thus, to enable children and parents to spend a greater proportion of the day together, the first practical measure he campaigned for was the reduction of factory work-hours for underage children.

Publicly confronting this perceived assault of the factory system on the family, Ashley argued that it not only estranged family members from one another, but, importantly, it reversed what he regarded as the traditional and divinely ordained pattern of family relationships with the submission of wives to husbands and the obedience of children to parents. Speaking of industrial labor in the House of Commons, he claimed that:

> It disturbs the order of nature, and the rights of the labouring men, by ejecting the males from the workshop, and filling

---

13. Davidoff and Hall, *Family Fortunes*, 109.

14. Kirby, *Child Labour in Britain*, 97–98.

15. Lord Ashley, "Reply to Lancashire Short-Time Committee" (pamphlet), Manchester, 26 Sep, 1842.

their places by females, who are thus withdrawn from all their domestic duties, and exposed to insufferable toil at half the wages that would be assigned to males, for the support of their families...[16]

Echoing Ashley, the *Record* decried the factory system in 1844 as "contrary to the design of providence" by "subverting" the "natural course of things" in the domestic sphere:

> ... a system has been introduced and has silently but rapidly spread through our operative population, contrary ... to the design of Providence and to the course of nature. It is man who is to go forth unto his work and to his labour till the evening; it is the woman who is to guide the house; and children are to be trained in useful knowledge, and strengthened by play and healthful exercise for the real labours of life, to which they are to be called in due season ... but this, the natural course of things, has been gradually subverted to a most hurtful extent ....[17]

As illustrated by these forgoing effects on family life, the existing factory system militated against every domestic value that Ashley, Oastler, Sadler, and the Victorian Evangelicals stood for, namely those of domestic paternalism, order, cleanliness, thrift, and a clear sense of "one's place" within the family structure. Ashley expressed his alarm at how the factory system had usurped the responsibility for husbands to provide for their wives, condemning this as a "perversion of nature" which had "the inevitable effect of introducing into families disorder, insubordination, and conflict."[18] He also described the "insubordination of children to their parents" as "one of the most frightful evils taking place in the manufacturing districts."[19]

For Ashley, as well as for Oastler and Bull, the campaign to curtail factory hours was all about reasserting the traditional primacy of the family within the social fabric of the nation. Resembling the most basic of "societies," the family was seen to represent a microcosm of how society at large should appear and how it ought to function as a cohesive unit. For Shaftesbury and other Tory paternalists, maintaining the cohesive, paternalist and deferential nature of the family was fundamental to realizing a society in which the various spheres of government, church, business, professional life, education and academe would reflect the same paradigm writ large.

16. Ibid.
17. Editorial, *The Record*, March 28, 1844, 4.
18. Ashley, "Hours of Labour in Factories," HC Debates, *Hansard*, 15 March 1844, Vol. 73, c. 1096.
19. Ibid.

Moreover, the family was also esteemed by conservatives as the primary conduit through which age-old traditions and values could be seamlessly transmitted from one generation to the next, thereby ensuring that unbroken continuity with the past which Edmund Burke and other conservatives had so highly valued as critical to a society's sense of its own heritage and identity. Meanwhile, for Ashley the Evangelical, the campaign for factory reform was about protecting and honoring the "first society" God had instituted on earth. Believing every word of the Bible to be "divinely inspired" and "authoritative," Ashley saw New Testament teaching on the need for wives to submit to their husbands and children to obey their parents as applicable to the present age; hence his idealized Victorian family reflected this deferential pattern of domestic relationships.

In addition to the factory reform campaign, Ashley's efforts to provide adequate housing for working class families was similarly driven by a desire to protect and uphold his family ideal. Reflecting common Victorian preoccupations with domestic order and cleanliness, Shaftesbury saw the construction and provision of clean, orderly and secure dwellings for working class families in 1872 as eminently conducive to fostering healthy domestic relationships:

> I am glad, then, to say that you have inaugurated this workman's city upon a sound and wise basis, and that every man shall have his house to himself . . . to maintain the great principal that the working man should be the master of his house, and the happy head of a moral and industrious family. I would urge you most sincerely, as long as you have breath, to hold fast to the great social family relations of life. That will be the first step in the prosperity of your city, and it is the grand security of empires.[20]

His family ideal melded the longstanding Tory paternalist emphasis on property ownership with traditional Evangelical teaching on male-headship within the family home. Drawing from these two traditions, Ashley's Victorian family ideal would represent the epitome of social respectability and moral rectitude, with its close ties providing the foundation for national prosperity and security. Under what he called "the holy sanction of domestic life," the family home contained the "seed of all virtue, decency, morality, comfort and true dignity."[21] Thus Ashley's conception of the family represented the product of a forgoing trend in nineteenth century society

---

20. Shaftesbury, *Speech on Laying the Memorial Stone*, 5.
21. Shaftesbury, *Speech at Working Men's Meeting*.

which Davidoff and Hall identified as the transposition of the traditional aristocratic concept of *stewardship* into religious discourse.[22]

In his personal life, meanwhile, Ashley's own domestic habits evidently reflected the public pronouncements he made on the nature of the family. Reflecting on his family life, Geoffrey Best remarked that Ashley tried to make his own home a model of his universal ideal for secure and harmonious families.[23] As early as 1828, thoughts of domestic life were on the mind of the twenty-seven year old bachelor when he remarked that he "rejoiced in the fancy of patriarchal duties."[24] Accordingly, he mused "what a purity of delight if God would bestow on me the wife of my heart, and a place for the exercise of imagined virtues!"[25] Marrying Emily Cowper (1810–72) in June 1830, Ashley enjoyed a felicitous and fruitful marriage with his wife for forty-two years.[26] As Ashley immersed himself in public affairs, his wife acted as his helpmate while assuming her primary responsibilities of homemaking and child-rearing. This division of labor in Ashley's household thus typified the Puritan and Evangelical marital ideal whereby the public vocation of the husband was complemented by the wife's domestic role.[27] In their married life, Ashley and Emily observed the Evangelical practices of reading the Bible together and conducting the religious education of their children upon an agreed plan.[28] Esteeming childbearing as a "high calling," Ashley and his wife bore ten children, with four of them predeceasing their father.[29] Ashley's relationship with his children was generally characterized by his biographers as one of "tender vigilance"[30] coupled with "absolute confidence and affection."[31]

Whilst this arguably was Ashley's basic disposition towards his children, in marked contrast to the detached severity of his father; Finlayson pointed out that family tragedy, such as the premature loss of a child, could

---

22. Davidoff and Hall, *Family Fortunes*, 73–74.

23. Best, *Biography of A. A. Cooper*, 31.

24. Ashley, Diary Entry (December 25, 1828) cited in Hodder, *Life and Work of the Seventh Earl*, 108.

25. Ibid.

26. Emily Ashley-Cooper died in 1872, predeceasing her husband, Shaftesbury, by thirteen years.

27. Davidoff and Hall, *Family Fortunes*, 323.

28. Best, *Biography of A. A. Cooper*, 30.

29. Ashley's son, Francis, died in 1849, followed by Maurice in 1855. The loss of his two sons was followed by the death of two daughters, Mary in 1861 and Constance in 1872.

30. Best, *Biography of A. A. Cooper* , 31.

31. Hodder, *Life and Work of the Seventh Earl*, Vol. II, 289.

also make him "fearful for the other members of his family."[32] Ashley's pangs of anxiety towards his children were particularly pronounced in his relationship with his eldest son, Anthony, the future Eighth Earl. Conscious that his eldest son would one day assume the "Shaftesbury" mantle, Ashley became profoundly disturbed by any hint of youthful rebellion or impropriety that besmirched the reputation of his heir. Upon hearing that Anthony had taken to smoking in 1846, Ashley despairingly wrote that "he was set for the trial, if not the grief of his parents."[33] It is a highly plausible irony that his eldest son's wayward behavior was an unwitting consequence of his overprotective parenting style, which, in turn, had been a conscious reaction to his own father's detached and cavalier parenting. Ashley's own family life therefore represented not only the domestic application of the Evangelical and Tory paternalist principles he espoused in public policy but also the outworking of his personal background and life circumstances.

Victorian Evangelical attitudes towards gender

With the Victorian Evangelical conception of family envisioning distinctive gender roles and responsibilities, this brought into obvious question the status of women and the extent to which the prevailing Evangelical perspective on women reflected that of Victorian society at large. In nineteenth-century Britain, the rise of industrialization heralded the absorption of women and girls into the labor force outside the home on an unprecedented scale. Prior to the Industrial Revolution, women generally worked with their husbands on the family property in an auxiliary capacity, taking primary responsibility for the care of young children and performing most of the domestic chores in the household. Opportunities for employment outside the family home were circumscribed and usually limited to work as either governesses or domestic servants.[34] For early Evangelicals such as Hannah More, the "ideal" woman was "active in charity, houseproud, taciturn, submissive to her menfolk and devout."[35] As Hilton had observed, English society in the first half of the nineteenth century remained ostensibly patriarchal.[36]

The subsequent advent of industrialization and its insatiable demand for human labor, however, would necessitate the employment of women

32. Finlayson, *Seventh Earl of Shaftesbury*, 324.

33. Ashley, Diary Entry (November 4, 1846), in Finlayson, *Seventh Earl of Shaftesbury*, 254.

34. Levine, *Victorian Feminism*, 85.

35. Hilton, *A Mad, Bad and Dangerous People*, 360.

36. Ibid., 353.

and children outside the home to help run the new industries mushrooming around the country, particularly those engaged in textile and cotton manufacturing. This influx of females into the industrial labor force had inescapable repercussions for traditional patterns of domestic life, whereby newly-employed women invariably had less capacity to attend to their domestic vocations as housewives and mothers.[37] This change in Victorian family dynamics received a mixed reception with Tories and many Evangelical Protestants decrying this change as a "perversion of the natural order," whilst liberals, radicals, Victorian feminists and other progressives welcomed it as an opportunity for women to become active contributors to society in their own right.

Ashley himself was aghast at this new order of gender relations and his agitation for factory reform sought to arrest this development. Thus, in this vein, his factory reform crusade was as much about conservation as it was about realizing genuine change. While the parliamentary social reformer saw agitation for the various Factory Acts in the 1840s as a means to achieving lasting reforms in industrial relations, workplace culture and childhood education, he also saw them as inherently conservative measures aimed at restoring the traditional pattern of domestic relationships. For Ashley, the preservation of traditional roles for men and women within the family was regarded as not only critical to the survival of the family, but also to the moral health of the nation. Drawing on the Report of the 1840 Commission into the factory system, Ashley argued that the absorption of women into the factories had diminished their capacity to fulfill their domestic duties of maintaining the "working man's home" and contributing to the morality of the "rising generation":

> how can it be possible that young women, whose labour has been so heavy and so prolonged, that they are in many cases unable to cook their own suppers, or even to eat the suppers prepared for them—how is it possible that they should learn the details of domestic life which constitute the comfort of the working man's home, and contribute so powerfully to the morality of the rising generation, because women must have, and ought to have, almost undivided influence on children during the earliest and most impressible years of their existence?[38]

For Ashley, maintaining the traditional gender roles of male "breadwinner" and female "homemaker" were deemed essential for ensuring both

---

37. Ibid., 362.

38. Ashley, "The Ten Hours Factory Bill," HC Debates, *Hansard*, 29 January 1846, Vol. 83, cc. 386–87.

domestic harmony and the morality of the next generation. Far from viewing such roles as fluid social constructs which could be readily renegotiated and adapted to suit changing times and cultural contexts, they were seen by him as fixed and universal ordinances of the divinely created order. Decrying the change to domestic relations precipitated by the factory system, Ashley argued that all things in the home "go to rack and ruin, because the men can discharge at home no one of the especial duties that Providence has assigned to the females."[39] For the Evangelical Ashley, this was not merely about the preservation of ancient human traditions but of "divinely instituted" vocations deemed to be eternally binding on all of humanity.

In particular, Ashley saw the maternal role of women as indispensable in shaping the character of the next generation. In the course of the 1842 parliamentary debate about the employment of women and children in mines, he argued that it was bad enough to corrupt the man, "but if you corrupt the woman, you poison the waters of life at the very fountain."[40] Thus one of the chief evils of the factory system for Ashley was its perceived effect of "wholly disqualifying women" from "even learning how to discharge the duties of wife and mother."[41] His abiding concern for the maternal upbringing of children reflected Victorian Evangelical beliefs that the moral character of women inescapably affected those of their children and, indeed, that of society at large. Ordained to "exercise an unlimited power over the years of childhood," he remarked that "all that is best, all that is lasting in the character of a man, he has learnt at his mother's knees."[42]

Ashley's views on the role of women essentially typified what Davidoff and Hall described as the "ambiguity among Evangelicals as to the strict definition of male and female responsibilities."[43] On the one hand, women were expected to be subordinate to their husbands yet; on the other hand, they had the potential to exert considerable spiritual and moral influence on their offspring. Sarah Williams similarly highlighted this paradox when she observed that while Evangelicalism reinforced the domestic duties of women, it arguably opened up a "radical dimension in women's lives" that was extra-domestic with its emphasis on mission, education, philanthropy,

---

39. Ashley, "Hours of Labour in Factories," HC Debates, *Hansard*, 15 March 1844, Vol. 73, c. 1099.

40. Ashley, "Employment of Women and Children in Mines and Collieries," HC Debates, *Hansard*, 7 June 1842, Vol. 63, c. 1335.

41. Ibid.

42. Ashley, "Hours of Labour in Factories," HC Debates, *Hansard*, 15 March 1844, Vol. 73, c. 1100.

43. Davidoff and Hall, *Family Fortunes*, 117.

and activism.⁴⁴ Williams cited the pioneering educationalist, Hannah More, and the Victorian social reformer, Josephine Butler, as two cases in point.⁴⁵ Victorian Evangelicals such as Ashley may not have welcomed the entry of women into the workplace and public sphere as agents for influence in their own right. Nonetheless, they placed considerable faith in the capacity for women, in the domestic and voluntary spheres, to determine the fundamental education, spirituality, outlook and character of the succeeding generation.

Mirroring the paternalist assumption that the "master" always understood the best interests of his "charges," Ashley was convinced that the (unreformed) factory system had been an unmitigated disaster for women. Thus he had no question that ensuing efforts to restrict female labor would be about advancing the welfare of all Victorian women. In fairness, his perceptions about the pernicious effects of the factory system on women and girls were not without foundation. Perusing through the voluminous reports of the Commissioners who had inspected the conditions of industrial workplaces, their first-hand accounts of females toiling under the most appalling conditions had horrified Ashley. Accordingly, he was eager to remind his parliamentary colleagues of the Commissioners' conclusion "that it was the universal opinion of clergymen, medical men, teachers, and others, that the condition of the women was one of the great and universally prevailing causes of the distress among the working classes."⁴⁶ In the female's discharge of onerous physical labor, Ashley appreciated the vulnerability of the female body. On debating female employment in agricultural gangs, Shaftesbury remarked to his fellow Lords in 1867:

> there is not a medical man who will not tell you that the most critical period of a woman's life is that between eleven and thirteen years of age. That is the time when a change in her constitution takes place, when maladies are most easily contracted, and when the female child requires to be watched with the most parental and minute care.⁴⁷

Expressing Evangelical concerns about sexual morality, Shaftesbury also voiced alarm at how the conditions of many industrial workplaces

---

44. Williams, "Evangelicals and Gender," in Lewis and Pierard (eds.), *Global Evangelicalism*, 292.

45. Ibid., 288–90, 293.

46. Ashley, "The Ten Hours Factory Bill," HC Debates, *Hansard*, 29 January 1846, Vol. 83, c. 387.

47. Shaftesbury, "Agricultural Gangs," Observation, HL Debates, *Hansard*, 11 April 1867, Vol. 186, c. 1468.

represented an affront to "female modesty." Concerning the mixed employment of genders on the Brickfields in 1871, Shaftesbury spoke of how "the want of respect and delicacy towards females exhibits itself in every act, word, and look for the lads grow so precocious . . . that in most cases the modesty of female life gradually becomes a byword instead of a reality."[48] Undoubtedly, Shaftesbury's sincere concerns about the welfare of female laborers were informed by his Tory paternalism and Evangelicalism as well as by the relatively impartial findings of reports and testimonies. His focus on female "modesty" and "sexual purity" in the 1870s reflected what Bebbington identified as the broader Evangelical concern about the sexual exploitation of women and children[49]—a preoccupation which propelled many Evangelicals to support such causes as Josephine Butler's Anti-Contagious Diseases Acts Movement and the campaign to lift the age of consent to sixteen.[50] At the same time, his paternalist assumption that all female laborers were hapless victims of oppression in need of deliverance overlooked the possibility that many women may have engaged in industrial labor by personal choice as well as by economic necessity.

Hence Victorian contemporaries who were not necessarily of the same Tory or Evangelical persuasion as Shaftesbury tended to view the absorption of females into the factory system in a somewhat different light. This, of course, included Victorian feminists who were determined to see these new fields of industrial employment opened to women.[51] Victorian feminists led by Jessie Boucherett and Millicent Fawcett had actively campaigned in the 1850s for the employment of women in the paid workforce and founded the Society for Promoting the Employment of Women in 1859. Possessing a two-fold aim, the Society was "formed for promoting the Training of Women and their employment in industrial pursuits."[52] The Society's campaign efforts were reinforced in the 1870s with the publication of a pamphlet collectively authored by leading feminists, Elizabeth Wolstenholme and the Evangelical-influenced Josephine Butler, together with female factory workers, Ada Smith and Dinah Goodall. Challenging the gender-specific factory reform legislation circumscribing female employment, the pamphlet argued that, though such legislation appeared to be in women's best interests, it "merely provides for reducing the paid labor of women by

48. Shaftesbury, "Children's Employment Commission—Brickfield—The Factory Acts," Motion for an Address, HL Debates, *Hansard*, 11 July 1871, Vol. 207, c. 1405.
49. Bebbington, *Dominance of Evangelicalism*, 226.
50. Ibid., 226–27.
51. Levine, *Victorian Feminism*, 86.
52. Ibid., 87.

that one hour daily . . . in order that the mother may employ it in unpaid labor at home."[53]

Indeed the pamphlet went on to suggest that if supporters of the legislation were so concerned for women's welfare, they should extend the purview of the legislation to working conditions in the home as well as the factory. This reflected their belief that women could experience oppression in the domestic sphere as well as the public sphere. Thus, in the eyes of such feminists, the two defects in the paternalism championed by factory reformers, such as Shaftesbury, was its failure to appreciate that the absorption of females into the labor force provided opportunity, personal autonomy, meaning and vocational purpose for a great number of women. Secondly, in this paternalism's otherwise laudable zeal to shield women from exploitation and harm in the industrial workplace, it neglected the reality that many women also encountered existing forms of oppression in the domestic sphere which the factory legislation could do little to remedy.

Notwithstanding his conservative Victorian attitudes towards the status of women, he was decidedly non-dogmatic on the question of women's suffrage in the early 1870s. Declining to oppose this measure outright, he essentially concluded that it was a matter for the "popular will" and conceded that the judgment of the people on this question should ultimately prevail without resistance. If women's suffrage was approved, the Earl argued that it should be universal and not confined to one class of women:

> The question of Women's suffrage . . . is manifestly a question which requires only perseverance on the part of its promoters, and that not a long perseverance, to attain success. In the days in which we live, there is little use in any opposition to the popular will. The grant of Women's Suffrage cannot be confined to spinsters . . . it must be extended to wives; and this, conjoined with certain changes in the laws of marriage, now apparently inevitable, will remodel, as it were the entire system of domestic life. It is possible that evil may be the result. The matter, however, rests with the holders of the suffrage, from whose repeated determination there is no appeal.[54]

By the time he proffered his views on the issue in 1871, Victorian society had shifted appreciably towards representative democracy and the grip of the aristocratic class had loosened palpably since his entry into British

---

53. Butler et al., *Legislative Restrictions*, 6; Nolland, *Victorian Feminist Christian*, 217.

54. Shaftesbury, letter to unidentified recipient (December 28, 1871), in Hodder, *Life and Work of the Seventh Earl*, Vol. III, 285–86.

public life almost half a century earlier.[55] While these changes may not have necessarily accorded with Shaftesbury's traditional Toryism, he was pragmatic enough to accept that the enfranchisement of the middle and lower classes was irreversible and, in a free society, it was only reasonable that their appeals on such questions as women's suffrage were acceded to. Given his speculation that evil 'could result' from changes to domestic life wrought by the extension of the franchise to all women, Shaftesbury's open stance on the issue owed more to a concession of contemporary political realities than any radical rethink on the status of women.

55. Mayer, *Growth of Democracy*, 48–50.

14

Sanctifying Sundays

In popular conceptions of Victorianism, the "quiet Sunday" has virtually attained iconic status as an enduring symbol of that epoch's religiosity, morality, and culture. As John Wigley appreciated, however, the Victorian Sunday "did not have one single form" as various social classes and subcultures each observed distinctive customs and manners on the day.[1] For large sections of the middle and upper classes, including those who were not devoutly religious, Sundays were routinely set aside for leisurely pursuits and family amusements such as card playing, countryside outings and high teas.[2] Within the Evangelical subculture inhabited by Ashley, Sundays assumed an integral place in not only the individual piety of believers but also in their collective vision for how society at large should live in accordance with the Fourth Commandment. As Wolffe noted, Evangelical attachment to the Sabbath had been evident since the Evangelical Awakening in the eighteenth century, with Sunday representing a spiritual high watermark in the weekly patterns of personal piety practiced by Evangelicals such as Wilberforce and Bickersteth.[3]

Notwithstanding subtle differences of opinion in how believers ought to observe the day,[4] Evangelical approaches to the state regulation of the

---

1. Wigley, *Rise and Fall*, 2.
2. Ibid., 2.
3. Wolffe, *Expansion of Evangelicalism*, 97.
4. Scotland, *Evangelical Anglicans*, 185. According to Scotland, the Recordite Evangelicals generally believed that the Sabbath must be "kept in strict accordance with the provision of the Fourth Commandment," whilst the Claphamites "were of the opinion that Jesus adopted a less rigorous understanding of the Sabbath day."

Sabbath remained fairly uniform from the Clapham generation to the Victorian Recordites. Despite the general aversion of Claphamite Evangelicals to paternalist state intervention in economic affairs, they were strongly in favour of legislation to protect the Sabbath in accordance with what Hilton diagnosed as their liberal Tory *moral* paternalism.[5] In 1795, Wilberforce and Lord Belgrave had unsuccessfully tried to introduce a bill to suppress Sunday newspapers. Determined to advance the sabbatarian cause, the Clapham Sect founded the Society for Promoting the Observance of the Sabbath in 1809 and eventually the Lord's Day Observance Society in 1831, of which Ashley became president.[6] From the 1830s, the *Record* continued the Claphamite tradition of sabbatarian activism, together with Evangelicals such as Ashley, Oastler, and Sir Andrew Agnew (1793–1843). In seeking the state's protection of the Sabbath, the succeeding generation of Evangelicals thereby embraced the moral paternalism of the Claphamites whilst spurning their *laissez-faire* economic outlook.

Against this background of a sustained Evangelical paternalism on the Sabbath question, it was little wonder Ashley emerged as a determined champion of the institution. In both its fidelity to Biblical precepts and its perceived utility of fostering social order, the Sabbath represented the apotheosis of his Evangelical-Tory worldview. In their discussions of the Victorian Sunday, Wigley, Bradley, and Scotland each mentioned the significant role of Ashley;[7] however they did not explore the motivating factors or justification for his support of the "Lord's Day" which featured in his pronouncements on the matter. For this reason, the rationales behind Ashley's reflections and speeches in support of the Sabbath merit closer examination. In the tradition of Oastler and Sadler in the factory reform movement, he saw the Sabbath as representing one of the chief junctions at which the interests of Evangelical Protestants and high Tory paternalists intersected.[8] As Shaftesbury expounded in a public speech in Glasgow in 1871:

> I look upon the Sabbath-day as a day of holy duties, a day of physical and mental recreation; I look upon it as a day in which you must devote a part—a good part—to the worship and

---

5. Hilton, *Mad, Bad and Dangerous People*, 323.

6. Scotland, *Evangelical Anglicans*, 184; Wigley, *Rise and Fall*, 34. Originally known as The Society for Promoting the Due Observance of the Lord's Day, the society was founded by Bishop Daniel Wilson (1778–1858), an associate of the Clapham Sect.

7. Wigley, *Rise and Fall*, 37, 114; Bradley, *Call to Seriousness*, 104–5; Scotland, *Anglican Evangelicals*, 191, 194, 197–200.

8. Like Richard Oaster, R. B. Seeley, and Michael T. Sadler, Shaftesbury recognized the Sabbath as not only inherently honoring to God but also as in the best interests of factory labourers.

> service of almighty God—but I look upon it as day that you may devote to many family affections, to many family duties, to many social intercourses, to many little innocent joys . . . .[9]

For Ashley, the mission to consecrate a day of reverence to God, where Christian families could uninterruptedly worship together and reflect soberly on spiritual matters, coincided with the paternalist imperative to institutionalize a day of rest for workers to unwind from the rigors and demands of the working week, thereby ensuring some modicum of social rhythm for both the family and the labor force. Like the high Tory paternalist Southey who had urged magistrates to "enforce the observance of the Sabbath" on the ground that it was congenial to "orderly conduct,"[10] Ashley believed that the institution could be employed to ensure the good health and order of society, aside from any explicitly religious or Evangelical purpose it could serve.

In his advocacy for the Sabbath, both inside and outside the parliament, Ashley publicly justified the universal observance of Sunday on each of these two grounds. In lauding the Sabbath for what he valued as its religious significance, his pitch was broadly ecumenical and non-sectarian. Unlike his campaigns against Tractarianism or Roman Catholicism, he did not concern himself with doctrinal specifics when commending the Sabbath to the House of Commons in 1850:

> Without entering into any theological argument . . . all who received either Testament, or both—the Jew, the Roman Catholic, the Church of England, all the reformed churches of the Continent, the Wesleyans, the Protestant Dissenters—all recognized the divine institution of the Sabbath, and carried into practice, as well as confessed, the obligation of the observance of one day in seven for the purpose of worship and repose. This obligation was universal. . . . The wonderful adaptation of this institution to the social, physical, and religious wants of man was, if there were no other, an argument for the divine character of the institution.[11]

For the Earl, the public institution of the Sabbath was pre-eminently about providing the necessary "space" for people to exercise their personal religious beliefs in whichever way they chose. While he may have had fairly specific ideas as to how he and other Evangelicals ought to observe the

---

9. Shaftesbury, *Full Report of the Great Meeting*, 16.
10. Southey, *Essays Moral and Political*, Vol. II, 158.
11. Ashley, "Post Office," HC Debates, *Hansard*, 30 May 1850, Vol. 111, c. 472.

Sabbath, his primary concern was about ensuring that the institution maintained its universal status. Whether one was Protestant, Catholic, or Jewish, the practice accorded with both the Fourth Commandment of Moses and the natural rhythm of creation believed to have been instituted in the Book of Genesis. For this reason, people of differing faith traditions could appreciate the "divine character of the institution." The great advantage for Shaftesbury on this issue was that he could advance the Sabbath cause on very broad religious grounds without compromising his Evangelical sensibilities.

Religious considerations aside, he turned to emphasize what he saw as the practical benefit of the Sabbath with its provision of a weekly rest-day for the labor-weary working classes. Against the mounting trend in Victorian society for public amusements to operate on Sundays, Shaftesbury told the House of Lords in 1881 that the wellbeing of the working classes was being trampled underfoot.

> I plead, my Lords, for a very large class of over-worked, toil-worn men; and, if you open your Galleries and Museums on Sunday you will greatly multiply the number of wretched victims—cab-drivers, omnibus men, tram-car men, railway officials, and other men, to say nothing of the attendants at these places of Science—who will have to work on that Day of Rest. Are these classes not entitled to be thought of as well as the people of leisure who wish to indulge their taste for Science and Art?[12]

As with the factory reform movement, his Tory paternalism impelled him to support and uphold a universal social order which *he*, but not necessarily *all* of the working classes themselves, saw as beneficial to their interests and conducive to maintaining national peace and order. Instituting the Sabbath was therefore primarily about putting the perceived interests of society as a whole ahead of any personal freedom for individuals to work on Sunday if they so pleased.

Warning of the consequences likely to stem from Britain following the French path of spurning the institutional Sabbath, Shaftesbury in 1881 attributed his country's relative social stability to its continued observance and contrasted this with the social chaos that had befallen France.

> In opening these places of amusement on the Lord's Day, what do you propose to do? You hope thereby to secure for this country an orderly population. Well, go through the City of Paris on Sunday, and what do you find? . . . The factories, shops, and streets are filled with labouring men as though it were a

---

12. Shaftesbury, "Sunday Opening of National Museums and Galleries," HL Debates, *Hansard*, 22 February 1881, Vol. 258, c. 1496.

> week-day, and every kind of ordinary employment is pursued on the Lord's Day . . . yet the very men to whom these places are accessible for the cultivation of their minds, the training of the heart, and the elevation of the human being, are the very class of men who burnt the Hotel de Ville and the Tuileries, disgraced the Place Vendome, and committed every form of excess.[13]

There was thus more than a hint of patriotism in the Earl's stance on the Sabbath. For Shaftesbury, there was something peculiarly British about instituting a day of rest designed to bolster the welfare and good order of society. As Nigel Scotland appreciated, Evangelicals since the late eighteenth century had been fond of juxtaposing the English Sabbath with the introduction of the ten-day week and abolition of Sunday in post-revolutionary France.[14] In the old British tradition of Tory paternalism, it was all about a benevolent government resolving to act for what it perceived to be the best interests of its citizens whether they would all personally agree to it or not. In contrast to those of a more liberal individualist persuasion, Shaftesbury saw this as infinitely preferable to a detached, *laissez-faire* government that would simply afford its citizens freer rein to act as they saw fit, regardless of any ensuing consequences their personal choices were likely to have for society.

Given that Ashley's esteem for the Sabbath owed much to his Tory paternalist politics as well as to his Evangelical Anglicanism, was his zeal for the cause characteristic of Victorian Evangelicalism as a whole? With the campaign for Sunday observance supported by sizeable numbers of Evangelical Anglican clergy and laity from Bishop Daniel Wilson to Lord Ashley, Wigley argued that it was the Evangelical party within the Established Church that proved to be the most significant influence.[15] Notwithstanding the pre-eminent role of Evangelical Anglicans, Owen Chadwick made the valid observation that their numbers were augmented by a wider Nonconformist coalition of Wesleyans, Baptists, and other free church members.[16] Larsen recognized that, whilst Nonconformists had been historically wary of state intervention in religious affairs, they were generally happy to support Sabbath legislation for the purpose of preventing people from being forced to work on Sundays.[17] Although they did not share Ashley's Churchmanship, many Nonconformists agreed with him that the Sabbath was the

---

13. Ibid., c. 1497.
14. Scotland, *Anglican Evangelicals*, 184.
15. Wigley, *Rise and Fall*, 146–47.
16. Chadwick, *Victorian Church*, Vol. II, 464, in Scotland, *Evangelical Anglicans*, 199.
17. Larsen, *Friends of Religious Equality*, 193.

"poor man's day" which protected his rest against the selfish interests of hard-driving masters.[18] Thus, while Nonconformist Evangelicals tended not to regard Sabbatarian legislation as the institutionalization of a core biblical precept, in the way that many Anglican Evangelicals were inclined to do, they supported such measures as conducive to the causes of conscientious objection, religious freedom and social justice for the working classes.

With this convergence of interests, Victorian Evangelicalism at large acquired a fairly solid reputation for its Sabbatarianism which Ashley was eager to exploit. In addition to serving as president of the LDOS, Ashley sponsored bills to curtail Sunday postal activity in 1850 and to secure the Sunday closure of the British Museum and National Gallery in 1856. According to Spence, Victorian Evangelical zeal for the Sabbath was also reinforced by a resurgent premillennial eschatology which cherished Sunday rest as an earthly foretaste of the rest expected to accompany the pending millennium.[19] The Sabbatarian Ashley succeeded in not only enshrining the Sabbath's status amongst Victorian Evangelicals as an "article of faith" but also in adapting it to his existing Tory paternalist ideology. The Sabbath accorded well with a political philosophy that stressed the necessity of state-regulated social order for both the wellbeing of society and the stability of traditional institutions such as the church and the family.

---

18. Ibid., 196.
19. Spence, "Time and Eternity," 300.

15

Evangelical Benevolence and Tory "Self-reliance"

The Victorian Evangelical 'third way' to resolving social disadvantage

As was evident in his attitudes towards the British Empire, Ashley's brand of Tory paternalism recognized that the role of the "paternal" party had its limits. While maintaining that paternalist intervention was necessary in the cases of both colonial dependencies within the British Empire and individuals within civil society, it was never his intention that such paternal governance continue indefinitely beyond the formative phase of the dependent party. Indeed, his ultimate purpose was to equip that party for independence and autonomy in its own right. In the realm of civil society, Ashley and the Evangelical Tory radicals argued that the state must intervene to help those deemed unable to help themselves. Such individuals included children, particularly those of the new industrial classes, paupers and those with disabilities, with Ashley identifying lunacy patients as a particularly vulnerable class. Likening the state to a responsible parent, Ashley argued that intervention was necessary not only to afford welfare and protection to such individuals in a season of need, but to equip them with the necessary wherewithal to become self-reliant contributors to society in the long term.[1] His approach to social welfare thus differed from that of the

---

1. Finlayson, "Victorian Shaftesbury," 35.

laissez-faire liberal Tories who argued that responsibility for advancing the wellbeing of the disadvantaged lay strictly in the private sphere and was no business of the state, whilst also differing from that of the Owenite socialists who agitated for the provision of a universal and perpetual state program of social welfare to combat disadvantage.

In the earlier stages of his public career, Ashley saw *laissez-faire* liberalism as the chief menace to advancing the welfare of the disadvantaged. Along with his fellow factory reform campaigners Oastler and Sadler, he denounced this political creed for being primarily responsible for the commercial excesses of the factory system and its callous indifference to the exploitation and oppression of child laborers. With Ashley and his fellow reformers subsequently succeeding in securing basic legislative protection for working-class children, Finlayson observed that he began to fear that the pendulum had latterly swung too far in the direction of state welfare.[2] Whilst earlier having supported greater state intervention for *ameliorative* purposes, Shaftesbury expressed concern towards the end of his life that excessive state intervention would sap the vital spirit of initiative and enterprise from individuals, inclined now to defer primarily to the state for the securing of their welfare. In 1883 Shaftesbury articulated his concerns about what he lamented as "the mischief of State aid." Reiterating his philosophy of moderate state interventionism, Shaftesbury wrote: "The State is bound, in such a case as this, to give every facility by law and enabling statutes; but the work itself should be founded, and proceed, on voluntary effort, for which there is in the country an adequate amount of wealth, zeal and intelligence."[3] The Earl warned that if the state encroached unduly on this voluntary principle, by way of providing houses for the laboring classes, it would "utterly destroy their moral energies."[4] Besides amounting to a kind of "legal pauperization," Shaftesbury claimed that the "mischief" of this unwarranted state intervention would give a "heavy blow and great discouragement to the spirit of healthy thrift now rising among the people."[5] Thus rejecting any state-run housing scheme, Shaftesbury commended the efforts of the private charity, the SICLC, for providing affordable housing based on "true commercial principles."[6]

Shaftesbury's shift in concern from the problems of inadequate state intervention in the 1830s and 1840s, to the perils of excessive government

2. Ibid.
3. Shaftesbury, "Mischief of State Aid," 936.
4. Ibid.
5. Ibid., 938.
6. Ibid., 935.

aid in the 1880s, was essentially a response to a broader trend in Victorian society that David Roberts identified as the "inexorable growth of government" fueled by a triad of population increase, industrialization, and urbanization.[7] Between 1833 and 1855, parliament passed 6,898 acts and created more than twenty central departments staffed by numerous commissioners, agents, inspectors and surveyors.[8] Given Ashley's own support for various factory and mining acts, together with his lead role on the General Board of Health, the Victorian social reformer could hardly absolve himself from the charge that he had contributed to this development. Nevertheless, his doctrine of state intervention had always been moderate with the view that government must supplement, rather than supplant, existing mechanisms for the provision of social welfare such as the family, the church, and the voluntary association.

In addition, Shaftesbury's concern about disproportionate state intervention and power stemmed from both his high Tory paternalist and Evangelical sensibilities. Given that elements of his paternalist philosophy were inspired by the landed gentry and its preference for localized administration, Shaftesbury shared the longstanding suspicions of British Tory paternalists towards centralized state authority. While, of course, defending authority as critical to an ordered society, the high Tory paternalists were committed to the subsidiarity principle, whereby it was preferable for power to be vested in localized institutions, such as the JP or the borough council, the parish church and the rural estate-owner, than for it to be heavily concentrated in a central seat of government such as Westminster. Given that power implied responsibility, it made sense for it to be close to the people it was intended to serve. Meanwhile, as an Evangelical, Shaftesbury believed that there was the potential risk for the overweening power of an excessively interventionist state to usurp the authority of the Almighty and intrude into the sacred sphere of an individual's conscience which was answerable to the laws of God before those of the State. Moreover, as his occasional rebukes of British imperial rule demonstrated, Shaftesbury feared the tendency for unfettered power to corrupt owing to 'natural' human pride and selfishness. Accordingly, the devolution of power across a range of authorities was always to be preferred since this would act as a proper check on its abuses.

Whilst by no means a doctrinaire capitalist, Shaftesbury appreciated the inherent merits of promoting individual enterprise and initiative, whether this was in commerce, education or philanthropy. In circumstances where this was deemed feasible, the conservative Earl saw privately run

---

7. Roberts, *Social Conscience of the Early Victorians*, 404.
8. Ibid., 396.

businesses as infinitely preferable to large-scale government enterprises as the principal generators of prosperity and vehicles for economic growth. Desiring to stimulate the growth of the cotton industry in colonial India, Shaftesbury appealed to the House of Lords in 1862 to give private enterprise a freer rein in navigating suitable zones for cultivating cotton:

> ... by resorting to private enterprise, the navigation of the Godavery [river] will be secured in much less time than if the work be reserved for execution by Government. ... I am entirely in favour of making this work over to a private company. ... My Lords, I do hope and trust attention will be given to this matter, and that everything will be done to encourage private enterprise. ... I trust, then, that private enterprise will be encouraged; that much will be done by the intelligence, the zeal, and the spirit of a large portion of our manufacturers, by the wise measures of our Government, and, above all, by the blessing of Almighty God.[9]

For Shaftesbury, the harnessing of private enterprise was eminently more conducive to realizing the economic ideals of efficiency and productivity. As an Evangelical, he also affirmed the worth of fostering private enterprise and wealth creation, believing these to be intrinsically pleasing and glorifying to God. Providing that such prosperity generated could remain unsullied by human greed and be utilized for the wellbeing of all people, this would attract divine favor.

As well as appreciating the value of private enterprise in the economic sphere, he remained committed to the "voluntary principle" in the realm of education. Whilst welcoming the expansion of education in the wake of the 1861 Report of the Select Committee on the Education of Destitute Children,[10] he recognized the voluntary ideal as the great driving force behind the success of the Ragged Schools and in no way desired to cede this to the state:

> Many persons of property now contribute their money towards the promotion of education because they think the obligation lies upon them, and that if they did not discharge the duty it would not be performed at all. But when the duty becomes recognized as devolving on the State they will be apt to regard themselves as freed from the obligation.[11]

---

9. Shaftesbury, "Cotton Supply (India)," Petition, Address for Papers, HL Debates, *Hansard*, 1 August 1862, Vol. 168, c. 1072.

10. Scotland, *Evangelical Anglicans*, 235. The 1862 Report had exposed the considerable dearth of educational opportunities in impoverished districts.

11. Shaftesbury, "Elementary Education Bill," Second Reading, HL Debates,

Speaking on the bill that would become known as the Forster Education Act of 1870, Shaftesbury feared that this legislation would irrevocably transfer the bulk of responsibility for education to state boards. Essentially, the Earl saw this trend as eroding the high Tory paternalist ideal of *noblesse oblige*, whereby wealthy landholders who had once regarded the patronage of education as one of their great prerogatives would now cede this responsibility to the state which had assumed greater control. With this abrogation of responsibility, the voluntary impulse would be extinguished and this would bode ill for the survival of voluntary systems such as the Ragged Schools. As Scotland pointed out, the number of pupils in the Ragged School system did in fact decrease dramatically after the passage of the legislation from 32,309 in 1870 to only 9,347 in 1872.[12]

Defying the growing trend towards the governmental regulation of education, Shaftesbury had insisted as early as 1859 that not only the provision of education, but the attainment of education itself, was a voluntary affair realized not so much by the provision of the state as by the efforts of the individual:

> The State, no doubt, may provide certain means to set men on the right path; but actual education must be acquired by a man himself—it must be done by his own efforts—by his own intellectual vigour; and there are no means by which the truth can be carried into any man's mind, if that man will not himself go nine-tenths of the way to receive it.[13]

Thus education was one of the primary means through which individuals would learn the lesson of being enterprising and self-reliant members of society. Significantly, they would learn not simply by instruction but by actually 'doing.'

Victorian Evangelical notions of 'self-help' and the primacy of the 'voluntary society'

For Shaftesbury, these conservative emphases on fostering the voluntary initiative and enterprise of individuals extended to the charitable sphere. In a realm where the needs of the disadvantaged appeared most acute—manifesting themselves in such afflictions as homelessness, destitution, squalor, and mental or physical impairment—the guiding objective of philanthropy

---

Hansard, 25 July 1870, Vol. 203, c. 849.
12. Scotland, *Evangelical Anglicans*, 236.
13. Lord Shaftesbury, *Speech to Literary Institutes*.

was essentially twofold. First, to ameliorate the immediate conditions of the afflicted, and second, to assist them, wherever possible, to cultivate the means of lasting self-improvement by way of undertaking appropriate education, training, or employment. Accordingly, charitable schemes such as model lodging houses, orphanages, mechanics institutes, and ragged schools were not only about providing accommodation or elementary education to destitute children but equipping them with the life skills to exist as able and respectable members of society.

Along with the ragged schools, Shaftesbury was gratified to witness other charity projects that evidently owed their success to private enterprise rather than government grants. Upon laying the foundation stone for a recently reconstructed housing estate in 1872, Shaftesbury paid tribute to the "individual efforts" of the residents who had not only benefited from the scheme but had voluntarily contributed to its ongoing success.

> We have founded this day a workman's city, and we have founded it upon the best principles. We have founded it upon the great principle of self-help, and upon the great principle of independence. By independence, I mean without any other assistance than that which every man has a right to receive from his fellow man— sympathy and kind aid—and that is what every man, either great or small, stands in need of from another.[14]

In extolling the virtues of "self-help" and "independence," Shaftesbury never conceived of society as being comprised of atomistic, isolated individuals possessing absolute autonomy to improve their own wellbeing independent of external agents such as the church, family, state or indeed other individuals. On the contrary, such virtues were only realized by individuals existing in the social context of interdependent communities where vital interaction with others helped to forge these attributes within oneself.

To Shaftesbury the Tory paternalist, the concept of a powerful, all-encompassing welfare state remained anathema to his lifelong political creed. In the final years of his life, he denounced such a state as "a melancholy system that tends to debase a large mass of the people to the condition of a nursery, where the children look to father and mother, and do nothing for themselves."[15] The Earl eschewed the emerging Christian Socialist movement of the 1860s on the basis of which Frederick D. Maurice and John Ruskin had favored the establishment of a British welfare state as the most compassionate and Christian response to social and economic

---

14. Shaftesbury, *Speech on Laying the Memorial Stone*, 4–5.
15. Shaftesbury, "Mischief of State Aid," 939.

disadvantage.[16] In contrast to Christian sympathizers of the movement, a regime of extensive state aid offended his Christian sensibilities as well as his political philosophy. As an Evangelical, Shaftesbury believed that the scriptures held ordinary human work in supremely high esteem, with God having assigned the first human beings to tend to the Garden of Eden. Before evil was understood to have corrupted the world, such work was deemed intrinsic to humanity's *Imago Dei* and basic sense of purpose. Although tarred by Original Sin, Evangelicals such as Shaftesbury nonetheless esteemed human labor as retaining its divine origin and purpose. Hence the new notion of the welfare state, which was seen as diminishing natural incentives for individuals to work, was denounced as an unwelcome innovation and one singularly incompatible with a Christian doctrine of labor. As a Tory paternalist, meanwhile, Shaftesbury saw Christian Socialism's tendency towards liberty, equality, and fraternity as incompatible with the traditional precepts of hierarchy and order.[17]

Given, however, that the Christian Socialists justified social action on the basis of Old Testament ethics in a not too dissimilar fashion to Evangelical Tories such as Seeley and Tonna, the antagonism of Tory Evangelicals such as Shaftesbury appeared surprising. As Hylson-Smith appreciated, the social philosophy of the Victorian Evangelicals and Christian Socialists had more in common than has often been assumed, particularly in light of their shared concern for working-class wellbeing.[18] As well as the Broad Church affiliation of Maurice and Ruskin, a plausible explanation for this Evangelical suspicion is that the Christian Socialists were *seen* to propose state intervention to a greater *extent* than what the Evangelicals thought was appropriately necessary for social flourishing. As exemplars of the voluntary spirit, one of the principal concerns Shaftesbury and the Victorian Evangelicals had about the welfare state was that its provision of social services could potentially obviate the need for church-run charities and societies.

According to James Stephen in 1849, the Victorian age was arguably the age of the voluntary society,[19] with a plethora of societies existing to help the homeless, the destitute, the imprisoned, widows, orphans, vagrants, penitent prostitutes, penniless governesses, and oppressed chimney sweeps.[20] Like their Claphamite predecessors, the Victorian Evangelicals undoubtedly took tremendous pride in the proliferation of these societies, viewing

16. Finlayson, "Victorian Shaftesbury," 31.
17. Hylson-Smith, *Anglican Evangelicals*, 209.
18. Hylson-Smith, *Anglican Evangelicals*, 210.
19. Bradley, *Call to Seriousness*, 135.
20. Roberts, *Social Conscience of the Early Victorians*, 229.

their activities as practical expressions of Christian charity and compassion. Epitomizing Ashley's fusion of Evangelical and Tory values, the voluntary society reflected his abiding belief, and that of his co-religionists, that voluntary organizations were eminently better-placed to minister to the needs of the poor than impersonal state-run agencies. These bodies stood as living testimony to their philosophy of taking direct personal responsibility for the relief of human suffering in their midst, rather than simply deflecting this obligation to the state.[21] Victorian Evangelicals feared, however, that if the state took the place of the voluntary sector in the provision of social welfare, the spirit of enterprise and charity which had kept such bodies afloat would be in danger of extinguishment, thereby spelling the certain demise of the Evangelicals' much-loved voluntary society. Given the high degree of aristocratic patronage, voluntary societies could also be regarded as serving the interests of class reputation, employed specifically by the nobility to debunk the accusations of radicals that they were indifferent to the suffering of the poor. Finlayson suggested that much of Shaftesbury's philanthropic activity was accordingly driven by his Tory paternalist desire to "disarm radical criticism" and thereby restore honor to his "own order."[22] Eager to maintain the hegemony of the aristocracy, Shaftesbury wrote that "his whole life had been spent in endevouring [sic] to build up the moral, social, political and religious estimation of the aristocracy."[23]

---

21. Bradley, *Call to Seriousness*, 120.
22. Finlayson, *Citizen, State and Social Welfare*, 53.
23. Finlayson, "Shaftesbury," in Hollis (ed.), *Pressure from Without*, 177.

Conclusion
A Conservative and a Reformer

Having imbibed Southey's romantic high Tory paternalism, together with Bickersteth's Anglican Evangelicalism, Ashley's personal religiosity proved most congenial to that of the Recordites who dominated the Anglican Evangelical culture of the early to mid-Victorian age. Although he was critical of the *Record* in its earlier days, principally because of its shrill *tone*, he came to resemble its similar absorption of conservative Protestant nationalism. Despite the tremendous indebtedness of Recordite Evangelicalism to the family piety of Wilberforce, the moral zeal of More, and the missionary impulses of Simeon, its defining Protestant nationalism originated not so much from the legacy of the Clapham Evangelicals but from the high Toryism of Southey and the *Quarterly Review*. As Lewis established, the issue of Catholic Emancipation had given rise to the formation of an alliance between Anglican Evangelicals and high Tory "Protestant Constitutionalists" which continued throughout the 1830s and 1840s, manifesting itself in the pages of the *Record*.[1] In the newspaper's petition to Queen Victoria to uphold the Sabbath, this combination of Tory and Evangelical preoccupations was still evident in 1850:

> As Protestant Englishman . . . we are determined as loyal and faithful subjects of your Majesty, by God's help, to hold fast the great principles of truth for which our martyrs died, claiming as our privileges, an open Bible with free access thereto, the Christian Sabbath, a free and full salvation through the merits and mediation of Jesus Christ alone, and the right of private judgment, with submission only to the law and to the testimony:

---

1. Lewis, *Lighten their Darkness*, 25.

thus discharging a solemn duty to our God, to our Queen and to our country.[2]

Together with the Tory Evangelical Michael Sadler, the *Record* regarded itself as the dual guardian of the English constitution and the Anglican Evangelical inheritance dating back to not only the eighteenth-century Evangelical revival but the martyrs of the English Reformation. Despite having supported the Catholic Relief Act in 1829, Ashley personified this alliance by advocating causes appealing to both Tory and Evangelical interests such as the Sabbath and the preservation of a confessional Christian state.

While the fusion of high Tory and Evangelical interests certainly galvanized Ashley on some causes, it also gave rise to innate tensions and paradoxes in Ashley's stance on other matters. On the one hand, his Protestant constitutionalism impelled him to defend the pre-eminence of the Established Church, whilst his Evangelicalism drew him towards a warm embrace of Nonconformist Evangelicals. Similarly, on the "Jewish Question," his Evangelical reverence for the Jewish origins of Christianity did not necessarily translate into support for Jewish Emancipation, at least initially, because he saw it as incompatible with his Tory ideal of preserving a monolithic, Christian state. Even on the issue of poor relief towards the end of his life, Shaftesbury found he had to navigate a "middle path" between the Tory paternalist approach of moderate state intervention he had defended in his lifelong campaign for factory reform and the traditional Evangelical philosophy of volunteerism and 'grassroots philanthropy' which underpinned his own voluntary societies. Notwithstanding such contradictions, the fact that Ashley and Anglican Evangelicals such as Haldane and Seeley could embrace high Tory ideals to the extent that they did in the Victorian period attested to the malleability and adaptability of Evangelical religion. In little more than a generation, Evangelicalism had shifted from accommodating Enlightenment thought, with the *Christian Observer* openly extolling the merits of Adam Smith's political economy, to the appropriation of high Tory principles popularized by the romantic movement.

Within the milieu of Anglican Evangelicalism and Victorian society at large, Shaftesbury became both a man *behind* his times and a man *for* his times, a paradox that became even more apparent in the latter decades of his life. In the midst of advancing biblical criticism, new revelations in science, and the dissemination of groundbreaking theories (such as those propounded by Charles Darwin), Hodder noted that Shaftesbury "stood

---

2. Petition to the Queen's Most Excellent Majesty 'Effects of the Observance of the Lord's Day," *The Record*, December 5, 1850, 3.

in the old paths."[3] His unyielding subscription to biblical literalism, for example, stood in stark contrast to the theological trajectory of the Seeley family. Whilst Shaftesbury's old friend and ally, Robert Benton Seeley, had stood firmly in the same Evangelical camp during the 1830s and 1840s, Seeley's son, Sir John Seeley, was swept along by the tide of biblical criticism and identified himself with Broad Church theology by the late 1850s.[4] Like many of his contemporaries from Evangelical backgrounds, the junior Seeley found traditional interpretations of Christian doctrine to be inadequate in light of biblical criticism and new discoveries in natural science.[5] On the contentious issue of public education, Ashley was again on the defensive as he pleaded for the cause of Ragged Schools in 1871 at a time when such elementary schools were coming under the aegis of government boards in the wake of Forster's 1870 Education Act.[6]

Despite his self-image, particularly after his wife's death in 1872, as "a lonely old man left behind by the tide of history,"[7] Shaftesbury availed himself of new causes where he regained a relevant, and even progressive, voice. His campaign to protect women and children from sexual exploitation in the early 1880s[8] coincided with the efforts of Josephine Butler, late-Victorian feminists and social purity activists to repeal the Contagious Diseases Acts. His mission to "watercress girls," costermongers, and homeless boys[9] paved the way for the urban mission of William Booth's Salvation Army. Meanwhile, as the British empire was consolidating its rule in India (with the Disraeli administration styling Queen Victoria as "Empress of India" in 1876), Shaftesbury not only repudiated the title but envisioned a future when this 'jewel' of the British imperial crown would become a "free and independent power" surrendered to its native inhabitants.[10] Given the paradox of Shaftesbury's public reputation as a conservative and reformer, together with his frequent juxtaposition of romantic idealism and visionary policy, it was only axiomatic that he would simultaneously be in front of, abreast of, and behind, the Victorian *zeitgeist* both inside and outside of his own church.

3. Hodder, *Life and Work of the Seventh Earl*, Vol. III, 383–84.
4. Wormell, *Sir John Seeley*, 14.
5. Ibid., 15.
6. Shaftesbury, "Letter to the Editor," *The Times*, November 13, 1871.
7. John Wolffe, "Cooper, Anthony Ashley-," 5.
8. Hodder, *Life and Work of the Seventh Earl*, Vol. III, 513.
9. Ibid., 321–23.
10. Shaftesbury, "Speech to the House of Lords," HL Debates, *Hansard*, 3 April 1876, Vol. 228, cc. 1043, 1047.

Enigma variations: Ashley and the complexity of Victorian Evangelicalism

Whilst guided by a resolute Evangelical faith, together with the paternalist outlook of the landed aristocracy, Lord Ashley remained a complex and enigmatic figure who frequently defied initial impressions. As a rising Tory-Evangelical, his guiding principles were simultaneously molded by the staunchly Evangelical Edward Bickersteth and the High Church-aligned Robert Southey. At once a conservative and a reformer, his traditional paternalist instincts were a motivating factor behind his far-reaching factory reform legislation. Convinced of humanity's depravity and helplessness, he nonetheless entertained hopes that the moral and spiritual improvement of the human condition was eminently possible through social activism. Despite being a creature of the old agrarian establishment, he appreciated the potential for the manufacturing system to raise the general standard of living, providing it did so by ethical means.[11] A devotee and apologist for the British Empire, he periodically surfaced as one of its unlikely parliamentary critics in cases where the unjust treatment of imperial subjects was apparent. A loyal son of the Established Church, he would do much to break down old denominational barriers by forging co-operation between Anglican and Nonconformist evangelicals through joint ventures such as the Evangelical Alliance and the BFBS. A sworn foe of socialism and Chartism, he nonetheless shared their grievances over the dire condition and exploitation of the working classes. Otherwise suspicious of Enlightenment-derived ideologies, he co-operated with Benthamite utilitarians to bring improvements to sanitation in Victorian towns and cities. While disdainful of *laissez-faire* liberalism, he would later voice grave concerns that the state was playing too great a role in the provision of social welfare and housing.

The seeming paradoxes of Ashley's various postures reflected the intriguing complexity of Victorian Anglican Evangelicalism generally. In the Victorian age, Evangelical Anglicanism did not simply exist in a vacuum but was molded and influenced by the competing ideological currents of the age. This religious movement was not only infused with Tory paternalist ideology but, also, to a significant degree, by the great ideological precursors of the Victorian age: the Enlightenment legacy and the romantic movement.

Reflecting the prevailing temperament of Victorian Anglican Evangelicalism, the Evangelical-Tory Ashley was both a product of the Enlightenment and the romantic movement. Although accepting the Calvinist

---

11. Ashley, "Hours of Labour in Factories," HC Debates, *Hansard*, 15 March, 1844, Vol. 73, c. 1101. Indeed Shaftesbury maintained that the prosperity of the manufacturing body was essential to the welfare and existence of the British Empire.

doctrine of "total depravity" and the hopeless destiny of humankind outside of Christ, his Evangelical pessimism about human nature, like that of Wesley and Wilberforce, was tempered by an Enlightenment-inspired faith in human progress. Indeed, as Trygve Tholfsen observed, an affinity existed between the classical Evangelical doctrine of progressive sanctification and the Enlightenment ideal of individual improvement.[12] Drawing on this correlation, Ashley's life mission was not simply to draw Victorians to the Christian gospel, critical for him as this was to their spiritual redemption and sanctification, but to elevate their level of education and standard of living.

In accordance with Enlightenment thought, the Earl was convinced that the expansion of educational opportunities and improvements to material wellbeing, particularly through the provision of adequate housing and sanitation, would appreciably lift the moral condition of the people. In his inspection of Victorian Britain's grim slum life, Ashley simply did not attribute the vices of the poor to "original sin" but cited the appalling state of their dwellings as a prime cause of their delinquent behavior.[13] Thus it followed that, if the urban poor could dwell in more salubrious surrounds, their moral character would invariably improve and it was to this end that Ashley proactively supported the construction of new housing estates to accommodate London's working poor. In a similar vein, his Ragged Schools movement was aimed at raising a kindlier and more civilized generation through the blessings of education. While the Evangelical Shaftesbury stressed it was the imparting of the gospel which ultimately changed hearts, he entertained no doubt that raising the standards of literacy, numeracy, and basic life skills amongst the young would create an infinitely better generation than the one preceding it. Shaftesbury's faith in human progress was by no means peculiar to his generation of Evangelicals, particularly those who shared his premillennial outlook. With its confidence that human agency could create a better world in preparation for the Second Advent, the historicist premillennialism of Ashley and the Recordites had inherited the Enlightenment's teleology of human progress.

The alignment of Ashley's outlook with Enlightenment thought was specifically evident in his cooperation with the Benthamite Edwin Chadwick on the issue of sanitary reform.[14] Drawing on the Enlightenment, the Victorian philosophy of utilitarianism pioneered by Bentham and consoli-

12. Tholfsen, "Intellectual Origins," 79.

13. Shaftesbury, *Addresses of the Earl of Shaftesbury and the Hon W. F. Cowper*, 3. According to Shaftesbury, the foul state of local alleys, dwellings and various localities were the cause of "moral mischief" amongst the poor.

14. Battiscombe, *Shaftesbury: A Biography*, 220.

dated by John Stuart Mill (1806–1873) emphasized the primacy of human happiness according to the maxim of "the greatest happiness of the greatest number that is the measure of right and wrong." All too conscious of the widespread human misery afflicting factory children and the mass of Britain's working poor, Shaftesbury and the Victorian Evangelicals embraced the utilitarian objective of maximizing human happiness, despite differences they had with the philosophical premises of the Benthamites. As Hilton observed, Evangelicalism and utilitarianism shared the ideals of individualism and humanitarianism with their joint opposition to slavery and other forms of oppression.[15] Both movements worked to know for certain all they could about themselves and, with this knowledge, determined how best to change the lives of others.[16] It was with this common aim to improve the material wellbeing of London's urban poor that Edwin Chadwick and Ashley served collaboratively as members on the Board of Health from 1848 to improve the sanitary condition of urban centres across England and Wales. While Ashley differed radically from the freethinking Benthamites in viewing the Bible, rather than the attainment of "maximum happiness for the greatest number," as the ultimate benchmark for civilization, he concurred with Bentham and his disciples that the eradication of human misery, to the extent possible, was a worthy temporal cause.

As well as the Enlightenment inheritance, Ashley was indebted to the romantic movement; not least through the influence of the romantic Lake poets on his evolving Tory paternalist philosophy. By virtue of his aristocratic station, the Earl's instinctive disposition to Tory paternalism was unremarkable but, given his Evangelical sensibilities, he happened to espouse the same romantic critique of industrialism and *laissez-faire* capitalism as Southey, Coleridge, Wordsworth, together with the *Quarterly Review* and the high Anglican-inspired Young England movement. Although the pragmatic and realist Ashley did not go to the same lengths as Young England and some of the Lake poets in calling for a return to a pre-industrial, agrarian "golden age," he keenly felt the romantic revulsion at the usurping of the old, hierarchical social order. While accepting that industrialization was irreversible, and indeed beneficial if it could be properly harnessed, Ashley's factory legislation essentially aimed to reconcile the modern factory system with the paternalist social paradigm of the romantics. As with his Enlightenment ideal of human progress, his romantic sentiments were by no means atypical amongst his generation of Victorian Evangelicals. Despite the antipathy between Evangelicalism and Tractarianism on matters of theology

---

15. Hilton, *Age of Atonement*, 32.
16. Meacham, "The Evangelical Inheritance," 93.

and ecclesiology, both Anglican traditions did share a romantic inheritance, albeit in different forms. Whilst the romantic strain of Tractarianism was evident in its idealization of the medieval church, the romantic flavor of Evangelicalism manifested itself in the writings of Evangelicals such as Seeley and C. E Tonna who harshly critiqued industrial society, railing against its "cold-hearted" utilitarianism and idolisation of market capital.

The romantic flavor of Victorian Evangelicalism was also evident in its historicist form of premillennial eschatology that Bebbington identified as "part of the Romantic inflow into Evangelicalism."[17] In their emotional feeling and affection for the Second Advent, Evangelicals such as Shaftesbury and Haldane reflected the romantic temperament of the age.[18] Their Evangelicalism tended to exhibit the romantic hallmarks of a special emphasis on moments of intense experience, a profound appreciation for the values of the past and a spirit of revolt against present conditions. The indebtedness of Ashley and Victorian Evangelicalism to both the Enlightenment and romanticism demonstrated that this religious tradition was not wholly a reaction to these movements, as was commonly perceived, but also, to some degree, flowed into these currents in the wider world.

Given his lifespan from the turn of the nineteenth century to the mid-1880s, Ashley witnessed the transformation of English Evangelicalism from the rationalist, measured, and postmillennial variety of the Clapham Sect generation to the more strident and premillennial version of the Recordites.[19] It has already been contended that Ashley, together with Bickersteth, represented a critical bridge between the old and new British Evangelicalisms of the nineteenth century. As such, it is difficult for Ashley to be pigeonholed into either one of Boyd Hilton's classes of "moderate" (Clapham) Evangelicals or "extreme" (Recordite) Evangelicals. Whilst the Hilton dichotomy is infinitely useful in highlighting many of the palpable differences between the old and new Anglican Evangelical generations, it is also problematic. Given the capacity for the Evangelicalism of Ashley and Bickersteth to simultaneously accommodate both Clapham and Recordite traits, it is critical not to view these two schools as mutually exclusive.

As Ralph Brown posited, there was common ground between the two variaties despite their differences: a moderate Calvinism, an attachment to the Church of England, a devotion to mission and social reform advocacy were just some of the enduring commonalities.[20] Moreover, Hilton's

---

17. Bebbington, *Evangelicalism in Modern Britain*, 84.
18. Ibid.
19. Hilton, *Age of Atonement*, 10.
20. Brown, "Evangelical Social Thought," 127 & 131. Brown suggested that owing to

designation of the label "extreme" to the newer school of Evangelicalism is somewhat lacking in nuance and again problematic in the case of Ashley. Whilst there was good reason to classify the radically escapist eschatology propounded by the futurist *Irvingite school* as extreme, this minority school of thought within premillennialism did not typify the views of Victorian Evangelicals more broadly, including those of Ashley and the Recordites. As Brown pointed out, most Anglican Adventists had completely rejected the fatalistic asceticism of Irving and Drummond's circle to embrace a historicist premillennialism that was outward-focussed and activist.[21] Far from being other-worldly, Spence established that this premillennialism was intensely preoccupied with the contemporaneous affairs of the material world with its quest towards the "restitution of all things."[22] Ashley, for one, exemplified this breed of Anglican premillennialism in his commitment to overseas mission and domestic social reform. Thus to lump such Anglican Evangelicals with the introversionist Irvingite school under the "extreme" label is simplistic and fails to do justice to the true Evangelical nature of Ashley.

Given Ashley's status as a "bridging figure" between the Claphamite and Recordite schools of Evangelicalism, the genius of his own faith lay in its adroitness to make Evangelical doctrines relevant and practical to the tumultuous economic and social vicissitudes of the Victorian age without compromise to their original integrity. In so doing, he was able to contribute to the preservation of the faith from one generation to the next amid a period of tumultuous social, political and economic change within his own lifetime. For all his enduring Evangelical conviction, however, he did not adequately envisage how the Evangelical faith would continue to be advocated once his time had passed. This was partly reflected in his singular failure to anoint a visible successor to continue charting either his parliamentary course in social reform and poor relief or his lay Anglican activism in mission and philanthropy.[23] As Wilberforce's parliamentary career drew to a close, the anti-slavery campaigner had groomed Buxton to carry on his parliamentary campaign against slavery. Likewise, Sadler had singled out the Earl himself to continue his pioneering campaign for factory reform.

---

their moderate, historicist premillennialism, the Recordites in fact had more in common with the earlier Claphamite generation than with contemporaneous Evangelicals who held to the extreme, futurist premillennialism of Edward Irving and the 'Albury circle'.

21. Brown, "Victorian Anglican Activism," 685.
22. Spence, "Renewal of Time and Space," 92.
23. *The Record*, October 2, 1885, 977.

By contrast, Ashley had groomed no such protégé. His profligate eldest son, who would eventually succeed him as the Earl of Shaftesbury,[24] proved unequal to the task and there was nobody in the modern Tory party to whom he could faithfully entrust his legacy. This was possibly because so much of the necessary work for factory reform and other causes was seen to have been accomplished by Ashley himself during his lengthy public career, thereby obviating the need for an immediate successor. Notwithstanding appreciable ameliorations to Victorian life under his watch, British society in the latter part of Victoria's reign remained plagued by a myriad of social and economic afflictions as documented in William Booth's damning exposé, *In Darkest England*.[25] Maladies such as ongoing urban poverty, widespread vagrancy, drunkenness and prostitution necessitated a fresh wave of social reform and philanthropic endeavor. Thus any need for Shaftesbury to groom a suitable successor from the 1880s seemed more than apparent.

An opportunity for Shaftesbury to bless such a successor arose as William Booth gained public prominence as leader of the newly formed Salvation Army in the 1870s and 80s. Like the Earl, the conscience of the breakaway Methodist preacher was kindled for the poor and helpless of Victorian Britain. In the British Evangelical tradition of Wesley, Wilberforce, and Shaftesbury, Booth and his 'Army' had combined evangelistic fervor with social action to redeem the bodies and souls of individuals. Shaftesbury's attitude towards the Salvation Army, however, was less than accommodating. Fixated more on the structure and outward appearance of the Army than on its motivating philosophy and objectives, Shaftesbury took issue with the novel paramilitary style of an organization that professed to be an evangelical Christian church: "When, however, I look at the constitution, framework, and organisation of the Salvation Army, its military arrangements, its Hallelujah Lasses, its banners, their mottoes, and a thousand other original accompaniments, I ask what authority we have, in scripture, for such a system and such discipline!"[26] He essentially saw its style as having no warrant in scripture, despite the lack of anything in the Bible suggesting its proscription.

Given this observation was made in light of his recent campaigns against Tractarian ritualism, it was perhaps not surprising that Shaftesbury was very quick to see the perceived dangers inherent in the symbols and

---

24. Anthony Ashley Cooper (1831–1886), The Eighth Earl of Shaftesbury, committed suicide six months after succeeding his father in the title in 1885.

25. William Booth published *In Darkest England and the Way Out* in 1890.

26. Shaftesbury, Diary Entry (November 7, 1881), in Hodder, *Life and Work of the Seventh Earl*, Vol. III, 435.

'externals' of Christian worship. Indeed, he drew a link between the nascent Army and the foregoing ritualism within the Established Church:

> I have no sympathy with that movement in the remotest degree; not so much as I have with that other extreme, Ritualism. Extremes meet, and I am disposed to think that, eventually, there will be an open alliance between the Ritualists and the Salvation Army. Both delight in show, both are dependent upon their leader—both are busy with externals.[27]

Unfortunately, his preoccupation with these externals obfuscated a reasonable appraisal of the movement's core doctrines and an appreciation of the extent to which its evangelical activism closely resembled his own. As Hylson-Smith noted, "Shaftesbury underestimated the contribution to be made to religious and social activity by the Salvation Army."[28] Whilst the Earl's inherent conservatism had been an asset in his stout defence of Evangelical doctrine, it also proved an obstacle in impairing his capacity to envision how his causes and ideals could be continued in new ways and in new forms. His inability, in this instance, to employ his customary Burkean strategy of "reforming to conserve," either by anointing successors to perpetuate his legacy or by lending his support to new but kindred-spirited movements, would do little to buoy the social action tradition within British Evangelicalism over the ensuing decades.

The limited influence of Shaftesbury in the British Evangelical world beyond the 1880s ensured his breed of Evangelicalism remained uniquely and unmistakably Victorian, having eclipsed almost five decades of Victoria's sixty-four-year reign. The tendency within much of Evangelicalism over the late nineteenth and early twentieth century to divorce evangelism from social action, as a conservative reaction to the nascent social gospel movement, would have alarmed the Victorian Shaftesbury. Owing to the activist legacy of Clapham, together with the early contribution of the radical Tory Evangelical factory reformers in the 1830s and 1840s, the great hallmark of Victorian Evangelicalism had been the largely successful marriage between the proclamation of the classic Christian gospel and the humanitarian social reform of society. Ashley personified this with his much-quoted dictum that "God had created the body as well as the soul." This was a maxim that guided his labors for factory reform and the education of the poor no less than his evangelistic efforts on behalf of the BFBS or the CMS. Returning to the central contention of this volume, above all Ashley's Evangelicalism

---

27. Shaftesbury, conversation with Mr Hodder (1885) in Hodder, *Life and Work of the Seventh Earl*, Vol. III, 440.

28. Hylson-Smith, *Evangelicals in the Church of England*, 180.

reflected the permeation of Tory paternalist values into Victorian Anglican Evangelicalism. According to Hylson-Smith, the "essential conservatism" of Shaftesbury and other Evangelicals was "undeniable" given their defence of the existing social order. Scotland added that it was this belief in a 'fixed social hierarchy' by figures such as Shaftesbury which perhaps explained why "Anglican Evangelicals gave almost no support to the emerging trade union movements of the 1870s and 1880s."[29]

Finally, G. M. Young's summation of Victorian Evangelical culture as one that imposed on all classes of society, whether religious or not,[30] its values of sabbatarianism, personal responsibility, philanthropy, domestic discipline, regularity in affairs and social conformity was a wide-ranging legacy that owed much to the pervasive political creed of Tory paternalism. The very notion of one class imposing its values on another, together with the ideals of personal responsibility, societal orderliness and loyalty to the English Protestant constitution, were long espoused by Tory paternalists such as Coleridge and Southey before their appropriation by Victorian Evangelicals such as Haldane, Seeley, Tonna, and Ashley. As a protégé of the high Tory Southey, as well as the Evangelical Bickersteth, Ashley's personal philosophy and outlook embodied many of the Tory paternalist motifs which helped define the evolving character of Victorian Evangelicalism.

---

29. Scotland, *Evangelical Anglicans*, 94–95.
30. Bebbington, *Evangelicalism in Modern Britain*, 105.

Bibliography

Primary Sources

Unpublished

Ashley-Cooper, Anthony. "Correspondence to Robert Southey." St Giles (September 12, 1830) [Maggs 10.12.54, Berg Collection, New York Public Library].
———. "Personal Diary." Vol. 2, (1838–45) [Broadlands Archives SHA/PD/2].
———. "Personal Diary." Vol. 3, (1834–45) [Broadlands Archives SHA/PD/3].
———. "Religious Notes and Reflections" (1835–37) [Broadlands Archives SHA/MIS /1].
Earl of Shaftesbury. "Correspondence to Charles Haddon (C H) Spurgeon" (1870) [Broadlands Archives SHA/PC/103–4].
———. "Correspondence to Lord Palmerston" (August 23, 1853) [Broadlands Archives PP GC/SH/24].
———. Letter to the Rev T G Bonney, January 10, 1878, 18–19, Correspondence between the Earl of Shaftesbury and the Archbishop of Canterbury, and also the Rev T G Bonney, on Publications of the SPCK, London, 1878 [Broadlands Archives SHA/MIS/41].
Southey, Robert, "Correspondence to Lord Ashley" (1832–33) [Maggs 10.12.54, Berg Collection, New York Public Library].
Spurgeon, c. H., "Correspondence to Shaftesbury" (1876–84) [Broadlands Archives SHA/PC/90–102].

Published

Ashley-Cooper, Anthony. *Address to the Gentry, Clergy and Freeholders of the County of Dorset*. Dorchester, September 27, 1831 [Broadlands Archives SHA/MIS/22].
———. *Condition of the Labouring Population*. Address to the Sturminster Agricultural Society, Sturminster, Dorsetshire, November, 1843.
———. *Dwelling-places of the Working Classes*. Speech delivered by Lord Ashley at the Hanover Square Rooms, May 22, 1846.

———. *Legislation for the Labouring Classes*. Address to the Lancashire Central Short Time Committee, Manchester, October 26, 1844.

———. *Social Condition of the Labouring Classes*. Speech in Bath, May 25, 1845.

———. *Speech of Lord Ashley from the Chair of the London Society for Promoting Christianity Amongst the Jews*. May 1845.

———. *Speech of Lord Ashley MP to Great Lay Meeting against Papal Aggression and Tractarian Novelties*. Freemasons' Hall, London, Thursday, December 5, 1850.

———. "Speech of Lord Ashley at the Late Election for the County of Dorset." (From the *Dorset Country Chronicle*, July 8, 1841) [Broadlands Archives SHA/MIS/9].

Author Unknown. "Obituary, Death of Lord Shaftesbury." *The Times*, Friday, October 2, 1885, 11 [Broadlands Archives SHA/MIS/47].

———. "Tribute article to Lord Shaftesbury." *The Times*, Friday, October 2, 1885 [Broadlands Archives SHA/MIS/48].

Bickersteth, Edward. *The Divine Warning to the Church*. London: Seeley, Burnside & Seeley, 1842.

———. *Family Prayers: Being a Complete Course for Six Weeks*. London: Seeley, Jackson and Halliday, 1841.

———. *Practical Remarks on the Prophecies: With Reference to their Fulfilment and to Personal Edification*. London: Seeley & Sons, 1832.

———. *The Restoration of the Jews to Their Own Land in Connection with Their Future Conversion and the Final Blessedness of our Earth*. London: Seeley & Burnside, 1841.

———. *The Signs of the Times in the East: A Warning to the West*. London: Seeley, Burside & Seeley, 1845.

———. *A Treatise on Baptism: Designed as a Help to the Due Improvement of that Holy Sacrament, as Administered in the Church of England*. London: Seeley & Burnside, 1840.

Bickersteth, M. c. *A Sketch of the Life and Episcopate of the Right Reverend Robert Bickersteth, Bishop of Ripon 1857–1884*. London: Rivertons, 1887.

Birks, Thomas R., ed. *Memoir of the Rev. Edward Bickersteth*, Vols. 1–2. London: Seeleys, 1852. (Reprinted by General Books LLC, 2009.)

Bredvold, Louis I, ed. *The Philosophy of Edmund Burke: A Selection from His Speeches and Writings*. Ann Arbor, MI: The University of Michigan Press, 1960.

Butler, Josephine, et al. *Legislative Restrictions on the Industry of Women: Considered from the Women's Point of View*. London: unknown publisher, ca 1874.

Buxton, Charles, ed. *Memoirs of Sir Thomas Fowell Buxton*. London: John Murray, 1855.

Carus, Rev William. *Memoirs of the Life of the Rev Charles Simeon: With a Selection from His Writings and Correspondence*. London: Hatchard & Son, 1847.

Chalmers, Thomas. "Causes and Cure of Pauperism." *The Edinburgh Review* 28.55 (March 1817) 1–31.

Coleridge, Samuel Taylor. *The Statesman's Manual; or the Bible the Best Guide to Political Skill and Foresight*. London: Gale and Fenner, 1816.

Conybeare, William J. "Church Parties." *The Edinburgh Review* 98.200 (October 1853) 273–342.

Earl of Shaftesbury. *Address at the Anniversary Meeting of the "Refuges for Homeless and Destitute Children."* Willis's Rooms, April 11, 1866.

———. "Address by the Earl of Shaftesbury." In *Full Report of the Great Meeting in the City Hall of the Glasgow Working Men's Association, The Earl of Shaftesbury's Visit to Glasgow*, 29th August 1871. [Broadlands Archives SHA/MIS/33].

———. *Addresses of the Earl of Shaftesbury and the Hon W F Cowper on the Health, Physical Condition, Moral Habits and Education of the People*. 12 October 1858. Liverpool: Benson & Mallett, 1858.

———. "Annual General Meeting of the Palestine Exploration Fund." *Palestine Exploration Fund Quarterly* 7.3 (July 1875) 115–17.

———. "Ch II: Work and Influence" and "Ch VII: Counsel to Young Men." In *Talks with the People by Men of Mark, Volume I: The Earl of Shaftesbury KG.*, edited by Charles Bullock, 17–24, 48–58. London: "Home Worlds" Publishing Office, 1882.

———. "The Earl of Shaftesbury on Sunday-Schools and Bible Teaching." Quoted by *The Record*, October 14, 1874, 3. [Broadlands Archives SHA/MIS/24].

———. *The Earl of Shaftesbury's Great Speech on Indian Cruelties*. Delivered at Wimborne, October 30, 1857.

———. *A Great Problem Solved: or, How to Reach the Heathen in Great Cities*. Address by the Right Hon. The Earl of Shaftesbury, KG, Chiswick House, London, July 16, 1878.

———. *Homeless Boys of London*. Speech delivered at the inauguration ceremony of the "Chichester" Training Ship, Blackwell, December 18, 1866.

———. *Inaugural Address of Lord Shaftesbury in the Proceedings Connected with the Inauguration of the Memorial Statue to Dr Isaac Watts*. Southampton, July 17, 1861, 10. [Broadlands Archives SHA/MIS/31].

———. "Introduction." In *Continental Sunday Labour: A Warning to the English Nation with an introduction by the Earl of Shaftesbury*, by Charles Hill, Secretary of the Working Men's Lord's Day Rest Association. London: Partridge, 1877.

———. "Introduction" to *These Fifty Years Being the Jubilee Volume of the London City Mission*, by John M. Weylland. London: Partridge & Co., 1884.

———. "Introduction." In *Light in Lands of Darkness: A Record of Missionary Labour with Introduction by the Earl of Shaftesbury Illustrated*, by Robert Young. London: Fisher Unwin, 1883.

———. "Introduction." In *Pantomime Waifs or a Plea for our City Children*, by Ellen Barlee. London: Partridge & Co., 1884.

———. "Introduction." In *Pictures of London Life: The Story of Mr Orsman's Mission in Golden Lane*, by Holden G. Pike. London: James Clarke and Co., 1876.

———. "Introduction." In *Round the Tower: or, the Story of the London City Mission*, by John Weylland. London: Partridge & Co., 1875.

———. "Introduction." In *Some Moral Miracles of the Gospel: A Record of Twenty-one Winters' Work of Preaching the Gospel in Theatres, Halls, and Mission Rooms [with an Introduction by the Earl of Shaftesbury].*, by Charles Sawell. London: Partridge and Co., 1881.

———. "Introduction." In *A Thought for the World; or, The Narrative of Christian Effort in Great Exhibitions*, by John M. Weylland. London: Partridge & Co., 1877.

———. *Lectures Delivered before the Young Men's Christian Association*. Exeter Hall, London, November 1862–February 1863. London: Nisbet, 1863.

———. "Letter to the Editor of the *Times* defending the value of the Ragged School Union." *The Times*, November 13, 1871. [Broadlands Archives SHA/MIS/46].

———. *Letter to Lord Kinnaird regarding Some Recent Ecclesiastical Matters connected with Scotland*, December 2, 1876.

———. *Lord Shaftesbury and the Revision of the Bible* [Consisting largely of a Letter to Canon William Selwyn, dated 24 Feb. 1870], London: Hunt & Co., 1870.

———. *The National Education Union and the Denominational System*. Speech Delivered by the Rt Hon The Earl of Shaftesbury at the Demonstration of the National Education Union, St James Hall, London, April 8, 1870.

———. "Notes and News." *Palestine Exploration Fund Quarterly* 8.3 (July 1876) 107–19.

———. "Preface." In *The Agricultural Labourer*, by a Wykehamist (reprinted from *Fraser's Magazine*), ix. London: Longmans Green and Co., 1873. [Broadlands Archives SHA/MIS/36].

———. "Preface." In *The Life of Thomas Wright of Manchester: The Prison Philanthropist*, by Thomas W McDermid. Manchester: Haywood, 1876.

———. "Preface." In *The Young People's Illustrated Edition of "Uncle Tom's Story of His Life (from 1789 to 1877)*, by John Lobb. London: Christian Age Office, 1877.

———. *Sanitary Legislation*. Address to the Social Science Congress of 1858, Liverpool, 1858.

———. "Seventh Annual Meeting for the Society for Improving the Conditions of the Labouring Classes." *The Labourer's Friend* (July 1851) 98–99.

———. *Speech to Bible Society* (Kensington Auxillary). March 9, 1877, 178.

———. *Speech Delivered at the Tenth Annual Meeting of the Manchester Young Men's Christian Association*. Manchester, March 25, 1856.

———. *Speech of the Earl of Shaftesbury at the Annual Meeting of the Church Pastoral Aid Society*. Thursday, May 8, 1873. London: Dalton, London, 1873.

———. *Speech of the Earl of Shaftesbury: On Laying the Memorial Stone of the First 1,200 Improved Dwelling Houses, to be erected by the Artizans', Labourers' and General Dwellings Company, Limited, on the Shaftesbury Park Estate, Lavender Hill, Wandsworth Road, London*. On Saturday, August 3rd, 1872. [Broadlands Archives SHA/MIS/35/2].

———. *Speech of the Earl of Shaftesbury, KG, at Working Men's Meeting*. Social Congress in Glasgow, October 2, 1874. [Broadlands Archives SHA/MIS/40].

———. *Speech to Literary Institutes for Working Men*. Delivered at the Opening of the Swindon Literary Institute, Swindon, November 22, 1859.

———. *Speech of Lord Shaftesbury in St James' Hall, March 1, 1872*. On Mr Dixon's Motion on the Education Question.

———. *Speech of the Right Hon Earl Shaftesbury*. Delivered in the Manchester Town Hall, October 6, 1866.

———. *Speeches of the Earl of Shaftesbury upon Subjects having Relation Chiefly to the Claims and Interests of the Labouring Class*. London: Chapman and Hall, 1868.

Cunningham, John William. *The Velvet Cushion*. London: Cadell & Davies, 1815.

Duncan, Robert. "An English Nobleman." *Britannia*, January 1900, 2. [Broadlands Archives SHA/MIS/19].

Gisborne, Thomas. *An Enquiry into the Duties of the Female Sex*. London: Cadell and Davies, 1797.

———. *An Enquiry into the Duties of Men in the Higher and Middle Classes of Society in Great Britain*, London: Printed for T. Cadell, 1824.

Haweis, Thomas. *A View of the Present State of Evangelical Religion throughout the World: With a View to Promote Missionary Exertions.* London: Williams and Son, 1812.

Hodder, Edwin. *The Life and Work of the Seventh Earl of Shaftesbury KG*, Vols. I–III. London: Cassell, 1886. (Reprinted by General Books LLC, 2009.)

Jeune, F. c. *A Charge Delivered to the Clergy and Churchwardens of the Diocese of Peterborough at His primary Visitation in October 1867 by France Lord Bishop of Peterborough.* Oxford: Parker & Co., 1867.

King, Walker, ed. *The Works of the Right Honourable Edmund Burke.* London: Rivington, 1801.

Kirk, Sir John JP. "First Shaftesbury Lecture." *This Way and that Way.* London: Shaftesbury Society and RSU, 1917. [Broadlands Archives SHA/MIS/6].

Kirton, John W. *True Nobility; or the Golden Deeds of an Earnest Life. A Record of the Career and Labours of Anthony Ashley Cooper, Seventh Earl of Shaftesbury, A Priceless Example for Youth.* London: Ward, Lock & Co., 1886.

Kosmos. "Letters to Eminent Persons. No. XV. To the Earl of Shaftesbury." *The World*, Wednesday, March 22, 1882, 5. [Broadlands Archives SHA/MIS/26].

Law, George Henry. *A Charge Delivered to the Clergy of the Diocese of Bath and Wells, at the Visitation of the Diocese,* May and June 1831, Wells, 1831.

Mill, John Stuart. *The Principles of Political Economy: with Some of Their Applications to Social Philosophy*, Vol. II. Boston: White and Potter, 1848.

Miller, R. E. "The Life and Labours of Lord Shaftesbury." *The National Philanthropist* 9 (March 1, 1885). [Broadlands Archives SHA/MIS/12].

More, Hannah. *Christian Morals.* London: Bruce, Slote-Lane, 1813.

———. *An Estimation of the Religion of the Fashionable World.* London: Cadell, 1791.

———. *The Life of Hannah More: with Selections from her Correspondence.* London, 1856.

———. *Thoughts on the Importance of the Manners of the Great to General Society.* London: Cadell, 1789.

Nash, Vaughan. "Sixty Years of Empire: XV—Factory & Mine Legislation." *The Daily Chronicle*, Thursday, June 24, 1897, 3.

Oastler, Richard. *Eight Letters to the Duke of Wellington: A Petition to the House of Commons: and a Letter to the Agricultural and Industrial Magazine.* London: Cochrane & Co., 1835.

———. *The Fleet Papers; being Letters to Thomas Thornhill Esq., of Riddlesworth, in the County of Norfolk; from Richard Oastler, His Prisoner in the Fleet, with Occasional Communications from Friends,* Vols. I–III. London: Cleaver, 1841.

Pretyman, George. *A Charge Delivered to the Clergy of the Diocese of Lincoln at the Triennial Visitation of that Diocese in May and June 1794.* London: Cadell and Davies, 1794.

Sadler, Michael Thomas. *Ireland; Its Evils and their Remedies; being a Refutation of the Errors of the Emigration Committee and Others, Touching that Country.* 2nd ed. London: John Murray, 1829.

———. *The Law of Population: In Disproof of the Superfecundity of Human Beings, and Developing the Real Principle of their Increase.* London: John Murray, 1830.

Scott, Thomas. *The Jews a Blessing to the Nations, and Christians Bound to Seek Their Conversion to the Saviour.* London: Goakman, 1810.

———. "Preface." *Commentary on the Holy Bible.* London: Nisbet, 1886.

Seeley, Robert Benton. *Memoirs of the Life and Writings of Michael Thomas Sadler.* London: Seeley and Burnside, 1848.

———. *Remedies Suggested for the Evils which Constitute Perils of the Nation.* London: Seeley, Burnside and Seeley, 1844.

Southey, Robert. *The Book of the Church*, London: 1824. Republished in London: Frederick Warne and Co., 1869.

———. *Essays Moral and Political,* Vol. I. London: Clowes, 1832.

———. *Sir Thomas More, Or, Colloquies on the Progress and Prospects of Society.* London: Murray, 1829.

Tonna, Charlotte Elizabeth. *Helen Fleetwood.* New York: Taylor and Co., 1841.

———. *Perils of the Nation: An Appeal to the Legislative, the Clergy, and the Higher and Middle Classes.* London: Seeley, Burnside and Seeley, 1844.

———. *Personal Recollections.* New York: Scribner, 1854.

Wilberforce, William. *A Practical View of the Prevailing Religious System of Professed Christians in the Higher and Middle Classes in This Country, Contrasted with Real Christianity.* London: Cadell and Davies, 1797. (Reprinted by Hendrickson LLC, 1996.)

Wilberforce D.D, Basil. Archdeacon of Westminster, "The Awakening." The Christian World Pulpit, May 24, 1905, 326 [Broadlands Archives SHA/MIS/20].

Journals and Periodicals

Blackwood's Edinburgh Magazine (1829)
The Christian Observer (1823 and 1832)
The Edinburgh Review (1817 and 1853)
The Quarterly Review (1839, 1840 and 1847)
The Record (1844, 1845, 1850 and 1867)
The Times (1867, 1871 and 1885)

Parliamentary Papers and Reference Works

Hansard, Parliamentary Debates, (3rd Series) Vol. 1 (October 1830) to Vol. 356 (August 1891).

Report from the Select Committee on Aborigines (British Settlements), *Parliamentary Papers* (1837) 7(425), 74–76.

Correspondence of the Rev George Stringer Bull to Short-Time Committees. London, February 6, 1833.

Secondary Sources

Adelman, Paul. *Peel and the Conservative Party, 1830–1850.* London: Longman, 1989.

Adler, Joseph. *Restoring the Jews to their Homeland: Nineteen Centuries in the Quest for Zion.* Northvale, NJ: Arnson, 1997.

Altholz, Josef L. "Alexander Haldane, *The Record*, and Religious Journalism." *Victorian Periodicals Review* 20.1 (1987) 23–31.

Bibliography

Anderson, Olive. "The Growth of Christian Militarism in Mid-Victorian Britain." *English Historical Review* 86.338 (1971) 46–72.

Andrews, Stuart. *Robert Southey: History, Politics, Religion*. New York: Palgrave Macmillan, 2011.

Atkins, Gareth. "Anglican Evangelical Theology, c. 1820–1850: The Case of Edward Bickersteth." *Journal of Religious History* 38.1 (2014) 1–19.

———. "Wilberforce and His Milieux: The Worlds of Anglican Evangelicalism, c. 1780–1830." PhD thesis, University of Cambridge, 2009.

Author Unknown. "The Seventh Earl of Shaftesbury: Incidents in His Life and Labours." *Leisure Hour*, January 1887, 56–61.

Bar-Yosef, Eitan. "Christian Zionism and Victorian Culture." *Israel Studies* 8.2 (2003) 18–44.

Battiscombe, Georgina. *Shaftesbury: A Biography of the Seventh Earl, 1801–1885*. London: Constable, 1974.

Bebbington, David. "Chapter 1: Evangelicalism and Cultural Diffusion." In *British Evangelical Identities Past and Present*, Vol. I, edited by Mark Smith, 18–34. Milton Keynes, UK: Paternoster, 2008.

———. *The Dominance of Evangelicalism: The Age of Spurgeon and Moody*. Nottingham, UK: IVP, 2005.

———. *Evangelicalism in Modern Britain: A History from the 1730s to the 1980s*. London: Unwin Hyman, 1989.

———. "Response." In *The Emergence of Evangelicalism: Exploring Historical Continuities*, edited by Michael A. G. Haykin and Kenneth J. Stewart, 417–32. Nottingham, UK: Apollos, 2008.

Best, Geoffrey F. A. *A Biography of A. A. Cooper: 7th Earl of Shaftesbury*. London: Batsford, 1964.

———. "The Evangelicals and the Established Church in the Early Nineteenth Century." *Journal of Theological Studies* 10.1 (1959) 63–78.

———. "Popular Protestantism in Victorian Britain." In *Ideas and Institutions of Victorian Britain: Essays in Honour of George Kitson Clark*, edited by Robert Robson, 115–42. London: Bell & Sons, 1967.

Bewley, Thomas. *Madness to Mental Illness. A History of the Royal College of Psychiatrists*. London: RCPsych, 2008.

Blackburn, Barbara. *Noble Lord: The Life of the Seventh Earl of Shaftesbury*. London: Home & Van Thal, 1949.

Bradley, Ian. *The Call to Seriousness: The Evangelical Impact on the Victorians*. Oxford: Lion Hudson, 2006.

———. "The Politics of Godliness: Evangelicals in Parliament, 1784–1832." PhD thesis, University of Oxford, 1974.

Bready, John W. *England before and after Wesley: The Evangelical Revival and Social Reform*. London: Hodder and Stoughton, 1938.

———. *Lord Shaftesbury and Social-Industrial Progress*. London: Allen & Unwin, 1926.

Brent, Richard. *Liberal Anglican Politics: Whiggery, Religion, and Reform 1830–1841*. Oxford: Clarendon, 1987.

Briggs, Asa. *Victorian People: A Reassessment of Persons and Themes 1851–67*. Chicago: University of Chicago Press, 1973.

Brinton, Crane. *The Political Ideas of the English Romanticists*. London: Oxford University Press, 1926.

Brown, David. *Palmerston: A Biography.* London: Yale University Press, 2010.
Brown, Callum G. *The Death of Christian Britain.* London: Routledge, 2001.
Brown, Ford K. *Fathers of the Victorians: The Age of Wilberforce.* Cambridge: Cambridge University Press, 1961.
Brown, Ralph. "Evangelical Social Thought." *Journal of Ecclesiastical History* 60.1 (2009) 126–36.
———. "Victorian Anglican Evangelicalism: The Radical Legacy of Edward Irving." *Journal of Ecclesiastical History* 58.4 (2007) 675–704.
Brown, Stewart J. *Providence and Empire: Religion, Politics and Society in the United Kingdom, 1815–1914.* Harlow, UK: Pearson Longman, 2008.
Canavan, Francis. *Edmund Burke: Prescription and Providence.* Durham, NC: Carolina Academic Press, 1987.
Carnell, Geoffrey. *Robert Southey and His Age: The Development of a Conservative Mind.* Oxford: Clarendon, 1960.
Chadwick, Owen. *The Victorian Church*, Part II 1860–1901. London: Black, 1972.
Clark, J. c. D. *English Society 1660–1832: Religion, Ideology and Politics during the Ancien Régime.* Cambridge: Cambridge University Press, 2000.
Carpenter, S. c. *Church and People 1789–1889: A History of the Church of England from William Wilberforce to "Lux Mundi."* London: SPCK, 1959.
Carter, Grayson. *Anglican Evangelicals, Protestant Secessions from the Via Media, c. 1800–1850.* Oxford: Oxford University Press, 2000.
Cobban, Alfred. *Edmund Burke and the Revolt against the Eighteenth Century: A Study of the Political and Social Thinking of Burke, Wordsworth, Coleridge and Southey.* London: Allen & Unwin, 1978.
Coleman, Bruce. *Conservatism and the Conservative Party in Nineteenth-Century Britain.* London: Arnold, 1988.
Constable, A. "ART. III.-The Life and Work of the Seventh Earl of Shaftesbury, K.G." *The Edinburgh Review* 165.338 (1887) 354–87.
Corsbie, Anne H. *A Biographical Sketch of Alexander Haldane.* London: Spottiswoode & Co., 1882.
Creighton, Colin. *Richard Oastler, Evangelicalism and the Ideology of Domesticity.* Occasional Paper No. 9 (1992). Department of Sociology and Social Anthropology, University of Hull.
———. "Richard Oastler, Factory Legislation and the Working-Class Family." *Journal of Historical Sociology* 5.3 (1992) 292–320.
Davidoff, Leonore, and Catherine Hall. *Family Fortunes: Men and Women of the English Middle Class, 1780–1850.* London: Routledge, 2002.
Day, Aidan. *Romanticism.* New York: Routledge, 1996.
Dicey, A. V. *Law & Public Opinion in England during the Nineteenth Century.* London: Macmillan, 1952.
———. *Lectures on the Relation between Law & Public Opinion in England during the Nineteenth Century.* London: Macmillan, 1920.
Driver, Cecil. *Tory Radical: The Life of Richard Oastler.* New York: Oxford University Press, 1964.
Dworkin, Gerald. "Defining Paternalism." In *Paternalism: Theory and Practice*, edited by c. Coons and M Weber, 28–31. Cambridge: Cambridge University Press, 2013.

Dzelzainis, Ella. "Charlotte Elizabeth Tonna, Pre-Millenarianism, and the Formation of Gender Ideology in the Ten Hours Campaign." *Victorian Literature and Culture* 31.1 (2003) 181–91.
Eastwood, David. "Robert Southey and the Intellectual Origins of Romantic Conservatism." *English Historical Review* 104.411 (1989) 308–31.
Edwards, David L. *Leaders of the Church of England 1828–1978*. London: Hodder and Stoughton, 1978.
Elbourne, Elisabeth. "Religion in the British Empire." In *The British Empire: Themes and Perspectives*, edited by Sarah Stockwell, 131–56. Oxford: Blackwell, 2008.
Ervine, W. J. Clyde. "Bickersteth, Edward." In *Blackwell Dictionary of Evangelical Biography*, 92–93. Oxford: Blackwell, 1995.
———. "Doctrine and Diplomacy: Some Aspects of the Life and Thought of the Anglican Evangelical Clergy, 1797–1837." PhD thesis, Cambridge University, 1979.
Finlayson, Geoffrey B.A.M. *Citizen, State, and Social Welfare in Britain 1830–1990*. Oxford: Clarendon, 1994.
———. *The Seventh Earl of Shaftesbury 1801–1885*. London: Eyre Methuen, 1981.
———. "Shaftesbury." In *Pressure from Without in Early Victorian England*, edited by Patricia Hollis, 159–82. London: Arnold, 1974.
———. "The Victorian Shaftesbury." *History Today* 33.3 (1983) 31–35.
———. "Wellington, the Constitution, and the March of Reform." In *Wellington: Studies in the Military and Political Career of the First Duke of Wellington*, edited by Norman Gash, 196–213. Manchester, UK: Manchester University Press, 1990.
Fryckstedt, Monica Correa. "Charlotte Elizabeth Tonna: A Forgotten Evangelical Writer." *Studia Neophilologica* 52.1 (1980) 79–102.
Gidney, W. T. *The History of the London Society for Promoting Christianity Amongst the Jews, from 1809 to 1908*. London: LSPCJ, 1908.
Gill, J. c. *The Ten Hours Parson: Christian Social Action in the Eighteen-Thirties*. London: SPCK, 1959.
Gleadle, Kathryn. "Charlotte Elizabeth Tonna and the Mobilisation of Tory Women in Early Victorian England." *The Historical Journal* 50.1 (2007) 97–117.
Gray, Robert Q. *The Factory Question and Industrial England, 1830–1860*. Cambridge: Cambridge University Press, 1996.
Greenleaf, W. H. *The British Political Tradition: Volume Two—The Ideological Heritage*. London: Methuen, 1983.
Hague, William. *William Wilberforce: The Life of the Great Anti-Slave Campaigner*. London: Harper, 2007.
Hammond, J. L., and Barbara Hammond. *Lord Shaftesbury*. London: Constable, 1923.
Hargreaves, John A. "Introduction: 'Victims of Slavery Even on the Threshold of Our Homes': Richard Oastler and Yorkshire Slavery." In *Slavery in Yorkshire: Richard Oastler and the Campaign against Child Labour in the Industrial Revolution*, edited by John A Hargreaves and E. A. Hilary Haigh, 1–40. Huddersfield, UK: University of Huddersfield Press, 2012.
Hart, Jenifer. "Nineteenth-Century Social Reform: A Tory Interpretation of History." *Past & Present* 31 (1965) 39–61.
Heasman, Kathleen, *Evangelicals in Action: An Appraisal of their Social Work in the Victorian Era*. London: Bles, 1962.

Hempton, David N. "Evangelicalism and Eschatology." *Journal of Ecclesiastical History* 31.2 (1980) 179–94.
Hennell, Michael. *Sons of the Prophets: Leaders of the Victorian Church*. London: SPCK, 1979.
Henriques, Ursula R. Q. *Before the Welfare State: Social Administration in Early Industrial Britain*. London: Longman, 1979.
Hilton, Boyd. *The Age of Atonement: The Influence of Evangelicalism on Social and Economic Thought, 1795–1865*. Oxford: Oxford University Press, 1988.
———. *Cash, Corn, Commerce: The Economic Policies of the Tory Governments 1815–1830*. Oxford: Oxford University Press, 1980.
———. *A Mad, Bad, and Dangerous People? England 1783–1846*. Oxford: Clarendon, 2006.
———. "The Role of Providence in Evangelical Social Thought." In *History, Society and the Churches: Essays in Honour of Owen Chadwick*, edited by Derek Beales and Geoffrey Best, 215–33. London: Cambridge University Press, 1985.
———. "Sardonic Grins and Paranoid Politics: Religion, Economics, and Public Policy in the Quarterly Review." In *Conservatism and the Quarterly Review*, edited by Jonathan Cutmore, 41–60. London: Pickering & Chatto, 2007.
Himmelfarb, Gertrude. *The Idea of Poverty: England in the Early Industrial Age*. London: Faber and Faber, 1984.
Hindmarsh, D. B. "Scott, Thomas." In *Biographical Dictionary of Evangelicals*, edited by Timothy Larsen et al., 591–93. Leicester, UK: IVP, 2003.
Holladay, J. Douglas. "19th Century Evangelical Activism: From Private Charity to State Intervention, 1830–50." *Historical Magazine of the Protestant Episcopal Church* 51 (1982) 53–79.
Holmes, Stephen R. "British (and European) Evangelical Theologies." In *The Cambridge Companion to Evangelical Theology*, edited by Timothy Larsen and Daniel J. Treier, 241–58. Cambridge: Cambridge University Press, 2007.
Hoppen, K. Theodore. *The Mid-Victorian Generation: 1846–1886*. Oxford: Clarendon, 1998.
Hutchinson, Mark, and John Wolffe. *A Short History of Global Evangelicalism*. Cambridge: Cambridge University Press, 2012.
Hylson-Smith, Kenneth. *Evangelicals in the Church of England 1734–1984*. Edinburgh: T. & T. Clarke, 1988.
Jay, Elisabeth, and Richard Jay. *Critics of Capitalism: Victorian Reactions to "Political Economy."* Cambridge: Cambridge University Press, 1986.
Jones, H. Stuart. *Victorian Political Thought*. Basingstoke, UK: Macmillan, 2000.
Keay, Mark. *William Wordsworth's Golden Age Theories during the Industrial Revolution in England, 1750–1850*. London: Palgrave, 2001.
Kirby, Peter. *Child Labour in Britain, 1750–1870*. Basingstoke, UK: Palgrave Macmillan, 2003.
Larsen, Timothy, et al., eds. *Biographical Dictionary of Evangelicals*. Leicester, UK: IVP, 2003.
———. "Bishop Colenso and His Critics: The Strange Emergence of Biblical Criticism in Victorian Britain." *Scottish Journal of Theology* 50.4 (1997) 433–58.
———. "The Book of Acts and the Origin of the Races in Evangelical Thought." *Victorian Review* 37.2 (2011) 35–39.

———. *Contested Christianity: The Political and Social Contexts of Victorian Theology.* Waco, TX: Baylor University Press, 2004.
———. "Defining and Locating Evangelicalism." In *The Cambridge Companion to Evangelical Theology*, edited by Timothy Larson and Daniel J. Treier, 1–14. Cambridge: Cambridge University Press, 2007.
———. *Friends of Religious Equality: Nonconformist Politics in Mid-Victorian England.* Woodbridge, UK: Boydell, 1999.
———. "The Reception Given *Evangelicalism in Modern Britain* Since Its Publication in 1989." In *The Emergence of Evangelicalism: Exploring Historical Continuities*, edited by Michael A. G. Haykin and Kenneth J. Stewart, 21–36. Nottingham, UK: Apollos, 2008.
Lawes, Kim. *Paternalism and Politics: The Revival of Paternalism in Early Nineteenth-Century Britain.* New York: Macmillan, 2000.
Lawrence, Jon. "Paternalism, Class, and the British Path to Modernity." In *The Peculiarities of Liberal Modernity in Imperial Britain*, edited by Simon Gunn and James Vernon, 147–64. Berkeley: University of California Press, 2011.
Levine, Phillipa. *Victorian Feminism: 1850–1900.* London: Hutchinson Education, 1987.
Lewis, Donald M., ed. *The Blackwell Dictionary of Evangelical Biography.* Oxford: Blackwell, 1995.
———. *Lighten Their Darkness: The Evangelical Mission to Working-Class London, 1828–1860.* Carlisle, UK: Paternoster, 2001.
———. *The Origins of Christian Zionism: Lord Shaftesbury and Evangelical Support for a Jewish Homeland.* Cambridge: Cambridge University Press, 2010.
MacDonagh, Oliver. *Early Victorian Government 1830–1870.* London: Weidenfeld and Nicolson, 1977.
Mandler, Peter. *Aristocratic Government in the Age of Reform: Whigs and Liberals 1830–1852.* Oxford: Clarendon, 1990.
———. "Cain and Abel: Two Aristocrats and the Early Victorian Factory Acts." *The Historical Journal* 27.1 (1984) 83–109.
Maxwell Fyfe, David Patrick (Lord Kilmuir). "The Shaftesbury Tradition in Conservative Politics." *Journal of Law & Economics* 3.70 (1960) 70–74.
Mayer, Annette. *The Growth of Democracy in Britain.* London: Hodder & Stoughton, 1999.
McCabe, Joseph E. "The Attitude of Edmund Burke (1729–1797) towards Christianity and the Churches." PhD thesis, University of Edinburgh, 1951.
McLean, Iain, and Camilla Bustani. "Irish Potatoes and British Politics: Interests, Ideology, Heresthetic and the Repeal of the Corn Laws." *Political Studies* 47 (1999) 817–36.
McDowell, Robert B. *British Conservatism 1832–1914.* London: Faber & Faber, 1959.
Meachem, Standish. "The Evangelical Inheritance." *Journal of British Studies* 3.1 (1963) 88–104.
Mohhan, T. G. "The Seventh Earl of Shaftesbury." *Churchman* 49.2 (1935) 131–40.
Morgan, Kenneth. *The Birth of Industrial Britain, 1750–1850.* Harlow, UK: Pearson Longman, 2004.
Morley, John. *Burke: A Historical Study.* London: Macmillan, 1867.

Munden, Alan. "Charles Simeon (1759–1836)." In *The Heart of Faith: Following Christ in the Church of England*, edited by Andrew Atherstone, 81–89. Cambridge: Lutterworth, 2008.

Nardinelli, Clark. "Child Labour and the Factory Acts." *The Journal of Economic History* 40.4 (1980) 739–55.

Newby, Howard et al. *Property, Paternalism and Power: Class and Control in Rural England*. Madison, WI: University of Wisconsin Press, 1978.

Noll, Mark A. "National Churches, Gathered Churches, and Varieties of Lay Evangelicalism, 1735–1859." In *The Rise of the Laity in Evangelical Protestantism*, edited by Deryck W. Lovegrove, 134–52. London: Routledge, 2002.

———. *The Rise of Evangelicalism: The Age of Edwards, Whitefield and the Wesleys*. Nottingham, UK: IVP, 2004.

Nolland, Lisa S. *A Victorian Feminist Christian: Josephine Butler, the Prostitutes and God*. Milton Keynes, UK: Paternoster, 2004.

Norton, Philip, ed. *The Conservative Party*. Hemel Hampstead, UK: Havester Wheatsheaf, 1996.

O'Gorman, Francis. *Edmund Burke: His Political Philosophy*. London: Allen & Unwin, 1973.

Oliver, W. H. *Prophets and Millennialists: The Uses of Biblical Prophecy in England from the 1970s to the 1840s*. Auckland, NZ: Auckland University Press, 1978.

Parsons, Gerald. *Religion in Victorian Britain. Volume I: Traditions*. Edited by Gerald Parsons, James R. Moore, and John Wolffe. Manchester, UK: Manchester University Press, 1988.

———. *Religion in Victorian Britain. Volume II: Controversies*. Edited by Gerald Parsons, James R. Moore, and John Wolffe. Manchester, UK: Manchester University Press, 1988.

———. *Religion in Victorian Britain. Volume IV: Interpretations*. Edited by Gerald Parsons, James R. Moore, and John Wolffe. Manchester, UK: Manchester University Press, 1988.

Perkin, Harold. *The Origins of Modern English Society 1780–1880*. London: Routledge & Kegan Paul, 1976.

Pollock, John. *Shaftesbury: The Reformer*. Eastbourne, UK: Kingsway, 2000.

Pope, Norris. *Dickens and Charity*. London: Macmillan, 1978.

Porter, Andrew. "Cultural Imperialism and Protestant Missionary Enterprise, 1780–1914." *Journal of Imperial and Commonwealth History* 25.3 (1997) 367–91.

Prochaska, Frank. *Christianity and Social Service in Modern Britain: The Disinherited Spirit*. Oxford: Oxford University Press, 2006.

———. *Royal Bounty: The Making of a Welfare Monarchy*. New Haven: Yale University Press, 1995.

Rashid, Salim. "David Robinson and the Tory Macroeconomics of *Blackwood's Edinburgh Magazine*." *History of Political Economy* 10.2 (1978) 258–70.

Raven, Charles E. *Social Righteousness and the Christian Gospel: A Study of the Work and Influence of Lord Shaftesbury*, The Tenth Shaftesbury Lecture, Monday, 30th April, 1934, Kingsgate Chapel, London. London: Shaftesbury Society & Ragged School Union, 1934.

Rennie, Ian S. "Evangelicalism and English Public Life, 1823–1850." PhD thesis, University of Toronto, 1962.

———. "Haldane, Alexander." *Blackwell Dictionary of Evangelical Biography*, Vol. II, edited by Donald M. Lewis, 500–501. Oxford: Blackwell, 1995.
Rennie, Ian S., and Donald M. Lewis. "Seeley, Robert Benton." *Blackwell Dictionary of Evangelical Biography*, Vol. II, edited by Donald M Lewis, 993. Oxford: Blackwell, 1995.
Roberts, David. *Paternalism in Early Victorian England*. London: Croom Helm, 1979.
———. "Tory Paternalism and Social Reform." In *The Victorian Revolution: Government and Society in Victoria's Britain*, edited by Peter Stansky, 147–68. New York: Franklin Watts, 1973.
———. *The Social Conscience of the Early Victorians*. Stanford, CA: Stanford University Press, 2002
———. "The Social Conscience of Tory Periodicals." *Victorian Periodicals Newsletter* 10.3 (1977) 154–69.
———. *Victorian Origins of the British Welfare State*. London: Archon, 1969.
Roberts, Michael. *Making English Morals: Voluntary Association and Moral Reform in England, 1787–1886*. Cambridge: Cambridge University Press, 2004.
Rose, E. Alan. "Oastler, Richard." *Blackwell Dictionary of Evangelical Biography 1730–1860*, edited by Donald M. Lewis, 839–40. Oxford: Blackwell, 1995.
Rosman, Doreen M. "Cunningham, John William." *Blackwell Dictionary of Evangelical Biography 1730–1860*, edited by Donald M. Lewis, 280–81. Oxford: Blackwell, 1995.
Sack, James J. *From Jacobite to Conservative: Reaction and Orthodoxy in Britain c. 1760–1832*. Cambridge: Cambridge University Press, 1993.
Schlossberg, Herbert. *The Silent Revolution and the Making of Victorian England*. Columbus, OH: Ohio State University Press, 2000.
Schmidt, Patricia L. "The Role of Moral Idealism in Social Change: Lord Ashley and the Ten Hours Factory Act." *Quarterly Journal of Speech* 63.1 (1977) 14–27.
Scotland, Nigel. "Bull, George (Stringer)." *The Blackwell Dictionary of Evangelical Biography*, edited by Donald M. Lewis, 162–63. Oxford: Blackwell, 1995.
———. *Evangelical Anglicans in a Revolutionary Age 1789–1901*. Carlisle UK: Paternoster, 2004.
———. "Francis Close: Cheltenham's Protestant Patriarch." In *Essays in Religious Studies for Andrew Walls*, edited by James Thrower, 126–35. Aberdeen: Department of Religious Studies, Aberdeen University, 1986.
———. *"Good and Proper Men": Lord Palmerston and the Bench of Bishops*. Cambridge: James Clarke, 2000.
Smith, David W. *Transforming the World? The Social Impact of British Evangelicalism*. Carlisle, UK: Paternoster, 1998.
Smith, Mark, ed. *British Evangelical Identities Past and Present*, Vol. I, *Aspects of the History and Sociology of Evangelicalism in Britain and Ireland*. Milton Keynes, UK: Paternoster, 2008.
Smith, Paul. *Disraelian Conservatism and Social Reform*. London: Routledge & Kegan Paul, 1967.
Speck, W. A. "Robert Southey, Benjamin Disraeli and Young England." *History* 95.318 (2010) 194–206.
———. "Robert Southey's Contribution to the *Quarterly Review*." In *Conservatism and the Quarterly Review*, edited by Jonathan Cutmore, 165–77. London: Pickering & Chatto, 2007.

Spence, Martin. *Heaven on Earth: Reimagining Time and Eternity in British Evangelicalism*. Eugene, OR: Pickwick, 2015.

———. "The Renewal of Time and Space: The Missing Element of Discussions about Nineteenth-Century Premillennialism." *Journal of Ecclesiastical History* 63.1 (2012) 81–101.

———. "Time and Eternity in British Evangelicalism, c. 1820–c.1860." PhD thesis, University of Oxford, 2007.

Spring, David. "Aristocracy, Social Structure, and Religion in the Early Victorian Period." *Victorian Studies* 6.3 (1963) 263–80.

———. "The Clapham Sect: Some Social and Political Aspects." *Victorian Studies* 5.1 (1961) 35–48.

St John-Stevas, Norman. "The Victorian Conscience." *Royal Society for the Encouragement of Arts, Manufactures and Commerce Journal* 120.5186 (1972) 96–105.

Stanley, Brian. *The Bible and the Flag: Protestant Missions and British Imperialism in the Nineteenth and Twentieth Centuries*. Leicester, UK: Apollos, 1990.

———. "British Evangelicals and Overseas Concerns, 1833–1970." In *Evangelical Faith and Public Zeal: Evangelicals and Society in Britain 1780–1980*, edited by John Wolffe, 81–96. London: SPCK, 1995.

Stewart, Robert. *The Foundation of the Conservative Party 1830–1867*. New York: Longman, 1978.

Stott, Anne. *Hannah More: The First Victorian*. Oxford: Oxford University Press, 2003.

Strachey, Lytton. *Eminent Victorians*, Harmondsworth, UK: Penguin, 1986.

Strong, Rowan. *Anglicanism and the British Empire c. 1700–1850*. Oxford: Oxford University Press, 2007.

Tholfsen, Trygve R. "The Intellectual Origins of Mid-Victorian Stability." *Political Science Quarterly* 86.1 (1971) 57–91.

Thompson E. P. *Customs in Common*. London: Merlin, 1991.

———. *The Making of the English Working Class*. London: Gollancz, 1980.

———. "Patrician Society, Plebian Culture." *Journal of Social History* 7.4 (1974) 382–405.

Tomkins, Stephen. *The Clapham Sect: How Wilberforce's Circle Transformed Britain*. Oxford: Lion Hudson, 2010.

Turnbull, Richard. "Eschatology and the Social Order: A Historical Perspective." *Whitefield Briefing* 3.2 (1998) 1–4.

———. "The Place of the Seventh Earl of Shaftesbury within the Evangelical tradition, with Particular Reference to His Understanding of the Relationship of Evangelistic Mission to Social Reform." PhD thesis, University of Durham, 1996.

———. *Shaftesbury: The Great Reformer*. Oxford: Lion Hudson, 2010.

Turner, Frank M. *John Henry Newman: The Challenge to Evangelical Religion*. London: Yale University Press, 2002.

Vierck, Peter. *Conservatism: From John Adams to Churchill*. London: Van Nostrand, 1957.

Ward, John Towers. *The Factory Movement, 1830–1855*. London: Macmillan, 1962.

Warner, Rob. *Reinventing English Evangelicalism, 1966–2001: A Theological and Sociological Study*. Milton Keynes, UK: Paternoster, 2007.

Weaver, Stewart A. *John Fielden and the Politics of Popular Radicalism, 1832–1847*. Oxford: Clarendon, 1987.

Whisenant, James C. *A Fragile Unity: Anti-Ritualism and the Division of Anglican Evangelicalism in the Nineteenth Century*. Milton Keynes, UK: Paternoster, 2005.

Wigley, John. *The Rise and Fall of the Victorian Sunday*. Manchester, UK: Manchester University Press, 1980.

Williams, Sarah C. "Evangelicals and Gender: Critiquing Assumptions." In *Global Evangelicalism: Theology, History and Culture in Regional Perspective*, edited by Donald M. Lewis and Richard V. Pierard, 270–95. Downers Grove, IL: IVP, 2014.

Wolffe, John, "Cooper, Anthony Ashley-." *Oxford Dictionary of National Biography*. Oxford: Oxford University Press, 2004. [online edition].

———. "The Evangelical Alliance in the 1840s: An Attempt to Institutionalise Christian Unity." In *Voluntary Religion*, edited by W. J. Sheils and Diana Wood, 333–46. Oxford: Blackwell for the Ecclesiastical History Society, 1986.

———. *The Expansion of Evangelicalism: The Age of Wilberforce, More, Chalmers and Finney*. Nottingham, UK: IVP, 2006.

———. *God and Greater Britain: Religion and National Life in Britain and Ireland, 1843–1945*. London: Routledge, 1994.

———. "Judging the Nation: Early Nineteenth-Century British Evangelicals and Divine Retribution." In *Retribution, Repentance, and Reconciliation*, papers read at the 2002 Summer Meeting and the 2003 Winter Meeting of the Ecclesiastical History Society, edited by Kate Cooper and Jeremy Gregory, 291–300. Woodbridge, UK: Boydell, 2004.

———. "Lord Palmerston and Religion: A Reappraisal." *English Historical Review*, 120.488 (2005) 907–36.

———. *The Protestant Crusade in Great Britain 1829–1860*. Oxford: Clarendon, 1991.

———. *Religion in Victorian Britain. Volume V: Culture and Empire*. Edited by Geoffrey Parsons. Manchester, UK: Manchester University Press, 1997.

Wormell, Deborah. *Sir John Seeley and the Uses of History*. Cambridge: Cambridge University Press, 1980.

Index

Agnew, Sir Andrew, 189, 283
Agricultural labor gangs, 57, 93, 96–97, 124, 170–71, 203, 278
Agriculture, 84, 86–89, 95–98, 109, 113, 115, 121, 175
Albury Circle, 73, 215, 223, 228, 303
Anglicanism. *See* Church of England
Anglo-Catholics. *See* Tractarians
Aquinas, Thomas, 33
Aristocracy, 3, 10, 14, 41, 56, 82, 88–89, 99, 107, 108–9, 111, 117, 129, 143, 176, 180–82, 186, 192–94, 221–22, 295, 299
Arminianism, 25, 30, 49
Ashley-Cooper, Anthony. *See* Shaftesbury, Seventh Earl of
Atheism, 157, 220, 247

Bebbington quadrilateral, 6, 26–27, 37, 74
Bentham, Jeremy, 3–4, 35, 90–91, 141, 154, 299–301
Bible,
  Authorized (King James) Version, 32, 73
  New Testament, 60–61, 253, 273
  Old Testament, 69, 166, 170–72, 177, 199, 229, 240–41
Bickersteth, Edward, 8–9, 13, 15, 18, 24–25, 28, 31, 35–37, 39, 47, 58, 61–73, 142, 147–53, 160–68, 206–10, 219, 221, 224–25, 228–31, 236–37, 241–42, 245, 250–51, 253, 255, 264–65, 269–71, 282, 296, 299, 302, 306

Bickersteth, Robert, 207
Birks, Thomas Rawson, 70, 72, 228, 250, 264
Blackwood's Magazine, 100–101, 113, 167, 196, 208
Book of Common Prayer, 40, 42, 118
Booth, William, vii, 298, 304
Boswell, James, 19
Boucherett, Jessie, 279
British and Foreign Bible Society (BFBS), 31, 36, 38, 42, 50, 65, 165, 191, 218, 221, 230, 265, 299, 305
British Empire, 80, 86, 89, 134, 220, 230, 233–38, 240, 288, 298–99
Bull, George Stringer, 14, 17–18, 131, 143, 147, 183–84, 186–91, 198–200, 202, 215, 219, 224–31, 249, 254, 270, 272
Burke, Edmund, 85, 102, 107–8, 115, 129, 176, 179, 273, 305
Butler, Josephine, 278–79, 298
Buxton, Thomas Fowell, viii, 8, 48, 50, 57–58, 303

Calvinism, 25, 30, 40, 49, 73, 107, 223, 228, 240, 299, 302
Canning, George, 129, 147
Catholic Relief Act (1829), 42, 65–66, 111, 128, 163, 165, 250, 297
Chadwick, Edwin, 4, 35, 90–91, 144, 154, 300–301
Chadwick, Owen, 286
Chalmers, Thomas, 33, 53, 71, 99, 141, 142, 147–48, 151–53, 155–56, 170, 208, 249–50, 264

Chartism, 2, 117, 151, 161, 186–87, 189, 225, 232, 299
Children's Employment Commission, 125
China, 60, 230, 237–38
Christ Church College (Oxford), 42, 262
Christian Influence Society (CIS), 156, 168, 173
Christian Observer, 8–9, 41, 48, 50, 53, 153, 162, 215, 223–26, 265, 297
Christian Socialism, 293–94
Church Missionary Society, viii, 9, 36, 42, 50, 58, 64, 86, 187, 230, 233, 305
Church of England, viii, 2, 5, 6, 8, 15, 18, 23, 34, 39–41, 45, 50, 52, 64–65, 86–87, 107, 119–20, 133, 144, 146, 163–64, 194–95, 200, 206, 210, 216–18, 233–36, 248–49, 252–67, 284, 302
Church of Scotland, 228
Church Pastoral Aid Society, 42, 86, 261
Clapham Sect, 8–10, 13, 16, 24–25, 33–36, 39, 42, 45–58, 61–65, 67–68, 71–74, 141, 147–55, 163, 166–70, 180–81, 195, 206–7, 210, 215–17, 223–26, 233–34, 237, 240–42, 249–51, 261, 268–71, 282–83, 294, 296, 302–5
Clarkson, Thomas, 116
Clerical Vestments (No 2) Bill (1867), 86, 257
Climbing boys (juvenile chimney-sweeps), 50, 57, 116–17
Cobbett, William, 143, 186
Colenso, John William, 261
Coleridge, Samuel Taylor, 11, 83, 86, 106, 118, 142, 144, 150, 163, 210, 255, 301
Colonialism, 112, 237–38, 288
"Condition of England" Question, 2, 4, 54, 71, 93, 136, 154
Conybeare, William J, 26, 41, 181, 248
Corn Laws, 4, 87–88, 128, 130, 138, 173
Cowper, Lady Emily, 12, 132, 274

Cunningham, John William, 42–43

Darwin, Charles, 297
Dicey, Albert V, 104
Dickens, Charles, 34
Disraeli, Benjamin, 130, 132, 219–21, 298
Dissenters. See Nonconformists
Doddridge, Philip, 28, 38, 59, 63, 209, 218
Drummond, Henry, 13, 147, 215, 223, 228, 303
Duncombe, Thomas, 186

Edinburgh Review, 99, 136, 153
Education Act (1870), 292, 298
Enlightenment, 36, 53, 106, 216, 297, 299, 300–302
Eschatology, 9, 13–14, 17, 36, 63, 67, 72–74, 142, 149, 166–68, 215–17, 225–28, 231, 233, 240, 242, 261, 270, 287, 302–3
Established Church. See Church of England
Evangelical Alliance, 38, 64–65, 219, 265, 299
Evangelicalism, viii, 1–20, 23–33, 37–44, 47–55, 58–59, 62–67, 72–74, 77–78, 86, 110, 141–49, 152, 159–60, 164–66, 168, 170, 174, 181–82, 184–85, 191, 195, 201, 205–11, 215–25, 228, 235, 245, 248–51, 258, 260, 264–65, 277, 279, 286–87, 296–97, 299–306
Evangelism, viii, 5, 16, 24, 28, 33, 36, 48, 61, 64, 70, 166, 207, 216, 221, 228, 231, 305

Factory Act (1802), 52
Factory (Ten Hours) Act (1847), 50, 87–89, 103, 128, 131, 135–36, 169, 188
Factory Act (1853), 134
Factory Commission (1840), 276
Factory Reform, vii, 1, 3, 12, 13–14, 18, 30, 34, 36, 49–56, 71, 83, 87–90, 93–104, 111–16, 122–25,

137, 141–43, 151, 154, 167, 174, 177, 183–203, 204, 209–10, 217, 239, 270–73, 276, 279–80, 283, 285, 289, 297, 299, 303–5
Fawcett, Millicent, 279
Feminism, 276, 279–80, 298
Fielden, John, 186
Fraser's Magazine, 100
Free trade, 15, 53–54, 99, 123, 128, 130, 147–48, 153, 164, 221

General Board of Health, 4, 35, 91, 132, 134, 136, 217, 290
Gisborne, Thomas, 49, 180, 269
Gladstone, William Ewart, 17, 131–32, 246
Grant, Charles, 50, 233
Grant, Robert, 241, 243
Guthrie, Thomas, 119

Haldane, Alexander, 9, 15–18, 24–25, 31, 37, 72, 215–16, 223–25, 226–30, 250–51, 255, 261, 297, 302, 306
Hodder, Edwin, 8, 18–19, 24–25, 36, 41, 59, 72, 96, 169, 182, 218, 249, 252, 297
Housing, viii, 3, 83, 88, 102, 116, 154, 230, 232, 273, 289, 293, 299, 300
Huntington, Countess of, 45
Huskisson, William, 99, 153, 186

Imperialism. *See* British Empire
India, viii, 50, 112, 127, 233–34, 236–37, 239, 291, 298
India Board of Control, 112, 127
Industrial Revolution, vii, 85, 99, 106, 108, 111, 121, 129, 275
Industrialization,
Ireland, 66, 124, 134, 162, 165, 203, 250–51, 257
Irving, Edward, 215, 223, 228, 303
Israel, 68–69, 72, 166, 171, 240, 242

Jerusalem, 60, 62, 69–70, 133, 240
Jerusalem Bishopric, 60, 62, 69–70, 133, 134

Jewish emancipation, 15–16, 45, 217, 221, 239, 243–46
Johnson, Richard, 233
Judaism, 68, 245–46

Keble, John, 255

Laboring classes, 99, 102, 121, 132, 148, 151, 157–58, 170, 176, 194, 289
Laissez-faire, viii, 2, 13–14, 54, 99, 102, 105–8, 114, 123, 136, 149, 154, 158–60, 170, 186, 189, 195–97, 202, 221, 270, 283, 286, 289, 299, 301
Lake Poets, 84, 106–7, 144, 157–58, 171–72, 202, 235, 301
Liverpool, Second Earl of, 107, 147, 258, 265
London City Mission, 209
London Missionary Society, 233
London Society for the Proclamation of Christianity amongst the Jews (LSPCJ), 36, 50, 60, 69, 240–41
Lord's Day Observance Society (LDOS), 283, 287
Lunacy Commission, 91, 112
Lutheranism, 38, 60, 133, 240

Malthus, Thomas, 99, 101, 123, 157, 170, 192, 202
Manners, Lord John, 88
Maurice, Frederick D, 293–94
Maynooth (grant), 66, 162, 165, 251–52, 264
Mercantilism, 99, 129–30, 132, 195
Methodism, 28, 33, 165, 185, 191, 195
Mill, John Stuart, 301
Millis, Maria, 8, 29, 41–43, 181, 209
More, Hannah, 8, 54–57, 178, 180–81, 269, 275, 278

Newman, John Henry, 255
Nonconformists, 2, 15, 28, 37–38, 44, 64, 118, 130, 163–66, 187, 194–95, 206, 216, 218–22, 234–35, 238, 246, 249, 258, 264–67, 286–87, 297, 299

Oastler, Richard, 14, 17–18, 49, 113, 131, 142–43, 147–48, 151–53, 162, 179, 183–88, 191–98, 199–200, 210, 215, 221, 225–26, 272, 283, 289
Opium Trade, 237–38
Owen, Robert, 83, 104, 160
Oxford Declaration (1864), 262

Palestine, 1, 60–61, 70, 239–40, 243–46
Palmerston, Lord, 12, 15, 70, 90, 132–38, 143, 198, 205–9, 215, 217, 224, 243
Papal Aggression, 249, 253
Peel, Sir Robert, 4, 10, 12, 52, 83, 87, 89–91, 99, 118, 129–32, 135–36, 147, 152, 162–65, 173, 175, 186, 191–92, 251, 264
Philanthropy, 1, 7, 16, 25, 33, 35, 37, 47–48, 52–53, 73, 77, 83, 152, 156, 184, 200, 205, 216–17, 219, 221, 229, 265, 277, 290, 292, 297, 303, 306
Pietism, 49, 68, 167, 240
Political Economy, 13–14, 71, 78, 94, 99–100, 108, 114, 123, 129, 132, 136, 142, 144, 147, 156–60, 169–70, 186, 189, 196–97, 202–3, 210, 297
Poor laws, 100
Pope Pius IX, 253
Postmillennialism, 60, 242
Premillennialism, 16–17, 60, 67–68, 73, 149, 167–68, 223, 225, 226–32, 233, 236, 240, 300, 303
Pretyman, George, 145
Protectionism, 4, 15, 87, 101, 130, 147, 165, 221
Protestantism, 4–6, 9, 14, 20, 47, 141, 180, 191, 196, 200, 207, 222–25, 240, 245, 249, 252, 254, 260
Protestant Constitutionalism, 163–66, 168, 170, 249, 297
Puritanism, 33, 43, 254, 258–60, 274
Pusey, Edward, 255–56, 258, 260, 262

Quarterly Review, 70, 100–101, 111, 113–14, 127, 136, 148, 151, 163, 167, 173, 176, 196, 208, 296, 301

Ragged Schools, viii, 28, 56, 73, 119–21, 123, 178–79, 204, 291–93, 298, 300
Ragged School Union, 27, 38, 50, 56, 82, 120–21, 156, 178–79, 209, 221, 256
Record, 9, 25, 50, 65, 71–72, 156, 162, 164–65, 170, 223–25, 254, 257–58, 261–62, 265, 272, 283, 296–97
Recordites, 24, 72, 163, 207, 215, 218, 250, 260–61, 268, 283, 296, 300, 302–3
Reform Act (1832), 130
Reformation, 5, 32, 40, 43–44, 64, 163–64, 249, 253, 255–57, 260, 265, 297
Ricardo, David, 99, 123
Ritualism, 86, 206–7, 225, 254–60, 263–64, 304–5
Roman Catholicism, 2, 31–33, 40, 63, 65–67, 73, 77, 149, 162–63, 165, 194, 200, 207, 216, 223, 225, 247–48, 249–54, 256–57, 259, 265–66, 284
Romanticism, 17, 74, 106, 216, 302
Ruskin, John, 293–94
Russell, Lord John, 12, 90–91, 133, 135–36, 138, 198
Ryle, John Charles ("J C"), 26, 258, 264

Sabbath, 16, 56, 63, 66, 170, 217, 230, 282–87, 296–97
Sadler, Michael Thomas, 14, 17–18, 50, 93, 95, 103, 108, 113, 116, 122–29, 131, 137, 142–44, 147, 149, 152–57, 162, 168, 175–79, 183–91, 195, 198–204, 208, 210, 215, 221, 225–26, 272, 283, 289, 297, 303
Salvation Army, vii, 298, 304–5
Sanitation, viii, 3, 35, 83, 91, 154, 198, 204, 230, 232, 299, 300

Scott, Thomas, 24, 28–29, 31, 33, 39, 47, 58–62, 70, 73, 148, 209, 218–19, 223, 228, 261, 264, 304
Seeley, Robert Benton, 13–14, 17–18, 52, 143, 156–58, 162, 166–68, 169–73, 175, 179, 196, 198–202, 210, 215, 221, 226, 228, 230–31, 294, 298, 302, 306
Seeley, John Robert, 261, 298
Shaftesbury, Sixth Earl of (Ashley's father), 5, 11, 93, 95–96, 98, 137
Shaftesbury, Seventh Earl of
  Childhood and education, 5–6, 19, 34, 42–43, 93, 137
  Evangelical conversion, 27–29, 35, 38, 148
  Entry to Parliament, 52, 82, 127
  Stewardship of St Giles, 11–12, 97–98, 100, 137–38, 182, 193
  Marriage and family life, 12, 132, 274–75
  Death and legacy, 51–52, 98, 159–60, 303–6
Short Time Movement, 125, 195
Simeon, Charles, 16, 24, 28, 30–31, 35–36, 49–50, 58–59, 61–64, 70, 73, 149, 240–42, 251, 261, 296
Slavery, 8, 33, 36, 48, 50, 52, 53, 57–58, 191, 193, 198, 301, 303
Smith, Adam, 99, 101, 114, 123, 297
Social gospel, 305
Socialism, viii, 104, 151, 160, 161, 168, 186, 225, 294, 299
Society for Improving the Conditions of the Labouring Classes, 205, 289
Society for Promoting the Employment of Women, 279
Southey, Robert, 6, 10–12, 16–18, 79, 86, 93, 95, 101–2, 106–32, 136–38, 142, 144–45, 147–51, 159, 163, 165, 168, 176–78, 186, 191–92, 196, 200, 202, 208–10, 216, 235–36, 255, 267, 284, 296, 299, 301, 306
Spurgeon, Charles Haddon, 43, 219–20, 222, 235, 265

St Giles Estate, 11, 42, 72, 79, 81, 93–98, 100, 112, 122, 124, 137–38, 171, 182, 193
State intervention, viii, 13–14, 53–54, 71, 91, 93, 101, 103, 105, 108, 125–26, 127, 130, 134–38, 142, 144, 147–58, 167–69, 177, 183, 187, 193, 198–99, 201–2, 210, 221, 270, 283, 286, 289–90, 294, 297
Stephen, James, 233, 294
Sumner, John Bird, 170
Sunday observance. *See* Sabbath

Tamworth Manifesto, 130
Test and Corporation Acts (1828 repeal), 38, 44, 163, 221
Thornton, Henry, 50, 233, 269, 270
Tonna, Charlotte Elizabeth, 13–14, 17–18, 143, 156, 166, 168–69, 173–79, 196, 198–99, 221, 226, 228, 230–32, 294, 302, 306
Tory Paternalism, 2, 4, 6, 10–14, 17, 19, 89, 99–100, 128–29, 131–32, 135–36, 141–44, 146, 149, 158–60, 166, 168, 170, 172, 174, 180, 184, 186, 191–96, 202, 205, 208, 210, 219, 245, 247, 279, 285–86, 288, 296, 301, 306
Tractarians, 16, 31–33, 42, 63, 67, 73, 149, 206–7, 216, 223–25, 248–49, 254–63, 284, 301–2, 304
Trade unionism, 306

Unitarians, 162
Urbanization, 2, 88, 99, 106, 290
Utilitarianism, 2–3, 13, 78, 90–91, 113, 141, 300–302

Venn, John, 42
Verney, Harry, 42
Victoria, Queen, 165, 296–98
Victorian age, vii, 3, 5, 7, 12, 51, 56, 70, 79, 106, 171, 210, 216, 218–24, 227, 231, 234–35, 239, 242, 248, 254, 294, 296, 299, 303

Voluntary societies, 5, 33, 49, 103–5, 120, 122, 155–56, 160, 162, 216, 290, 292–95, 297
Volunteerism, viii, 120, 155, 297

Watts, Isaac, 265
Wellington, Duke of, 17, 107, 127–28, 130, 137, 194, 196, 250–51
Wesley, John, 6, 25–27, 29–30, 33, 49, 63, 165, 185, 190–91, 238, 284, 286, 300, 304
Whiggism, 3–4, 10, 12, 57, 77–78, 82–83, 89–91, 99–100, 127–38, 141, 147, 154, 162, 164–65, 189, 193, 195–98, 209, 219
Whitefield, George, 6, 25, 30, 37, 49
Wilberforce, Basil, 1
Wilberforce, Samuel, 141, 262
Wilberforce, William, viii, 1, 8, 13, 30, 33, 36, 49–59, 62, 65, 141–42, 148–49, 153, 179–81, 199, 233, 241, 249, 251, 282–83
Wilson, Daniel, 286
Wolstenholme, Elizabeth, 279
Women's suffrage, 280–81
Wordsworth, William, 11, 83, 85, 88, 106, 144, 159, 301

Young England (movement), 88, 102, 301
Young Men's Christian Association, vii

Zionism, 16, 47, 61, 216–17, 239

www.ingramcontent.com/pod-product-compliance
Lightning Source LLC
Chambersburg PA
CBHW070013010526
44117CB00011B/1548